Comparative
National
Economic
Policies

A READER FOR
INTRODUCTORY ECONOMICS

Comparative National Economic Policies

A READER FOR INTRODUCTORY ECONOMICS

William Moskoff

SANGAMON STATE UNIVERSITY

D. C. HEATH AND COMPANY
Lexington, Massachusetts   Toronto   London

To Sarah, Leah, and Rachel:
in the hope that all
their alternatives
will be humane

7-29-74

Published simultaneously in Canada.

Printed in the United States of America.

International Standard Book Number: 0-669-83188-3

Library of Congress Catalog Card Number: 72-3397

Preface

For most students, the introductory economics course is a terminal experience with formal economic education. In addition, if the student is using one of the standard textbooks designed for such a course, his attention is usually focused solely on the economy of the United States. While this appears to be a logical locus of inquiry, there is a substantial cost conferred upon the student by narrowing his geographical perspective. The student is essentially denied the opportunity of seeing how other countries tackle major economic problems, and is thereby thrust into intellectual isolation from viable alternatives to the American economic system.

This book is an attempt to fill the existing vacuum. A basic premise is that the American economy cannot be viewed as the Omega point in the evolution of political-economic systems. While America's economy has witnessed an increasing intervention in the market by the public sector, the variety of pragmatic policy responses within the U.S. economy has hardly exhausted the possibilities of dealing with the problems of a mature economy. In addition, American capitalism definitionally operates within a political-economic framework which at the present time does not admit of certain solutions which have been successfully implemented in other societies.

In order to broaden the perspective of students and afford them the opportunity to reflect on a variety of international experiences, I have selected a series of readings covering the policies pursued in Western Europe, the Soviet Union, Japan, Canada, Australia, and Yugoslavia. Altogether, the policies of 14 countries are covered. The three broad areas covered by the readings are: (1) macroeconomic policy, (2) microeconomic policy, and (3) domestic economic issues.

The choice of these countries is rooted in the belief that the experiences of other countries or economic systems is made more credible as potentially applicable to the U.S. if the countries are developed industrial nations and/or are countries with similar political and legal structures.[1] Thus, while the Soviet Union is clearly not a country with a democratic political framework, its status as a major industrial power might provide some interesting lessons for the U.S.

As a corollary to this, the experiences of individual less-developed nations, while important, and possibly possessing the virtue of transferability to other less-developed nations, are not nearly as likely to be applicable to countries performing at substantially higher levels of economic development and socially acculturated to different work habits.

The readings emphasize policy rather than theory. While a theoretical approach would be extremely interesting, it would fail to provide the student with a view of how other capitalist nations or other economic systems actually respond to the problems of their economies. In conjunction with the emphasis on policy, the readings are biased in favor of the successful experiences of these countries. It goes without saying that other countries endure failures in implementing policies and create their own massive social problems. The Japanese and the Russians have demonstrated that they are as capable as the U.S. in polluting their environments. The emphasis on success is designed to show the student that other industrial nations, some capitalist, others socialist, can solve problems that we have failed to conquer and that there are a variety of approaches to macro- and microeconomic policy questions. Thus, the readings evidence the positive potential of *industrial man,* not his ignominious defeats.

The selection of the readings has been guided by the assumption that the student has had no previous contact with economics. Therefore, the level of economic sophistication is within the reach of all students taking an introductory course. It is also assumed that the readings are used in conjunction with a principles textbook as supplementary material, not as an independent learning vehicle.

In sum, this book aims at widening the student's view of the universe of economic policies while, at the same time, narrowing the overall concept of the book to an offering of alternatives which are at least within reasonable bounds for a comparison with U.S. economic policy and problems. For the teacher, the book provides a vehicle for relieving the frustrations of the many students who want to know if there are alternative ways of conducting economic affairs. Such an answer need not necessarily be given in a "radical" economics course, nor should the student have to take another economics course to learn what the alternatives are. It is possible to satisfy his curiosity at the level of the first economics course. This is the end to which this book is directed.

I wish to express my appreciation to my research assistant, Carter Bacon, for all the important and unimportant tasks which he performed so competently. I also owe a debt of thanks to my former colleagues Rosemary Hale and George Weiner for their advice at various points in the development of the book.

William Moskoff

---

[1] The obvious exception is Yugoslavia, which is generally considered on the borderline of being classified as a developed nation, and does not have a democratic political structure. However, as the outstanding practitioner of market socialism, its exclusion would demonstrably detract from the purposes of the book.

Contents

Government and the Firm 168

Income Distribution and Wage Determination 200

International Trade 223

PART 3 DOMESTIC ECONOMIC ISSUES

Pollution 241

Health 259

Women 289

Urban Development 323

Poverty and Welfare 349

1 *MACROECONOMICS*

Fiscal Policy

The role of government in affecting the level of employment and prices through its expenditure and taxation policies constitutes the basic goal of fiscal policy. Consideration in this section is given to two kinds of policies: (1) revenue sharing, and (2) the "Concerted Action" program in West Germany.

What is revenue sharing? Basically it refers to the flow of funds from one governmental unit to another; for example, funds flowing from the federal government to a state government, or from state government to a municipality. Such flows already exist in the United States. About 20 percent of the revenue of state and local governments comes from federal aid. However, these flows appear to be inadequate relative to the magnitude of the problems with which governors and mayors must cope. Local governments, especially the big cities, are asked to deal with the burgeoning problems of providing quality education, cleaning up the environment, and constructing decent housing with a revenue base that has been squeezed almost to the limit. Fiscal crises have already caused certain school systems to close for a period of time due to a lack of funds. It is obvious that property owners can bear only so much of the burden of providing the revenue for these programs. An additional problem is that some states are wealthier than others and are therefore financially more capable of dealing with these problems. Per capita expenditures for public education in 1964 ranged from a high of $201 in Utah to a low of $91 in South Carolina. In the same year, the per capita revenue collections of the top five states were $396 compared with $197 in the five bottom states. Such a situation reflects the concentration of low-income families in the poorer states and calls for the relief of their fiscal pressures by the federal government, the only institution with sufficient resources to deal with the problem.

The first selection deals with attempts made by Canada, Australia, and West Germany to deal with the problem of redistribution from the wealthy areas of their countries to the poorer areas via revenue-sharing schemes. The article demonstrates that there are a variety of ways in which revenue-sharing policies can be designed.

The second selection deals with West Germany's so-called "Concerted Action" program which was begun in 1967. The program involves the federal government, acting in concert with the major interest groups of society, in developing a program to achieve the fundamental macroeconomic objectives of growth and stability. As such, "Concerted Action" is an official part of West German economic policy. It is an explicit attempt to wed overall governmental economic policy with private interests.

Michael E. Levy and Juan de Torres are economists with the National Industrial Conference Board. Dr. Otto Schlect is with the West German Federal Ministry for Economic Affairs.

Grants and Revenue Sharing Abroad: Canada, Australia, West Germany

MICHAEL E. LEVY and JUAN DE TORRES

In the developed nations revenue sharing is employed in such countries as Australia, Canada, Sweden, the United Kingdom, and West Germany; among the developing nations, Argentina, India, Nigeria, Pakistan, and Rhodesia have all made use of some form of revenue sharing. The developing nations will be omitted altogether from this study, because their economies and institutions are too different from those of the United States to permit useful inferences.

Among the developed nations, revenue sharing occurs in unitary states as well as in federal states. In a unitary state, there is only one sovereign level of government, whereas in a federal state sovereignty is divided functionally among two or more levels of government. Summarized here are the experiences of three federal states—Canada, Australia, and West Germany—because revenue sharing within the framework of a federal government structure is most likely to provide instructive parallels for the United States.

Federal constitutions nearly always draw a distinction between *exclusive* and *concurrent* powers. An exclusive power is exercised by only one level of government. Concurrent powers may be exercised by more than one level of government. In the United States, for example, the federal government is the only government allowed to levy taxes on foreign trade; state governments, in turn, are the only ones that can charter local governments such as towns and counties. These are exclusive powers. However, the federal government as well as the states may levy income

Reprinted from *Federal Revenue Sharing with the States,* by Michael E. Levy and Juan de Torres, © 1970, National Industrial Conference Board, pp. 59–79, by permission of the publisher.

and excise taxes. These are concurrent powers. It is well to keep this distinction in mind when examining the revenue structure of federal states.

In connection with the present summary of revenue sharing in Canada, Australia, and West Germany, the following general considerations are also worth bearing in mind. The institutions of Canada and Australia are quite similar to those of the United States, even though Canada exhibits a much greater cultural, economic, and geographic diversity than the United States. Australia is less diverse but includes a frontier section (like that of the United States in the nineteenth century), namely, Western Australia. West Germany, in contrast, represents a much more closely knit economic and geographic market for goods, labor, and capital than the United States; moreover, its institutions differ substantially from those of the United States. Thus, these three countries exemplify a diversity of experiences that should prove useful in assessing the direction that revenue sharing in the United States may take.

Canada

The background of the Canadian federal government is great diversity among its ten provinces, nine of which form extensions of neighboring geographic or economic regions in the United States. On the West Coast, British Columbia is more closely related to the Pacific Northwest of the United States than to other Canadian provinces. On the East Coast, there are the four maritime provinces (New Brunswick, Newfoundland, Nova Scotia, and Prince Edward Island) related in many ways to New England. In the center, three prairie provinces (Alberta, Manitoba, and Saskatchewan) continue the Great Plains into the Arctic; and Ontario dips so deeply into the manufacturing belt of the United States that the shortest land-route from Detroit to Buffalo passes through it. Only the Province of Quebec constitutes an economic entity that is relatively free of links to the United States.

Constitutional Subsidies

The combination of extreme diversity and proximity to the attractive United States markets explains a peculiar feature of the Canadian constitution (British North America Act of 1867): the provinces are prohibited not only from using customs duties—as is common under most federal constitutions—but also from using excise taxes. To all appearances, Canada's founding fathers feared that a multiplicity of excise taxes in the various provinces would hamper the development of a common market in Canada. As a result of this policy, written into the Constitution, the provinces could utilize only direct taxes, that is, income and property taxes. In the nineteenth century, this restriction meant virtual fiscal impotency because of the high resistance among the population to taxation in general, and to property and income taxation in particular. Consequently, the provinces were compensated by a subsidy from the Dominion government provided for in the constitution. During the early years, this subsidy amounted to 50 percent of provincial general revenues.

The peculiarity of this tax-sharing arrangement, however, was that the amount was fixed for each province and rose with the increase in population only as long as the population remained under 400,000. This payment was not revised upward until 1918. Consequently, constitutional subsidies became progressively less important as the economy and population of Canada grew and as provincial governments took on more responsibilities. Currently, constitutional subsidies are negligible, having already dropped to 9 percent of provincial revenues by 1930. The provinces did not miss this subsidy because, throughout this period, the attitude of taxpayers to direct taxation was rapidly changing. Personal income, corporate income, and estate taxes were developed in a small way during this time, while the property tax proved to be a rapidly growing and very suitable means of financing urban public services.

Specific Grants

In 1912, the Dominion enacted its first specific grant. It was for agricultural education and required matching funds from the provinces. But unlike the United States—where specific grants have provoked few constitutional controversies—Canadian specific grants were attacked as an infringement on the autonomy of the provinces as early as 1919, particularly by Quebec's spokesmen. The first big Canadian specific grant, enacted in 1927, established that if a province instituted an old age pension plan, the Dominion would pay 50 percent of the costs. The Provinces of Quebec and New Brunswick were strongly enough opposed to this federal scheme to stay out of it until 1936, despite the considerable financial sacrifice entailed by this stand.

Nevertheless, the combination of the Great Depression and World War II had the same effect in Canada as in the United States—a great strengthening of the central government relative to the provinces. The Dominion moved into the income tax field and provided emergency grants to the provinces when their own finances collapsed during the depression; and it instituted specific grants to handle welfare and other services.

Because of profound concern over the way in which Dominion and provincial taxes were functioning under the Canadian Constitution, the Rowell-Sirois Commission was set up in 1937 in order to conduct a study and make recommendations for constitutional changes. One of its main recommendations, three years later, was a proposal to centralize personal income taxes, corporate income taxes, and estate taxes ("succession duties") in the Dominion and to compensate the provinces through general grants which would be negotiable every five years.

At first the provinces rejected this arrangement; but under the pressure of World War II financing, they abandoned personal income and corporate income taxation in return for general grants from the Dominion. During the war years and until 1947, the Dominion established important new specific grants, such as grants with matching requirements for vocational training, grants to universities, and grants for the construction of the Trans-Canada highway. In addition to its assumption of old age pensions and unemployment insurance during the depression, the Dominion took on important new responsibilities such as the monthly payments (family allowances) for all children under 16. These measures led to serious strains in the Federation by 1947, and to a serious constitutional crisis in 1953, revolving around the issues of taxation and specific grants. This constitutional crisis has not yet been resolved (though its virulence appears to have subsided); consequently, the Canadian tax structure has been in transition ever since 1947. Every five years, the provinces and the Dominion meet and come to a compromise agreement, a Federal-Provincial Financial Arrangements Act, which settles these issues for that period. Currently, tax sharing and taxation are governed by the 1967 Act which provides a moratorium until it is renewed or revised in 1972.

The general tendency in postwar Canada has been to reverse the 1930–1947 trend. In 1947, a year of disarmament, the Dominion accounted for 58 percent of all government expenditures, that is, both purchases of goods and services and transfer payments; by 1963 this share had dropped to 43 percent, and by 1967 it was down further to 42 percent.

Tax Sharing or Tax Credits:
A Transitional Arrangement

After 1947, the provinces began to move into income taxation (particularly Ontario and Quebec). The Dominion permitted this by belatedly enacting full or partial tax credits (or "abatements," as they are called in Canada). But this arrangement was unfair to provinces that had not enacted income taxes and did not intend to do so. In effect, relative to the income tax base, the Dominion was now collecting more income taxes from those provinces than from the provinces that had enacted their own income taxes and whose taxpayers benefited from the new Dominion tax credits. Therefore, when new agreements between the provinces and the Dominion were negotiated in 1957, the whole system of tax credits and tax sharing was revised.

To those provinces that did not wish to set up their own tax-administration apparatus, the Dominion offered "tax renting," a form of tax sharing. The new system worked in the following way, "Standard rates" were adopted—initially at 10 percent of the Dominion personal income tax collections, 9 percent of the Dominion corporate income tax collections, and 50 percent of the Dominion estate tax collections. If a province administered its own personal income, corporate income, or estate taxes, its taxpayers received a tax credit at the "standard rate," that is, they would deduct tax payments from the corresponding Dominion tax up to a maximum of the "standard rate." Any province that did not enact its own taxes was entitled to receive a general grant from the Dominion equivalent to a proportion of the Dominion's tax collections determined by the "standard rate." Hence, provinces without income or estate taxes received general grants equal to the maximum amount of tax credit that could possibly be claimed by the taxpayers of those provinces that had instituted their own taxes. The benefit to the taxpayer in the one case (tax credits) became a payment to the provincial government in the other case ("tax renting").

Ontario and Quebec were the first provinces to avail themselves of the tax credits or abatements; the other provinces received general grants determined by the standard rates. Thus, at its initiation, "tax renting" provided sizable general grants to most provinces. However, tax renting proved to be transitional. All the provinces now have adopted their own taxes under the tax credit system. At the same time, tax abatements have been increased substantially. The latest Federal-Provincial Fiscal Arrangements Act, that of 1967, sets the standard rate for the Dominion income tax at 28 percent (compared with 10 percent in 1957); for the corporation income tax at 10 percent (compared with 9 percent in 1957); for the estate tax at 75 percent (compared with 50 percent in 1957). In essence there has been a partial, but noticeable, withdrawal of the Dominion from income and estate taxation.

Equalization

The 1957 Act also set up a system of revenue equalization among the provinces by means of tax sharing. In the Canadian system of equalization, a certain norm for taxation is adopted and provinces that fall below this norm are compensated by the exact amount needed to bring their tax yield up to the norm. This is best illustrated by an example. If the adopted norm is a 10 percent tax rate on per capita taxable income of $4,000, it provides a per capita yield of $400. Provinces with per capita taxable incomes above $4,000 would receive no equalization payment from the Dominion. But if the per capita taxable income were only $3,900, the per capita yield at a 10 percent rate would be only $390; hence, in this case, the province would be entitled to a per capita payment of $10 from the Dominion.

Variations on this simple arrangement arise in two ways. First, the number of revenue sources to be equalized may be multiplied. In this case, "deficits" and "surpluses" are computed on the basis of the norm for each tax and become additive. Thus a province may have a deficit with respect to the personal income tax base, but a surplus with respect to oil royalties. The surplus in oil royalties would then offset the deficit in the yield of the personal income tax for calculation of the equalization payment. When equalization was first adopted in Canada in 1957, only the three revenue sources of direct taxation (personal income, corporate income, and estate taxes) were equalized in this way, but subsequently, other revenue sources were added. The 1967 Act prescribes the use of 16 revenue sources, including such taxes as the general sales tax and such nontaxes as sales of leases on oil and natural gas lands.

The second source of variation in the equalization scheme relates to the rate, or per capita yield, used for establishing the norm that is going to regulate equalization payments. Initially, the norm was based on the average tax yield in the two wealthiest provinces. This, of course, maximizes the number of provinces qualifying for equalization payments as well as the total amount of these payments. The 1967 agreement incorporated a less generous arrangement by basing the norm on the *national average* per capita yield. Consequently, the equalization payments flow to fewer provinces and raise the revenues of these provinces to the average yield rather than to that of the wealthiest provinces.

In addition to the equalization payments, the Dominion instituted in 1958 special grants to its low-income Atlantic or maritime provinces (New Brunswick, Newfoundland, Nova Scotia, and Prince Edward Island). In this context, "special grant" is merely a general grant given to certain governments and not to others. No special formula has been used to determine the amount of these special grants. They have been negotiated with an eye to the financial resources of the Dominion and the needs of the maritime provinces. However, they have further reinforced interprovincial equalization.[1]

Opting Out

As may be gathered from the changes in fiscal arrangements of the Canadian Federation outlined above, the 1957 Federal-Provincial Fiscal Arrangements Act was by no means definitive. One of the principal developments since that date was the adoption, in 1965, of the "opting out" principle as a part of Dominion-Provincial relations. According to this principle, any province can opt out of a list of Dominion programs negotiated between the Dominion and the provinces. If it wishes to do so, it is entitled to financial compensation for the loss that it would incur by opting out. Compensation is extended through tax sharing as well as tax credits. In four Dominion health and welfare programs, tax credits are provided against the Dominion personal income tax if the province opts out. Quebec has opted out of all four programs and therefore receives an additional 19 per-

---

[1] These special grants were discontinued after fiscal 1967.

centage points against the federal personal income tax collections over and above the regular "standard rate" used for tax abatements. General grants are given to provinces that opt out of any one of five other programs; these payments are calculated on the basis of the extra expenditure that a province incurs if it opts out of the federal program and institutes its own program. Thus, the opting-out principle gives rise to another tax-sharing arrangement in Canada.

As of 1969, only the Province of Quebec had made use of the opting-out provisions. In general, the opting-out principle permits differential treatment among provinces or states of a federation by their central government. While such a special treatment runs counter to the constitutional practice of the United States, where every state has the same rights and obligations, it has by no means been uncommon in other countries. Despite the looseness of this type of federalism, it can function effectively and over long periods of time, the only requirement being that the number of states be relatively small. Switzerland is a good example; there, as a legacy from the feudal arrangements of the Middle Ages, the cantons have long differed in their specific relations with the central government.

Summary

At the beginning of Canada's history as a nation, tax sharing appeared as the logical result of a policy of economic development. Canada's statesmen felt that economic development required uniform taxation—that is, federal taxation—even though the provinces and their local governments had to provide many governmental services. Tax sharing became an important part of the solution to this dilemma. It allowed for a high degree of uniformity of taxation throughout the Dominion while providing the provinces with the revenue resources required to meet their responsibilities.

In fiscal 1969 the provinces will, it is estimated, receive from the Dominion government $1,500 million in the form of specific grants, $954 million in general grants or tax sharing, and additional benefits from tax credits valued at about $2,200 million. Tax sharing, however, now has a very different rationale. About 62 percent represents equalization payments; the remaining 38 percent arises from various compromises concerning the respective roles of the Dominion and the provinces which have been institutionalized in the form of tax-sharing agreements. The latter proportion had formerly been much higher (about 58 percent of total general grants in fiscal 1959) because of "tax rentals," which have since given way to tax credits.

Australia

Australia is less diverse than Canada; yet it includes Tasmania—an isolated, remote, and relatively small island confronted with difficult problems of economic development—and Western Australia, one of the last "frontiers" among developed nations. Victoria and New South Wales are urbanized and developed. Queensland and South Australia contain both developed areas and frontier. These six states, together with the Northern Territory, which is federally administered, constitute the Federal Commonwealth of Australia.

At its birth, in 1901, the Australian Federation reserved customs duties for the Commonwealth. Because of the unpopularity of direct taxes on income and property at that time, this prohibition left the states financially weak, though they retained excise taxation. In Australia there was one additional reason for adopting tax sharing. The Australian propensity to import was generally high; but it was much higher in the frontier areas than in Victoria and New South Wales. Since customs duties served as a sizable source of revenue, covering nearly all federal expenditures, the burden of taxation fell most heavily on the frontier areas. Therefore, the general grants to the states were calculated in ways designed to compensate these areas for their heavier tax burden. This arrangement was then incorporated into the constitution and slated to continue for 10 years before being renegotiated.

The Commonwealth soon began to view general grants as "fiscally irresponsible." Therefore, the general grant was fixed at 25 shillings per capita in 1910 and allowed to remain at this level for the next 18 years. With the rapid increases in Australia's population and income and the expanding use of income taxes by the states, the importance of the general grant declined sharply from 57 percent of state revenues in 1911 to 20 percent in 1928. However, the underdeveloped states were dissatisfied because they claimed they bore a heavier burden of customs taxation and had a greater need for support. Therefore, "special grants" were instituted for Western Australia (in 1911), Tasmania (in 1922), and South Australia (in 1929). This arrangement of giving "special grants" to "claimant" states above and beyond the general and specific grants has continued to this day as a characteristic of Australian tax sharing.

Specific Grants

Despite its aversion to tax sharing, the Commonwealth provided considerable financial assistance to the states during 1910–41; but it relied increasingly on the specific grant. In 1923, the Commonwealth instituted a specific grant for roads. Initially, distribution among the states was based three-fifths on population and two-fifths on area. In 1926, this grant was made quite specific and conditional: its use was limited to construction; it was supervised by a federal executive board, and it required 75 percent matching of the Commonwealth funds. During the Great Depression, these conditions proved burdensome and were lifted. However, supervision and matching were reinstated in 1964, although on a more modest scale. In

1959, the formula for distribution was modified to one-third population, one-third area, and one-third vehicle registrations, thus reducing the tendency to aid heavily the thinly populated states. At present, the roads grant remains the single most important specific grant, accounting for 56 percent of all specific grants. (However, general grants are much more important in Australia than specific grants, and the roads grant is of real financial importance only in Western Australia, where it accounts for about 18 percent of the state's revenues.)

During and after World War II, specific grants were instituted for universities, hospitals, public works, and housing. Only the program for universities gained real importance. On the whole, specific grants have not developed very far in Australia. In addition, present specific grants are quite "general" in comparison with the restrictions commonly imposed on specific grants in the United States. Perhaps this is due to the earlier experience with the roads grant as a highly specific and conditional grant —and to the distinctly unfavorable reaction of the states to these features of the grant.

Australia has developed an interesting and somewhat unusual specific grant: a subsidy on the interest payments on state loans and on the sinking funds for such loans. Partly in return for this subsidy, the states allow the Commonwealth to regulate their borrowing through a "loan council." This arrangement dates back to the Financial Agreement of 1927, which converted the former per capita flat general grant of 25 shillings into this type of subsidy. The fundamentals of this agreement have persisted to the present day. Its suitability is explained at least in part by the heavy responsibilities for economic development that have traditionally been assigned to the states. Through this grant for interest payments and sinking funds, Australia is operating much as developing nations do when they form subsidized and government-owned industrial development corporations. Technically, this is a specific grant, but in actual operation it resembles more closely a general grant, or the federal income tax exemption of interest on state and local bonds in the United States.

General Grants and Equalization

When World War II broke out, the Commonwealth judged that centralization of all income taxes, personal as well as corporate, would be necessary. The states disagreed, but the Commonwealth prevailed in the constitutional tussle that followed, and by 1942 the states had relinquished all income taxes. After the war, the states attempted to regain their former prerogative, but the Australian tax-payer had become accustomed to filing only one income tax form and Australia kept the system instituted in war time. Under this system the states retained great responsibilities which they no longer could meet from their own tax resources. Thus, general grants became an important feature of Australian governmental finances.

At first (1942–46), the states were merely paid annually the average amount which had been collected by each state during 1939–41. This arrangement was inadequate because it reflected the prewar income-tax policies of the states and did not allow for economic growth. In 1946, in order to come to a new agreement the Commonwealth offered the states £40,000,000 and invited them to divide this among themselves. At the same time, the states were promised an annual increase in this "tax reimbursement" fund according to a formula that took into account population and the increase in the level of wages. The states reached an ad hoc agreement on the initial division of the fund, but provided that in the future the fund should be divided according to an "adjusted population" formula based on population weighted by two "cost factors": school population and population density. This formula was to be phased-in by applying it to one-tenth of the fund during the first year and an additional tenth during each successive year until 1957–58, when the entire amount of the fund was to be distributed according to the new formula.

This arrangement did not settle the issues, either as to the total amount of the fund or as to its distribution. Each year the state premiers prevailed upon the Commonwealth premier to add "supplements" to the amount provided by the formula. (Supplements amounted to 28 percent of the formula grants in 1951–52; they never dropped below 9.8 percent.) These supplements were divided among the states in different ways and became the subject of unwelcome annual negotiations.

At the expiration of this 10-year agreement, the Commonwealth and states adopted a new 6-year agreement, effective in 1959. Distribution according to "adjusted population" was abandoned; instead, flat payments were negotiated for 1958–59 for each state. These new payments—renamed "financial assistance" grants—increase with population, wages, and a 10 percent "betterment factor." Supplements were needed in only three of the six years during which this new agreement was in operation. It was continued with slight modifications in the 1965 agreement, which expires in 1970; this agreement follows the main lines of the 1959 agreement except that the base amount was adjusted in favor of Queensland and the "betterment factor" was raised to 20 percent.

As is evident from the above, general grants in Australia are handled in an informal manner. Their history also shows that the amount and distribution of such grants can become a potent annual political issue. Australia has been able to settle the issue through ad hoc agreements because it is a federation composed of only six states. Federations with a greater number of states would probably have to develop more objective methods to achieve any generally agreeable solution. Moreover, the system has worked in Australia partly because the Commonwealth has provided separate economic support to its economically weakest states, Western Australia, Tasmania, and (until 1959) South Australia. These special grants are determined with considerable sophistication.

Special Grants

By 1929, the Commonwealth had distinguished three "claimant" states, Western Australia, Tasmania, and South Australia; and three "standard" states, New South Wales, Queensland, and Victoria. In 1933, the Parliament decided to establish a Commonwealth Grants Commission to report on what special grants the claimant states needed. The work of the Commission proved so successful that it is still in existence 36 years later. The reason for its success is probably that it has managed to come up consistently with "objective" solutions to the requests of the claimant states. For example, is the same quality of hospital service costlier in thinly populated Western Australia than in more densely populated Victoria? The Commission studies this matter and attempts to establish "objective" cost differences. By means of such determinations, based largely on well-chosen studies of tax effort and the cost of providing public services, the Commission has kept such questions outside the political arena of Parliament and the Premiers' Conferences. This seems to satisfy the claimant states. When South Australia was persuaded to abandon claimancy in 1959, it was compensated by an increase in its general grant that exceeded the amount it had been receiving in special grants.

Summary

Given the exclusion of the states from the taxation of income and their continuing heavy responsibilities, Australia necessarily has relied heavily on general grants. In 1964–65, these came to £356.5 million, 72 percent of all Commonwealth grants to the states and 48 percent of the states' total revenues. (In the case of Tasmania, general grants amounted to 78 percent of total grants and 68 percent of total revenues.) Large general grants date back to 1942; yet there have been no reports of the "fiscal irresponsibility" which had been dreaded in Australia in the 1920s and had prompted the Commonwealth to virtually eliminate general grants at that time.

The main trouble associated with large general grants in Australia has been not fiscal irresponsibility, but exhausting political struggles over the size and distribution of such grants. The solution found by Australia for this problem—for each state a negotiated flat amount that increases with population and cost factors—may not be suitable for federations that comprise a larger number of diverse states and are likely to require more "objective" formulas.

In the case of special grants, however, the Australian approach of providing special support for "claimant" states on a basis of differences in tax effort and public service costs is of considerable interest and applicability wherever there are states which can be clearly classified as "claimant" states. It is a cross between handling special grants in the legislature or in "governors' conferences," a highly political process, and handling them within a special department of the executive branch, as is done in the United States in such cases as the Appalachia programs. Apparently, the Commonwealth Grants Commission has been able to combine the strengths of each of these two approaches while avoiding most of their weaknesses.

West Germany

West Germany is a federation with a highly urbanized and integrated economy (though marked cultural differences may exist). The Basic Law of 1949 divided governmental power among a central government (*Bund*), and 11 states (*Länder*). Three of the Länder are city-states (somewhat like the District of Columbia), that is, they combine state and local functions; they are Bremen, Hamburg, and West Berlin. The other eight are North Rhine-Westphalia, Bavaria, Baden-Württemberg, Lower Saxony, Hesse, Rhineland-Palatinate, Schleswig-Holstein, and Saarland. These eight have a local level of government (formed of *Kreise* or *Gemeinden*) as in Australia, Canada, and the United States.

Interestingly, in Germany tax sharing has been a very important constitutional and political issue. This is because when the German Empire (Reich) was formed in 1871, the Reichstag, or central legislature, was allotted taxing powers only over customs and excise taxes; consequently the central government had to rely to some extent on contributions from the states (Matrikularbeiträge). These contributions (ranging from 2.5 percent of the central government budget to 11.0 percent during 1871–1913) were never so great as to seriously weaken the central government, but they were one of the means by which the Kaiser's chancellor could—and often did—rule without the confidence of the Reichstag. It was a valuable threat against the Reichstag; if the Reichstag rejected some parts of the budget, the chancellor could appeal to the states.

In reaction, the Weimar Republic (1919) placed all tax administration under the central government. The states now depended on the central government for their revenues, as the power of the purse was consolidated under the Reichstag.

But this consolidation may have had an undesirable effect. When the National-Socialist party gained the chancellorship in 1933 as the largest minority party, the other parties (Catholic Center, Social Democratic, and Communist) were unable to maintain separate bases of power in the states, even though two of the parties (Social Democrats and Catholic Center) actually had majorities in some of the states.

In political theory, federalism is often considered to be a strong defense against one-party rule. The classic example is the United States from 1865 to 1929, when the Republicans often had overwhelming majorities but the Democrats were never in danger of being wiped out because of their base of power in the South. The framers of the Basic Law of 1949, in their attempt to incorporate in the constitution every possible device designed to prevent a repetition of one-party rule in Germany, included federalism. Weimar federalism, however, had failed in this respect—perhaps because of the financial weakness of the states. The Basic Law of 1949, as a result, is one of the few written constitutions which contain permanent provisions about tax sharing. The new measures were intended to make the states financially independent of the central government but not to strengthen them to such an extent that the central government would become largely dependent on them (because this would favor executive power). The constitution tried to pick its way between the two extremes. This task was complicated because uniformity of taxation was highly esteemed in the closely integrated West German economy.

Division of Tax Legislation

West Germany proceeded toward the solution of this problem in the following way. As in any federation, in West Germany there are exclusive and concurrent powers. In the case of taxes, only two taxes are exclusively within the legislative sphere of the Bundestag: customs duties and fiscal monopolies. These two are very minor revenue sources; in 1968, they represented only 4.1 percent of total Bund and Länder tax revenues. Other taxes fall in the area of concurrent powers. However, since uniformity is of value in such a tightly integrated economy, the constitution established the principle that in the case of concurrent powers "federal law breaks state law." The Bundestag (the successor of the Reichstag) has availed itself of this privilege and legislated widely in the area of concurrent powers.

Thus all the major taxes fall in the area of concurrent jurisdiction, where the Bundestag has legislated widely. However, in this area the powers of the Bundestag vary. The Bundestag may legislate as it wishes if the proceeds of the tax accrue entirely to the Bund; but if the proceeds flow in part or entirely to the Länder, then the Bundestag can legislate only with the concurrence of the Council of States (Bundesrat). This body is composed of representatives from the Länder, which are given 3 votes if their population is under 2,000,000; 4 votes if under 6,000,000 but over 2,000,000; and 5 votes if over 6,000,000. Each delegation must vote as a unit and is bound by resolutions passed by the Länder. Tax legislation, division of the proceeds of shared taxes (see below), and constitutional amendments—which must secure a two-thirds majority in the Bundesrat to be passed—constitute the major functions of the Bundesrat. On these questions, its concurrence is necessary. On others, it can be overruled by the Bundestag.

This complex setup divides taxes into three basic categories: (1) taxes that only the Bundestag may legislate; (2) taxes that the Bundestag may legislate on its own, if it wishes; (3) taxes that the Bundestag may legislate only with the concurrence of the Bundesrat.[2]

Division of Tax Proceeds

Having established this division, the Basic Law of 1949 went on to assign the proceeds of taxes. The Bund receives the proceeds from the following; customs, fiscal monopolies (at present there is only a spirits monopoly), turnover taxes (now being converted to a value-added tax to comply with the requirements of the Common Market), the transportation tax on carriage of freight and passengers for profit, and all excises excepting the beer tax. Currently the Bund taxes only two commodities, tobacco and fuel oil (Mineralöl). Altogether, these Bund taxes came to 46 percent of Bund and Länder tax revenues in 1968. The Länder are assigned the proceeds of numerous taxes, but these add up to much less revenue than the Bund taxes. They are the following: the "property" or net worth tax, the beer tax, all "transactions taxes" except the turnover and transportation taxes (for example, taxes on insurance, lotteries, drafts and bills of exchange, sales of motor vehicles, and so on), inheritance tax, and taxes "of exclusively local application" (for example, a fire protection tax). Altogether, the taxes of the Länder came to 8 percent of total Bund and Länder tax revenues in 1968.

Proceeds of taxes on income, which in 1968 accounted for 45 percent of tax revenue, must be shared by the Bund and the Länder; the precise distribution pattern is determined by the Bundesrat. This is one of its most important powers. In 1950, the Bund received no revenue from income taxes; it was given its first share in 1951. This share increased quickly over the years to a peak of 39 percent in 1964–66; at present it is down somewhat to 35 percent.

Division of Tax Administration

West Germany has proceeded further constitutionally in the area of tax sharing than other countries by providing for a division of tax administration. In West Germany, the right to administer a tax belongs to the government that receives its proceeds. In principle, this could lead to much duplication of tax administration. West Germany has dealt with this problem in two ways. First, the Bund is allowed to delegate its power to administer a tax. Second, West Germany has established 15 Regional Finance Offices (Oberfinanz-directionen). These offices perform the tax-collecting

---

2 The right of the Bundestag to legislate taxes in the second and third categories is, moreover, subject to review by the Federal Constitutional Court, which may invalidate the legislation if the Bund does not need the revenues from such taxes or if it is not proved that there is an advantage in such nationwide legislation (in the case of taxes whose proceeds flow wholly or in part to the Länder).

functions of both the Bund and the Länder. In some of the bigger Länder, there is more than one Regional Finance Office, but in no case do Regional Finance Offices cross the boundaries of the Länder. The head of each Regional Finance Office is appointed by the Land in which the office is located with the concurrence of the Bund. His salary is paid half by the Bund and half by the Land, and he heads both a Land Tax Division and a Bund Tax Division. The Land Tax Division is by far the more important; it administers all taxes whose proceeds go entirely to the Länder, those taxes whose proceeds go partly to the Länder, and taxes whose administration has been delegated by the Bund to the Länder (that is, the turnover tax and the transportation tax). The Bund Tax Division handles only customs and the two excises on tobacco and fuel oil, or about 12 percent of total Bund and Länder tax revenue. However, the Bund appoints the personnel in the Land Tax Division who administer the taxes the Bund has delegated—the turnover tax and the transportation tax—which, together, constitute another 24 percent of total Bund and Länder taxes. It also has the spirits monopoly, which accounts for about 2 percent of tax revenues of both the Bund and the Länder. This leaves the Länder with full responsibility over personnel who administer about 62 percent of the tax revenue collected, although only 37 percent of Bund and Länder taxes flow to the Länder.

Equalization of Burdens and Specific Grants

The Basic Law of 1949 mandated equalization, that is, that the richer parts of Germany help the government finances of the poorer parts. In meeting this mandate, Germany has worked out a system based on the following three principles:

First, West Germany has adopted what it calls "horizontal equalization": the richer Länder pay into an "equalization-of-burdens fund" and the poorer Länder draw payments from this fund. The Bund sets the formulas that determine these payments and withdrawals. This arrangement is designed to assist the poorer states without making them unduly dependent on the central government.

Second, although payments flow only to the Länder (without any pass-through requirements), the computation of these payments takes into account not only the taxes of the Länder but also the taxes of the local authorities within each Länder. This arrangement recognizes the fact that the Länder extend substantial financial aid to their local authorities (and also the existence of the three city-states where local and state revenues are amalgamated).

Third, the distribution formula is based on actual tax collections. Payments flow to those Länder whose per capita tax collections are below the average per capita tax collections for West Germany as a whole. Using actual tax collections simplifies computation of equalization payments but gives rise to adverse incentive effects at the state (and, possibly, at the local) level. The richer states find that the more they tax the more they have to pay to the equalization-of-burdens fund, whereas the poorer states may increase their drawings from the fund by reducing their taxes. If this system appears to have functioned reasonably well—despite its adverse incentive effects—this may be partially due to the enlightenment of the Länder, and even more to the extensive powers of the Bund, which may legislate the taxes used by the Länder (according to the constitutional forms described above). Any competition among the Länder to lower taxes could thus be quickly arrested by the Bund.

Finally, despite the strong emphasis of the Basic Law of 1949 on the financial independence of the states vis-à-vis the central government, West Germany's central government has found it desirable to stimulate certain types of state and local expenditures by means of specific grants. This program of specific grants, based on national priorities, is less important than in the United States—yet it came to 12 percent of total state and local revenues in 1967 (compared with the present 18 percent in the United States).

Recent Revisions

The preceding analysis covered the West German tax structure as it has existed since 1950. But the Common Market nations are currently engaged in a process of tax harmonizing that is producing important changes in the West German tax structure. Among these changes, the substitution of the value-added tax for the turnover tax is the most far reaching to date. Moreover, the second half of 1969 witnessed an important fiscal agreement among the Bund, the Länder, and local authorities, concerning fiscal reform. Several changes in the tax-sharing arrangements were introduced which will become effective in 1970. The projected effects of these various changes are summarized in Table 1. As indicated there, the net result of these changes will be to strengthen the finances of local authorities at the expense of the Bund—leaving the financial strength of the Länder virtually unaffected (even though the relative contribution of the major taxes changes drastically). On balance, however, this redistribution of financial strength between the Bund and the local authorities will be rather modest.

Summary

The framers of the Basic Law of 1949 had to exercise considerable ingenuity in re-establishing the financial independence of the Länder in a strongly integrated economy which stresses uniformity of taxation. This uniformity seems to have been achieved to a much greater extent than in the United States. As a rule, the German taxpayer—whether a person or a corporation—need keep only one set of books for taxation by the various

Table 1. Impact of the 1969 Fiscal Reform on Tax Distribution

Category of tax		Federal government	Länder governments	Local authorities *
		Percentage distribution		
Wage tax and assessed income tax	1969	35	65	—
	1970	43	43	14
Corporation tax and capital yield tax	1969	35	65	—
	1970	50	50	—
Capital transactions tax, insurance, and bill taxes	1969	—	100	—
	1970	100	—	—
Turnover tax	1969	100	—	—
	1970	70	30	—
Trade tax	1969	—	—	100
	1970	20	20	60
		Increase (+) or decrease (−) in DM billion		
Wage tax and assessed income tax		+ 3.5	− 9.6	+ 6.1
Corporation tax and capital yield tax		+ 1.9	− 1.9	—
Capital transactions tax, insurance, and bill taxes		+ 1.2	− 1.2	—
Turnover tax		−10.0	+10.0	—
Trade tax		+ 2.6	+ 2.6	− 5.2
Total		− 0.8	− 0.1	+ 0.9

SOURCE: Deutsche Bundesbank.
* Including taxes levied by Berlin, Bremen, and Hamburg.

levels of government. He deals with a local government finance office for payment of most of his taxes; this local office, in turn, reports to the Bund Tax Division and/or the Land Tax Division of its Regional Finance Office. Thus, tax sharing has been used to attain a high degree of tax co-ordination and integrated tax administration; at the same time, it has served as an important interstate revenue equalization device.

Conclusions

The foregoing review of the intergovernmental fiscal relations within three federations demonstrates that discrepancies between revenue-raising power and expenditure responsibilities are widespread. Grants and tax- or revenue-sharing devices are common tools for bridging the revenue-expenditure gaps at the state and local level. Yet there are considerable variations in the specific techniques, legal provisions, and administrative arrangements used by different federations.

Moreover, the balancing of revenues with expenditure responsibilities is not the only major function of tax sharing. All three nations reviewed here make extensive use of revenue sharing for equalization purposes, that is, for redistribution of revenue from the wealthier to the poorer states or regions of the country. In addition, Canada has used revenue sharing to provide an alternative to tax credits for those provinces that did not wish to set up their own tax administration. Australia used it initially to modify the incidence of taxes on imports which placed a particularly heavy burden on its less-developed states. Finally, in West Germany, economic goals have been joined with political considerations in connection with tax sharing: the federal fiscal balance and the financial strength of the Länder have been shaped by the constitution with political safeguards against one-party rule in mind.

The Role of the "Concerted Action" Program in the Economic Policy of the Federal Republic of Germany

DR. OTTO SCHLECHT

A government policy intended to achieve and safeguard stability of the price level, reasonable growth of the national economy, and full employment cannot disregard the connection between overall economic development and the development of income. Within a free, Western social system, over-all economic development is influenced also—and to a very substantial extent—by how autonomous groups, particularly labor and management, exploit their freedom of movement in reaching wage-policy decisions. Within the limits set by the prevailing state of macroeconomic development, labor and management contribute with their decision on the wage level and on the price level (via demand and costs) toward laying down the degree of employment and the chances of growth. Hence, government economic policy can hardly attain its prescribed objectives for over-all economic development solely with the means of monetary and fiscal policy. It has to depend on the big autonomous groups of economic society behaving in a manner consonant with those objectives. It is this behavior of the groups, which is oriented to the common objectives for over-all economic development, that is meant when "Konzertierte Aktion" (Concerted Action) is referred to in the Federal Republic of Germany. This voluntary behavior of

Reprinted from *The German Economic Review*, Vol. 8, No. 3, 1970, pp. 255–260, by permission of the publisher.

the big social groups is the aim of the government initiative for "Concerted Action."

So in the Federal Republic of Germany, "Concerted Action" is the attempt, within the framework of government economic policy and within a market economy system, to harmonize the development of income with overall economic development by harmonizing objectives. This sort of income policy differs in essential respects from the course set for income policy in the past few decades in other Western industrial countries. As demonstrated by the examples of Great Britain and the Netherlands, within a fundamentally liberal system in the long run government compulsion in income policy is not very successful and basically benefits no one. Government compulsory requirements and controls on the movement of wages and salaries, which would restrict autonomy in negotiating wage rates and would then have to be extended to free price setting, and so on, lead to a trend in which either government control would have to become ever more drastic or which would only end in an even worse explosion of suppressed demands. For this reason, German economic policy has dispensed with "wage guidelines" and all similar things, and instead, with its initiative for "Concerted Action," has worked in the direction of voluntarily harmonized behavior of the groups concerned.

Since early 1967, the "Concerted Action" program has been one of the instruments of official economic policy in the Federal Republic of Germany. At that time, Professor Karl Schiller had become Federal Minister for Economic Affairs; it is to him that thanks are due for placing economic policy in the Federal Republic of Germany on a footing embracing modern economic methods. Over-all guidance of macroeconomic development in the market economy became a program. And from the beginning, "Concerted Action" was part of it.

The ground had been prepared for it in economic policy debate in our country. The Economic Advisory Council in the Federal Ministry for Economic Affairs had recommended as far back as 1956, in an annual report on the economic situation, that "labor and management should be provided with new material with which they can assess the effects of their planned wage policy measures on the economic process as a whole and the resulting consequences for themselves."

Similar proposals made by this Advisory Council in spring 1960, by the German Trade Unions Federation in its statement of basic principles issued in 1963, and by the Board of Experts for the Assessment of Overall Economic Trends in its annual expert opinions, and also considerations which originated from the beginning of the sixties among officials of the Federal Ministry for Economic Affairs finally brought success after the change of government in December 1966 had created the required internal political conditions.

In summer 1967, the new "Act to Promote the Stability and Growth of the Economy," the new "basic law on the policy of the economic process," was promulgated. In English translation § 3 of this act reads:

1. In the event of the jeopardization of one of the objectives enumerated in § 1, the Federal Government shall make available orientation data for simultaneous, co-ordinated action (Concerted Action) of regional public authorites, trade unions and associations of firms for the attainment of the said objectives. The said orientation data shall include in particular a description of overall economic relationships in the light of the given situation.

2. At the request of any of those concerned, the Federal Minister for Economic Affairs shall explain the said orientation data.

Hitherto the "Concerted Action" program has been pursued in the spirit of this statutory formulation. To re-emphasize the point: the only party placed under an obligation is the federal government. It must provide and explain orientation data; by way of its economic and fiscal policy it must create the basis on which concerted behavior is possible for and can be expected of the autonomous groups. Whether and how the big, organized, economic and social associations adapt their income policy decisions to the objectives of over-all economic development and thus integrate their behavior into the economic and fiscal policy influencing over-all economic trends is, and remains, voluntary. So the government must attempt to co-ordinate; it cannot and may not issue orders. From case to case it has to derive up-to-date orientation data from economic policy objectives and actual developments; that is, with respect to orientation data for wage policies it is not permitted to proceed simply according to certain, rigid, patent wage-theory formulas. As far as content is concerned, with its orientation data it can gain persuasive power only if those data are consonant with the judgment reached by the affected parties, in a joint dialogue, on the desired over-all economic development.

In the German economic policy debate, the term "Concerted Action" is mostly also used erroneously to designate the conference convened several times a year by the government. In that conference, the exchange of information and opinions takes place among the government and the autonomous groups, without which voluntary concerted action would hardly be possible. The government invites only the most important associations to these talks. The number of participants is intentionally kept relatively small, so that the exchange of ideas can remain fruitful. Regular participants are: (1) about ten trade union chairmen—from both important specialized unions and the peak organization, the German Trade Unions Federation, and also from the "Angestelltengewerkschaft" (Salaried Employees' Union); (2) from the employers' side, the chairmen of the peak associations of industry, wholesale and foreign trade, retail trade, handicrafts and trades, the farmers, the banking business, and the chairmen of the Union of German Chambers of Industry and Commerce and the National Union of German Employers' Associations; (3) in an advisory capacity, members of the above-mentioned Board of Experts for the Assessment of Overall Economic Trends and the president of the German Bundesbank; (4) as government representatives, the Federal Ministers of Finance, Labor, and Agriculture or their delegated representatives; the Federal Minister for Economic Affairs takes the chair. The associations participating in the talks are selected so that as far as possible all firms in the German economy are represented by one of the associations and that, on the other hand, all important employees' associations take part. The object is to ensure that the results, conclusions, and information emanating from the talks can also be effectively disseminated on as broad a basis as possible in the various groups of economic society.

During the talks, no resolutions of any sort are passed which would impose obligations on the participants. There are no formal votes or the like. Moreover, the talks are largely confidential; otherwise it would hardly be possible—for all participants, not only the government—to provide really complete information and bring about a genuine exchange of views, that is to avoid "hot air." And wage policy is not the only issue dealt with in these talks. They also cover general trade cycle policy, the trend of employment, the investment and price policy of firms, government competition policy, and long-term income and wealth distribution. Without an exchange of information and views on these questions, too, it is impossible to induce willingness in the participating groups to orient their behavior to the objectives of over-all economic development. Those concerned must be sure that general economic and fiscal policy will be pursued in such a manner that concerted action does not become an incalculable risk.

This mode of conducting economic policy talks with the autonomous groups is something fundamentally new for the Federal Republic of Germany. By way of this exchange of information and opinions in the talks of the "Concerted Action" program, the participants have a chance to take part in shaping economic policy opinions and decisions. These talks provide them, so to speak, with an official addressee for their wishes in respect of a broad variety of decisions by government authorities on economic policy and income policy. It is manifest that this facet of the talks also changes both the position of the pressure groups in a free, pluralistic society and the picture these associations present to society. These talks are, we might say, a sign that nowadays co-operation of all decision makers in a liberal society is necessary, and that there is no longer on the one side the sovereign—though democratically controlled—ruler and on the other the ruled society.

The consequences and the successes of the talks within the framework of the "Concerted Action" program since 1967 have shown in the first place that the idea and action of introducing this instrument for the over-all control of the economic circulatory system have proved an expedient means of tackling a generally appreciated problem. The "Concerted Action" program was able to start with a large amount of advance trust in it, and it rapidly gained great popularity among the public. As a result, however, it also awakened great hopes which simply could not be fulfilled. It can achieve positive effects only if it is capable of convincing those affected. The only pressure that can be exerted on the behavior of the participants must emanate from public opinion. A group which deviates to an extreme degree from the jointly elaborated objectives and data for over-all economic development is obliged, so to speak, to justify its action to the public; if it fails to prove the necessity of its diverging behavior, it risks being accused of having caused undesirable over-all economic development by its behavior. The quantifying target projections set up by the government for over-all economic development constitute the yardstick for the public's judgment of such deviations by individual groups. Those projections make it more difficult for the various groups to lay an ideological smoke screen over their diverging objectives with the innocence of pure, self-centered "logic." All this, of course, presupposes that, in its turn, the government will institute in good time the measures for which it has a mandate and suitable instruments for the preservation of over-all economic equilibrium.

"Concerted Action," moreover, cannot lead to, say, anticyclical wage policy—however ideal that might be considered by many people. To make such demands would be asking too much of this instrument. What can be achieved is at best an improvement in the constancy of income development; extreme, procyclical swings of the income pendulum can be avoided, if it is possible, within the ambit of the "Concerted Action" program, to attain a consensus of the participants on the desired development.

In 1967, the year of the economic recession, all concerned agreed that —as it was put—no negative wage policy should be pursued. And indeed there were hardly any wage cuts in the crisis. At the time, this was a success that was attributed generally to the "Concerted Action" talks. It was possible because the macroeconomic and income policy interdependences were demonstrated to the participating groups, their understanding was gained for the necessary decisions in the areas of government over-all control, regulatory and structural policy, and the participating groups autonomously oriented their decisions thereto. By way of clarification it must be added that wage policy cannot be made a residual factor, nor is it possible, even with the most ingenious wage-policy guidelines, to swim against the tide of overdemand or underdemand resulting from government laissez-faire. Harmonization of modes of behavior running counter to the basic direction in which the forces of the market are exerted would be doomed to fail at an early stage. Within the framework of trade cycle policy, therefore, wage policy can play only a supplementary, or rather an accompanying, role, but in no circumstances a dominant role. Monetary and fiscal policy must form the nucleus of over-all control. For this reason, too, no pronounced anticyclical wage policy is possible—any demand for such a policy would be problematical if only on account of the double function of wages as a demand and cost factor.

Another success of the "Concerted Action" program, which naturally cannot be expressed in terms of figures, is the fact that over-all economic considerations and arguments play a considerably bigger role than formerly in the internal and public debates among labor and management. The remarkable objectivization and "economization" of bargaining has certainly also had positive effects in social respects. The "Concerted Action" talks cannot eliminate social conflicts. The interests in question are of too massive proportions for that. But they can—and this they have definitely achieved—limit the legitimate conflicts and make the significance and cause of those conflicts more easily perceptible.

The talks, and the "Concerted Action" idea in itself, have also, of course, been subjected to considerable criticism in the course of the German economic policy debate. Some critics see in these talks the constitutional danger that private groups may penetrate too deeply into the sphere of government decisions. Conversely, others criticize the fact that the government does too little to ensure that through the medium of "Concerted Action" the binding establishment of "correct" wage increases is effected. The wage-increase rates should be decided on by the participants like bank rate by the central bank. Further basically aggressive criticism is leveled against the fact that supposedly the "Concerted Action" program is intended only to preserve the existing, unjust distribution relationships.

The future will show whether this instrument of voluntary advance coordination will remain useful. The decisive prerequisite is an economic policy which, on the whole, is convincing and is successfully oriented to the objectives of stability, growth, and full employment. If such a policy is lacking, nobody can demand of management and labor that they voluntarily waive their own short-term market chances in favor of long-term benefits for all.

Discussion Questions

1. How would you evaluate the worth of revenue sharing plans in Canada, Australia, and West Germany?
2. What benefits do you think would accrue to the United States if revenue sharing were adopted?
3. Discuss the goals of the West German "Concerted Action" program.
4. Would a "Concerted Action" program be applicable to the United States?

The Banking System

The Federal Reserve System in the United States is a hierarchical system consisting of (1) the policymaking Board of Governors at its head, (2) 12 regional Federal Reserve Banks, and (3) the member banks of the system, which account for about 85 percent of all demand deposits in the country. In reality, even those banks which are not officially member banks of the Federal Reserve System correspond with the larger commercial banks, and thus it is fair to say that, for all intents and purposes, we have a unified banking system operating under the aegis of the Fed.

The two articles in this section describe two alternative banking systems. The second article, written by Yoshizane Iwasa, Board Chairman and former president of Japan's largest bank, explicitly treats the differences between Japan's banking system—a nationwide multi-branch structure—and our own. The first article, written by Jane Nelson, an economist with the Federal Reserve Bank of Richmond, Virginia, examines the banking system which probably most fascinates Americans—the banking system of Switzerland. When the term "Swiss banks" is mentioned, it conjures up visions of American actors depositing untaxed incomes in banks which sit in the shadow of the actors' luxurious chalets, or organized crime using the secrecy of Swiss banks to hide illegal wealth, or the international intrigue of an author depositing royalty advances on a phony autobiography of Howard Hughes. But the Nelson article dispels some of this mystery.

Swiss Banks

JANE NELSON

As a rule, the subject of banking generates little interest outside the business world. Few people, however, fail to perk up their ears at the mention of Swiss banks. This unusual reaction is not due to widespread knowledge concerning these institutions but, on the contrary, may be attributed to popular misconceptions and to the general air of mystery which seems to surround their operations. This article will attempt to dispel some of the mystery and explain why Swiss banks do, indeed, occupy a very special niche in the financial world.

Background

The Swiss banking system differs from its European counterparts primarily in the unusually large degree of freedom exercised by individual banks and in the rigid enforcement of bank secrecy. These characteristics are rooted deeply in Swiss history.

The present Swiss state began as a military alliance between three German cantons, or states, in 1291. In 1648 the confederation became independent of the Holy Roman Empire, and 200 years after that a federal constitution was written. Shielded by an exceptionally rugged terrain, Switzerland remained aloof from the turbulent European scene, and her neutrality was officially recognized by the major powers in 1815 by the Treaty of Vienna. At an early stage, the Swiss emerged as an independent, hard-working people, skilled in the arts and crafts. Today Switzerland is a confederation of 22 cantons and three half cantons, each of which has its own legislature, executive, and judiciary. Just as Swiss citizens jealously guard their personal privacy, the cantons guard their prerogatives, and the federal government has relatively little authority in areas other than those explicitly specified by the Constitution, namely, foreign affairs, money and coinage, post, and railroads. Taxes have remained predominantly a cantonal affair, and tax offenses are generally treated as administrative, not criminal, matters.

Until World War I the development of Swiss banking had paralleled that of most other continental banking systems. Among other things, these systems differ from their American counterpart in that checking accounts play a much less important role. In Switzerland, most small transfers of funds which are handled in the United States with checks are cleared through giro accounts administered by the Federal Post Office. Another

Reprinted from the *Monthly Review* of the Federal Reserve Bank of Richmond, December 1968, pp. 8–10, by permission of the publisher.

contrast is that banks, acting as brokers, are the principal members of stock exchanges.

The dramatic rise in the international importance of Swiss banks occurred after World War I. With the breakdown of the gold standard in the early 1930s, most European countries turned to isolationist economic policies including restrictions on the export of currency and capital. These policies, in conjunction with a number of other factors, contributed to the severity of the depression which spread throughout the Continent. In contrast, Switzerland, which emerged virtually untouched by the war, adopted no such policies. Thus, as most European nations grappled unsuccessfully with inflation, depression, and political instability, Switzerland stood out more and more clearly as a haven for savings, investment, and business enterprises.

Bank Secrecy

Secrecy is the aspect of Swiss banks which intrigues the world. It reflects the Swiss view that one's finances are as private a matter as one's religion and equally deserving of freedom from governmental control. While most banks maintain a confidential relationship with their customers, few go to such lengths as Swiss banks to preserve this relationship intact. The Swiss do not feel obliged to enforce laws not of their own making. A bank must open its books when so ordered by a Swiss criminal court. As long as their customers do not break Swiss law or international law, however, the banks protect the depositors. Even the existence of an account is not acknowledged to a third party. The numbered account, which came into being in the 1920s, is another safeguard of privacy, although in practice an unnumbered account is equally secret. The numbered account is not an anonymous account; a client's identity is always known to the top two or three executives of a bank. The origin of the funds deposited is also generally known, particularly in regard to large deposits, since no bank will knowingly accept stolen money. Indeed, most large Swiss banks will refuse any sizable deposit with a dubious past, or where tax evasion is the obvious motive for opening an account.

In the early 1930s the sanctity of Swiss bank accounts was put to a severe test when Hitler ordered all German citizens to declare their foreign holdings. Gestapo agents dispatched to ferret out Swiss accounts of German nationals scored some initial successes. Partially in response to this violation of financial privacy, the Swiss federal government passed the Banking Act of 1934 which authorizes fines and/or imprisonment for any bank employee who gives information respecting any account to any third party not specifically authorized by the account holder. All foreign governments, the Swiss federal and cantonal governments, and all foreign and domestic revenue authorities, are classified as third parties.

Strict bank secrecy often involves problems in the matter of beneficiaries. If a depositor dies or disappears without leaving a designated heir, the bank will search for any legal heirs. Should the search fail, Swiss law stipulates that the account escheats to the bank after having lain dormant for 20 years. Following World War II, Swiss banks were left with numerous unclaimed deposits as many depositors had perished with their beneficiaries. For years the supposed existence of these unclaimed deposits generated fierce controversy and litigation, but Swiss law remained unchanged.

Banking Structure

Switzerland is often described as "overbanked" with approximately one bank per 4,000 citizens in a territory twice the size of New Jersey, compared to a ratio of one bank per 14,000 citizens in the United States. Swiss banks may be divided into seven categories.

Big Banks

The five big banks account for about one-third of the assets of all Swiss banks. The three largest, the Swiss Credit Bank, the Union Bank of Switzerland, and the Swiss Bank Corporation have assets of approximately $2.5 to $3.0 billion each. As members of the Cartel of Swiss Banks, the big banks establish common interest rate policies but compete vigorously in other areas. Big bank activities cover a wide range, but lately they have come to specialize in short- or medium-term loans, especially in the export-import field. The big banks are also the most important stock brokers in Switzerland, with dealings on both domestic and foreign exchange, and are the principal underwriters of domestic stock and bond issues. Moreover, they are large dealers in foreign exchange and in gold. The big banks provide investment advisory and custodial services to their depositors who wish their funds put to work. Much of Switzerland's prominence in international finance derives from the status of big banks as international lenders. Switzerland currently supplies about one-third of all funds in the growing European currency market, a good portion of which comes from the big banks. While these banks may receive substantial deposits from underdeveloped countries, very little money is reinvested there. The big banks have numerous branches throughout Switzerland and a small number abroad. Through subsidiaries, they run the largest Swiss investment trusts.

Private Banks

The 50 private banks are among the oldest in Switzerland, with many dating from the late eighteenth century. They are not incorporated and the partners are liable to the full extent of their private fortunes. As long as private banks do not advertise or publicly seek business, they are not required to publish any financial statements and are exempt from certain provisions of the National Bank Law governing the ratio of capital to liabilities, and the maintenance of reserve funds. However, they must file financial statements with the Swiss National Bank. Any bank which does not publish financial statements may not accept savings deposits. The significance of private banks lies almost entirely in the world of international finance.

Cantonal Banks

Virtually every canton owns and operates its own bank, and the deposit liabilities of each bank are guaranteed by its cantonal government. Their activities, predominantly mortgage financing, are generally confined to the canton. Cantonal banks account for about one-third of total Swiss bank assets.

Other Banks

While these banks are Swiss corporations on Swiss soil, they are owned wholly by foreigners and their business is almost entirely foreign. The number and size of other banks has mushroomed since World War II and some are as large as big banks.

The remaining three categories include local banks, savings banks, and loan associations. Local banks, some of which are quite large, generally specialize in mortgage loans. While virtually all Swiss banks offer some type of savings account, savings banks proper serve the small depositor and balances exceeding a certain amount receive a lower interest rate. Loan associations, or banks, are found in nearly every small community. Their activities resemble those of credit unions in this country.

Regulation and the Swiss National Bank

Compared with banks in other countries, Swiss banks have always been uniquely unregulated. They issued their own circulating notes until the Swiss National Bank, established in 1905, began to exercise its note-issuing monopoly in 1907. In addition, the National Bank was authorized to store the national gold reserve, act as a national clearinghouse, and provide a limited degree of credit regulation. For the most part, regulation of Swiss banks has been directed at insuring efficient banking services and protecting private depositors. Following the failure of a number of banks in 1929, liquidity and capital requirements were established to be enforced by regular audits. Banks are audited by independent, authorized firms and irregularities, if uncorrected within a specified time, are reported to the Federal Banking Commission. Audits and reports of condition are not available to the federal or cantonal governments. All banks must submit balance sheets to the National Bank at least annually to expedite its function of money and credit regulation. Banks establish their own interest rates; neither the government nor the National Bank is empowered to set ceilings, although the National Bank may express approval or disapproval in regard to certain rate changes. Until 1964, banks were not legally required to maintain reserves with the National Bank, but in accordance with "gentlemen's agreements" they usually maintained a minimum ratio between their liabilities and their deposits with the National Bank. These agreements also included measures designed to counter threatening inflation.

In 1964, gentlemen's agreements proved inadequate in stemming the inflationary pressures caused by a tremendous inflow of foreign capital. The Swiss legislature felt compelled to enact a series of temporary measures aimed at curbing a domestic real estate boom, discouraging the inflow of foreign funds, and preventing such funds from entering the Swiss domestic money supply. These controls, which were administered by the central bank, included among other things the prohibition of interest payments on foreign deposits, the requirement that net inflows of non-interest bearing funds be paid into a frozen account at the central bank unless they were re-exported, and the placing of ceilings on the growth of bank credit. With the subsiding of inflationary pressures, all of the mandatory controls were removed by the spring of 1967. A few, however, were shifted to a voluntary basis under the auspices of the Swiss Bankers' Association. Because inflation fostered by inflows of foreign capital has continued to threaten Swiss economic stability, the Swiss Parliament is currently considering legislation which would broaden the hitherto limited control of the Swiss National Bank over monetary policy. Compulsory reserve requirements would be the principal policy tool. The passage of this controversial legislation depends largely upon the willingness of the Swiss banks to surrender a portion of their highly prized freedom from central control. Should the proposed changes become law, Swiss banks would remain among the world's least regulated banks.

International Reputation

The international reputation of Swiss banking can be said to have three aspects. The first arises from Switzerland's role as an international clearinghouse, featuring the Swiss-chartered Bank for International Settlements in Basel. In recent years, frequent meetings in Basel among prominent financial leaders seeking to bolster confidence in the international monetary system have heightened the prestige of this small country. While Swiss neutrality and desire for financial independence precludes membership in the International Monetary Fund, her influence in the area of international finance is substantial.

The second aspect derives from the extensive activities of Swiss banks as brokers and underwriters in the Euro-capital market, and as brokers and dealers in gold and foreign exchange. In the latter capacity, Swiss banks have sometimes been criticized for abetting disturbing movements in the foreign exchanges and in the gold market, thereby undermining key currencies. It should be borne in mind, however, that the veil of secrecy prohibits the disclosure of the origin of their transactions regardless of whether the bank is acting for its own account or as agent for a client.

The third aspect is somewhat ironic in that Swiss banks, a majority of which are very conservative, have achieved an air of notoriety. Because of rigid secrecy, statements made about the identity of Swiss bank depositors cannot be proved or disproved, and are left hanging. For example, swindled funds are often suspected of having been spirited off to Swiss vaults; international rackets, dope rings, and spy rings are said to use them behind legitimate fronts; and many a current or deposed strong man is thought to have siphoned off his country's wealth into a personal Swiss bank account. In the United States, Swiss banks have been accused of acting as fronts in corporate raids and proxy battles.

The use of Swiss banks for tax evasion is another cause of notoriety, particularly in this country where willful evasion is a felony. A portion of any interest or dividends earned on a Swiss account is withheld in Switzerland for Swiss taxes, but may be credited against United States taxes by filing the appropriate papers. Upon doing so, however, the Internal Revenue Service is alerted as to the existence of the account. Capital gains go completely untaxed if they are not reported or repatriated. Since failure to report such gains is illegal, such funds naturally are seldom repatriated. Compared to the number of French, German, and Italian depositors, it is thought that relatively few Americans have Swiss accounts.

Banking in Japan

YOSHIZANE IWASA

The substantial growth and development of the Japanese economy during the postwar era has received considerable publicity and is well understood abroad. At the same time, Japanese commercial banks which have played a most significant role in the nation's economy, remain comparatively unknown.

Japan's banking system was established about 100 years ago, copied to a great extent from the United States national banking system. The organization and function of financial institutions, however, differ according

Reprinted from *The Bankers Magazine,* Winter 1968, pp. 35–48, by permission of the publisher.

to a particular country's economic development processes, as well as with prevalent social and economic circumstances. For example, in Japan, commercial banks:

- Process few mortgages.
- Provide no personal trust services (this is done by trust banks).
- Do no securities underwriting.
- Handle no leases (though several banks are looking into this field).
- Do no factoring.
- Offer no bank credit cards (though many banks have arrangements with department stores for debiting customer accounts for purchases made).

On the other hand, banks in Japan do provide a number of services that are somewhat unique. Most valued bank customers receive a visit of their bank's official every day. All bank branches act on behalf of the Internal Revenue Service. Some metropolitan government and municipality offices have a bank window at their offices. Only a few banks such as Fuji Bank maintain windows at such places as public markets and raceways. And several banks offer consulting services (business development, legal, tax) to medium-sized and small firms at no charge.

In addition, some banks have arrangements with travel agencies and airlines to promote travel with a "fly-now, pay-later" service.

To understand the nature of Japanese banking, however, it is necessary to examine more closely some of the services, managerial techniques, and the organizational structures that give our banks their character and strength.

Financial Institutions of Japan

In contrast to the banking system of the United States, banking in Japan is based on the nation-wide, multi-branch system. As a result of the government's wartime policy which urged the amalgamation of commercial banks, the number of banks which totaled 519 in 1935, is now only 87.

Naturally, the characteristic forms and functions of financial institutions differ according to the stage of economic growth and social customs of the respective countries. In Japan, financial institutions had already developed prior to the capitalization of industries, which occurred after the Meiji Restoration in 1868, and by around 1905, the formal modernization of banking had been completed. Since then, of course, there have been significant improvements in the banking system.

After World War II, the nation's banking system was extensively reorganized. Long-term credit banks and a foreign exchange bank were established by special law. The establishment of medium-scale financial organizations such as mutual loan and savings banks and credit associations is also a notable feature of postwar banking.

Classification of Japan's Financial Institutions

* Central Bank: The Bank of Japan.
* Ordinary Banks: City banks (12), local banks (63)—established on the basis of the Bank Law.
* Trust Banks: Seven.
* Special Banks: Long-term credit banks (3)—established on the basis of the Long-term Credit Bank Law; Foreign exchange bank (1)—established on the basis of the Foreign Exchange Bank Law.
* Governmental Financial Institutions: Japan Development Bank; Export-Import Bank of Japan; People's Finance Corporation; Housing Loan Corporation; Small Business Finance Corporation; Agriculture, Forestry and Fisheries Finance Corporation; Hokkaido and Tohoku Development Corporation; Local Public Enterprise Finance Corporation; Small Business Credit Insurance Corporation; Medical Care Facilities Finance Corporation.
* Small and Medium Scale Enterprise.
* Finance Corporations: Mutual loan and savings banks (72); Credit Associations (528); Labor Credit Associations; Credit Cooperatives; Shoko Chukin Bank (Central Bank for Commercial and Industrial Cooperatives).

When we say "bank" in Japan, we mean ordinary banks, foreign exchange banks, trust banks or long-term credit banks. As shown in Table 1, the funds of these banks are much larger than those of other financial institutions. In step with the trend in Western countries, however, the commercial banks' share of total funds is declining. Along with the rise in national income, mutual loan and savings banks and credit associations, more closely allied with medium-and-small enterprises as well as the general public, have proven increasingly popular.

The financial institutions conducting commercial banking business are ordinary banks, the foreign exchange bank, and 15 foreign banks in Japan. All are based on the Banking Law. Main business lines of these banks are:

* Deposits: current deposit, ordinary deposit, deposit at notice, time deposit, installment savings, deposits for tax payments, and foreign currency deposits.
* Loans: loans on deeds, loans on bills, overdrafts, bills discontinued.
* Securities: national bonds, corporate bonds and debentures, and stocks.

Table 1. Deposits and Savings of Financial Institutions *

	(Unit: 1,000 million yen; end of year)				
	1950	*1955*	*1960*	*1965*	*1966*
Banking accounts	1,048	3,724	8,872	20,653	23,790
	(59.9)	(53.8)	(50.0)	(45.3)	(44.7)
Trust accounts	19	318	1,437	3,536	3,882
	(1.1)	(4.6)	(8.1)	(7.8)	(7.3)
Mutual loan and	50	412	1,084	3,220	3,728
savings banks	(2.9)	(6.0)	(6.1)	(7.1)	(7.0)
Credit associations	43	294	958	3,114	3,688
	(2.5)	(4.2)	(5.4)	(6.8)	(6.9)
Agriculture	137	386	823	2,432	2,986
cooperatives	(2.5)	(5.6)	(4.6)	(5.3)	(5.6)
Life insurance	32	173	690	2,094	2,563
companies	(7.8)	(2.5)	(3.9)	(4.6)	(4.8)
Trust fund bureau	249	843	1,930	4,705	5,850
	(1.8)	(12.2)	(10.9)	(10.3)	(11.0)
Post-office life insur-	33	244	701	1,204	1,370
ance and postal annuity	(14.2)	(3.5)	(3.9)	(2.6)	(2.6)
Total	1,749	6,918	17,759	45,546	53,206
Including others	(100)	(100)	(100)	(100)	(100)

SOURCE: Bank of Japan.
* Items in parentheses in percent.

- Others: domestic and foreign exchange business, guarantee, receipt
  of stock subscriptions, payment of stock dividends, representative
  business for the Bank of Japan, consignment of secured debenture
  bonds, safe-keeping deposit, and other subordinate business.

Each of the city banks has an average of some 160 domestic branches,
while local banks average about 60 branches. Originally, the local banks
were established on the principle of "one local bank in each prefecture" to
contribute to the local economy. However, in keeping with the progress
of the economy, the government policy of regional economic development,
as well as of traffic and communications facilities, local banks have gradually extended their business beyond their own communities.

World War II forced Japanese banks to change in various aspects.
Those connected with *zaibatsu* concerns (industrial combine) such as
Yasuda, Mitsubishi, Sumitomo, and Mitsui were affected most seriously.
These giant banks maintained their dominant positions by controlling big
enterprises. After the war, however, the *zaibatsu* concerns were dissolved
and the respective banks lost their control over affiliated companies. Moreover, the fragmentation of heavy industrial enterprises centered on muni-
tions production was a serious blow to these *zaibatsu*-connected banks.

As a result, they have turned to the general public as a large—and growing—source of funds.

Flexibility in Banking Administration

In the United States, the banking system permits multiple regulation by various government organizations. In Japan, however, the Ministry of Finance is in charge of administering commercial banks on the basis of the Banking Law, and the Bank of Japan (central bank) regularly audits their business accounts. The Ministry of Finance gives administrative guidance in various phases of banking, issuing licenses, and authorizing establishment of branch offices, capital increases, change of name, holding of concurrent posts, amalgamation and changes of statute, all according to the Banking Law. Also, the commercial banks have to get finance ministry approval for the acquisition of immovable property and account settlement.

The government helps commercial banks conduct business soundly by examining their reports and formulating the standards of capital structure and the balance of account. Some of these standards are:

- The deposit-loan ratio should be 80 percent or less.
- Ratio of current assets to total deposits should be over 30 percent.
- Ratio of current income to current expense should be within 78 percent.
- Ratio of fixed assets for business to net worth should be within 50 percent.
- Dividend ratio should be 12.5 percent or less per annum.
- Owned capital should not be less than 10 percent of the total.

The current Banking Law, enacted in 1927, has continued to play an important role in the administration of banks, although the currency system and the financial situation have changed phenomenally since then. The composition of assets of commercial banks has been much improved in the postwar period, so that the application of the Banking Law, which was originally for protecting depositors and perfecting the banking system, has been used for encouraging commercial banks to serve the economic and financial policy of the government.

For instance, the government, which used to be very reluctant to authorize the establishment of new branch offices for fear of excessive competition, relaxed the ban (see Table 2). This came about because of changing financial conditions, distribution of population, and increasing public dependence upon banking services.

Short-Term Foreign Capital

Short-term foreign capital, which has been introduced in the form of import funds, Euro-dollars, and free-yen, has played a more important role

Table 2. Spread of Commercial Banking Offices

	1950	1955	1960	1965	1966
City Banks:					
Number of banks	11	13	13	13	13
Number of offices	1,595	1,821	1,791	2,040	2,087
Local Banks:					
Number of banks	56	65	64	63	63
Number of offices	3,515	3,702	3,822	4,262	4,337

in Japan than in any other industrial country. This is because in Japan, where interest rates are comparatively high and foreign exchange reserves are insufficient, short-term foreign capital provides less expensive funds for trade finance and contributes to improving the country's balance of payments. However, the excessive inflow and rapid outflow of short-term capital has an adverse effect on the payments balance. As a result, foreign exchange banks are restricted in their foreign exchange holdings, though they are obliged to hold considerable amounts of foreign exchange as liquid reserves.

Because of positive efforts to establish authorized foreign exchange banks overseas, Japan's foreign exchange banks now have 56 overseas branch offices, 10 each in the large money markets of New York and London. Through transactions based on correspondent contracts, these overseas branches are playing a key role in facilitating the foreign exchange business.

Capital Structure of Japanese Banks

Banking accounts are settled semiannually in Japan, the first term ending September 30, and the second on March 31. The breakdown of major accounts in the total assets of Japanese commercial banks at the end of September 1965 is as follows: cash, checks, bills, and deposits—11.0 percent; loans and discounts, 58.5 percent; and securities, 11.9 percent.

In U.S. banks, by comparison, cash, checks, bills, and deposits, accounted for 15.4 percent, loans and discounts for 54.1 percent, and securities for 27.7 percent. The difference may be attributed to the fact that Japanese commercial banks are the main suppliers of industrial funds, that Japan's capital market is not fully developed, and that the average ratio of loans to deposits is higher than in the United States.

The major share of loans extended by city banks are used for business, while only 1 percent are for individuals. Of the bank loans for business purposes, 90 percent are for the operating capital and the rest for equipment. This is in sharp contrast to the Bank of America's loans in 1965, which break down into loans for business, 48 percent; loans for paying off on installment debts, 31 percent; and secured loans, 31 percent.

Most securities held by Japanese banks consist of corporate debentures and stocks; the proportion of national bonds is very small, since Japan's fiscal policy has been conducted in accordance with a balanced budget policy since the war. However, our government recently decided to issue national bonds, and more than 40 percent of these are expected to be absorbed by city banks. Also, in view of the reserve requirement system, a gradually rising intake of national bonds is to be expected. Holdings of other securities are also expected to increase as the securities market improves.

The Interest Rate System

Japan's official bank rate system is comprised of four items as of September 1, 1967: discount rate on commercial bills (5.84 percent), interest rate on loans against collateral of national bonds (6.21 percent), interest rate on loans against bond collateral other than national bonds (6.57 percent), and overdrafts.[1] Among these, the discount rate on commercial bills has been most important in recent years. The maximum loan interest rate of private banks is restricted by law, but commercial banks have made a voluntary agreement of a standard rate lower than the legal maximum. However, interest rates on loans with a term of more than one year and of those less than 1 million yen are excluded from the agreement.

The loan interest rates of the city banks were tending to decline in accordance with the efforts of both industrial firms and banks to reduce a heavy interest burden and the government's general policy of depressing rates. Though Japan's interest rates are higher than those in the United States, the differential is becoming less as rates rise in the U.S.

Dependence on External Liability

The liabilities of Japanese banks, expressed as a percentage of total working capital, are composed of deposits (64.4 percent), borrowings (8.8 percent), and capital funds (2.9 percent). Borrowings from the Bank of Japan constitute 5.1 percent of total liabilities, and call money 3.7 percent. The high dependence on external borrowing results from fund demand exceeding deposits, and became conspicuous during the past economic-growth period. We have already pointed out that the deposit-loan ratio of Japanese banks is remarkably high. However, the city banks,

---

[1] The rate was fixed at 6.57 percent per annum for the period from June 1965 to August 31, 1967. However, since September 1, 1967, because of the tight money policy taken by the government, no rate is quoted under this system although the system itself remains.

which have the larger enterprises as their clients, differ from local banks in terms of deposit-loan ratio as well as degree of dependence on external borrowings.

The reserve requirement rate (the ratio of liquid funds to customers' deposits) was set by the Bank of Japan at about 1.7 percent on the average for all banks and remained at this level for some six years, but in 1965 it was changed to the level indicated in Table 3. This percentage does not

Table 3. Reserve Rates Under the Reserve Deposit System

City Banks	Time deposits	Other deposits
With deposits of more than	percent	percent
¥100,000 million	0.50	1.00
¥100,000–¥20,000 million	0.25	0.50
Less than ¥20,000 million	0.25	0.50
Mutual Loan and Savings Banks and Credit Assns.		
Amount of deposits more than		
¥100,000 million	0.25	0.50
¥100,000–¥20,000 million	0.25	0.50

seem so high, however, if we take into account that time deposits are proportionally large. They determine the percentage of funds the bank is required to deposit with the Bank of Japan, which also sets the rates in accordance with the business situation. Compared to reserve rates of the Federal Reserve System in the U.S., those of Japan are very low.

Interest on External Borrowings Hampers Profits

The structure of assets and liabilities reflects the profit characteristics of Japanese banks. As for earnings, income from loan interest and discount charges account for 75 percent of the total, while income from interest and yields on securities accounts for less than 15 percent. Concerning expenses, interest on deposits is 40 percent of total expenditures. Another major factor which affects profits is the interest on external borrowings, the rate of which fluctuates with the call-money market situation. In our country, as in the United States, banks have been affected by the profit squeeze. Interest rates on deposits have remained unchanged since 1961. However, there are some factors hampering the increase of profits. Among these are the downward tendency of interest rates on loans for enterprises, intake of large amounts of national bonds yielding less than the average interest rate on loans and yields on securities, and interest on external borrowings, which is influenced by the financial policy. In order to overcome the declining trend in profit margins, Japanese banks are trying to reduce dependence on external borrowings.

Bank Loans and Economic Growth

In terms of capital structure, Japan's enterprises are very dependent upon bank loans; thus, banks and industries are closely connected with each other. Under the economic circumstances prevailing in the postwar period when the capital accumulation of industries was small and the capital market poorly developed, it was very difficult for enterprises to raise funds by issuing stocks or debentures. In prewar days, the average capital structure of Japanese enterprises consisted of 45 percent net worth and 55 percent external funds of which borrowings from financial institutions accounted for only 16 percent or so. Today, however, the average capital structure of major enterprises breaks down into 26 percent owned capital, 18 percent short-term borrowing, and 17 percent long-term borrowing, mostly bank loans.

As shown in Table 4, the ratio of bank loans to total industrial funds is over 40 percent.

In the past period of rapid growth, the fund demand by business firms on city banks was so strong it surpassed deposits. Moreover, the government's financial policy of avoiding flotation of public bonds, plus the immaturity of the bond market and the shortage of capital accumulation, made it necessary for banks to execute over-loans. This phenomenon was unfavorable for commercial banks, and after that the economy slowed down, and over-loans were unnecessary. Measures to eliminate these over-loans and improve the situation have been taken.

The ability of Japanese banks to supply such enormous amounts of industrial funds, including long-term funds, can be attributed mainly to the fact that time deposits account for over 50 percent of all deposits. Of these, 1-year time deposits account for 80 percent. Moreover, most of them are renewed. Loans are composed of discounted commercial bills, exchange bills, loans on bills, loans on deeds, and overdrafts. Of these, loans on bills account for the lion's share (about 55 percent of all loans), followed by discounted bills (around 30 percent). Except for discounted bills, bank loans always call for security.

Short-Term Money Market and City Banks

Modernization of Japanese business required considerable equipment investment. Much of this was financed through over-borrowing from banks. Meanwhile, the dependence of city banks, as major suppliers of industrial funds, upon external funds such as borrowings from the central bank and

Table 4. Net Supply of Industrial Funds *

	1960	percent	(Unit: ¥1,000 million) 1964	percent	1966	percent
Stocks	472 (363)	16.1	724 (546)	14.4	335 (235)	6
Industrial bonds	153 (151)	5.2	157 (157)	3.1	225 (225)	4.1
Loans, all banks	1,326 (288)	45.3	2,007 (403)	39.9	2,629 (370)	47.4
Loans by other private financial institutions	757 (375)	25.9	1,732 (659)	34.5	1,820 (699)	32.8
Loans by governmental organization	160 (118)	5.5	337 (207)	6.7	446 (281)	8.1
Special account	59 (59)	2	66 (66)	1.4	86 (86)	1.6
Total	2,927 (1,354)	100	5,023 (2,038)	100	5,541 (1,866)	100
Reference (Foreign capital)	39 (39)		108 (72)		†43 (†27)	

* Figures in parentheses show funds for equipment investment.
† Indicates outflow of foreign capital.

call money, was also very heavy. Restrictions on central bank loans to commercial banks made the city banks rely on the call money market, imposing a burden because of the high interest rates. Thus, short-term money, which should go to the securities market, became concentrated in the call market, bringing an imbalance between the long- and short-term interest systems. This imbalance continued until the fall of 1965.

Reflecting the relatively high rate of call money, short-term government securities and discounted bills (interest rates of which are comparatively low), had been prevented from circulating in the short-term money market; therefore, such short-term government bonds were held largely by the Trust Fund Bureau and the Bank of Japan. Since late in 1965, however, the interest rate on call money has declined to a level reflecting the official discount rate. Since government policy has turned toward conducting flexible measures not only for long-term capital, but also the short-term money market, the abnormal phenomena once prevailing in the capital market have disappeared.

Public Bonds and Debentures Purchasers

Issuance of public bonds and debentures has increased remarkably since 1958, financial bonds since around 1958, debentures since 1959, and government-guaranteed bonds since 1960. Reflecting insufficient capital accumulation and the immaturity of the securities market in Japan, city banks and long-term credit institutions have played key roles in purchasing such securities.

Bond and debenture purchases by individuals and investment trusts is increasing year by year. However, the circulation market of bonds and debentures is still inadequate. Accordingly, the conditions for issuing bonds and debentures which should ordinarily be created through the mechanism of the money market, have been decided by representatives of The Bank of Japan, trust banks, and the securities underwriting firms, in accordance with conditions for issuing government-guaranteed bonds and short-term public bonds bearing low interest.

Although city banks cannot act as underwriters for the issuance of bonds and debentures, they have influence on the bond market as trustees and main purchasers. City banks have purchased bonds as a means of financing enterprises. Such bonds can be posted as security for borrowings from the Bank of Japan. Also, bonds held by the Bank of Japan are subject to bonds operations by that bank.

Purchase of bonds and debentures by financial institutions other than city banks is small in amount because the cost of funds is higher in these institutions, and because interest rates on their loans are generally higher than the yields of debentures, in contrast with the situation in city banks.

Such purchases by individuals and corporate investors have been impeded by the immaturity of the market. However, since the beginning of 1966, the bond market has reopened after a 4-year suspension to cope with a situation brought about by the flotation of national bonds. All in all, securities investments are expected to grow further in line with the rise in national income.

Remarkable features of bond and debenture issuance are that the total amount of bank debentures issued is larger than that of corporate debentures, and that long-term funds procured through bank debentures are supplied from long-term credit banks as a form of long-term loans for enterprises. Loans from long-term credit institutions often take the form of joint financing with city banks; on the other hand, city banks purchase bank debentures from long-term credit institutions, thereby establishing mutual relationships between the two types of institutions.

There are two types of bank debentures, one-year discount debentures and five-year interest-bearing debentures. The former are purchased mainly by individuals and corporate investors, and the latter by financial institutions.

The flotation of public bonds started in January 1966 for the first time since the war. Continued flotation of national bonds shall strengthen the position of city banks in the bond-and-debenture market. At the same time, city banks intend to get authorization to handle national bond transactions for their customers, in view of growing diversification of individual's portfolio investment and the policy of expanding the bank's customer services.

Securities Market and Commercial Banks

During the past period of rapid economic growth, the securities market advanced significantly. The stock market experienced two booms during the periods: one from around 1955, when Japan had almost finished its economic reconstruction, and another from 1961, when ultra-rapid economic growth started. Stock prices continued to rise steadily, supported by substantial capital increases by enterprises. Rising individual income levels were also a factor boosting stock prices. The turnover ratio of stock sales reached nearly 100 percent and there were undoubtedly speculative factors.

Another factor boosting the stock market was the investment trust, introduced in 1951. The balance of investment trust was only ¥59,500 million in 1955, but reached ¥1,180,000 million in 1961. During the stock boom, the catch phrase, "Farewell to banks, welcome securities," was indicative of the mood of investors. Banks and securities firms competed aggressively for available funds as time deposits or as securities investments.

From the autumn of 1961, however, interest in investment trusts declined along with stock prices. Nevertheless, the balance of investment trusts maintained a high level of ¥1,200,000 million at the end of 1965, despite stagnation of the stock market during the same year. Thus, stock investments still have a strong influence on the savings market.

It can be said that the stock market has been more highly developed than other securities markets. However, there has been insufficient attention paid to establishing the interest system, through which the liquidity of funds should be adjusted to prevent the abrupt overflow of money from one sector of securities markets to the other. Accordingly, the stock market could not avoid being seriously affected by fluctuation of business activities.

In July 1965, the government announced measures to counter the business recession. Since then, the stock market has regained its active tone. The stagnation that prevailed for more than four years, until 1965, can be attributed to an over-supply of stocks through capital expansion in excess of the normal capacity of the stock market; this brought the same results as over-loans and over-borrowing in the monetary market.

A series of measures to rescue the stock market were undertaken successively by the newly-established Japan Joint Securities Company, Ltd. and the Japan Securities Holding Association, which purchased dead stocks; capital increases were suspended by all industries; the Bank of Japan offered exclusive loans to some of the big securities firms which were threatened with financial difficulties; and the reorganization of the securities market was undertaken by revising The Securities Exchange Law.

Japan's commercial banks are fostering the securities market in order to develop closer mutual relations as suppliers not only of long-term funds but also of short-term operating funds. For instance, city banks, together with leading securities firms have established the Japan Joint Securities Company, Ltd. and, in order to stabilize stock prices, the banks purchased lots of excess stocks through the stock market.

In addition, city banks have suspended the loan interest due from big securities firms which faced financial difficulties.

The Securities and Exchange Law was revised in spring 1965, and the 429 firms now in existence must obtain authorized licenses to continue their business until 1968. Considering the fact that 70 percent of the present securities firms are quite small, the securities field is being forced to change greatly. Japan's securities firms handle consignment sales, purchase of securities, sales and purchase for their own account, and underwriting business as well. A remarkable feature is that these business lines are not segregated. In order to operate their business smoothly, securities firms require liquidity of funds. To meet this demand these securities finance companies now operate with funds supplied by banks and the call-money market.

Assisting the Smaller Enterprise

Since it is difficult for small and medium sized firms to raise funds in capital markets, the national and local governments are supplying them money through such agencies as the Small Business Finance Corporation, the People's Finance Corporation, and the Small Business Credit Insurance Corporation. Although the government has fostered mutual loan and savings banks, credit associations and co-operatives, and other sources of fund suppliers, city banks still extend 45 percent of all loans to these enterprises.

Some smaller firms, while otherwise sound, are hampered by lack of experience and knowledge, and they also hesitate to go to specialized management consultants. It is very convenient, however, for these enterprises to consult their banks. In 1960, the Fuji Bank started systematic business consulting services aiming at extending the function of the bank beyond its normal boundaries. Since that time, all of the leading city banks have followed suit by introducing such services.

Major city banks offer these consulting services free of charge, since they are not authorized to conduct any business other than that specified by the Banking Law. Of course, banks benefit through improvements in the customers' businesses and closer bank-client relations.

Bank Deposits Advantageous

Thrift is part of the Japanese character, and the ratio of saving to the individual disposable income amounts to 20 percent. This is phenomenally high compared with that of the United States, which is around 7 percent. Of individual financial properties in Japan, savings deposits account for 41.5 percent, while temporary deposits, trust and insurance and securities account for 20 percent, 13.7 percent, and 20.3 percent, respectively (in 1963). The comparable figures for the U.S. are: securities, 55.6 percent; savings deposits, 18.9 percent; trust and insurance, 18.6 percent; and temporary deposits, 6.2 percent. Thus, as shown in Table 5, Japan's ratio

Table 5. Comparison of Savings with GNP *

Japan (Unit: ¥1 billion)

	GNP	Bank deposits	Ratio of bank deposits to GNP
1955	9,056	3,724	41 percent
1966	34,936	23,756	68 percent
Growth rate	3.9 times	6.4 times	

U.S. (Unit: $1 billion)

	GNP	Bank deposits	Ratio of bank deposits to GNP
1955	397.5	220.4	55 percent
1966	759.3	407.6	54 percent
Growth rate	1.9 times	1.8 times	

* Bank Deposits: Japan—all 87 banks. U.S.—commercial banks and mutual savings banks 1955—14,243 banks, 1966—14,271 banks.

of bank deposits to the GNP stands very high, as does the growth rate of bank deposits over that of the GNP.

The breakdown of all bank deposits in Japan at the end of December 1966, is as follows: private and corporate deposits, 86.9 percent; deposits by financial institutions, 5.7 percent; and government deposits, 2.4 percent. In comparison with U.S. banks, the weight of private and corporate deposits is much higher, while deposits by financial institutions are relatively small. (In the United States at the end of 1965, private and corporate deposits accounted for 74.0 percent, followed by deposits of financial institutions at 11.2 percent, and government deposits at 10.5 percent. This is mainly due to the difference between the banking systems of the two countries.)

Of private and corporate deposits, the former account for about 60 percent. Corporate deposits are sensitive in the reflecting business trend, while private deposits have continued to grow in keeping with growth of national income. In the past decade, private ordinary deposits tripled, while time deposits increased sevenfold.

Popularity of Ordinary and Time Deposits

Among the various kinds of bank deposits, ordinary and time deposits have proven most popular. Time deposits account for 73 percent in amount of all private deposits, while ordinary deposits account for 23 percent. Ordinary deposits which bear interest at the rate of 2.19 percent per annum, are convenient because they can be withdrawn at any time upon request.

One type of ordinary deposit of the Fuji Bank is called the "Circle Deposit," and the depositor can withdraw from any office of the bank by showing his deposit passbook. Considering the current situation in which the personal check system is not used as extensively as in the United States, the bank also provides various customer services such as transfer of deposits for payment of public service charges, including electricity, gas, water supply, and other utilities. Ordinary deposit is also transferable into a long-term time deposit.

At present, there are three kinds of time deposits—3-month, 6-month, and 12-month. Their annual interest rates are 4 percent, 5 percent, and 5.5 percent respectively. In other classifications, there are such kinds as time deposits issued in uninscribed form, automatic renewal time deposits, and time deposits for credit card users.

Future of the Personal Check

The rise in personal income has brought a change in the distribution of personal financial properties, as shown in the decline of savings deposits and an increase in trusts and insurance and securities. In line with brisk diffusion of durable consumer goods, the characteristics of private deposits have gradually changed along with the depositors' requirements. To meet such demands and to facilitate much more functional banking services which cannot be expected in a conventional ordinary deposit system, the personal check system has come into the spotlight since 1961, along with the new policy of banks to attract the general public.

This system is proving more popular year by year but is used by only some 700,000 of Japan's 78,550,000 personal depositors as of March 31, 1967. Thus, the degree of diffusion is far below that in the United States. This is mainly due to the difference in consumer habits, immaturity of the credit investigation system, and cautious screening of personal check applicants. Since the mishaps concerning personal checking accounts are very rare, public recognition of the merits of this system has improved considerably, and much greater diffusion is expected with the rise in national income levels.

In Japan, personal check depositors need make no marginal payments, nor keep a minimum balance, since most of the depositors using personal checking accounts have other kinds of accounts such as time deposits and ordinary deposits which can be considered as security.

Consumer Loans

Consumer loans extended by Japan's financial institutions are steadily increasing. The balance of consumer loans extended by banks, mutual loan and savings banks, and trust and banking companies as of the end of March 1967, reached a total of ¥168,300 million, almost double that of a year ago. In July, major life insurance companies started to extend consumer loans, centering on housing loans. However, the use of consumer loans is far lower than that of the U.S. and other Western countries.

As of the end of March 1967, the balance of consumer credit accounted for only 0.6 percent of total loans extended by financial institutions. Although the consumer loan system is expected to expand at a rapid pace, rationalization of such business in banks and improvement of loan terms are required. At present, unsecured consumer loans cannot be extended because of insufficient credit investigation, and it may be a long time before this system is adopted.

Certainly the consumer loan system in Japan has grown rapidly in the past several years. However, the percentage of consumer credits in total loans is extremely small. The balance of loans extended by all banks, mutual banks, and credit co-operatives as of the end of March 1967, amounted to ¥22,736,100 million. Of this amount, consumer loans accounted for only 0.6 percent. It can be said, then, that although the growth rate is significant, the weight of consumer loans in fund operations is quite low.

Japan's consumer credit system started formally in 1960 as a means of purchasing automobiles. Since then, it has been applied to purchases of durable consumer goods as well as houses. Since the latter half of 1964, when the relaxation of money stringency became effective, consumer loans have been in the banking spotlight.

As a result, the ratio of consumer credits by financial organizations to all consumer credits has risen remarkably. Consumer credits are also extended by installment payment stores, organizations issuing credit cards and house construction firms, but figures for such loans are not available. According to the Bank of Japan, the balance of loans extended as operation funds to firms handling installment payment business by all banks and mutual loans and savings banks at the end of March 1967, reached a total of ¥800,200 million. Not all of these funds are necessarily destined for installment payment sales, but if we consider this figure as the balance of consumer credits extended by various organizations other than banks, the latter (banks) could account for about 16 percent of the total. At the end of 1964, the estimated balance of consumer credits amounted to ¥530,600 million, of which ¥32,500 million or 6 percent were extended by financial institutions. Taking this fact into consideration, we can appreciate the vigor of financial institutions in extending consumer loans during these three years.

At the end of March 1967, the balance of consumer loans extended by city banks amounted to some ¥40,000 million as compared with ¥29,300 million a year ago, an increase of 36.5 percent. Meanwhile, those extended by local banks rose from ¥31,800 million to ¥61,800 million, a whopping 94.3 percent increase by the same comparison. Likewise, consumer credits extended by mutual loans and savings banks increased by 71 percent, from ¥18,600 million to ¥31,800 million.

At present, the repayment term for consumer loans extended for the purchase of durable consumer goods is usually two years at a maximum. As for housing loans, the average repayment term has been extended from about 6 years to 10 or 15 years. The average interest rate is 6 percent per annum and is applied under the add-on system, in which the interest is considered as part of the loan. In the case of education loans, the interest rate is slightly lower, averaging 5 percent per annum, and it is also figured on an add-in basis.

The maximum amount of a single loan for purchasing durable consumer goods or for services is 1 million yen, while that for housing loans is ¥3 million. Most consumer loans call for guarantees from makers or dealers (in purchasing goods) or real estate firms (in purchasing land or houses). The bank has co-operative tie-ups with such enterprises. When a bank extends these loans in the absence of tie-up, they are generally granted against negotiable securities or real property.

Significant features of consumer loans in the current phase are the granting of housing loans combined with life insurance on the borrower, and extension of the repayment term. In the case of housing loans combined with life insurance, if the borrower should die, the bank receives the full amount of the insurance to offset the loan's balance, and the family is discharged from repayment. This system is familiar in the U.S., where it was inaugurated in 1917.

For the promotion of consumer loans in Japan, improvement of conditions, especially extension of the repayment term, will be accelerated. At the same time, procedures for extending loans will have to be rationalized, since at the present stage consumer loans are small in value and less profitable.

Unsecured consumer loans, which are so popular in the U.S., will not prosper in Japan until a more reliable credit investigation system is established.

The Competitive Situation

There is sharp competition among Japanese banks in every phase of business. Competition is most severe in the securing of deposit accounts and in extending business by utilizing sizable funds. This has been due mostly to the need for improving the deposit-loan ratio and fund position, and to the slower increase of deposits in commercial banks as compared with non-banking institutions.

Each commercial bank is eager to strengthen its services and gain new customers. All are active in modernizing offices, advertising, and public relations. There is also strong competition to establish branches in newly developed residential areas, to expand new business departments, and to approach clients to have them extend loans.

Branching and Mergers

When talking about competition, the increase in the number of bank branches must be stressed. In Japan, the establishment of new banks has been prohibited since 1955, but restrictions against new branch offices were relaxed in 1960. Although two local banks were recently absorbed by city banks to which they had been closely linked historically, there is no possibility of any widespread amalgamation. In line with structural changes in the economy and industrial reorganization, there are factors accelerating the reorganization of financial institutions.

In general, city banks are closely connected with their affiliated trust and banking companies and life insurance companies, each group comprising a financial unit. Also, each city bank has considerable power to dominate several local banks, mutual loan and savings banks, and credit associations in terms of staff and capital.

The administrative guideline for bank mergers is as follows:

- Mergers of local banks will be recognized only when they will produce no regional economic problems and strengthen business of the banks.
- Mergers of city banks are welcome if they help to eliminate excessive competition. However, excessive growth of any bank and bad effects of amalgamation should be carefully avoided.
- Mergers of city and local banks are inadvisable because such mergers will possibly bring excessive competition among city banks to expand their businesses. However, if a local bank cannot expect further growth, it is allowed to merge with a city bank with which it has close connections.

Foreign Exchange Business

Foreign exchange business is one of the most important activities of Japan's commercial banks. Japan, lacking natural resources, has to import almost every kind of raw material. Most of Japan's foreign trade is handled by the integrated trading houses. According to the Ministry of International Trade and Industry, the volume of exports handled by 16 leading trading firms accounted for 61.7 percent of all exports and 71.2 percent of all imports in 1966.

At present, foreign exchange business is conducted by the following banks: The Bank of Tokyo, which was established under the Foreign Exchange Bank Law; 10 class "A" authorized foreign exchange banks, such as the Fuji Bank, Ltd., the Sumitomo Bank, Ltd., the Mitsubishi Bank, Ltd., the Sanwa Bank, Ltd., the Daiichi Bank, Ltd., the Mitsui Bank, Ltd., the Nippon Kangyo Bank, Ltd., the Daiwa Bank, Ltd., the Bank of Kobe, Ltd. and the Tokai Bank, Ltd.; the Industrial Bank of Japan; and 15 foreign banks in Japan. In addition, there are 54 class "B" authorized foreign exchange banks which cannot contract direct correspondent agreements with overseas banks. Among these are local banks, trust banks, and long-term credit banks, excluding the Industrial Bank of Japan.

In this field, competition among authorized foreign exchange banks is very severe, since each enterprise ordinarily deals with a number of banks. Thus, the conditions for trade finance, forward exchange, and various other services are matters of sharp competition among banks. In addition to ordinary foreign exchange business, the banks also handle exchange control business assigned by the government. This includes collecting foreign exchange bills, certifying exports, licensing imports, and paying the government's overseas bills.

The introductions of foreign capital and foreign investments into Japanese enterprises were activated by the liberalization of capital transactions, and the foreign exchange banks have played an important role as intermediators, consultants, and guarantors. Because of the shortage of capital in Japan, long-term foreign funds have greatly contributed to the modernization of Japan's industry and the growth of the domestic economy.

Management of Japanese Banks

Since the management system of Fuji Bank is representative of major Japanese banks, its organization chart is discussed here. Fuji Bank's functions and organization are arranged by business categories under direct control of executives. So far, the regional management system has not been adopted.

The Fuji Bank's Organization Chart

Smooth communication and quick policy decisions are most important factors in modern big business. Fuji Bank exerts great effort to improve these functions by delegating responsibility to lower management. Through such activities as regular meetings of middle-management of each department in headquarters, various inside committees, house organs, and inter-office announcements by each department and branch manager before the start of business, communication is facilitated.

Executives share responsibility for their own departments in headquarters or regional blocs comprising several branches. The bank's activity is decided at a vice chairmen's meeting. The decision is then approved by the chairman and president and the deputy chairman. Activities concerning more than one department are adjusted by the Planning and Coordination Division, while decisions on policies for branches are made by a joint staff of related departments in headquarters.

Fuji Bank has 210 branches all over the nation, and the operation of each branch is based on an autonomous accounting system. All branches are linked by the bank's automatic relay teletype, and concentration of business activities is promoted in order to ensure rational and systematic management. Administration of business promotion in each branch is conducted by the Business Development Division. Each branch belongs to a regional group with one supervising branch as a core. The supervising branch provides leadership among the group in carrying out managing policies suggested by headquarters.

A meeting of branch managers is held twice a year and is aimed at driving home management policies and examining the business situation. In addition, meetings of supervising branch managers are held occasionally.

Personnel

Every country has its own system of personnel management based on the employment market, social customs, and economic circumstances. Most Japanese businesses have used a traditional system incorporating such features as lifetime employment and the seniority wage scale. While applying this system, Fuji Bank also uses a professional qualification system, in which professional abilities are classified into 11 groups, and each employee falls within one of these groups. Personnel management uses the classification system as a guide to employee status; such factors as promotion, removal, training, and payment are determined in consideration of discovering and developing individual ability, and encouraging the will to work. Through this system, wages are decided fairly according to the individual's contribution to Fuji Bank.

It is the Western custom to employ new persons as needed by enterprise; however, most enterprises in Japan make it a rule to accept employment applicants from among new college and school graduates every spring. In the case of Fuji Bank, new college graduates account for 30 to 40 percent of new employees every year; about 20 percent of these are males. In line with the development of centralized business operations, the number of female employees has come to exceed that of males since 1963.

The service period of female employees is generally around four years. Thus the work assigned to female employees is inevitably limited to routine or supplementary tasks. As a result, women employees rarely become officers.

Every year, the percentage of college graduates among new employees increases. This is because of the employment conditions and social attitudes in Japan, where labor forces of good quality are comparatively abundant, and banking is considered a secure and highly respectable business.

Particularly necessary is the orientation of new employees who have no business experience. For this purpose, Fuji Bank provides programs for specific females, males, high school graduates, and college graduates respectively. And to cope with technological changes in office work and modernization of management, the bank has been conducting group training of middle-management since 1959. In addition, considerable numbers of clerks are sent to English conversation institutes to prepare for increased foreign business along with the internationalization of the Japanese economy. Each year, several clerks of exceptional ability are also sent to overseas universities with the aim of cultivating high-level bank officers with an international viewpoint. On top of this, many commercial banks in Japan are sending able employees to overseas banks to study, research, and collect information on the banking business.

In 1947, the employees of Fuji Bank organized a labor union based on the union shop system. All bank employees except those in management positions are union members.

Each of city banks has its own labor union, and the interunion relation is maintained by the Federation of City Bank Labor Unions. The labor union and the management of the bank sign a labor agreement annually. The management council, composed of management and employee representatives, is considered an organ for maintaining and improving contact and communication between the two sides so that differences of opinion may be resolved amicably.

Age of Automation

Japan has more electronic computers than any country except the United States. City banks and leading local banks in Japan have introduced electronic computers in a massive and concentrated way to facilitate the management business. IBM's accounting machines (PCS) have come into widespread use since the mid-1950s. Fuji Bank began to use electronic computers (EDPS) in 1960, and has concentrated electronic computer centers in Tokyo and Osaka. These centers are equipped with a total of 7 computers, including the UNIVAC 418. However, in order to speed the ever growing volume of business, the Fuji Bank, during 1968, will augment their computer operations with three high performance computers—two units of UNIVAC 1108 and one NCR 315.

Currently computers are employed for a variety of calculations based on the real-time system. These include accounting of all the necessary procedures or ordinary deposit; time deposit; interest and discounts on loans on bills; interest and handling charges on import usance bills, wages; and custody of commercial bills, calculation related to consumer financing, compilation of statistics for management control. In addition, the bank undertakes business from outside sources such as consignment business from the Japan Travel Bureau in connection with the settlement and adjustment of travel coupons, the calculation of social securities, and so on.

U.S. banks were the first to use computers for centralized management of checking accounts. On the other hand, Japan was first to use computers for managing ordinary deposit business, because ordinary deposits are the most popular and interest is computed on the daily basis. For example, Fuji Bank has more than 4 million ordinary deposit accounts all over the nation and, the use of electronic computers in this field relieved the business burden phenomenally. Some city banks have already adopted the "on-line real-time system," and all are expected to follow suit.

Business rationalization through the use of electronic computers also makes adoption of new customer services possible. When the Tokyo Olympic Games were held here in 1964, the computer centers of Fuji Bank handled all the business dealing with custody, receipts and payments, and control of admission tickets.

Uniquely Japanese

As we have seen, there are many features of Japanese banking that are similar to banking in the United States, as well as other industrialized countries. Although the dominant position of commercial banks remains unchallenged, their share of the nation's funds has been gradually declining in favor of non-bank financial institutions. At the same time, severe competition among banks to increase deposits and earnings has resulted in the conduct of "creative" business development procedures new to the country and its culture.

Yet, banking in Japan retains a flavor all its own, dictated by the needs and demands of the nation and its people.

Discussion Questions

1. What are the essential similarities and differences between the U.S. and Japanese banking systems?
2. What special role does the Swiss banking system play in the international financial arena?
3. If you had to defend the U.S. banking system against Swiss and Japanese economics students, what arguments would you present?

Monetary Policy

The basic function of monetary policy is to control the supply of money in the economy. Through control of the money supply, a monetary authority works toward its goals of high employment and price stability. It accomplishes this through action on the amount of credit which it makes available, and by controlling the price of credit, that is, the interest rate. In the United States, the Federal Reserve, the country's central bank, uses three major weapons to effect its policies. In order of importance they are, (1) open-market operations, or the buying and selling of securities to commercial banks and the public, (2) the discount-rate mechanism, or the rate at which member banks can borrow from the Federal Reserve, and (3) the legal-reserve requirement.

The first article in this section deals with the Canadian anti-inflationary monetary policy first implemented in the fall of 1968. The author, Louis Rasminsky, has been the governor of the Bank of Canada since 1961, and he addresses the issue of the efficacy of monetary policy in his own country. The article is interesting because of the intimate relationship which exists between Canada and the United States. Rasminsky's argument is that because the Canadian economy is profoundly effected by prices in the United States, Canadians are really at the mercy of U.S. anti-inflationary policies, and their own policies can only have marginal effects.

The second article examines the West German perception of the role of monetary policy. In perspective, it should be noted that western Europeans have, in general, placed great emphasis on the role of monetary policy. In this context it is useful to see the changing role of German monetary policy. The authors assert that monetary policy has to be seen in the total context of achieving a number of macroeconomic goals. Thus the article examines the relationship of monetary policy to other policies, such as wage policies, and, in particular, the relationship of monetary policy to the "concerted action" program. Professors Klaus and Falk are on the faculty of the University of Erlangen-Nuremberg.

Canadian Monetary Policy and the Problem of Inflation

LOUIS RASMINSKY

For about a year now, the immediate objective of Canadian monetary policy has been to help to bring about and maintain credit conditions. From the autumn of 1968 until the spring of 1969, the impact of Bank of Canada operations on the banking system took the form of a substantial reduction in the liquid assets of the banks and a progressive reduction in the rate of expansion of their total assets. By May 1969 the more liquid assets of the banks, which provide the cushion which enables them to expand their lending activity, had been reduced by three-quarters of a billion dollars; and the ratio of their more liquid assets to their total assets had fallen from 32.5 percent to 28 percent, a level which is very low by historical standards. A further $250 million of bank liquidity was immobilized last April when the Bank of Canada used its power to increase the secondary reserve requirements of the banks. Beginning in the autumn of 1968, the cost of credit in financial markets and institutions rose sharply and the availability of funds in the domestic bond market was greatly reduced.

By the spring of this year the level of liquidity of the banks as a group had declined to the point where they felt obliged to take steps to reduce the rate of increase in their loans. Since there are always large unused loan commitments outstanding at any time, this process took a while to have its full effect on the trend of bank loans outstanding. By July the impact of changes in lending policies became clearly evident. The banks' general loans, which include both business loans and personal loans, continued to rise very strongly in the first four months of the year, rose less rapidly in May and June, and did not rise at all from June to September. Thus by the early summer, potential borrowers were finding that credit, besides being very costly, was becoming much more difficult to obtain.

The central banks' management of the cash reserves since then has continued to constrain the overall liquid position of the chartered banks. Their more liquid assets declined sharply in July and have remained approximately level since then.

Credit conditions in Canada have become very tight. The increase in the money supply, using any definition one chooses, has been negligible in recent months. Defined as public holdings of currency and Canadian dollar bank deposits, there has been no increase in the money supply since February, and the increase amounts to less than 6 percent over the past 12 months. Bank credit is hard to come by. In spite of the sharp reduction

Reprinted from *The Conference Board Record,* December 1969, pp. 57–60, by permission of The Conference Board.

in the demands of the government of Canada on the capital market this year, other borrowers have not been able to raise as much money in the domestic bond market. Interest rates are very high. They range from about 7.6 percent on 3-month treasury bills to 10–10.5 percent on first-class conventional mortgages. Since the rise in interest rates is a world-wide phenomenon, there has been little room for escape from high interest costs by borrowing abroad, although funds may be somewhat more readily available for some borrowers outside Canada than at home.

I do not believe that one can explain either the insistence of lenders on receiving such high interest rates or the willingness of borrowers to pay them, without reference to the strong expectations of continued inflation that have developed. Borrowers have been reluctant to postpone expenditures for fear of incurring higher costs later, and lenders have sought to protect themselves against the impact of rising prices by refusing to lend except at high rates. Inflationary expectations have unhappily become a central feature in our economic situation, and it is a central task of economic policy to try to eliminate their causes.

In the 12 months ending September 1968, the government's over-all cash requirements, excluding those of the Exchange Fund, were $1,200 million. In the 12 months ending September 1969, there was a net cash availability of nearly $100 million. This large swing has been of great assistance to the central bank in controlling bank liquidity during the past year. Had it been necessary to deal with a large increase in public debt at a time when monetary policy was directed toward reducing the liquid assets of the banking system, it is obvious that the increase in interest rates would have had to be even greater than it was, or the growth of the money supply would have had to be larger.

Policies of Restraint

Anti-inflationary monetary and fiscal policies operate by restraining the rate of increase in total spending in the economy. In an ideal world a moderately lower rate of increase in the dollar value of spending would have all of its impact on the rate at which prices and costs were rising and none at all on the real growth. If this happened, one would move smoothly from an unsustainable rate of increase in spending to a sustainable rate of increase, without any risk of loss of output in the process. Unfortunately, our markets are not that sensitive; prices and costs are not that flexible; competition in our economy is not that close to being perfect. Some producers, faced with a dampening of market conditions, may continue for a while to obtain increased prices, at the cost of a slower increase or a reduction in the volume of their output. But other producers may confront more competitive situations, and in the face of a slackening in demand in dollar terms for their products begin more quickly to find it difficult or impossible to continue to raise prices, even if they are only trying to pass on cost increases to final consumers. In order to avoid too great a squeeze on their profit margins, they must make determined efforts to check increases in their costs. Sooner or later virtually all producers are in this position. That is fundamentally the way in which the control of the total level of spending affects prices and costs in the private sector of the economy. It works entirely through market forces.

One difficult feature of this process is that there are bound to be important lags between the time when the rate of increase in total spending in dollar terms slackens off and the time when the full impact on the rate of price and cost increase in the economy is felt, unless the policies of restraint are drastic. The lag will be that much longer if those in a position to influence prices, wages, and other incomes use their market power to resist the process rather than to facilitate the return to non-inflationary conditions. It should not be too surprising, given the lags involved, if there is a temporary, rather discouraging period when we seem to be getting the worst of both worlds because the rate of expansion of the economy in real terms has slowed down but prices continue to rise for a while at much the same rate. It is important that we should understand the reasons why the economy may perform in this way, and not be too quick to lose heart in such a period or too ready to abandon policies of restraint before the job is done.

There seems to be accumulating evidence that policies of restraint are beginning to take hold, both in Canada and in the United States. In the United States, the evidence of a pronounced slowing in the growth of over-all demand has become a good deal more convincing during the past two or three months. Although a slowing trend had been suggested by the quarterly estimates of real Gross National Product for some time, corroboration in the important monthly indicators of the labor market and of industrial production has only been discernible in the very recent statistics.

Unfortunately, an accurate assessment of most of the Canadian economic indicators since the first quarter has been complicated by a number of major strikes which have had an influence that is difficult to isolate. Even so, after making due allowance for all the temporary dislocations, it would seem that the underlying trend of demand in this country is no longer increasing nearly as rapidly as it was in the period up to the first quarter of this year. For example, consumers appear to have been behaving more cautiously since the end of the winter. Exports, quite apart from the special difficulties in selling wheat, have clearly lost much of their upward momentum which was such an important expansionary factor last year. Most areas of investment spending still appear to be strong in Canada on the basis of surveys now available, but housing starts have been declining from the high levels reached earlier this year. Industrial production and non-farm employment (both of which, of course, have been seriously affected by strikes) have shown weakness in recent months, and this has been reflected in an edging up of the unemployment rate, which is now 5 percent.

It is early to expect to see much impact of these developments on the trend of prices and costs, here or in the United States. It is, however, worth noting that in both countries profits, which increased very strongly during 1968, have leveled off or declined slightly in the first half of this year, and further pressure seems to be developing on profit margins. In Canada, the most widely used measure of prices shows slightly greater rates of increase over this year to date than they did during 1968. After seasonal adjustment, the Consumer Price Index increased at an annual rate of 4.5 percent in the first nine months of 1969.

The greater increase in the Consumer Price Index this year is almost wholly attributable to the more rapid rise in shelter and other service costs. While such costs bear just as heavily on consumers as other prices, it has to be remembered that this area of the index is particularly slow to respond to any general easing of demand pressures since it includes many items that directly reflect wage and salary costs, as well as regulated charges, mortgage interest rates, and property taxes. When one confines the analysis to the prices of goods, one does find in the recent statistics a few instances of reversals of earlier sharp increases of certain major commodities, but one does not find convincing evidence of any general moderation of price trends. Similarly, the typical wage and salary increases continue to be very large in relation to productivity, without evidence of a moderating trend. Nor is there conclusive evidence to date that inflationary expectations are on the wane.

The Real Goal

So while there are indications that policies of restraint are beginning to work and that we are on the right track, it is perhaps too optimistic to conclude that these policies have now done the full job of creating conditions that will eventually lead to a significant reduction in the rate of price and cost increase, despite the inevitable time lags that exist both in the adjustment of prices and costs to easier demand conditions and in the response of the economy to policy changes.

The Bank of Canada has no love for policies of restraint or for high interest rates in themselves. In the world as it is constituted the effort to bring inflation under control may involve some slowing for a period in the rate of real growth of the economy. The Bank does not wish to see any under-utilization of productive resources or any increase in unemployment. This is not the objective of an anti-inflationary monetary policy. On the contrary, the objective of policy is to create conditions which will encourage a prolonged and sustainable increase in output and employment.

Inflation is not such a condition. Quite apart from the serious inequities it involves and the unfair sacrifices it inflicts on those in the weakest bargaining position, including older people, the process of inflation and the attempts to adjust to inflation introduce tensions and distortions into the economic process which are bound to result in unsatisfactory economic performance. As more and more people try to adjust to inflation, more and more pressure is put on costs and prices and restrictive policies are needed simply to keep inflation from accelerating. Nothing is gained in the process in terms of output and employment, and people are put to a substantial and unnecessary degree of inconvenience and anxiety in the attempt to keep up with inflation. It is taking a very short-run view to believe that the tolerance of inflation can result in a higher level of real output or less unemployment. Inflation jeopardizes the kind of long-run economic expansion on which durable growth in employment depends.

The antithesis which is sometimes set up between concern about inflation on the one hand and concern about employment and growth on the other is therefore, in my judgment, a false antithesis. There are undoubtedly real costs involved in the short run in bringing inflation under control. But these have to be weighed against the eventual real costs and inequities involved in failing to control inflation. For my part, I am certain that the real costs, in terms of output and employment, of failing to control inflation would in the end be much more serious. We need reasonable monetary stability for a number of reasons, but primarily as a means of maximizing our prospects of achieving high and efficient employment in the years ahead.

We must, of course, do all we can to keep the real costs of anti-inflationary policies to an absolute minimum. Because of concern about minimizing these costs and obtaining the best performance from the economy over the longer run, I have for a number of years advocated that monetary and fiscal policies to influence aggregate demand should be supplemented not only by "supply" policies designed to improve the use, efficiency and mobility of our economic resources but also by an organized effort to influence public opinion in the direction of exercising restraint in the determination of prices and costs. It is for this reason that I have attached, and continue to attach, importance to the work of the Prices and Incomes Commission.

Self-Restraint and Self-Interest

To succeed in controlling inflation, the fact that there is a very limited number of basic policies on which one can rely in a market economy must be faced. "Supply" policies, vitally important though they are, are necessarily long-term in character and cannot be expected to produce quick effects. They are more relevant to long-term productivity performance and regional balance than to the actual control of inflation. In the short run, major reliance has to be placed on the control of aggregate demand supplemented by voluntary restraint, if this can be arranged, or without it if it cannot.

To the extent that those with market power are prepared to facilitate a return to non-inflationary conditions, the degree and duration of fiscal and monetary restraints will be reduced. It is obvious that much remains to be done to convince all groups in the economy that self-restraint is not altruism but a matter of practical self-interest because it can minimize the cost to the whole economy of controlling inflation. Therefore, business should exercise restraint in its pricing policies.

In formulating monetary policy it is, of course, necessary to look not only at the current indicators of the economy, but also to form as good a judgment as one can regarding possible developments in the future. The responsible authorities must keep their policies under constant review. Monetary policy is essentially forward-looking. This does not mean, however, that we can avert our gaze from what is going on around us. And it does not mean that in looking ahead we should take a very limited time horizon and be so concerned with the next few months that we fail to pay enough attention to the next few years.

Future Prospects

All policy is in some degree based on forecasts, and experience has shown that economic forecasts are not always as accurate as one would like them to be. The prospective strength of the economy at any time is open to under-estimation as well as over-estimation and in recent years the tendency has been to err in the direction of under-estimation. It is necessary to appraise the risks in both directions. In a non-inflationary environment with the economy operating well below its potential, there is likely to be, and often should be, a willingness to take the risk that the economy may turn out to be stronger than is foreseen. On the other hand, in an inflationary period, and particularly one in which inflationary expectations have become very strong, and in which there is a firm underpinning of demand favorable to resumed expansion, one must be very conscious of the risks of premature relaxation. This would run the serious danger of confirming the expectations of those who think that when it comes to the crunch the authorities will lack the will to persist in policies of restraint and that inflation is here to stay.

One occasionally hears it suggested that we should not press the fight against inflation on the ground that since external prices have an important influence on our price level there is not much we can do on our own, and that we might as well leave the job to the Americans and spare ourselves all the inconveniences and the risks of anti-inflationary policies. I consider this course of action totally unrealistic. If this were to become the policy of this country, can there be any doubt as to what would happen to the expectations of Canadians in regard to inflation, or what would happen in the bond market (on which not only industry depends for finance for expansion but on which provinces and municipalities depend to raise money for social capital needs), or as to what would happen in foreign exchange markets, or as to what would happen to domestic cost and price levels? Such a policy might be defensible if our inflationary pressures were entirely due to developments in the United States. While it is the case that prices in that country, particularly at the consumer level, have been rising more rapidly than in Canada this year, there is still plenty of evidence of domestically generated inflation here, particularly on the cost side. There are important areas of the Canadian economy where recent cost performance is worse than that of the United States.

If Canada fails to do as well as the United States in controlling inflation, the weakening of our competitive position over a period of time will damage our economic prospects for the future. On the other hand, if Canada were to do a little better in controlling inflation than the United States—something which may well be within its power—this would not constitute a problem. Such an outcome would be rewarding. There would be a pay-off in increased employment and output from the improved competitive position and prospects for sound and sustained economic growth would be enhanced.

In times like these it is always heartening to stop for a moment to think of the capacity of the Canadian economy for growth and for the improvement of standards of life in this country. Much can be accomplished in a relatively few years with the right policies.

In my opinion, the greatest threat to the full achievement of this fine potential is posed by inflation. There is no sector of our society which does not have a vital interest in the success of the effort that is now being made to deal effectively with this problem.

Monetary Policy and Overall Control

JOACHIM KLAUS
HANS-JÜRGEN FALK

The Problems

In recent years, monetary policy has experienced a renaissance in scientific debate which is remarkable as compared with the importance assigned to it in the early postwar years. New theoretical knowledge and practical experience have again strengthened the formerly greatly reduced confidence in its effectiveness. Thus today there are scarcely any doubts that it is

Reprinted from *The German Economic Review,* Vol. *8,* No. 2, 1970, pp. 97–114, by permission of the publisher.

capable of exerting substantial influence on the economic process, if its instruments are utilized to the full and properly applied. However, there is also widespread agreement that monetary policy cannot be applied in isolation from other spheres of economic policy. This becomes especially clear in a system with overall control of the market economy, in which it is desired to achieve several macroeconomic objectives simultaneously by means of purposive level and structural control. This sort of policy employs three big levers:

a) government agencies and their revenue and expenditures policy

b) the Bundesbank and its monetary policy

c) management and labor and their wage policy

and endeavors ". . . to place the whole arsenal of means in the service of the complete array of objectives."

The new function of monetary policy resulting from these changes calls for a reappraisal of its location. In this connection, two sets of questions require clarification.

1. What is the relationship of monetary policy to the catalogue of official, macroeconomic objectives, and to the other instruments of economic policy?

2. What institutional consequences result from the inclusion of monetary policy in a consistent system of overall control?

The Changed Function of Monetary Policy and Its Integration into an Overall Control System

The official array of objectives has been set forth in Germany by the parliament in the "Act for the Promotion of Stability and Growth" (Stability Act). Hence the aim of price stability, which was given priority for a long time, has lost its predominance and can now only be given consideration as one among several objectives which are in principle of equal rank. The mandate of the legislature obliges the federal and Laender governments to institute their measures in such a manner ". . . that, within the framework of the market economy system, they contribute simultaneously to stability of the price level, a high level of employment, and external trade equilibrium while maintaining steady and reasonable economic growth." Since the central bank, "while performing its mission," is required to support the general economic policy of the federal government and is expressly called upon to make allowances for the objectives of the Stability Act in all its actions, it now has to bear also formally part of the responsibility for trade cycle and growth policy. Consequently, the monetary policy which was formerly oriented more or less one-sidedly to the objective of preserving the value of money must be modified. In doing so, we must proceed from the fact that the four official objectives which are to be achieved simultaneously are not independent of each other so that measures undertaken by the various agencies responsible for economic policy may—intentionally or unintentionally—affect several objectives at the same time. Such a highly differentiated pattern of effects makes isolated action seem hazardous.

If conflicts of objectives are to be avoided, co-ordinated action is necessary, in which mutually countervailing measures can be precluded from the outset. If such co-ordination is waived, then, in consequence of the pluralism of agencies implementing economic policy and the pluralism of objectives, monetary policy will be faced with the danger of

1. lack of efficiency.
2. conflicts between its objective of preserving the value of money and the other macroeconomic objectives.
3. limitations on its scope of action.

The possible lack of efficiency of monetary policy may be due to a large number of factors, not all of which can be excluded by co-ordination with the other instruments of economic policy. However, some of them can be moderated in this way, so that it is possible to enhance the effectiveness of monetary policy. To demonstrate this, it is necessary to undertake a more detailed classification of the factors that generally reduce efficiency. The most important of them are

a) tardy employment of the instruments.
b) too long a "braking distance" of the measures employed.
c) ineffectiveness where there is a liquidity trap or similar situations involving only slight responsiveness of investment decisions.
d) countervailing inflows of liquidity from abroad.
e) countervailing fiscal policy action.
f) countervailing wage changes.

The delay between situation analysis and application of means—the inside lag—is responsible for the tardy employment of instruments. It is the result of two separate lags: the recognition lag and the action lag. Tardy diagnosis results from inadequate information, especially with regard to future developments. Rapid recognition of the situation is made extraordinarily difficult for the central bank as long as it remains uninformed about the lines of action to be expected of government agencies, and labor and management. The uncertainty may lead to a wait-and-see attitude and finally to tardy application of the instruments. So if only in the interests of an exchange of information, co-ordination of monetary policy with the other spheres of economic policy is expedient and necessary. It is true accurate forecasts are still problematical, but situation analysis is facilitated so that the recognition lag, even though it cannot be eliminated, can be shortened. The action lag on the other hand can scarcely be influenced by co-ordination of action. Although it is conceivable that co-ordination talks could accelerate the decision-making process at the central bank, there is no certainty that this effect would occur.

The long "braking distance" between the application and the effect of measures can likewise hardly be shortened by co-ordinating action. This outside lag is immanent in the system, that is, it is a consequence of the forms of control and the structures of the market economy. At best it might be reduced by improvement of the instruments of monetary policy, with which, for instance, redeployment of banks' assets and the activity of financial intermediaries could be brought under control.

There are better prospects of successful co-ordination, if the monetary policy instruments remain "blunt" owing to too little responsiveness of investment decisions (say, in the case of a liquidity trap and/or of a relatively high degree of independence of investments on credit costs) or if they cause only structural changes. If central bank measures affecting interest rates, the quantity of money, and the liquidity of the economy are coupled with appropriate modifications of government expenditure and revenue and wages, their efficiency may be substantially enhanced by the simultaneous and, under certain circumstances, cumulative effect of several instruments.

As a rule, special difficulties arise for monetary policy from foreign trade relations and international capital flows, if—as is usual—exchange rates are rigid and the decision on parities lies with the governments. Especially in Germany, it has repeatedly proved that all central bank measures to preserve the value of money give rise to countervailing inflows of liquidity from abroad (owing to inflationary trends prevailing there or on account of other factors of economic uncertainty). The Board of Experts attempted to set forth how a way can be found out of this dilemma in its 1968/69 annual expertise: If adaptive inflation is rejected, the only way out is economic policy action by the government (influencing of foreign trade and capital movements) with, or if necessary without, exchange rate corrections. Only by way of such external safeguards can monetary policy at home be given the efficiency required for success. So precisely in this sphere, co-ordination between monetary policy and government agencies is manifestly of special importance.

However, it is also equally necessary for monetary policy and general fiscal policy to be adapted to each other. In an economy in which from 30 to 40 percent of the national income flows through public treasuries, the government is capable of making any central bank instrument ineffectual by way of budgetary policy. This is particularly true of an expenditure or taxation policy which counteracts central bank control of the quantity of money, but also of government debt policy affecting interest rates. Only accurate mutual information and co-ordinated action can provide security against such countervailing effects. However, in a state with a federative structure like that of the Federal Republic of Germany this involves considerable difficulties, though they are by no means unsolvable.

A pure increase in the efficiency of individual monetary policy instruments can hardly be achieved by coupling with wage policy measures. On the other hand, such a combination is desirable in another respect. Wage changes, acting via cost and demand effects, influence certain objectives in a direction which the central bank is intent on preventing. In this instance, co-ordination can provide a way out. Hence, with regard to possible *conflicts of objectives* wage policy is of substantial importance for monetary policy.

This leads to the question of how far co-ordination of monetary policy instruments with the other instruments of economic policy can *ameliorate* conflicts. In general,

— the more numerous the objectives
— the more precisely they are fixed
— the less parameters that can be taken as action parameters
— and the more numerous the limitations and restrictions
— the more aggravated will be the conflicts of objectives.

Since the number of official, macroeconomic objectives—as already mentioned—is laid down by parliament, it cannot be reduced by a constant consultation or information process. Indeed, it is increased by co-ordination efforts, because also the distribution policy viewpoints of employers and employees must be given consideration. To this extent, integration of monetary policy into the overall control system not only brings this instrument no advantages, but direct disadvantages owing to the increased danger of conflicts.

On the other hand, by co-ordination talks among all agencies which have an influence on economic policy it is possible to achieve agreement on the interpretation of the various objectives, which are not quantified by the legislature. This affords the possibility of eliminating conflicts between objectives which arise from differing conceptions of their content. Moreover, joint, concrete definition of objectives also offers the chance of fostering the willingness to accept compromises on the basis of a better understanding of macroeconomic interdependencies and appreciation of the necessity of certain actions of other participants. In this way conflicts resulting from obstinacy and dogmatism could be avoided.

A consideration of the relation between the number of objectives and the available action parameters shows the compulsion to co-ordinate even more clearly. On the one hand, despite all efficiency-reducing factors, if all its instruments are employed consequentially monetary policy alone is capable, under certain circumstances, of checking inflationary trends so effectively by curbing demand that price stability results. But then, as a rule, it endangers the maintenance of "reasonable" economic growth and full employment. On the other hand, in some cases it is possible for the other agencies responsible for economic policy to attain on their own special objectives to which in each case they assign priority. In such cases, however, there is a danger that the value of money may be influenced in an undesired direction. Due to isolated efforts, therefore, objective conflicts may be caused both by the wage policy of the employers and employed and by government fiscal policy. But if these agencies agree on joint action, their various instruments can be combined and co-ordinated. Then additional action parameters are available for each objective, the correct dosage and combination of which helps to avoid incompatibilities, that is, they exert a conflict-reducing effect. This facilitates considerably the attainment of the official catalogue of objectives. At the same time, such limitations and restrictions as are set up by individual agencies responsible for economic policy in order to protect themselves against disadvantages in the event of isolated application of certain instruments are no longer needed. This touches on the third problem, which is linked up with an autonomous monetary policy: the danger of a narrowing down of the central bank's range of action, interpreted as the domain ". . . in which relatively conflict-free monetary policy action is possible."

The central bank's range of action has been substantially increased in the past few decades by quantitative expansion and qualitative modification of the instruments. Owing to the already described possible impairment of the effectiveness of its instruments, under certain circumstances the central bank may find itself compelled to employ these means with the greatest possible rigor. Such action increases the number of those affected, the severity of the effects, and the danger of conflicts of objectives. In many instances, these changes afford an isolated monetary policy only two possible alternatives:

a) efficient but highly conflictive, or

b) conflict-free but inefficient implementation.

However, since the central bank, being an "institution without assured political power," cannot continually engage in political conflicts without endangering its independence, but should also not lose its importance as one of the most important institutions responsible for economic policy as a result of ineffectual action, the sole remaining way out of this dilemma is co-ordination with the other agencies responsible for economic policy. The incidence and severity of effects can be dosed better by objective-adapted and co-ordinated employment of several instruments than by isolated action.

To summarize, it can be said that co-ordination of monetary policy instruments with other economic policy instruments not only brings advantages, but constitutes a *conditio sine qua non* for an effective overall control system.

In addition to these instrumental aspects, however, institutional considerations must also be taken into account. Co-ordination of behavior demands a minimum of contact among a given group of participants and hence also certain institutional arrangements. In order to attain a consensus, it is necessary for each participant to sacrifice functional independence to a certain extent.‘ This becomes especially problematical, if the assessment of objectives is likewise to be subject to mutual agreement. This sacrifice and the de facto limitation of the various ranges of autonomous action provide grounds for assuming that consequences affecting constitutional law will be involved. Since precisely the autonomy of the central bank is stressed repeatedly, but will possibly have to be newly interpreted or even modified as a result of the combination of monetary policy and over-all control, at this juncture a more detailed analysis of the position of the central bank is necessary.

Co-ordination and Autonomy of the Central Bank as a Problem of the Economic Constitution

The question as to the position of the central bank within the structure of the constitution and the state is by no means new. Ever since the abolition of the gold redemption mandate, the position of the central bank has been controversial. While under the gold standard it had a fixed and closely defined range of action and its activity was chiefly of a declaratory nature; with a "managed currency" it has a broad range of action. Its consequent significance as one of the most important economic policy makers is the cause of the controversial conceptions of the location of the central bank within the system of political powers, and especially of its relation to the government. Fundamentally, it is possible to regulate this relationship in four different ways:

1. Subordination; the central bank is obliged to comply with government instructions.
2. Integration; the central bank has the character of a ministry, its president is a member of the cabinet and hence fully integrated into the government.
3. Co-ordination; the central bank is independent and ranks on a par with the government, but its actions must be agreed upon with the government.
4. Autonomy; the central bank operates completely independently.

None of these arrangements can be assigned to any specific order of the state although, for example, the integration principle is often put into effect in centrally controlled economies. "Political systems which all conceive themselves as parliamentary democracies and constitutional states and are derived in one form or another from the classical principle of separation of powers, have arrived at quite different, and in fact contradictory results in integrating their central banks into the framework of their systems." Since, in Germany, experience with dependent central banks had been unsatisfactory and the population had, and still has, a particularly marked fear of new inflations caused by the state, when the monetary system was reorganized, the central bank in this country was given a relatively large degree of independence, though the latter is tied up with various co-ordination elements. Its autonomy derives in three respects from the provisions of the Bundesbank Act:

a) institutionally.

b) with regard to personnel.

c) functionally.

The institutional position of the Bundesbank has not been cleared up completely, however, which may result in controversy with regard to the requirements of the Stability Act. The Act merely states that it is a "federal juristic person under public law." So although in the Act no use is made of the terms "Anstalt" (statutory institution which may be a public corporation), corporation or foundation, and none of these legal forms can be deduced from its overall make-up, the Bundesbank is nevertheless often defined as an "Anstalt," an "Anstalt with an exceptional status," or an "Anstalt-like establishment with its own peculiar nature and—contrary to the rule—limited administrative supervision." These attempts to describe the special position of the Bundesbank with the aid of traditional instruments of legal theory must be regarded as unsatisfactory. The lack of administrative supervision, equality of status of the Central Bank Council and the Bundesbank Directorate with supreme federal authorities, the lack of possibilities of imposing sanctions in the event of objections by the Federal Audit Office in conjunction with the personal and functional independence permit rather the conclusion that in this instance a legal form has been created which is completely new in our legal system and that the Bundesbank has become an *institutum sui generis*. True, it is a part of the executive—that is it cannot be interpreted as a "fourth power" in addition to the legislative, executive, and judicial—but in contrast to other government organs it remains free from government control. Precisely this fact may raise special problems in respect of co-ordination in a system of over-all control.

Over and above this, the hindrance and facilitation of co-ordination depend on the personnel and the composition of the central bank organs. The arrangements in this respect have been made relatively complicated. The organs of the German Bundesbank are the Central Bank Council, the Directorate, and the boards of management of the Land Central Banks. The topmost body is the Central Bank Council—consisting of the Directorate and the presidents of the Land Central Banks—which lays down the bank's monetary and credit policy. The members of the Directorate are appointed by the federal president on nomination by the federal government; in this connection the latter must give the Central Bank Council a hearing. The presidents of the Land Central Banks are likewise appointed by the federal president, the nominations in this case coming from the Bundesrat, the second chamber of the federal parliament, which in turn reaches a decision on the basis of proposals made by the competent agencies under Land law and after hearing the Central Bank Council. The other members of the boards of management of the Land Central Banks are appointed by the president of the Bundesbank on nomination by the Central Bank Council.

So there is a substantial amount of political influence (through the federal government and the Bundesrat) on the appointment of the leading personalities in the central bank organization. However, the pluralism of the nominating bodies and the opinion of the Central Bank Council (which should not be underestimated) in conjunction with the nature and duration of the employment contracts result in relatively great independence of the leading members of the central bank with regard to pressures exerted by political parties and associations.

The strongest guarantee of Bundesbank autonomy, however, lies in the functional sphere: "In the exercise of the powers vested in it by the Act it shall not be subject to instructions of the Federal government." This precludes any direct influence being exerted by the federal government. A limit is set here also to the federal Chancellor's authority to issue directives, so that within its functional domain the Bundesbank is on a par with the government. Over and above this, however, under the prevailing law it is also independent of parliament, since the Bundesbank Act makes no provision for possible controls and sanctions. Nevertheless it is possible to modify the autonomy of the Bundesbank by legislative means. "The behaviour of the leading persons in a central bank will not remain unaffected by this fact." The political range of action is therefore more limited than the legal one. This may possibly facilitate co-ordination efforts.

All in all, it can be said that the Bundesbank has a relatively high degree of independence. The governing factors are

a) its legal construction as an *institutum sui generis,*

b) the pluralism of its executive organs and the bodies nominating them, and

c) its non-subjection to instructions from the federal government.

That independence is further increased by the fact that direct influence by pressure groups is precluded.

Nevertheless, even the Bundesbank is not completely autonomous. It is required by the Bundesbank Act "while duly performing its functions, to support the general economic policy of the Federal government." In more concrete terms the Stability Act demands of all federal corporations, "Anstalten" and foundations—which, according to prevailing doctrine, also include the Bundesbank—that, within the ambit of their assigned tasks, they should give consideration to official objectives when instituting their own measures. Experience in the field of economic policy has shown that the demand for support of official economic policy may conflict with the "performance of its functions." In order to examine what consequences may arise for the overall control system from such a conflict, it is necessary to inquire more closely into the Bundesbank's functions.

In the Bundesbank Act the functions of the Bundesbank are circumscribed only vaguely in a not particularly informative general clause. For all that, it outlines two spheres of functions:

1. safeguarding of the currency and
2. settlement of payments.

As the second function and the resulting position of the Bundesbank as a bankers' bank are more of a technical nature the sole remaining economic policy function is the safeguarding of the currency. But this latter function is by no means clear. In the Bundesbank Act—as in numerous other central bank acts—the legislature refrained from defining this stabilizing function in concrete terms. Moreover, in the case of a managed currency it is hardly possible ". . . to find a substitute definition which, from the standpoint of legislative precision, would be equally as satisfactory as the gold standard." In addition, it must be taken into account that the Bundesbank alone would certainly not be in a position—even if the requirements of the Act were formulated in such manner—to safeguard the stability of the currency, since the latter is not dependent on the Bundesbank's measures alone. Nearly all financial, social, wage, and general economic policy decisions, and the pricing behavior of enterpreneurs and government price fixing and tariffs have an effect on the value of money. Furthermore, it may be endangered by foreign forces which can hardly be influenced by the Bundesbank, since it is not the latter, but the federal government which decides on flexibility or rigidity and parities for the exchange rates. Hence the Bundesbank cannot be required to perform the task of ensuring monetary stability. That would be demanding too much. The function of "safeguarding the currency" laid down in the Bundesbank Act can be regarded only as an orientation point for the employment of monetary policy measures with the object of stabilizing the value of money.

Here the already mentioned problems inherent in the demand for the Bundesbank to support general economic policy are clearly evident. The lack of a concrete definition of its tasks means a broad scope for the bank's own discretion. In the light of the comprehensive monetary policy instruments and in consequence of the general interdependence of all economic policy measures and the monetary situation, the use of that discretion easily results in the difficulties mentioned at the beginning, which can be ameliorated only by co-ordination measures. The possibility of conflicts was certainly realized when preparing the Bundesbank Act. For this reason the relationship between the Bundesbank and the other agencies responsible for economic policy was thoroughly ventilated. The following proposals were submitted for discussion:

1. In order to preclude conflicts from the outset, the federal government should have the right to issue instructions. This would nullify the autonomy of the Bundesbank.
2. The central bank and the government should be equally constrained to observe the "principle of monetary justice" on pain of penal or disciplinary sanctions. Apart from the question of the judicability of this principle, in this instance it also remains unclarified how the conflict is to be solved *prior* to the resulting negative effects.
3. The central bank should be compelled by rulings of the administrative courts or the Federal Constitutional Court to support general economic policy. In this instance the same difficulties are encountered as in the case of the second proposal.
4. The conflicts should be resolved by a court of arbitration, a mediation procedure or by way of a conciliation committee.

However, none of these proposals were incorporated in the Bundesbank Act. The legislature was of the opinion that no arbitration body with a better grasp of the subject could be formed ". . . than that possessed by the two institutions involved in the conflict and that therefore the matter would certainly be referred back to parliament for more exact legislative regulation." The only step the federal government can take is to postpone a decision by the Central Bank Council for up to two weeks. If agreement has then still not been achieved—that is, if there is a "dramatic" conflict— the Bundesbank decides autonomously. In so doing, owing to its only inadequately definable tasks, it has a relatively high degree of flexibility and is quite capable of endeavoring to find a compromise between conflicting objectives. Nevertheless, in the final analysis the decisions eventually made are always based solely on its own interpretation of duties imposed by the Act. Precisely for this reason, in the light of the relationship between the Bundesbank and the federal government the danger of conflicts must be regarded as particularly great. And that danger is hardly diminished by the few rudimentary co-ordination provisions contained in the Bundesbank Act. True, the members of the federal government are entitled to participate in the consultations of the Central Bank Council and to enter motions, but they have no vote. In his turn, the Bundesbank president has no decision-making authority in the consultations of the federal government on "issues of monetary importance," which he should be invited to attend.

Thus the antimony in the current situation of the economic constitution is clearly manifest. The Bundesbank enjoys a relative maximum of independence. At the same time, however, it is obliged, while duly performing its functions, to support general economic policy without this task being adequately defined in concrete terms and without any delineation of the institutional solutions in genuine co-ordination between Bundesbank and federal government. Possible conflicts are consciously accepted as inevitable hazards, instead of overcoming the difficulties involved in a combination of autonomy and co-ordination.

The Linking of Monetary Policy and Concerted Action

It is by no means an unsolvable problem to find an institutional arrangement which does justice *both to the compulsion to functional co-ordination and the position of the central bank under constitutional law*. A solution is offered by a monetary-economic policy coordination process which satisfies the following criteria:

1. Coordination talks among agencies responsible for monetary, fiscal, and wage policies at a *single* round table. Above all, this would require that the ministers of finance and economic affairs, and representatives of management and labor be called in to take part in making monetary policy decisions.
2. Possibility of freely bringing conflicts to a conclusion in respect of appraisal of measures and objectives.
3. Simultaneity of possible decisions coupled with the greatest possible transparency and information on the probable reactions of the participants.
4. Upholding of the co-operative element during consultation and preparation of the decisions.

Institutionalization of co-ordination of behavior on these lines has the advantage that in the Concerted Action program action patterns are already available, from which utilizable know-how can be taken over.

An even more important point is that, by means of a solution designed according to these criteria, Concerted Action can be combined with monetary policy to facilitate the task. This would mean amelioration of a number of the functional co-ordination problems and simultaneously of the conflict between the autonomy of the central bank and the requirements concerning its integration into the conception of an overall control system, which conflict hitherto seemed to be an institutional subordination problem.

As compared with the present position of the Bundesbank, in the event of real coordination with other agencies responsible for economic policy this arrangement would mean ad hoc a limitation of the bank's freedom of action, but its autonomous position would be strengthened by the functionally improved integration into the over-all control system. This is true in three respects. First, the danger of subordination of the central bank and abrogation of its autonomy, that is the compulsory (legislative) integration of its policy into the over-all control system (which danger grows with the intensity of government control activity), would be diminished to a considerable degree. Secondly, the de facto enjoinment of the co-operative element in the consultations provides the necessary safeguard against tutelage and being outvoted, since all decisions require the agreement of all participants. Thirdly, in the final analysis a large group of agency representatives which meets continually affords protection against the narrowing down of argumentation; the expansion of the range of action of economic policy which is thus attained, or made evident, in favorable situations benefits the monetary policy makers equally as much as the other participants.

The enumerated criteria for the institutional solution of the co-ordination problems from the standpoint of monetary policy are largely the same as those applicable to a macroeconomically oriented wage policy in a Concerted Action framework consonant with functional efficiency. Hence the co-ordination problems of monetary policy closely parallel those of the Concerted Action program. This relationship makes it seem an obvious step to integrate monetary policy and Concerted Action. Such a functional and institutional supplementation of the instruments of overall control is the easiest means of ensuring co-ordination of control authorities and measures, while preserving the autonomy of the central bank and of managment and labor associations.

Discussion Questions

1. How did the Canadians use monetary policy to fight inflation?
2. Discuss the use of monetary policy in West Germany as a macroeconomic policy weapon.
3. How does German monetary policy relate to the "concerted action" program?

Unemployment and Manpower Policy

Unemployment is a harsh state of being. It brings with it not only material deprivation, but psychological hardships that are beyond quantification. A decade ago economists were quite convinced that our unemployment problem was essentially caused by a lack of aggregate demand, a level of spending by households, businesses, and government which was insufficient to maintain a full employment level of output.

Today, however, many believe the character of unemployment in the United States has changed. The phenomenon of rapid technological change has produced a situation in which existing skills become obsolete more quickly than in the past. Thus, unemployment in this case is not a function of a lack of aggregate demand, but of the lack of conjuncture between the skills demanded and the skills supplied in the labor market. In other words, even if demand expanded, there would still be a certain proportion of the labor force which would not be absorbed into gainful employment. This is known as structural unemployment. Structural unemployment calls for a policy mix quite different from the traditional notion of expanding total demand. In particular, manpower policies, such as retraining or relocation, must be used to supplement expansionary monetary and fiscal policies.

The following articles treat the ways in which West European countries have used manpower policies. David Bauer's article provides a survey of Western Europe while Bertil Rehnberg's focuses attention on Swedish manpower policies and the success they have had in battling unemployment. Bauer is in the International Economics Department of the National Industrial Conference Board. Rehnberg is Deputy Director-General of the National Swedish Labour Market Board.

Low Unemployment Rates Abroad

DAVID BAUER

Between 1960 and 1968, unemployment in Germany never exceeded 1 percent of the labor force and in Japan rarely moved above 1.3 percent. While unemployment in Italy edged past the U.S. rate last year, previously joblessness in that country—as well as in France, Great Britain, and Sweden—was usually well below the U.S. average. Only Canada has experienced unemployment rates significantly higher than in the United States (see Figure 1). These comparisons, it should be noted, are based on unemployment data from abroad that are adjusted so as to conform in definition and coverage to U.S. rates.

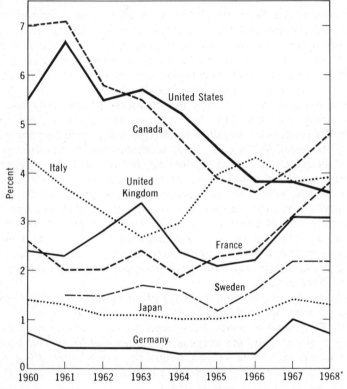

* Preliminary.

Figure 1. Unemployment Rates in Selected Countries, 1960–1968. *(Data from U.S. Department of Labor, Bureau of Labor Statistics; and the Conference Board.)*

Reprinted from *The Conference Board Record*, August 1969, pp. 51–56, by permission of The Conference Board.

Such differences in rates can be attributed to a host of factors. These include, above all, the rate of expansion of economic activity in individual countries, variations in the use of monetary and fiscal measures to control such activity (and hence the unemployment level), and the general nature of the economic system and of economic endeavor. But beyond largely economic influences, there are others that may be said to have contributed to differences in unemployment rates among the major industrial countries. (See Table 1.) One such factor is manpower systems and personnel policies specifically designed to eleviate, shorten, or altogether prevent unemployment, another is the degree of self-employment among the labor force.

Manpower Programs and Personnel Policies

The various programs and policies used abroad to initiate the effects of unemployment are frequently in the form of joint undertakings by government and private industry. They consist primarily of apprenticeships and other vocational training for those leaving school, relocation assistance, and retraining courses. Additionally, personnel policies in many firms are structured so that employees can be retrained throughout periods of slack business activity or are notified of impending layoffs far in advance of the actual termination date, such practices often reflect both legal regulations and voluntary efforts on the part of employers.

Common Market Programs

European efforts to mitigate unemployment have been supported by the European Economic Community's Social Fund, from which member countries receive sums for retraining and relocation programs. These payments, which underwrite 50 percent of the cost of many national manpower programs, helped retrain approximately 256,000 persons and relocate an additional 298,000 between 1961 and 1967. (In contrast, the U.S., which has a labor force slightly larger than the Common Market's, relocated approximately 13,000 workers through federal programs between 1965 and 1968.)

Relocation of workers is made both within and outside of the country sponsoring the program. Placing them outside the home country is eased by Common Market policies designed to facilitate free movement of labor. Information offices in countries where there is a surplus of labor advise workers of job vacancies in other countries; social security systems are being reorganized so that a relocated worker will retain many of the benefits which accrued to him in his home country; and, with some exceptions, employers are forbidden to discriminate between native job applicants and those from another Common Market country.

Retraining and relocation programs financed by the Fund are long-range efforts; payments to participating countries are not made until a

Table 1. Labor Force and Unemployment in Selected Countries, 1960–1967 *
(in thousands)

	United States	Canada	France	Germany	Great Britain	Italy	Japan	Sweden
Labor Force								
1960	69,628	6,411	19,690	25,080	24,008	20,320	na	43,940
1961	70,549	6,521	19,580	25,300	24,301	20,270	3,635	44,300
1962	70,614	6,615	19,610	25,430	24,604	20,090	3,709	44,800
1963	71,833	6,748	19,940	25,540	24,711	19,740	3,773	45,190
1964	73,091	6,933	20,100	25,600	24,844	19,820	3,737	45,810
1965	74,445	7,141	20,220	25,750	25,040	19,620	3,751	46,530
1966	75,770	7,420	20,330	25,670	25,166	19,380	3,794	47,620
1967	77,347	7,694	20,510	25,190	24,974	19,530	3,769	49,630
1968	78,737	7,919	20,620	25,060	24,850	19,480	3,825	49,790
Unemployed								
1960	3,852	446	520	180	580	880	na	630
1961	4,714	466	400	100	550	750	56	580
1962	3,911	390	400	90	700	640	56	510
1963	4,070	374	470	110	830	530	65	510
1964	3,786	324	360	80	590	590	60	470
1965	3,366	280	450	70	520	780	45	480
1966	2,875	267	470	70	550	830	61	530
1967	2,975	315	620	250	780	740	82	710
1968	2,817	382	720	180	760	750	86	670

* Based on U.S. definitions.
SOURCE: Bureau of Labor Statistics.

worker has been employed for six of the twelve months following his training or relocation.

Establishment of the Social Fund has provided a means whereby the resources of the entire Common Market can be focused on unemployment problems within particular countries. Italy, which contributes 20 percent to the cost of the fund, received 37 percent of the payments made between 1961 and 1967; the Netherlands has accounted for 7 percent of total contributions, but 9 percent of total payments.

Under another program, approximately 219,000 unemployed coal and steel workers received payments between 1960 and 1967 that helped them finance retraining programs and meet relocation expenses, and partially reimbursed them for wages in new jobs which were below those previously received.

Training Programs for Youth

The difficulties encountered by young persons seeking work in the U.S. contribute in a major way to this country's relatively high unemployment rate. Nearly one out of every three persons job-hunting last year was between 16 and 19 years of age, and while the unemployment rate for the entire labor force has averaged slightly under 5 percent since 1960, the rate for youths has been nearly 15 percent.

To be sure, teen-agers abroad generally are unemployed more frequently than older, more experienced workers, but the unemployment rates are often much closer to those of adults than is the case in the U.S. The success of European youths in finding jobs is particularly noteworthy since a substantially large proportion of them are in the labor market. According to the International Labour Office, between 50 percent and 80 percent of European males 15–19 years of age are either employed or looking for work, as compared to approximately 44 percent in the U.S.

Entry into the labor force via vocational education programs is more common abroad than in this country. In Germany, for instance, over 60 percent of youths currently between 20 and 23 years of age participated in vocational education programs *before* they had reached 18 years; the pertinent ratio for the U.S. is 19 percent. In Great Britain, staff members of the Youth Employment Service interview every 15-year-old who leaves school (these account for over half of students terminating studies), and most of those who leave between 16 and 17. Career possibilities are discussed on the basis of a student's preferences and on the results of aptitude tests. Through such tests, interviews, and the cooperation of employers (who are encouraged to register appropriate job openings), approximately two-fifths of all youths are placed in their first jobs by the Service. In Sweden, compulsory education for those who do not plan to attend college is begun in the eighth grade, when they spend three weeks with potential employers learning about a particular industry and about the tools, machines, and work skills used in specific occupations.

Apprenticeship

Apprenticeship and other forms of post-school vocational education are, in many countries, considered an extension of formal education, which for most youths ends at age 15. At that time, students have the option of (1) continuing their education in preparation for university study or a career, or (2) entering the labor market, often through an extended period of industrial training. In some countries, vocational school is compulsory for students leaving secondary school. In the U.S., probably less than 50 percent of high school graduates not entering college enroll in apprenticeship or vocational training. The ratio is frequently higher in Europe; over 70 percent get such training in Germany and Austria. And this comparison does not fully indicate the importance of industrial training in keeping the unemployment rate lower abroad. Over half of the high school graduates in the U.S. learning work skills do so in vocational courses which, in spite of recent revisions, are heavily oriented toward agriculture and home economics. Apprenticeship training, both in the U.S. and abroad, often offers more difficult courses and consequently a better opportunity for full-time employment, but the estimated ratio of eligible U. S. high school graduates accepted into apprenticeships in 1967 is less than 20 percent.

Two of the features which most distinguish between apprenticeship training here and abroad are the financial support that programs abroad receive from government agencies, and the low level of wages paid to trainees (although reduced wage rates for younger workers are not limited to apprentices). Subsidies in Italy, Japan, Netherlands, Norway, Sweden, and Switzerland are of two types. Nonfinancial assistance is provided in the form of free instruction for trainees in government facilities, or direct grants are given to employers conducting classes in their own plants. In France, industrial, craft, and commercial establishments must pay an apprenticeship tax equal to 0.6 percent of wages, but exemption may be claimed if the firm provides training. Employers in Great Britain also pay an apprenticeship tax which may be partially offset by grants made to those who are training apprentices.

Wage rates for younger workers abroad are frequently below those of other workers—in some instances, firms are granted exemption from minimum wage laws for their teenage employees. Workers between 14 and 15 in France can be paid as much as 50 percent less than the legal minimum, and workers 17–18 can receive 20 percent less. Wage rate differentials for younger workers in Great Britain exist for those up to 21 years of age, and up to 23 years in Sweden and the Netherlands. The differentials, which are frequently subjects for negotiation in collective bargaining agreements, are based on variations in work skills and experience. Lower wages are more readily accepted by younger workers because they are apt to be living with their parents and their living costs are therefore low. Additionally, parents in a few countries receive child allowance payments even though their children are enrolled in apprenticeship programs.

Apart from the success of apprentice programs in reducing unemployment by teaching work skills, the indenture contract itself is a guarantee of job security. During layoffs, younger persons abroad usually fare better than in this country because seniority is less important in determining which workers are to be dismissed. The chances of a young apprentice being retained are excellent. Apprenticeships are usually considered as binding on the employer, and thus assure the trainee of a job for the life of the contract (usually three–five years).

In Japan, where employers feel very nearly a social obligation not to discharge employees, apprenticeship usually marks the beginning of lifelong employment. Apprentices are schooled not only in work skills, but also in work attitudes and a sense of identification with the company—vital for an employee whose attachment to the firm is expected to be permanent.

It should be noted, however, that in Great Britain and several other countries, doubts have arisen concerning the benefits of early vocational training received in lieu of time spent in secondary school. Although industrial training has helped to reduce unemployment among teen-agers, some observers feel that such a reduction occurs at the expense of the productivity and mobility of the labor force. Youths have often chosen training (particularly in the jobs at which their fathers are employed) because they lack the formal education required to qualify for more productive jobs elsewhere. Extending the years of secondary education beyond the customary European practice might, according to some educators, provide the academic background necessary for entry into professional and scientific fields.

A related criticism is that apprenticeship training does not always result in greater productivity among industrial workers. According to one British commentator, apprenticeship is

> perhaps the greatest single cause of inefficiency in British industry. It leads to an absolute shortage of skilled labour, and to rigid rules of demarcation between the crafts that may be practised by people who have served different types of apprenticeship. The Amalgamated Engineering Union— with its million members by far the most important voice in the matter— . . . has consistently prevented grownup men from being recognised as fully skilled, however good their individual accomplishments.

Protection Against Layoffs

The U.S. is one of the few major industrialized countries that does not have a comprehensive program for advance notice of layoffs. The timing and procedures to be followed in the event of layoffs are often not mentioned in collective bargaining agreements; in contrast, advance notice of layoffs are required by law in Germany and Great Britain. In Belgium, Great Britain, and Italy, workers' compensation is also required. English dock workers are protected not only by national legislation, but also by a board composed of union and employer representatives, who must approve an employer's decision to cut his work force. In no instance can a dock worker be laid off because labor-saving machinery has been installed. In Germany, the personnel directors of coal and steel firms are appointed by the union, which is also represented (on an equal basis with management) on the board of directors. Formulation and administration of personnel policies are also functions of the 4,000 Works Councils (made up of labor and management representatives) in Sweden.

In addition to legal restrictions, many European firms have voluntarily avoided layoffs. Some have done so as a result of past labor shortages which have made them willing to retain skilled workers during periods of slack demand. Also, most firms feel a social responsibility to their employees that does not permit dismissal except under the gravest circumstances. One writer stated:

> For example, reports confirm that the German employer's attitude still tends to be somewhat patriarchal, resulting in a feeling of heavy responsibility for the job security of those dependent upon him for employment. In addition, he may also be somewhat afraid of loss of prestige among his fellow employers, because employee layoffs might be interpreted as proof of his failure as a businessman. Similarly, surviving paternalistic trends in small Italian enterprises may still make employers reluctant to lay off or dismiss. However, management's approach in large, modern enterprises probably differs very little from that of its American counterpart. Even prior to the introduction of strict legal regulations, employers in the Netherlands have frequently appeared to be reluctant to separate employees during short slack periods. In France, where trade unions take the position, as does also a large part of the general public, that the employer is under a moral obligation to make great efforts to protect his workers from the hardships of temporary or final job loss, mass dismissals or layoffs are likely to cause retaliatory action.

Layoffs resulting from seasonal fluctuations in agriculture, construction, and other industries account for roughly one-fifth of all unemployment in the U.S. In Europe, unemployment during winter months has been partially curbed by financial incentives available to firms who minimize dismissals during these months. Successful as some of these incentives have been in averting unemployment, however, their main purpose in many instances was to overcome the problems resulting from labor shortages that have plagued many countries. Particularly in the building trades, where a scarcity of labor led to lagging construction of homes and public facilities and rapidly rising wage rates, firms have been encouraged to utilize crews as fully as possible on a year-round basis.

In Germany, trade unions were instrumental in formulating legislation giving construction firms grants equal to 11 percent of wages paid between December and March; low-interest loans are also available to firms buying equipment for use during the winter months. Over 30 percent of appropriations for federally constructed projects in Germany are spent between November and March. Builders in Austria, Belgium, the Netherlands, and Sweden qualify for payments if they continue operating during the winter, while home buyers in Canada can receive $500 if most of the construction of the house they purchase was done during the winter months. Construction layoffs in Great Britain have been limited by a rescheduling of government projects (including those undertaken by nationalized industries), which account for roughly half of all construction activities.

The Role of Self-Employment

Still another reason why unemployment generally tends to be lower in other industrial countries than in the United States is that a relatively large proportion of the labor force abroad is either self-employed or works in family-owned businesses. This means that a large number of Europeans and Japanese who are working on their own farms or in their own shops and establishments are not likely to become unemployed in the strictly statistical sense. It does not mean, of course, that they are protected from fluctuations in business activity, or that they may not be underemployed part or most of the time.

In the United States, roughly three-quarters of all farm labor consists of owners and unpaid family workers. While unemployment for these persons is negligible—many return to school or household duties in winter months—they constitute less than 4 percent of the nation's work force. In other countries, however, agricultural workers account for a much larger share of the labor force—only 4 percent in Great Britain, it is true, but roughly 11 percent in Sweden and Germany, and upward of 20 percent in Italy and Japan (see Figure 2). Workers wishing to remain in farming experience little unemployment, while labor shortages in manufacturing assure jobs for those willing to work off the farm. The rural-to-urban area migration has actually worked to curb labor supplies in countries such as Italy, where many women who formerly worked as farm laborers withdrew from the labor force entirely when their families relocated.

Unemployment among nonagricultural workers in the U.S. is relatively high because of the predominance of wage and salary employment. Only about 10 percent of this country's nonagricultural work force is self-employed or works in family-owned enterprises; the vast majority work in establishments owned by others and are thus prone to layoffs or dismissals if business slackens. Only the nonfarm labor force in the U.K. (94 percent wage and salary) and Germany (89 percent) is comparable to the U.S. in this respect (see Figure 2). Wage and salary personnel in France account for approximately 86 percent of all non-agricultural workers, and in Italy and Japan the ratio drops to about 75 percent. According to one estimate, unemployment in the United States in the early 1960s

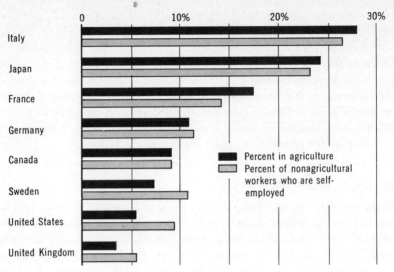

Figure 2. Occupational Characteristics of the Labor Force in Selected Countries, 1966. *(Data from Organisation for Economic Co-operation and Development; and the Conference Board.)*

would have been about one-third lower if the self-employed (including unpaid family workers) had constituted as large a portion of this country's labor force as they do in Japan.

The prevalence of wage and salary employment in the United States partly offsets the low unemployment rates which might otherwise prevail in a country where a relatively high proportion in the labor force is in the service industry. In this sector unemployment rates tend to be lower than in manufacturing, since service employment and output fluctuates only moderately over the course of the business cycle. Over 50 percent of all U.S. workers are employed in service occupations, contrasted with a ratio of under 35 percent in France, Germany, Italy, and Japan. On the other hand, the proportionately small number of self-employed and family members working in service establishments in the United States (17 percent, as compared to 22 percent in France and Germany and 36 percent in Japan) results in higher unemployment rates for many service workers than for their counterparts abroad.

The level of unemployment rates thus is partly a reflection of the occupational characteristics and structure of an individual country's labor force, but a low rate does not necessarily indicate that the labor force is being utilized in the most effective and most productive way. While self-employment may afford workers a certain measure of "job security," such a guarantee may be illusory if it does no more than prevent a worker from swelling the unemployment statistics. Moreover, job security attained in this guise may come at the expense of gains in productivity and hence in overall output. Italy, for instance, has large pockets of underemployed, working on small, undercapitalized farms and commercial establishments. Many of these workers probably would be reluctant to work for others. But from an aggregate point of view, the country's total manpower resources would be more productive if such persons were to be shifted to other jobs, particularly in industries where the ratio of capital per worker is high. The importance of similar shifts in fostering the growth of the economies of Western Europe during the 1950s has been amply documented in recent years.

Active Manpower Policy in Sweden

BERTIL REHNBERG

The Rehn Model

Swedish labor market policy has in recent years been increasingly correlated with the economic policy. The explanation is to be found in the efforts during the postwar period to check the recurrent strain between full employment and inflation, that is full employment achieved through general economic measures, a situation which usually includes both excessive demands for manpower in certain regions and sectors and unemployment in others. The Swedish Confederation of Trade Unions (LO) strongly claimed from the government a restrictive economic policy combined with a selective labor market policy. (In a constant boom there are not many "natural" tasks left for the trade union movement, which is instead forced to help check wage claims.) According to the Rehn model the economic activity should be balanced at an employment level corresponding to about 96–97 percent of the labor force. The gap should be selectively filled through labor market policy measures to avoid unemployment. This could create the conditions rendering it possible to come nearer to attaining the main economic aims. An essential objective of the labor market policy is also to facilitate and even to make it possible to accelerate the structural changes in the economy. This can be done primarily through measures to facilitate the readjustment of manpower to new jobs.

Our knowledge of the functioning of the labor market is fairly limited. However, through labor force surveys now carried out every month, we know that there is a continuous flow of people into and out of the labor force from one sector to another of the labor market. Business cycles and seasons, changes in the technological and economic conditions of produc-

Reprinted from the *Three Banks Review,* December 1969, pp. 22–32, by permission of the publisher.

tion, and so on, continuously influence manpower requirements. The Swedish labor force numbers some 3.8 million persons, but the labor force sample survey shows that during 1967, 4.4 million persons simultaneously have been in the labor force. The number of persons employed on the Swedish labor market has been on the increase for several years. It is true that this has in part been due to the fact that Sweden has had for some years a net influx of labor, but another very important factor in this process has been a gradual rise in the rate of participation in the labor market— particularly among married women. The definition of "full employment" is therefore no longer the same as it was a few years ago, and today it is generally accepted that it should be possible further to raise the employment rate by means of an active labor market policy without coming into conflict with the other aims of the economic policy.

The increasingly rapid changes in the economy require greater labor mobility. Changes in production, for example, new materials, new machinery and methods, require continuous adjustment of staff within the enterprise. Many workers can take up other tasks without previous training. Others are retrained within the enterprise. This is done without the support of public authorities, that is at the expense of the enterprise. There are no branch funds or other funds that can be utilized for this purpose. Out of a total of 1.6 million members of the LO, 350,000 had to change jobs within the enterprise in which they were employed during the period 1966– April 1968. Many, though not all of them, obtained better paid jobs.

The Advance Warning System

Early information on expected changes on the labor market is an important basis for the labor market policy. We have for many years had an agreement between a central governmental body, the National Labour Market Board and the employer organizations on advance warning of production cut-backs. It is a voluntary agreement, thus without legal backing, which now also includes the employee organizations. The agreement stipulates that anticipation of layoffs of more than two weeks shall be made to the county labor board concerned at least two months in advance. Notification shall be made of dismissals affecting more than 50 persons at least three months in advance. When the warning has become public, the county labor board, the trade unions, and representatives of the enterprise inform all employees affected about problems and measures connected with the production cut-back. This is done at a joint meeting. The management explains the causes of the production cut-back and the pace at which the change-over is planned to take place. The trade unions give information on the stipulations concerning advance warning and layoffs included in the collective agreements, on conditions for redundancy payment, unemployment benefits from the unemployment insurance funds, and so on. The county labor board provides information of the services offered by the employment offices: employment opportunities, retraining facilities, transfer grants, employment-creating measures, and so on.

The possibility of finding good solutions to the employment problems depends to a high degree on the possibility of creating trustful co-operation between all parties concerned. According to the agreement on advance warning, the county labor board can request that a joint committee consisting of representatives of the employer, the employees, the municipality, and the employment office be set up. The most important task of the committee is to support and facilitate the work of the employment office. The committee discusses all measures that may be required to facilitate the re-employment of the workers concerned and may also consider the particular problems of individual workers. The experience gained in recent years shows that these committees have played a very important role and have effectively contributed to the smooth development of the comprehensive structural changes in recent years.

Obstacles to Mobility

However, there are many obstacles to rapid and adequate mobility on the labor market. The rising standard of living leads to increased local ties. Strong social and psychological ties keep people attached to the place where they have long earned their livelihood. Many persons who are forced to consider other employment lack information on the employment opportunities available. Those who have been unemployed for some time often lack the economic resources required for moving to another place. In our rapidly changing economy many people are unable to adjust to new tasks because they lack the occupational qualifications required. Other unemployed persons cannot move because they own a house in a place where no buyer can be found. In other cases the removal comes to nothing because it is impossible to find a flat or house in the place where a new job is offered.

These examples could be multiplied. It is a primary task of the labor market policy to remove or reduce these obstacles in the way of desired mobility. It is of greatest interest to society, the employers, and the individual workers, that this adjustment should be as rapid, smooth, and successful as possible. This is particularly important in the present situation when the capital behind each person employed in production grows at a rapid rate. All parties are also aware of the value of rapid and successful adjustment. The employers regard the public Employment Service as a service institution which is able to follow the development on the whole labor market and to give them valuable information and practical help when they have to hire or layoff labor. The trade unions are equally prepared (wholeheartedly) to support the Employment Service in its activity, since an effective Employment Service promotes the interests of their members.

A network of public employment offices collects data every day on vacancies and job-seekers. The National Labour Market Board publishes every week a gazette containing, in addition to general information, short descriptions of some 15,000 vacancies of every kind, from simple jobs to the most qualified posts for graduate engineers. The number of copies printed every week is generally 35,000. The vacancies are not advertised anonymously and the job-seekers are free to contact the employers direct. An increasing number of employment offices also have what is called an open reception where the job-seekers can obtain a vacancy list without any registration procedure and then themselves contact the employers direct. The list is renewed once or several times a week. This system has proved successful and the possibility of using Automatic Data Processing to get the lists printed more rapidly and to eliminate errors is now being studied. The Employment Service has some 250 branch offices provided with modern equipment and everything they need for rapid communication all over the country, that is teleprinters.

Measures to Facilitate Mobility

An example may illustrate the efforts to improve the geographical mobility between different parts of the country. The labor requirements for agriculture and forestry have for many years been declining in northern Sweden. For various reasons it has not been possible to create a sufficient number of new employment opportunities in this relatively sparsely populated part of the country. Consequently, the measures have to a great extent been directed at facilitating the removal of the unemployed to other areas. For this purpose employment service staff from places in southern and central Sweden reporting manpower shortage have been sent to help the employment offices in the northern area. These officers have arrived with firsthand information on job opportunities in their home districts and have therefore been able to give detailed information on these vacancies. The applicants have then been able to gain further knowledge of them by personal visits to the employers which unemployed persons can make. This means that the employment office arranges visits to potential employers in other places and pays the traveling expenses, including a daily allowance, for these visits. The employment offices in these surplus areas have further intensified their activity by having their staff visit underemployed and unemployed persons who have not themselves visited the employment offices and grant them information on employment opportunities, removal grants, and so on. In this way it has been possible to get into touch with those who have been least aware of the employment offices and who might otherwise have been left behind in a period of rapid and fundamental changes in the local economy.

Grants to facilitate geographical mobility are given to job-seekers who have to move to other localities in order to find suitable employment. They include traveling and removal expenses, a starting allowance when taking up new employment, and a separation allowance to persons who, due to the housing situation or other reasons, have to maintain two households. Within certain regions with exceptionally high employment it is also possible for the labor market administration to buy owner-occupied houses which cannot be sold on the open market, when the owner is taking up employment elsewhere. To some extent it is also possible— through co-operation between the Labour Market Board and the National Housing Board—to give workers immediate access to a house or flat in the new place of work. Around 30,000 job-seekers receive mobility grants during a year. The average cost of moving a family from the depressed areas in the north to central Sweden is about £500.

Retraining—An Important Instrument

Many workers who have to leave a job can without great difficulty directly take up a new one or can otherwise receive the training they need at their new place of work. However, a great number of the unemployed must be trained for a new occupation before they can get a job. In such cases private employers also do much to help their new workers and this is done without government grants. Nevertheless, in many cases, in particular during a recession, public training facilities are required to render the unemployed attractive on the labor market. Often the cause of the difficulty is the age or the handicap of the unemployed person. In Sweden we have therefore for many years had a government-financed training program called training for labor market purposes. The employment offices decide if such training is to be considered. Those eligible are persons who are, or are expected to become, unemployed or underemployed or who suffer from a handicap. However, for several occupations in which there is a great shortage of manpower, unemployment is not a condition. Thus, persons who have a job can also be offered training in these occupations. The duration of the training varies between a couple of months to two years (for handicapped persons it can be considerably longer). The training is provided at special training centers operated by the National Board of Education, at courses arranged by private organizations but paid for by the Labour Market Board, in ordinary schools, and to some extent in private enterprises. As regards the occupations, the training program in principle covers the whole labor market. The special courses arranged by the National Board of Education at present offer training in some 250 occupations or occupational specialties.

Training for labor market purposes is free and the trainees receive a training allowance. For a person with a wife and two children it amounts to about £90 a month. The usual practice has been to let the scope of the training program vary to meet seasonal and business cycle requirements. Thus, training for labor market purposes has in principle had the same stabilizing effect on the labor market as the selective employment-creating measures described in the following paragraph. The total number of persons undergoing training at some time during 1968 was 84,000. In mid-March 1969 there were 36,500 persons undergoing training.

Job Creation Measures

In spite of the greatest efforts, it is not possible immediately, or even in the long run, to find jobs for all the unemployed. The reason may be personal obstacles or local ties. The labor market program therefore also includes the possibility to create employment. The Labour Market Board thus has considerable funds at its disposal to finance government, municipal or private relief works. These works can be started at short notice in districts where employment is in need of reinforcement, be carried out during a certain time of the year or be reserved for certain categories of unemployed.

The Labour Market Board is also able to use these funds to finance extra government orders to provide the time required to find new jobs for the labor affected by advance warnings or to bridge over a temporary decline in production. For the same purpose grants-in-aid can also be given for municipal orders. What is characteristic of all these employment-creating measures is that they are initiated on labor market policy grounds and can accordingly be timed, aimed at a certain geographical area or at a given branch of industry, and that they can even be reserved for certain unemployed categories. For handicapped persons, older workers, and workers with local ties there are special workshops and simple outdoor jobs. In mid-January 1969 there were about 29,000 in such sheltered employment. In addition to this, the Employment Service can also offer employers willing to employ handicapped persons who cannot be placed in the open market in the normal way a grant amounting to about £400 per person a year.

When it is desirable for labor market purposes, employment can also be selectively increased through changes in private and public investments. This was the case during the last European recession, when the situation in Sweden did not permit a general stimulation of demand. The investment funds of industry were released in the winters of 1967/68 and 1968/69 to promote employment in the construction and engineering industries. For the same reason housing construction and the building of schools and hospitals have also been allowed to expand. The government is responsible for these matters and bases its decisions on proposals presented by the Labour Market Board.

By selective measures—including training for labor market purposes—it was possible during the winter 1967/68 to provide employment for some 100,000 persons or about 3 percent of the Swedish labor force. During the winter of 1968/69 this part of the labor market policy program provided employment and training for about 110,000 persons simultaneously. The efforts have to a great extent been aimed at northern Sweden which, due to structural changes in forestry, has had the highest unemployment rate in the country. Otherwise the activity was largely comprised of persons whom it has not been possible to fit into the open market. Another part of the labor market policy is to further a long-range increase in employment in certain underdeveloped areas, primarily in northern Sweden. Grants and loans can be made for the expansion of firms already established or for the setting up of new manufacturing enterprises. During the period 1963–68 such aid was granted to 767 establishments, and to a total amount of £65 million. The result in employment is calculated to be 26,000 new job opportunities.

Tangible Results

Has this policy been successful in the sense that it has brought us nearer to the various economic objectives? The answer must be 'Yes.' There was an increase in unemployment between 1966 and 1967, and during the first three-quarters of 1968 there was a further slight increase in the number of unemployed. However, the changes may be said to have been modest. The highest differences registered at any time between 1966 and 1968 did not exceed one percentage unit. Building investments were, due to the various steps taken, maintained on a high and even rising level throughout the recession. Productivity within manufacturing has risen at a faster pace than usually. Consumer prices have been more stable (during 1968 in reality completely stable) than earlier during the 1960s, and industry seems to have been able to manage the cost problems. Exports have kept pace with imports and the balance of payments improved. The growth of the GNP, which was 3.1 percent in 1966 and 3.3 percent in 1967, is calculated at 4.5 percent in 1968. Furthermore, the serious shortage of manpower in important service sectors such as health care and other public services has been considerably reduced.

Discussion Questions

1. What are the basic factors which led to low levels of unemployment in Western Europe and Japan throughout the period of the sixties?
2. What manpower policies does Sweden use to assist in the achievement and maintenance of full employment?
3. Given the apparent success of government supported manpower policies abroad, do you think the U.S. government should increase its role in the labor market in pursuit of full employment?

Inflation

Few problems raise a greater tempest than that of inflation. Every consumer measures it in goods not bought and in the rising price of food; every officeholder fears for his political life because of it. If everybody knows it is present and if everybody likewise abhors inflation, it cannot be said that unanimity exists in explaining different annual rates of inflation or ways to bring the rate of price rise down to a tolerable level.

In this country, the debate has centered around these two issues of cause and treatment. Two general causes for inflation have been put forth, each assigned different weight by different economists. The first argument is that as the economy expands and national income rises the forces of demand outstrip the more slowly increasing supply, and prices rise as a consequence. This is the "demand-pull" argument. The second hypothesis is that inflation is induced by the so-called "cost-push" factor. The argument is that as costs rise, particularly wages, this constitutes a good and sufficient reason for management to raise prices. Embedded in this argument is the belief that large powerful unions and equally powerful corporations have the ability to impose on society prices which are not determined by market forces.

Economic theory in the macro-policy area suggests that tight monetary policy and a reduction in government spending (and/or a rise in taxes) provides the best method for curbing inflation, at least when it is of the demand-pull variety. But economic theory was proven wrong when it was applied to the United States economy at the end of the 1960s and into the beginning of the 1970s; prices kept on rising even while unemployment remained high. Thus, on August 14, 1971, President Nixon announced Phase 1 of the wage-price freeze, and on November 14 set up the machinery to administer a set of controls on prices, wages, rents, and interest.

The two following selections discuss methods used in Western Europe to combat inflation. The first deals with Western European construction costs and inflation, a problem not unfamiliar to the American scene. The second describes the operations of the Belgian Prices Commission, an organ set up in 1951, some 20 years before our own Prices Commission.

Both articles appear to offer some interesting lessons for the United States.

E. Jay Howenstine is an economist in the U.S. Department of Housing and Urban Development. M.A.G. van Meerhaeghe, formerly chairman of the Belgian Prices Commission, is presently a Professor of Economics at Rijks University in Belgium.

Rising Construction Costs and Anti-Inflation Policies: A Report on Western Europe

E. JAY HOWENSTINE

The special cabinet committee on Price Stability gave particular attention to inflationary pressures in the construction sector in its report published in January 1969. The construction industry will again receive special attention this year when the Secretaries of Labor and Commerce submit their joint report to Congress (under Title IV of the amended Manpower Development and Training Act) on opportunities for lessening construction seasonality.

The United States is not alone in such preoccupations. A recent study completed for the Organization for Economic Cooperation and Development (OECD) in Paris reveals that in most West European countries the problems of general inflation and of inflationary pressures in the construction sector have been considerably more intense and persistent during the 1960s than in the United States. Experience of other OECD governments in dealing with these problems may, therefore, be of some relevance to the American scene. This article reviews the European experience.

Reconnoitering the Problem

Excessive rises in construction costs are important not only because they limit the market for certain kinds of construction, such as housing, but also because they may have far-reaching effects on the growth of the economy. Because in-place construction constitutes a large part of the Nation's stock of capital, inflated construction costs become built into the economy's cost structure.

During the period 1943–63, according to an OECD study, construction prices in West European countries, with the exception of France, Portugal, and the United Kingdom, rose more rapidly than did prices in general. (See

Reprinted from the *Monthly Labor Review,* June 1969, pp. 3–10, by permission of the U.S. Department of Labor, Bureau of Labor Statistics.

Table 1.) In those countries where data are available for a much longer period, there was a considerably more rapid rise in construction costs than in the general price level. For example, from 1914 to 1958, housebuilding prices in France rose 80 percent more than wholesale prices, while in the Netherlands they were 120 percent higher. A considerable degree of caution must be exercised, however, in drawing conclusions from such data concerning the cause and cure for rapidly rising costs in the construction industry. It may not be a simple case of demand exceeding supply.

Table 1. Indexes of Price Changes in Gross National Product and Construction, Selected OECD Countries, 1963

[1953 = 100]

Country	Gross national product	Total construction	Residential construction	Other construction	Construction prices as percentage of GNP prices
France	159.6	157.5	173.4	146.6	98.7
Netherlands	139.6	159.3	159.9	159.1	114.1
Austria	139.1	157.1	158.3	156.3	112.9
Greece *	137.1	144.1	134.2	152.8	105.1
Sweden	136.4	137.1	135.0	138.5	100.5
Norway	133.7	145.5	135.8	151.8	108.8
United Kingdom	133.7	124.9	124.4	128.4	93.4
Italy	133.2	139.0	140.7	137.6	104.4
Denmark *	133.0	135.7	134.3	136.5	102.0
Switzerland	131.3	—	†	—	—
Germany (F. R.)	131.0	157.5	162.5	153.9	120.2
Ireland	127.8	129.8	138.1	126.0	101.6
Canada	121.6	125.4	128.1	124.2	103.1
United States	119.8	122.7	118.1	126.1	102.4
Belgium	118.3	—	139.6	—	—
Portugal	111.8	106.2	109.6	105.2	95.0

* 1953–62.
† In Heinz Kneubühler "Housing Construction Policies and Techniques in Switzerland," OECD Observer, October 1965, it was indicated that house building costs have risen much faster than the cost of living.
SOURCE: Mary S. Painter, "Construction in OECD Countries," OECD Observer, April 1966, p. 13; OECD, National Income Accounts 1950–61 and General Statistics, January 1965.

One reason for caution is that the statistical data in this field leave much to be desired. Care must also be exercised in choosing base periods for comparing inflationary pressure in different industrial sectors. If, during the base period, a state of relative balance does not exist, an element of bias immediately enters.

Second, it is extremely difficult to determine to what extent the nature of the construction product is changing as a result of improvements in size, quality, standards, and equipment. If rising costs reflect greater economic value going into the product, this is quite different from higher costs for an unimproved product. Improvements that are obvious in the long term may be difficult to identify and quantify in the short run.

A third consideration, suggested by Colin Clark, is that there is probably a long-term trend toward relatively higher costs in the construction industry compared with other industries, because the technological and managerial difficulties of industrializing it are greater. An important characteristic of the construction industry is the immobility of the final product. Since the resources of the industry must go to the site dictated by demand, the possibility of developing a mass production industry to meet a nationwide demand is limited in comparison with those in other manufacturing industries. During the postwar period, these limitations have been circumvented in part as a result of prefabrication, industrialized building systems, and rapid improvements in the materials and equipment incorporated into structures. Nevertheless, the construction industry will probably always operate under a comparative handicap in this respect. In this light, rising construction costs may not reflect either demand or cost pressures, but merely that costs in other industries are declining relative to those in construction because of more rapid increases in productivity.

The inefficient use of productive capacity is another factor making for higher costs. Because of seasonal habits of thought and operation, construction resources are overemployed in summer and underemployed in winter even though, from a technological point of view, work on many types of construction could continue at a high level year round.

There may also be strong cost-push pressures operating in the construction industry. Its traditional instability of employment for both climatic and economic reasons has caused workers to seek higher hourly wage rates as compensation for anticipated loss of working time.

Other factors making for cost-push pressures are the restrictive practices of employers, workers, and manufacturers of building materials. These include contractors' comparisons of tender prices before tenders are actually submitted for jobs, and subsequent adjustment of the lowest tender to arrive at a "fair price." Specialist subcontractors and manufacturers of construction materials are sometimes accused of forming "price rings," which prevent the lowering of costs. Trade unions in the industry are often criticized for such practices as restricting output, resisting the introduction of new materials or machines, restricting entry of new members, and designing regulations to keep certain operations within the jurisdiction of a particular craft union.

It would seem to be clear, therefore, that as a result of technical and institutional factors, rising costs in the construction industry may require a variety of remedial measures. To the extent that rising costs are caused by inefficient use of resources, the solution lies in removing the barriers to higher productivity. To the extent that they are attributable to cost-push factors, the solution consists in attacking them. To the extent that they arise from excess demand, the problem calls for restrictions on demand. In any specific inflationary situation, it is likely that all three elements will be present in varying degrees. For policy-making purposes, it will be difficult to determine the relative importance of these factors. In fact, construction policies in OECD countries have proceeded along all three lines.

Using Resources Efficiently

Since World War II, an increasing amount of attention has been given to the problem of achieving more efficient use of resources in the construction industry, particularly in OECD countries that have been confronted with continuing inflationary pressures. Several main lines of action have emerged.

A major first step has been to reduce seasonal unemployment. Although certain extreme climatic conditions place absolute limits on the possibilities of continuous work on certain types of construction, winter construction work in most climates is now technically feasible as a result of far-reaching technological improvements in the last several decades. Nevertheless, as one moves from Northern to Central Europe, where winters are less severe, there has been, surprisingly, a tendency toward greater rather than less instability of activity in the construction industry.

There is serious doubt, therefore, that adopting measures to curb excess demand for construction during the summer period will be effective if nothing is done to alter traditional methods of thinking, financing, and managing in the winter season. In Austria, for example, the construction trade unions have taken a strong stand on this issue. In 1965, the Advisory Committee on the construction industry, a tripartite subcommittee of the National Advisory Committee (BEIRAT), in its first report stated that the output of the industry could be increased by 50 percent with existing resources, mainly through the elimination of seasonal unemployment. If the Central European countries—with comparatively mild winters—adopted winter stabilization methods similar to those adopted in Norway and Sweden—with comparatively severe winters—this would undoubtedly lead to more effective utilization of resources throughout the year and would tend to lessen demand pressures during the summer season.

Secondly, a wide range of measures are being taken to improve productivity in the construction industry, but in general the possibilities have only begun to be realized. In France, for example, one general principle behind the Fifth National Economic Plan (1966–70) is to avoid restrictive measures in coping with inflationary pressures, if at all possible. The emphasis is rather on measures to increase output through better management, the promotion of capital-intensive techniques, accelerated training programs to increase skill levels, and the promotion of a greater spirit of competition within the national and European markets. The deputy director of the United Kingdom National Building Agency, A. W. Cleeve Barr, has maintained that the volume of housebuilding could be doubled with the same labor force through rationalization and industrialization of the building process. In view of the long term technological disadvantage that construction must cope with in comparison with most other industries, particular attention should be given to the promotion of research and to efforts to achieve a wide application of findings. In Austria and Denmark, employers and workers are collaborating on a number of progressive steps in this direction.

The awarding of long term contracts has been a third major step in achieving a more efficient use of construction resources. Such awards would exert a stabilizing influence on the industry by enabling contractors to organize and plan their work ahead over a period of years, providing workers with long periods of stable employment under the same employer. Under such a contract, the contractor has greater incentive to utilize expensive but cost-reducing machinery in the knowledge that he will be able to amortize his investment over the long term through relatively continuous use. At the same time, workers have a more effective guarantee of employment. Even during periods of "full employment" in the construction industry, the worker is continuously faced with the problem of securing new employment as each job ends. In some countries, a guaranteed weekly or annual wage many encourage greater stability in the industry from the workers' point of view.

Fiscal policy has been designed to encourage cost-reducing methods of construction. Accelerated depreciation allowances may encourage the introduction of more capital-intensive methods, and tax concessions to producers collaborating in officially approved programs of modular coordination would tend to promote simplification in building methods. The possibilities of achieving a reduction in costs are also affected by the size, type, and conditions of subsidies that may be offered. In the case of private housing, subsidies may be granted only for meeting conditions of cost reduction. In the Netherlands, for example, the Ministry of Housing and Building provides a special incentive for labor-saving building methods by granting a 25 percent extra allocation of housing funds to those local authorities who use building methods requiring less than nine hundred man-hours per dwelling.

Another important means of increasing construction output—assuming that sufficient capital is available—is to increase manpower resources in construction, either by recruitment from another sector with lessening employee requirements (such as agriculture) or by increasing the number of foreign workers. In France, for example, it is estimated that between 90,000 and 115,000 excess agricultural workers were moving into other sectors annually between 1965 and 1970. Most of the highly industrialized European countries have utilized foreign workers in combating their inflationary labor shortages; for example in 1964, 32 percent of the construction labor force in Switzerland consisted of foreign workers. In some countries—for example, Austria—there is a rather widespread view that it would be desirable to utilize considerably more foreign workers in attempting to cope with the excess demand for construction.

It is clear that imposing restrictions on construction activity before all possible measures are taken to improve the efficiency of existing construction resources may be not only socially undesirable but also a poor use of valuable resources. It would certainly be undesirable for employment stabilization measures to reduce incentives for improving productivity. In fact, there is a rather widely held view in several countries—the Federal Republic of Germany and the United Kingdom among them—that a state of mild excess demand is desirable as a constant spur to higher productivity in the industry.

Coping with Cost-Push Factors

Since cost-push factors are principally rooted in the traditional instability of the industry, success in implementing measures for more effective use of resources and promoting greater stability will, in the long run, tend to reduce the pressure of such factors. Thus, the assurance of reasonable profit margins and the reduction of high bankruptcy rates among construction contractors resulting from full employment should foster greater cost stability. Manufacturers of construction materials and equipment might gain economies of scale arising from relatively full employment of productive capacity, which could result in more stable prices for materials and equipment. Workers might obtain a decent annual wage by working more hours per year, resulting in less pressure for abnormally high hourly rates to compensate for fewer hours worked per year.

Efforts to promote greater competition among firms and different kinds of construction materials and methods is another approach. This is particularly important since the localized character of the construction industry frees it from some of the competitive pressures that exist in the national and international market for most other products. Postwar technological progress has contributed greatly to increasing the substitutability of materials and methods, and many possibilities exist for providing the small contractor with better information and improved methods for increasing his competitive efficiency.

A third means of combating cost-push tendencies in some countries has been that public works departments have carried out some of their programs directly with their own work organization, when it is felt that competitive bidding has not yielded "fair" contract prices. For example, local public housing authorities in the United Kingdom have adopted this procedure with the additional objective of encouraging the use of new building materials and techniques. Certain controversial problems of full and fair costing have been encountered, however, in comparing dwelling unit costs of public housing with those of privately produced housing.

On a broader front, widespread attention has been given in Europe to the possibilities of an "incomes policy"; that is, the exercise of a degree of collective control over the level and structure of incomes, particularly in relating increases in economic return to increases in productivity. However, such a policy, particularly with regard to wages, will probably be less successful than measures to increase annual income through steadier employment. As noted earlier, man-hour productivity in construction tends to rise less than the average for the economy as a whole. Thus, while it may be useful to relate economic return to increases in productivity as one means of raising output and lowering costs, it would hardly be fair to construction workers to maintain that the rate of productivity increase establishes a limit of permissible wage increases.

Cost reduction may also be achieved through tripartite collaboration among employers, workers, and government. Such collaboration has already reached a comparatively high state of development in the construction industry in many OECD countries. If a government has embarked on a national policy of stabilizing the construction industry at its equilibrium rate of growth, it would appear justified in using this full employment commitment as leverage to help bring about a reduction of costs and a removal of restrictive practices. If continuous full employment can be achieved, there is a possibility of reconciling lower unit costs to the ultimate consumer with higher annual incomes for those in the industry.

Curbing Excess Demand

One final step before taking measures to curb demand for construction is to determine whether the intense demand pressures may not reflect long term structural shifts calling for a higher rate of construction activity. If relatively more productive resources should be devoted to construction in order to meet consumers' preferences, then demand pressure has an important role to play in resource allocation. This has been true in some of the less industrialized OECD countries, where acceleration of the rate of economic development requires relatively more resources allocated to the construction industry.

Even though all possible steps have been taken to increase construction output and capacity, inflationary deviations arising from excess demand for construction may still be going beyond tolerable upper limits. In this case, restrictive action, either through monetary and fiscal controls or by physical control mechanisms, may be unavoidable.

Monetary and Fiscal Controls

With regard to public construction, it would appear that government should be able to place necessary restrictions on its own level of construction activity. This, however, has not been the case, since national governments have often lacked authority to control or influence the investment expenditures of local, provincial, and regional bodies, as well as publicly owned and controlled industries. Nevertheless, considerable progress is being made in developing a co-ordinated public construction policy in a number of countries, including Austria, Denmark, the Netherlands, Norway, and Sweden.

With regard to private construction, there is a strong body of opinion in some West European countries—Denmark and the Federal Republic of Germany—that favors giving practically free rein to all private construction demand. This view would place the full, or nearly full, burden on the public sector. However, this type of policy not only conflicts with recognized national social priorities in the field of public works, but risks an unbalanced curbing of public construction that may seriously impair the development of the infrastructure the country needs to support expanding private investment and to achieve national growth objectives. As a result, most European governments, even those most favorable to free enterprise—such as Belgium, Germany, and Switzerland—have applied anti-inflationary curbs to both private and public construction sectors.

The classical means of dealing with excess private demand has been monetary policy. If private firms and individuals are attempting to invest more in new construction than the productive factors in the industry can supply, traditionally the central bank has adopted a restrictive credit policy. The difficulty with such a policy, however, is that it conflicts with social priorities. Although in principle general credit restrictions are nondiscriminatory, in practice they have affected sectors of the construction industry unequally. They have been highly discriminatory toward those types of construction—such as housing, particularly low-income housing—which are sensitive to small increases in capital costs. Such treatment can only be avoided by adopting a policy of selective credit restriction where high priority construction is protected against inequitable cut-backs.

If the effectiveness of monetary controls is undermined by the existence of private savings, as happened in Sweden during 1955–57, then the state can supplement such measures by curtailing any loan facilities that it may have extended to the private construction sector or by imposing taxes on new construction. If such supplementary fiscal methods are not politically practicable, or are ineffective in achieving the desired reduction in private construction, it is possible that there may be no other recourse than the use of physical control mechanisms.

Controls on Construction Output

During the World War II, most governments felt compelled to adopt output controls over goods and resources, including construction, but in peacetime conditions some countries—such as Canada and the United States—are not only reluctant but are strongly opposed to adopting such measures. Aside from practical problems of political administration, the allocation of physical resources by a central authority—even when limited to certain sectors of the economy—tends to be regarded as incompatible with free market processes.

In other countries, however, including Denmark, the Netherlands, Norway, and Sweden, limited physical controls have proved fairly effective instruments not only in achieving socially desirable objectives but also in coping with excess demand. In Sweden, a comprehensive system of collection and analysis of information on building demand and capacity has been operated by the National Labor Market Board since World War II. In an effort to avoid some of the disadvantages attached to the compulsory licensing system, Sweden has experimented in a number of regions for several years with a voluntary licensing system for private construction projects based on tripartite collaboration between government, employers, and workers. In 1966, this voluntary system was made nation-wide. Each governmental Provincial Labor Market Board has an Advisory Planning Committee composed of representatives of employers' and workers' organizations in the construction industry and the secretary of the committee is a member of the provincial board. The committee's objective is to work out a program that will permit use of the region's construction resources continuously at full capacity.

The committee discusses the general timing of projects with clients, examines occupational requirements and the availability of workers, and fits the project into the manpower map made up by the board with a view to adjusting projects to the region's available manpower. In general, the construction labor force is split two to one between new construction and maintenance and repairs. After discussions with the client end, the Advisory Planning Committee recommends the best quarter in which to start the project.

Recommendations go to the Provincial Labor Market Board and are normally approved by it. Clients who feel discriminated against in the recommendations of the advisory committee have the right to appeal the decision to the National Labor Market Board. In practice, there are few appeals. To insure against the possibility of the advisory committees becoming exclusive clubs advancing their own vested interests, the national board has the right to investigate and alter the advisory committees' recommendations.

Two important safeguards have helped to guarantee the success of the system. (1) The former compulsory system could be restored if the voluntary system does not work. (2) Perhaps more importantly, employers and trade unions have made an agreement with the Labor Market Board under which any contractor who starts a project earlier than the date recommended by the advisory committee is expelled by the employers' federation; and trade unions are also pledged to boycott the firm. Moreover, the expelled firm would no longer come within the scope of the collective agreement covering the industry.

According to some authorities in the industry, the next stage in the development of the Swedish programing of construction will be the introduction of a national "network system," which will create an overall control system to ensure the scheduling and utilization of the available stock of machinery and equipment for the maximum number of hours in a given work period.

The Netherlands' Ministry of Housing and Building prepares a building program a year ahead, based on assumptions relating to the labor force available, the number of productive hours expected, changes in man-hour productivity, and so on.

Total building capacity is subdivided into major sectors of activity, such as residential construction, schools, hospitals, and commercial buildings. The allocation among the sectors is based on a number of assumptions and political priorities and is subject to revision after consultation with relevant government departments.

In a second step, the building program is then allocated among the 12 provinces, which in turn make allocations to individual local authorities on the basis of estimated needs. Large urban municipalities are, however, invited to submit multi-annual programs of their building requirements and to suggest suitable priorities. In Sweden, the adjustment of demand to capacity is based upon a detailed analysis of local needs and resources which are eventually integrated into a national program; in the Netherlands, by contrast, the overall building capacity is estimated at the national level, broken down into sectors, and allocated to provinces, which divide it among local authorities.

Other European countries have attempted to manage their construction resources in similar, though less comprehensive, ways. Even in countries where there is strong general opposition to public intervention, governments have been compelled to adopt some physical controls because of the severity of inflationary pressures. As an example, the Swiss federal government in 1964 adopted a comprehensive program of restrictions to curb excess construction demand without jeopardizing the construction of essential projects, including low-cost housing. Cinemas, theaters, dance halls, and other amusement centers; museums, exhibition halls, sports buildings, luxury apartments, and petrol stations; and one-family houses having more than 1,200 cubic meters or costing more than 200,000 francs were postponed for one year as nonessential.

General Inflation, Stable Construction

Assuming that the rate of savings from current income is sufficient to support the rate of construction, it is generally desirable that construction continue at more or less its normal pace despite inflationary conditions in other sectors and balance of payments disequilibrum. Construction provides the sinews that an economy requires to create new jobs for its growing labor force, to maintain and strengthen its position in the international market, and to meet the growing domestic demands for better living conditions. Most construction requirements must be met in order for the government to achieve the two basic national objectives of full employment and economic growth. If, on the other hand, the rate of construction is not being supported by the rate of saving from current income, then steps must be taken to curtail construction or increase savings by decreasing the rate of consumption.

Moreover, insofar as there are substantial unemployed resources, it is generally desirable to exempt compensatory employment programs from anti-inflationary cut-backs. As examples of such tailored anti-inflationary measures, both the governments of Canada and the United Kingdom exempted "depressed areas" where unemployment rates were substantially above the national average.

However, in certain types of monetary and fiscal crises, particularly those involved in balance of payments difficulties, governments have sometimes been forced to curtail construction activity as part of over-all anti-inflationary policy, resulting in substantial unemployment in the industry. The Economic Commission for Europe, in its survey of housing policies in 1960, concluded that "many Western European countries found it necessary to impose restraining monetary, budgetary, or physical control measures designed to reduce demand for residential building as a means of alleviating strains in their internal economies."

"Stop and go" construction policies, particularly when applied with the severity and frequency found in Denmark and the United Kingdom, have, however, had far greater adverse repercussions than short term unemployment of construction resources. By disrupting and slowing down the rate of capital formation, such policies—while making short term contribution to coping with inflationary and balance of payments difficulties—have nevertheless lowered the rate of economic growth, which is crucial in achieving long-term price stabilization and balance of payments equilibrium.

While it may happen that governments are confronted with crises requiring emergency action that may be in basic conflict with other fundamental national objectives, the aim should be to adopt domestic and international measures that will prevent such crises from arising. Compensatory policies should be formulated well in advance of the need for them so that if the general situation deteriorates, it will be possible to avoid—or at least minimize—the application of makeshift "stop and go" policies to the construction industry.

European Summary

European experience with inflationary pressures in the construction industry yields several findings relevant to contemporary anti-inflation construction policy in the United States. (1) It points up the problem's complexity and militates against simplistic notions—for example, that high trade union wage rates are the cause of inflationary construction costs. (2) It suggests the importance of defining the volume of construction resources that is required to achieve the national goals of economic growth and full employment. If an expansion in capacity is required, a national manpower policy of recruitment, training, and development for the construction industry is indicated. (3) The necessity of a wide range of measures to promote greater productivity in construction, particularly in eliminating seasonal unemployment, is indicated. (4) European experience demonstrates the value of a stabilization policy aimed at the maintenance of full employment in the construction industry, when the size of the sector is geared to other national objectives. If there is excess construction demand, restraints on demand are in order. If there are substantial idle construction resources, other things being equal, demand stimulants are desirable. (5) The short-sightedness of "stop and go" policies applied to construction, particularly public works, as instruments for coping with general inflationary and balance of payments difficulties, is clearly shown. Emphasis should be placed on measures that deal with the basic causes of such difficulties rather than on stopgap measures at the eleventh hour, which are basically in conflict with other national objectives. (6) Finally, it indicates how tripartite collaboration between government, employers, and workers in the construction industry can cope with excess construction demand in an orderly and equitable—though not necessarily desirable—manner, if monetary and fiscal restraints fail, and if strong inflationary pressures become a permanent feature of the American economy under conditions of continuing full employment.

The Belgian Prices Commission

M. A. G. VAN MEERHAEGHE

Before embarking upon a discussion of the most important provisions relating to the Belgian Prices Commission, a consultative body—the like of which exists in no other country—it will be as well to outline the main legal enactments concerning prices.

Legislation on Prices

While other Ministers have a certain amount of authority in the field of prices (the Minister of Communications, for instance, has to approve prices of various services), it is usual for them to consult their colleague at the Economic Affairs Department or to raise questions on the subject with the Ministerial Committee for Economic and Social Co-ordination or the Cabinet. As will be seen from the further text, responsibility for price policy is in fact borne by the Minister for Economic Affairs. In this task he is assisted by the Prices Commission.

Maximum Price

The Statutory Order of January 22, 1945 prohibits:

a) the sale, offering or purchase on the domestic market of products, basic materials, foodstuffs, merchandise or animals.

b) the offering, acceptance or performance of any services (with the exception of those arising out of a labor, employment, apprenticeship or domestic service contract)

at a price higher than the maximum price fixed by the Minister for Economic Affairs. The latter may also determine sellers' and intermediaries' profit margins.

By the Ministerial Order of May 9, 1966, all prices of goods and services were pegged at the level at which they stood on May 6, 1966. The Order was withdrawn on September 2, 1966.

At the present time, ceiling prices or prices prevailing at a certain date are in operation in respect of the following products:

a) *Foodstuffs*

  1. Beef and veal, pigmeat (trade margins).
  2. Biscuits.

Reprinted from *Weltwirtschaftliches Archiv,* Vol. *99,* No. 2, 1967, pp. 257–270, by permission of the publisher and author.

3. Roasted chicory.

4. Pudding powder, self-raising flour, vanilla-flavored sugar, cornflower.

5. Flour.

6. Belgian and imported butter (trade margins).

7. Liquid milk.

8. Rice.

b) *Industrial products*

1. Low-voltage electricity.

2. Public gas supply.

3. Tires and inner tubes.

4. Proprietary medicines.

5. Domestic electrical appliances.

6. Bricks.

c) *Services*

Taxi fares.

The Orders must be applied to an entire sector, even if aimed at only one particular enterprise.

Certain Orders concerning ceiling prices stipulate that prices must be "ratified." This is required when the price has to be calculated in accordance with specific directives (for example, in the case of tires and inner tubes).

Normal Price

When no ceiling prices are fixed, it is prohibited to sell at prices higher than the normal price. Decisions as to whether a price is normal or abnormal are left to the courts, who take into account such factors as profit, market position, and operating costs.

In actual practice, the courts base their judgments on the customary prices, thereby overlooking the fact that such prices are not necessarily normal prices.

Where a ceiling price has been laid down, it is still obligatory to sell at the normal price, even if the latter is below the former. In this case too, no price may result in ". . . the realisation of an abnormal profit, more particularly through the overvaluation of one of the cost factors."

Competition

The Royal Decree of January 13, 1935 relates to the protection of producers, traders, and consumers "against certain practices aimed at distorting normal conditions of competition." These same terms are incorporated in the Law of May 27, 1960 on the curbing of abuses of dominant economic positions. The regulations deriving from Articles 85 and 86 of the Treaty establishing the European Economic Community are of particular importance in this context.

Notification of Price Increases

Producers and importers are required to submit notifications to the Prices Division of the Ministry of Economic Affairs, if appropriate through their trade or industrial associations, not later than 21 days prior to the proposed date of introduction, in respect of any price increase which they intend to apply on the Belgian market for "all products, materials, commodities or merchandise and . . . all services."

Prior to September 6, 1966, the obligation to submit such a notification related only to:

a) goods subject to resale price maintenance.

b) goods or services, the collective scales of charges for which were fixed jointly by or for various enterprises.

c) a hundred-odd other products, where not as yet included in the two foregoing categories—in particular, margarine; salad oil; coffee; bread; macaroni; spaghetti and similar products; vegetable, fish and meat preserves; sugar; jam; beer; soap; paint and varnish; tires and inner tubes; bicycles; radio and television sets; footwear; rayon fibers; blankets; mattresses; wood and metal furniture; bricks; cement; oil products; fertilizers; rice; insurance and hairdressing charges.

The notification must state in particular:

a) the name, Christian name, address and occupation or, in the case of a firm, the trade name of the producer or importer.

b) specification of the products or services.

c) the conditions of sale (ex producer or importer or delivered domicile, with or without tax).

d) the currently applied selling price.

e) the new selling price and the date from which it is to apply.

f) the grounds on which the increase is warranted by the cost factors; the Ministerial Order of September 2, 1966 stresses that these grounds must be expressed in terms of figures.

In the case of imported products, the Department's Prices Division requests applicants to supply, *inter alia,* the following data (as regards both the ruling and the proposed prices):

a) the C.I.F. or free-frontier price, in Belgian francs. If an increase takes place, it is also required to state whether this is in operation on the domestic market of the country of origin.

b) the import duties.

c) the taxes (luxury, standard rate or turnover tax).

d) the customs clearance costs (including bank charges, health control fees, acceptance costs).

e) the importer's cost.

f) the importer's distribution margin.

g) the importer's selling price: with or without tax; delivered or ex warehouse.

h) the wholesaler's distribution margin.

i) the wholesaler's selling price: with or without tax; delivered or ex warehouse.

j) the retailer's distribution margin.

k) the selling price to the consumer.

The information under h, i, j and k is only required in the case of fixed, catalogue or recommended prices. It must be stated whether the importer is the sole distributor. Considerable importance is attached to the reasons given in support of increases in distribution margins.

The provisions governing notifications of price increases do not affect new products or products which have been subjected to fundamental processing.

Distributors may only increase their prices to the extent that the producers, importers or distributors have raised theirs by an amount permitted by the regulations. In addition, distribution margins, expressed as percentages, must be maintained.

In order to prevent the system of compulsory notification of price increases from arresting a downward movement, the Ministerial Order of October 8, 1959 was supplemented on September 8, 1961 by an article, namely Art. 3· *bis,* providing that producers and importers giving notice of price decreases not later than the date upon which such decreases come into operation may, if they make application at that time, be exempted from the conditions laid down in Articles 1 and 2 concerning the time limit or statement of reasons, in accordance with procedures to be determined by the Minister for Economic Affairs in each individual case, when submitting subsequent notification for increases.

The Prices Commission

Task

The Prices Commission was set up on February 16, 1951. The members were appointed on March 22, 1951 and the first meeting was held on

April 2, 1951.

The task of the Commission is:

a) to make recommendations, whenever requested by the Minister for Economic Affairs, on all problems relating to the cost of living.

b) to follow the trend of prices and submit suggestions on price policy to the Minister for Economic Affairs.

The Commission is thus a consultative body but has the right to act on its own initiative. It must not be confused with the Index Commission, whose function consists mainly in approving the authorities' monthly proposals concerning the level of the Index of Retail Prices.

Within the Commission a Standing Committee has been created. Its terms of reference comprise:

a) observation of the price trend.

b) submission to the Minister of all problems which it wishes to be studied by the Commission.

c) collection of the necessary documentary material and preparation of the ground for the Commission's activities.

Structure

The Commission consists of a Chairman, Vice-Chairman, and members representing:

a) employees' organizations (9 members).

b) industry (4 members).

c) wholesale and retail trade (4 members).

d) large distribution enterprises (4 members).

e) family interests (4 members).

f) agriculture (3 members).

g) self-employed persons (2 members).

h) import trade (1 member).

i) transport (1 member).

j) credit institutions (1 member).

k) the following government departments: Economic Affairs, Trading Classes, Prime Minister's Office, Agriculture, Finance, Employment and Labour, National Insurance, Communications and Post Office, Public Works (1 member each).

The Minister for Economic Affairs appoints the Chairman, the Vice-Chairman and the active members of the Commission and their deputies, as well as determining their term of office. The Commission has an equal number of active and deputy members.

The Standing Committee consists of the Chairman, the Vice-Chairman, a representative of the Ministry of Economic Affairs and members appointed by the representatives of:

a) employees' organizations (3 members).

b) industry (1 member).

c) agriculture (1 member).

d) trade (1 member).

e) family interests (1 member).

The Secretariat of the Commission and the Committee is staffed by officials of the Ministry of Economic Affairs.

The Commission's structure is such as to ensure that account is taken of all aspects of the problems with which it is called upon to deal. The Chairman may, moreover, invite "any competent person" to attend the meetings of the Commission in order to obtain his opinion on a specific question.

Activity

The Commission has on many occassions conducted an inquiry into the situation in the field of prices and price policy. On certain questions opinions have been divided, a case in point being the recommendation (April 4, 1955) concerning resale price maintenance. It is, however, noteworthy that many of the Commission's recommendations on price policy have been unanimous. On October 1, 1956, for instance, it advocated a restriction of credit and rejected measures such as an export levy and a general price freeze without a dissentient vote. The same consensus marked the recommendation issued on May 18, 1966, at the Minister's request, concerning the possible reduction of indirect taxes on certain products.

The bulk of the Commission's activities, however, are centered on the application of the Orders governing prior notifications of price increases.

All such notifications are submitted to it for an opinion. As a general rule, those relating to an entire sector are dealt with by the Commission and those relating to individual cases by the Standing Committee. Sector representatives are asked to outline their standpoints to the Commission and also answer questions put by its members. Should additional information be required, the persons concerned are afforded the opportunity to comment on them during subsequent sessions.

If the inquiry appears liable to take more than the 21 days referred to above, the parties concerned are requested to postpone their price increase. In point of fact, the 21-day period only begins to run from the time when the file is complete—in other words, when the requests for information have been satisfied. When files are examined in the Standing Committee, it is usually found to be less necessary to call upon experts from the enterprises concerned.

In a resolution dated January 10, 1958, the Prices Commission expressed its desire to be provided with the following data (for the last five years, or since the last price increase if it dates from before this period):

a) production or turnover.

b) manpower.

c) relative importance of the parties concerned in the sector to which they belong.

d) system of price determination—for example, competition, cartel, catalogue price.

e) trend of selling prices.

f) distribution margins, where selling prices to the consumer are fixed by the producer or the importer.

g) duties and taxes.

h) exports in volume and value.

i) imports of the same or similar products (volume, value, quotas, agreements, and minimum prices).

j) internal consumption in volume and value.

k) profit as percentage of capital and reserves or of turnover, with any appropriate comments.

The motivation of the rise must show the incidence of the rise in the cost factors on the price to the consumer. Information must also be given on any factors which have had a favorable influence on the cost. The notification must further contain details of the trend of:

a) prices of basic materials and wage-costs (in absolute figures and as a percentage of the selling price).

b) aggregate wages and quantities of basic materials used.

What in fact is required is the detailed cost structure.

The Commission's recommendations are the result of an inquiry conducted with the greatest possible thoroughness. Whereas in wage negotiations on an equal-representation basis, the representatives of the trade unions usually assume as axiomatic that wage increases will bring about price rises in the sector concerned, the union members of the Commission consider themselves primarily as representing consumer interests; they do not necessarily express a favorable opinion regarding a notification of a price increase, even when such an increase involves a rise in wages.

As said, recommendations are in many cases unanimous, which sometimes calls for concessions from all members. If it proves impossible to reach unanimity, all standpoints are incorporated in the recommendation. Although, of course, the members representing the government departments participate in the discussions, their views are not embodied in the recommendations.

The Chairman of the Commission notifies the Minister of the recommendation. The Minister, who also receives a report from his department on the application in question, may naturally exercise his discretion as to whether he adopts it or not.

If the enterprises concerned choose to ignore the Minister's decision, he may issue an Order for the freezing of prices or the fixing of a ceiling price.

Needless to say, the number of applications is conditioned by the cyclic phase. Thus it rose steeply in 1956 after the Suez crisis. Statistics on the subject, however, are only available from 1964 onwards, this being the result of questions asked in Parliament (see Table 1).

Table 1. Number and Nature of Decisions Concerning Price-Increase Notifications Since 1964

Period	Number of decisions	Approved by Minister	Partially approved	Rejected	Files under examination
1964 [a]	327	121	99	107	24
1965 [b]	311	131	81	99	84
1 Jan. May 9, 1966 [c]	177	69	45	63	—

SOURCE: [a] Question parlementaire no. 20 (February 10, 1965); *Bulletin des Questions et des Réponses du Sénat,* no. 18, Bruxelles, 1964–1965, p. 466.
[b] Question parlementaire no. 19 (December 2, 1965); *Bulletin des Questions et des Réponses du Sénat,* no. 11, 1965–1966, p. 430.
[c] Ministry of Economic Affairs.

The same applies to action taken on notifications, the data on which have only been obtainable since 1964. However, analysis of such data is of less significance because no distinction is made between, on the one hand, collective and individual cases and, on the other hand, between important and less important cases.

In order to forestall criticism, the Minister naturally avoids systematically restraining the rise in prices of items in the Index of Retail Prices while allowing others free rein.

Appraisal

It would be an exaggeration to say that there is enthusiasm among employers concerning the compulsory notification of price increases and the concomitant activity of the Prices Commission. The business sector agrees with the Minister's being thus kept informed of the trend of prices but regrets that he "is increasingly exploiting the compulsory declaration system in order to exert pressure on enterprises to restrict, postpone or even simply waive price increases."

This overlooks the fact that the compulsory notification system is designed precisely to enable the authorities to give expression to their reactions in advance. In this connection reference may be made to statements by Economics Ministers of various political persuasions. During the inaugural meeting of the Commission (April 2, 1951), Minister A. Coppé (Social Christian Party) defined the Commission's task as "preventing excessive price rises . . . ironing out peaks." At a meeting held on October 15, 1954, Minister J. Rey (Liberal Party) asked the Commission to devote the main weight of its attention to products "the prices of which appear to be too high." On June 23, 1961, Minister A. Spinoy (Belgian Socialist Party) said: "It is upon you [the Commission] . . . and upon your Chairman that I rely for information as to the necessity of modifying or reviewing our price policy." Dealing with the notification system, Minister J. van Offelen (Liberal Party) pointed out at a press conference on September 11, 1966 that the persons or firms concerned were obliged "to submit notification of proposed increases to the Department . . . several weeks in advance *and to discuss the necessity and the extent of such increases.*"

While generally speaking the larger enterprises comply with the legislation on compulsory notification of price increases, the attitude of the smaller and medium-sized enterprises frequently leaves something to be desired. In a recommendation dated January 8, 1962, the Central Council for the Economy expressed the opinion that the fairly severe sanctions for non-observance of the Order of October 8, 1959 might serve as a warning. In this connection, however, the ineffectuality of the juridical power is to be deplored. It is even reasonable to ask whether it has not been saddled with tasks which are really more within the province of the government. It is as all events desirable to update the legal basis of official intervention in the field of prices.

The following are some reflections concerning the activity of the Prices Commission:

a) Although the members are pledged to secrecy, it has been known for the Commission's recommendations to have come to the ears of pressmen. When it is considered that some papers publish reports of secret political meetings, this cannot be said to be surprising. Even so, we feel that a reduction of the number of persons who have access to the Commission's files would help to ensure that its discussions and reports are treated more confidentially. In the Standing Committee, moreover, no leaks have so far been detected.

b) The organizations represented in the Commission would like the number of the Prices Division's officials to be increased so as to provide the Commission with better and quicker information. This is all the more necessary following the extension of the notification system to all goods in September

1966. Supervision over the application of the regulations also leaves something to be desired.

c) These organizations consider it wrong that increases in charges made by public services are not systematically submitted to the Commission for recommendations. They rightly hold the view that the private and public sectors must be treated on the same footing. The authorities have no interest in setting bad examples and undermining the Commission's prestige.

d) The members wish to have prior notice of the standpoint adopted by the government in problems relating to European integration, and more particularly as to the probable repercussions of the proposed decisions of the European Economic Community. This desire is understandable: in contrast with what has been repeatedly proclaimed, the development of the Community has brought little in the way of price decreases. Indeed, the authorities concerned would appear to have little regard to the movement of prices and a common price policy.

e) Finally, the members take exception to the fact that certain unanimous or quasi-unanimous recommendations have been disregarded for political reasons. It must not be forgotten, however, that the Commission is a consultative body, whose recommendations the Minister is free to follow or not as he thinks fit. Even when they are not acted upon, they may nevertheless be assumed to have influenced the Minister's decision.

Despite the foregoing objections, it may be said that notification of proposed increases and examination of them by the Prices Commission have contributed to slow down the pace of the upward tendency of prices. "The fact that over years prices have increased less in Belgium than in neighboring countries is due in some measure to the work of the Prices Commission." Because of the numerous factors which have an influence on the level of prices, the effects of the Prices Commission's activity cannot be accurately assessed. Its chief service has been to foster a "psychological restraint."

The system of compulsory notification allows the Minister a few days to gauge the repercussions of a given price increase on price policy. He can make use of this "to enter into negotiations with the parties concerned and endeavour to secure, if called for, a reasonable compromise." As far as ever possible, moreover, the Economics Ministers have employed negotiation in preference to direct intervention.

As a result of the Commission's initiatives, numerous suggestions have been submitted to the Minister. In some cases, they have given rise to measures which have brought about a fall in prices, noteworthy instances being provided by the fields of pharmaceuticals and domestic electrical appliances.

Last but not least, the Commission is a manifestation of economic democracy. It is, indeed, designed to act as ". . . the link between Government policy and the aspirations of consumers in general and our business circles in particular."

Consumers are in a better position to keep track of price movements and to influence the Minister's decisions. The organizations represented in the Commission acquire experience with regard to the price-shaping machinery. Thus in many cases they appreciate the necessity of a price increase and refrain from doing anything untoward where this measure is concerned. Furthermore, such experience may stand them in good stead in other consultative bodies.

Discussion Questions

1. What kinds of anti-inflation policies have West Europeans used in dealing with the problem of rising construction costs?
2. How applicable is the European experience with construction costs to the U.S. scene in the late sixties and early seventies?
3. Discuss and evaluate the goals and results of the Belgian Prices Commission's activities.
4. Compare the Belgian experience with a prices commission with the United States' more recent experience with a similar institutional mechanism to combat inflation.

Economic Growth

Economic growth is one of the magic terms in economics. For the under-developed countries of the world where the vast majority of the population wallows in hideous poverty, growth may mean the difference between life and death. For the developed industrialized nations, economic growth is translated into increasing the number of options available in an already viable economy. Growth may be translated into the movement toward or the maintenance of a full-employment economy. At the household level, economic growth may mean a second family-car or a summer trip to Europe. For society as a whole, economic growth creates the possibilities for allocating resources toward collective goods such as education, water conservation, and medical research.

But growth does not take place without attendant costs. The price of growth is pollution, crowded cities, and the dissipation of non-renewable resources. Later in the book specific attention will be given to the urban and pollution problems.

The two countries examined in this section on growth are Japan and Finland. The experience of Japan provides the most phenomenal example of economic development in the post-World War II period. Japan literally rose from the ashes of its devastated dreams of an empire to take its place as one of the five great industrial powers in the world. Miyazaki's article examines a number of the crucial reasons for Japan's unique successes.

The article on Finland brings to light a problem facing a large number of the industrialized nations, that of regional disparities in development. In the United States it is obvious that the fruits of growth have by-passed the Appalachian region and the rural south. Similarly, West European countries have suffered from regional underdevelopment, for example, Brittany in France. This article describes the policy mix which the Finns have implemented to cope with the problem of reducing the gap between its developed and less-developed regions.

Pekka Lahikainen is Secretary General of the Regional Development Board of Finland. Yoshikazu Miyazaki is a member of the economics faculty at Yokohama National University.

Rapid Economic Growth in Postwar Japan

YOSHIKAZU MIYAZAKI

Three Aspects to the Postwar Japanese Economy

In the ten years from 1954 to 1963 Japan's real national product rose by more than 2.2 times, showing an annual average growth rate of 9.4 percent. In the light of the fact that during this period the annual average growth rate of real national product was 7.4 percent in West Germany, 6.5 percent in Austria, 6.1 percent in Norway, 6 percent in Italy, 4.9 percent in France and, in particular, 2.8 percent in the United States, and 2.5 percent in England, we see that Japan's growth rate was of a remarkable order.

The economic bodies which actually attained this high economic growth are, of course, the individual enterprises. The growth of Japanese enterprises in the postwar period has been such as to fit the word "miraculous" exactly. For example, the sales and sales profits of Matsushita Electric Industrial, a representative manufacturer of domestic electrical appliances in Japan, increased by as much as thirteen times in the ten years from 1954 to 1963. Even in its most flourishing ten-year period (during the 1920s) the Ford Motors, famous for its mass-production "Ford system," proved incapable of exceeding an increase of the order of ten times. In postwar Japan, however, not only Matsushita but also such manufacturers of domestic electrical appliances as Sanyo Electric, Sony, and Hayakawa Electric have all realized sales increases of from ten to twenty times in the last ten years, while Toyota Motor and Nissan Motor are also no exceptions to this phenomenon.

Nevertheless it is well known that behind the splendid spectacle afforded by this rapid growth there has developed a fierce market-sharing competition among the various enterprises. The large enterprises of Japan have been vying desperately with one another, competing fiercely in the introduction of foreign technology, in investments in equipment in their factories, and in advertising and sales. The term "excessive competition" secured immediate acceptance throughout the country as an expression of this state of affairs. The situation is exemplified by the following facts: 64 Japanese trading companies are engaged in business in New York and 38 in Hong Kong; 53 Japanese manufacturers have been importing electronic technology from Radio Corporation of America, and 17 Japanese companies have been paying patent fees for the Sanforizing process to the Peabody Company.

Thus, because the Japanese economy grew at a high rate it provoked

Reprinted from *The Developing Economies,* Vol. *5,* No. 2, pp. 329–350, by permission of the Institute of Developing Economies and the author.

"excessive competition" among enterprises, and "high economic growth rate" and "excessive competition," being, as it were, the two sides of a coin, have been the driving force of the postwar economy, with "excessive competition" acting as the driving force for the attainment of high growth rate. From the point of view of the relations between various enterprises this economic situation has tended to strengthen large-scale enterprises. As is well known, there used to be the Mitsui, Mitsubishi, Sumitomo, and other *zaibatsu,* the enterprise groups which ruled prewar Japan, but these *zaibatsu* were dissolved under the postwar Occupation policy. Recently, however, the companies formerly affiliated to the *zaibatsu* have come to be reintegrated anew as enterprise groups known by the name of *"keiretsu"* (a word signifying a closely tied complex of industrial and financial corporations).

Viewing this development from *"zaibatsu"* to *"keiretsu"* as a whole, the following two points seem characteristic. First, in the prewar *zaibatsu* the links in the enterprise groups were centered on the commercial sector of their businesses. (Consider, for example, the influence wielded by Mitsui & Company in the prewar Mitsui *zaibatsu* and by Mitsubishi Shoji in the Mitsubishi *zaibatsu.*) But in the postwar *"keiretsu"* the enterprise groups are centered on the heavy and chemical industry sector. Second, the prewar *zaibatsu* took the form of "family konzerns" linked vertically and topped by a holding company for the whole group. On the other hand, the postwar *"keiretsu"* are centered on financial institutions and take the form of konzerns in which the enterprises are linked horizontally.

The postwar *"keiretsu"* include not only enterprise groups formerly affiliated to the Mitsui, Mitsubishi, Sumitomo, and other *zaibatsu,* but also newly formed enterprise groups such as the Toyota Group, the Hitachi Group, the Toshiba Group, and the Yawata Group. All of these are making unceasing efforts to strengthen their own groups, and at the frontiers of the new industries which have been developed in Japan since the war, they have been competing against one another without quarter in equipment investment. When, for example, the Mitsubishi Group built an oil and chemicals refinery at Yokkaichi, competitive construction of a similar plant was pressed forward by the Mitsui Group at Iwakuni, and the Sumitomo Group at Niihama, then by the Nippon Oil Group at Kawasaki, and lastly by the Idemitsu Kosan at Tokuyama. At present no less than nine oil and chemicals refineries are producing within the narrow confines of Japan. This is so not only in the case of the oil-chemicals industry. In the field of motor vehicles, too, nine manufacturers in addition to Toyota and Nissan are competing to increase their shares in the market. Similar competition is being carried on by all other industries from iron and steel to food processing. As a result, Japan's productive potential has risen rapidly, and she has realized a degree of high growth which is literally the highest in the world.

In the above account we have likened "high economic growth rate" and "excessive competition" to the two sides of a coin, but in fact there is another aspect to the Japanese economy. It would be more accurate to say that "high economic growth rate," "excessive competition," and "the *keiretsu* form of organization" are the three aspects which build up three-dimensionally the reality of the Japanese economy in the 1950s. Thus, in order to reveal the secret of rapid economic growth in postwar Japan it is necessary to reveal the process by which "excessive competition" developed among the large enterprises of Japan, that is to explain the method of capital accumulation in the various *"keiretsu"* and the process by which the enterprises were organized in the form of *"keiretsu."*

The key to the secret of the rapid economic growth in the postwar period, particularly since 1955, is to be found in the following four questions: First, how did the large enterprises get the necessary funds? Second, how did they get the necessary labor? Third, what instigated the enterprises to invest so furiously? And fourth, to what extent were the policies adopted by the government effective? The labor question can be answered quite simply. Until quite recently (or at least up to 1956), a continual supply of superior labor, both of good quality and readily adaptable to modern technology, was available, and the enterprises' propensity to invest was never subject to restriction from this aspect. Consequently, in the following sections we shall consider the remaining three questions in some detail.

The Establishment of Indirect Financing

First, we must consider the method of obtaining funds for an enterprise. The following three main methods are normally employed: Under direct financing when an enterprise is about to embark on an undertaking it issues debentures or shares and obtains funds directly from the public. Under indirect financing it does not obtain funds directly from the public but obtains the funds indirectly in the form of a loan from some financial institutions which have collected funds from the general public in the form of deposits. This method is characterized by the existence of a financial institution standing between the public, the providers of the funds, and the enterprise, the source of demand for funds. Lastly, under self-financing the funds needed by the enterprise are provided out of the internal funds of the enterprise itself, for example, out of depreciation funds or profits held over.

Table 1 shows the precentages of funds obtained by enterprises in Japan, the United States, England, and West Germany in the last five years. As we see from the table, the advanced countries were practically wholly dependent on self-financing, and Japan alone is conspicuous as having adopted indirect financing. We would expect there to be some relation between this method of obtaining funds and the highest growth rate in the world.

In what way, then, did this indirect financing come into being? That it was not, of course, of natural origin will be apparent from the fact that

Table 1. Percentages of Funds Obtained by Enterprises in Various Countries

Source of funds	Japan average 1958–62	United States average 1958–62	England average 1958–60	West Germany average 1958–62
Internal funds				
Depreciation	20	39	28	50
Held over	4	26	34	5
Shares	13	14	15	11
Debentures	7	} 11	4	
Bank borrowings	34		6	} 34
Other	22	10	13	
Principal method employed	Indirect financing	Self-financing	Self-financing	Self-financing

SOURCE: Statistics Department, Bank of Japan, *Nippon keizai wo chūshin to suru kokusai hikaku tōkei* (Japan and the World: A Comparison by Economic and Financial Statistics), March 1964.

West Germany, which, like Japan, made a recovery after defeat in war, adopted a method of obtaining funds which differed from that adopted by Japan. To state our conclusion in advance, an important factor is that in the postwar measures for currency reform—the ending of war subsidies, the dissolution of the *zaibatsu,* and the dispersal of concentrations of economic power—more care was taken in Japan than in West Germany to see that the city banks would always be in an advantageous position.

First, in the change to the new yen currency in Japan carried out in February 1946 (the Emergency Financial Measures), new yen was given in exchange for old yen at par only up to a sum which was insufficient even for living expenses for one month. All remaining yen assets were compulsorily paid into savings accounts, which, furthermore, were blocked, and free disbursements from the banks were stopped. For the city banks, which had on their books vast sums in bad debts owed by armaments firms which were bankrupt due to the defeat, this blocking of deposits was, needless to say, a welcome measure promising recovery from a desperate situation. In contrast to this, the currency reform effected in West Germany in June 1948, was a measure extremely unfavorable to the creditor banks, since it provided for the exchange of old Reichsmarks for new Deutsche Marks at the rate of 10 to 1, and debts in the old Reichsmarks were in principle also scaled down to one-tenth. Conversely, this may be said to have been a measure very much in favor of borrower enterprises. Nor was this all, for in West Germany measures were also taken to evaluate firms' assets at market prices and to grant temporary exemption from taxation for appreciation resulting from this evaluation, so that extraordinarily convenient conditions were provided for manufacturers directly participating in industrial production. In Japan the ground was made firm for the banks, but on the other hand, in the course of the subsequent inflation the manufacturers were obliged to suffer inroads made in their capital through lack of redemption funds, because the revaluation of their assets was delayed. Here we find the earliest instance of the banks being given preferential treatment over industry.

Second, we must consider the ending of wartime subsidies. In West Germany no particular problem arose regarding wartime subsidies, since all debts were reduced to one-tenth. In Japan problems arose over the bad debts owed to the banks and the disposal of the rights on them. In this matter, too, the banks enjoyed favorable treatment. The "special losses" of the armaments firms resulting from the ending of wartime subsidies were not charged to the account of the banks, the former creditors, but a fair proportion of them were charged to the account of the shareholders of the armaments firms. In particular it is worthy of note that before anything was charged to the account of the creditors (chiefly the banks) an amount of up to 90 percent of capital funds chargeable to the account of the shareholders was first calculated, and only if this were insufficient was anything ever charged to the account of the creditors. Thus the banks who in the previous instance found themselves in a favorable position at the time of the change to the new yen currency as *debtors* of their depositors now received preferential treatment as *creditors* of the armaments firms.

Third, it is a well-known fact that, as a part of the measures for the dissolution of the *zaibatsu,* private enterprises or combinations of such enterprises which either (a) had large assets, (b) had many employees, (c) were engaged in branches of activity unrelated to one another, (d) exercised managerial control over other enterprises, or (e) supplied the greater part of important products, were designated enterprises in which "an excessive concentration of economic power in private hands" was present, and measures for deconcentration were taken in respect to them. While there was a fair number of companies in the manufacturing and mining, and the commerce and services sectors which were designated as subject to deconcentration under these measures and which were actually split up and their factories disposed of (257 companies were designated in the manufacturing and mining sector and 68 in the commerce and services sectors, but only 18 companies were made subject to action), the main banks, headed by the city banks, were not designated either as holding companies or as companies subject to deconcentration, and they survived unscathed.

Finally, the point that the banks were consistently afforded preferential treatment due to the success of some measures and the failure of others was a great factor in the development of the Japanese indirect financing method. These measures included such things as the collapse of the movement for the democratization of securities holdings which aimed at the promotion of direct financing, the collapse of the Shoup Recommendations (measures for preferential treatment of dividends as opposed to interest on deposits in tax policy), and the revival of the debenture-issuing banks which had been prohibited by GHQ.

The term "indirect financing," however, does not adequately describe the methods for obtaining funds employed in the postwar Japanese economy. This is because, though we speak of "indirect financing," it is not true that all enterprises of all their variety of size are equally being financed from financial institutions.

Next, let us go further into the matter and see what concrete form indirect financing took after 1955.

First, in Table 2 we can see, within the funds supplied for the purposes of industry, the breakdown of the funds obtained from sources outside the enterprise and the relative importance of each source. The most conspicuous fact would seem to be that, after 1955, the importance of government financial institutions declined greatly while the proportion of funds supplied by private financial institutions, in particular by the city banks, rose.

Table 2. Sources of Funds Supplied to Industry (by percentage)

| | | Securities market | | Private financial institutions | | | | | |
| | Total external funds supplied | Shares | Debentures | Total | City banks | Long-term credit banks | Others | Government financial institutions | Finance special account |
Year									
1954	100.0	23.23	3.01	66.21	14.96	9.79	41.45	16.35	2.67
1955	100.0	14.12	3.92	68.91	17.68	7.47	43.76	11.07	3.32
1956	100.0	12.53	4.06	76.78	40.87	3.94	31.97	4.98	2.33
1957	100.0	15.89	2.91	73.36	33.90	4.87	34.59	6.08	1.94
1958	100.0	14.28	3.54	72.44	24.82	8.30	39.32	7.29	2.46
1959	100.0	11.17	6.88	73.06	24.78	6.94	41.34	6.42	2.48
1960	100.0	16.12	5.22	71.19	24.83	6.34	40.02	5.46	2.01

SOURCE: Compiled from Statistics Department, the Bank of Japan, *Hompō keizai tōkoi* (Economic Statistics of Japan), 1962.

A closer examination of the content of this advance on the part of the city banks throws into relief the fierce competition in loans among the city banks, and the consequent competition for deposits to be used for this purpose. Table 3 lists the banks in order of their balances on loans at the end of each year from March 1955.

All the banks show spectacular increases of up to five times in the last ten years, but we can see from the figures how fierce the competition for loans was among the city banks, as was exemplified in the struggle for first

Table 3. City Banks in Order of Balances on Loan, 1955–1964 (March of each year)

Banks	1955	1956	1957	1958	1959	1960	1961	1962	1963	1964
Fuji	1	1	1	1	2	2	1	1	1	2
Mitsubishi	2	2	2	2	1	1	2	2	2	1
Sanwa	3	3	4	3	3	3	3	3	3	3
Sumitomo	4	4	3	4	4	4	4	4	4	4
Kangyo	5	5	5	6	5	7	6	5	7	6
Mitsui	6	6	6	5	6	6	5	6	6	7
Tokai	7	7	7	8	8	5	7	8	5	5
Dai-Ichi	8	8	8	7	7	8	8	7	8	8
Kyowa	9	9	9	9	9	10	10	11	11	11
Daiwa	10	11	12	11	11	11	11	10	9	9
Kobe	11	12	11	12	12	12	12	12	12	12
Tokyo	12	10	10	10	10	9	9	9	10	10
Hokkaido Takushoku	13	13	13	13	13	13	13	13	13	13

SOURCE: Compiled from any analysis of financial statements published by the Japanese banks.

place between the Fuji Bank and the Mitsubishi Bank, and Tokai Bank's ascent to a higher place in the table. The figures for March 1964 show that the balances on loan from the four great A-class banks, Mitsubishi, Fuji, Sanwa, and Sumitomo, were all over ¥600,000 million, with the B-class banks, Tokai, Kangyo, Mitsui, and Dai-Ichi, in ¥400,000 million, and the remainder below $300,000 million.

Fierce lending competition among the city banks is thus one of the characteristics of recent times, but this is not all. It is an important point that over two-thirds of the amount on loan from the city banks has been lent to large enterprises, as is clear from Table 4. If we add to these loans those made by the long-term credit banks, the trust banks, and the development banks, we see that an immense sum in capital funds is being supplied entirely for the purpose of financing large enterprises.

What is more, carrying our analysis of the loans from the city banks to the large enterprises one step further, we can draw attention to a most singular tendency. This is the fact that these loans are supplied as concentrated finance to enterprises belonging to the same *keiretsu*. This is shown statistically in Table 5.

In the table b/a indicates the percentage of loans made by city banks which are made to enterprises belonging to the same *keiretsu*, and b/c indicates, from the point of view of the enterprises belonging to the same *keiretsu*, the percentage of the funds required by the enterprises borrowed from banks belonging to their own *keiretsu*. Generally speaking, b/c is greater than b/a. This shows that the lending power of the city banks is the greater, and that they easily have more than enough funds with which to

Table 4. Borrowings by Large Enterprises in Manufacturing Industry
(enterprises with more than 1,000 employees)

Sources	percentages
Private financial institutions	
City banks	68.68
Local banks	36.61
Long-term loan and trust banks	86.39
Financial institutions for medium and smaller enterprises	10.31
Total	70.75
Government financial institutions	
Development bank	34.31
Small business finance corporation	0.12
People's finance corporation	12.20
Total	37.64
Business associates	16.39
Professional moneylenders	—
Relatives and acquantances	0.78
Others	59.44
Grand total	58.04

SOURCE: *Chūshōkigyō chōsa saishūkei shiryō* (Recompiled Data from Surveys of Medium Smaller Enterprises), balances on loan on December 31, 1957.

Table 5. Proportion of *Keiretsu* Financing in Loans Made by the
Principal Banks (average of 1956–60) *

Banks	b/a	b/c	Banks	b/a	b/c
Fuji	13.27	24.21	Sumitomo	9.73	19.33
Mitsubishi	19.32	21.97	Mitsui	24.27	17.16
Sanwa	10.05	25.08	Dai-Ichi	16.65	18.11

* (a) denotes total loans; (b) loans made to enterprises in the *keiretsu;* and (c) total borrowings by the enterprises in the *keiretsu*.
SOURCE: Compiled from Negotiable Securities Reports.

meet the requirements of the *keiretsu* enterprises. An exception is the Mitsui Bank. In spite of the fact that 24 percent of the loans made by the bank are to enterprises in the Mitsui *keiretsu,* the bank is not supplying to the full the funds demanded by the *keiretsu* enterprises because such an extremely large sum in funds is required by the Mitsui *keiretsu.* We may say that this reveals most strikingly one of the weaknesses of the postwar Mitsui *keiretsu.*

To summarize, we have made clear: (1) that after 1956 the importance of government financial institutions declined and the indirect financing centered on private financial institutions, particularly the city banks, was established; (2) that fierce competition in loans occurred among the city banks; (3) that the greater part of the loans made by the city banks went to finance large enterprises, and (4) that *keiretsu* financing was particularly conspicuous. These are the characteristics of indirect financing peculiar to the economy of postwar Japan.

The Principle of "Set Control" of the New Enterprises

What raised the enterprises' propensity to invest? In a word we may say that it was "investment behavior aiming at control by the *keiretsu*" of a complete set of all industries related to one another.

While he was still president of the Mitsubishi Bank, Makoto Usami, the president of the Bank of Japan, spoke as follows regarding the principle of set control:

> We are not doing it under any definite principle of aiming at set control. Within our group alone there are a large number of undertakings and if, for example, it happens that we have to go into business in, say, the oil-chemicals industry, Mitsubishi Rayon has connexions with oil-chemicals, and so does Mitsubishi Chemical Industries. As a result it appears as though we had a general principle of getting set control of industries. I think the truth is not that we have the idea of getting a complete set of everything there is, but that these things happen out of the necessities of business.

This may indeed be so. When we speak of set control, we, too, do not mean a mere unreasoning "getting a complete set of everything there is." It is no doubt natural that these events should have taken place under the pressure of necessity, but what were these necessities? Why did they result in the principle of set control? This is what I wish to analyze.

As we have seen above, indirect financing has been prevalent in postwar Japan. What is more, through the pipe lines of the giant prewar *zaibatzu* banks and the other city banks have passed the postwar recovery funds and modernization investment funds. The companies which were in an advantageous position for obtaining funds were those backed by the powerful banks, headed by the companies formerly affiliated to the *zaibatsu* and connected with these pipe lines. That is to say, in the natural course of events funds were supplied in the form of long- or short-term loans by the Mitsui Bank to the Mitsui *keiretsu*, by the Mitsubishi Bank to the Mitsubishi *keiretsu*, by the Sumitomo Bank to the Sumitomo *keiretsu*, by the Fiji Bank to the Yasuda *keiretsu* and the former Asano *keiretsu*, and by the Dai-Ichi Bank to the Kawasaki Dockyard, Kobe Steel, and so on. It is nevertheless true that investment in coal and mining, shipbuilding, marine transport, and other industries which have had difficulty in paying their way since the war, as well as in electricity, roads, railways, airways, telecommunications, and other branches of the basic industrial sector, has been increasingly dependent on state capital financed by the Development Bank or direct investment out of government funds.

Thus the companies backed by powerful banks, such as those formerly affiliated to the *zaibatsu* and in possession of advantageous positions for obtaining funds, took steps to rebuild and expand themselves. It was not merely the rebuilding, rehabilitation, and expansion of enterprises which had existed from the war years that took place. All of the *keiretsu,* backed by funds from the banks, eagerly entered new fields, including some with which they had no connection before the war. For example, up to 1952 the Integrated Steel Manufacturers were confined to the so-called "three integrated companies"—Yawata Iron & Steel and Fuji Iron & Steel (the two companies which were formerly Nippon Iron & Steel) and Nippon Kokan. Recently Kawasaki Steel, Sumitomo Metal Industries, Amagasaki Iron & Steel, Kobe Steel, Nakayama Steel, Nisshin Steel, and Osaka Iron & Steel have been added to the number of steel manufacturers, making a total of 10 large producers.

In the automobile industry the situation is the same. In 1949 small 4-wheeled vehicles were all produced by the three firms Toyota, Nissan, and Ota Motors. Since that date Prince (formerly Fuji Precision Machinery), Hino, Isuzu, Shin Mitsubishi, Toyo Kogyo, Daihatsu Kogyo, Honda Motors, Fuji Heavy Industries, and others have joined the field and by 1964 had expanded their production by as much as 40 times in their efforts to overtake Toyota and Nissan. On the other hand, Ota Motors and Tokyu Kurogane became entirely eclipsed by the rise of these new companies. In the paper industry, Oji Paper, which before the war produced 72 percent of all the paper (excluding *Japanese paper*) in Japan, was not only divided up into three companies(Jujo Paper Mfg., Oji Paper, and Honshu Paper Mfg.) but also came into competition with Daishowa Paper Mfg., Kokusaku Pulp, Tohoku Pulp, Kanzaki Paper Mfg., Chuetsu Pulp, Mitsubishi Paper, and so on.

In addition to these, similar relations are to be found both in synthetic fibers and in electric refrigerators, the typical durable consumer's goods products. This will be clear from the degree of concentration of production in industries conspicuous for the number of new enterprises, as shown in Table 6.

What we can read from this table, however, is not merely the large numbers of new enterprises entering these fields but that practically all these new enterprises, as closer inspection will show, had the backing of such powerful banks as the following:

1) Mitsui Bank: Hino Motors, Kanegafuchi Spinning.
2) Mitsubishi Bank: Honda Motors, Shin Mitsubishi Heavy Industries.
3) Sumitomo Bank: Nippon Electric, Daishowa Paper Mfg., Sumitomo Metal Industries, Toyo Kogyo, Kanzaki Paper Mfg., Sanyo Electric.
4) Fuji Bank: Hayakawa Electric.

5) Sanwa Bank: Teikoku Rayon, Amagasaki Iron & Steel, Nisshin Steel, Nakayama Steel, Nippon Rayon, Osaka Iron & Steel, Daihatsu Kogyo.
6) Dai-Ichi Bank: Isuzu Motors, Fuji Electric, Kobe Steel.
7) Nippon Kangyo Bank: Tohoku Pulp.

Large business organizations in competition against one another in entering new industries and connected in *keiretsu* on the finance side were also

Table 6. Percentage of Concentration of Production in Industries Conspicuous for Their Number of New Enterprises *

(A)   Iron & Steel Manufacturing

Name of company	1937	1949	1958	1960	1963
Former Nippon Iron & Steel	83.9	65.9			
Yawata Iron & Steel	——	——	29.8	33.2	25.8
Fuji Iron & Steel	——	——	28.2	26.6	23.7
Nippon Kokan					
Nippon Kokan	10.1	22.6	13.8	13.4	13.8
Tsurumi Iron & Steel	3.8	——	——	——	——
Kawasaki Steel	——	——	7.9	8.0	11.0
Sumitomo Metal Industries (3)	——	——	4.8	4.9	9.1
Kobe Steel (6)	——	——	——	3.2	4.8
Amagasaki Iron & Steel (5)	——	——	4.7	4.4	3.2
Nakayama Steel (5)	——	——	5.0	4.0	2.3
Nisshin Steel (5)	——	——	——	——	2.3
Osaka Iron & Steel (5)	——	——	——	0.8	1.0
Others	2.2	11.5	5.8	1.5	3.0

(B)   Small Four-Wheeled Vehicles

Name of company	1949	1954	1958	1960	1963
Toyota Motor	34.5	47.7	45.7	33.3	39.6
Nissan Motor	52.7	28.9	33.5	41.9	34.8
Prince Motors	——	13.7	9.4	8.4	8.7
Isuzu Motors (6)	——	——	2.3	5.9	7.4
Hino Motors (1)	——	——	2.9	5.2	4.7
Shin Mitsubishi Heavy Industries (2)	——	——	——	4.8	2.6
Toyo Kogyo (3)	——	——	3.1	——	1.4
Daihatsu Kogyo (5)	——	——	0.6	——	0.4
Honda Motor (2)	——	——	——	——	0.2
Fuji Heavy Industries	——	——	——	0.4	0.1
Ota Motors	12.8	9.3	——	——	——
Tokyu Kurogane	——	——	0.9	——	——
Others	0	0.4	1.6	0.1	0.1

Table 6.—Continued

(C) Paper Manufacturing

Name of company	1937	1949	1958	1960	1962
Oji Paper	71.7				
Jugo Paper Mfg.	——	25.0	19.1	15.5	15.8
Oji Paper	——	27.0	8.4	13.0	15.3
Honshu Paper Mfg.	——	10.7	8.1	6.1	4.2
Daishowa Paper Mfg. (3)	——	2.9	7.4	8.0	8.8
Kokusaku Pulp Industry	——	——	——	2.6	5.0
Tohoku Pulp (7)	——	——	2.9	3.7	4.6
Kanzaki Paper (3)	——	——	3.5	4.7	3.9
Chuetsu Pulp Industry	——	——	4.6	3.9	2.9
Mitsubishi Paper	6.0	4.8	3.1	3.1	2.8
Hokuetsu Paper	5.4	6.9	3.6	3.2	2.6
Daio Paper	——	——	3.3	——	——
Others	16.9	22.7	35.6	36.2	34.1

(D) Synthetic Fiber Manufacturing

Name of company	1950	1955	1958
Toyo Rayon	22.0	1.3	45.6
Kurashki Rayon	57.4	3.8	21.9
Nippon Rayon (5)	——	——	8.9
Dai Nippon Spinning	3.4	5.2	5.6
Teikoku Rayon (5)	——	——	4.9
Asahi-Dow	——	7.0	3.9
Kanegafuchi Spinning	16.9	0.1	2.2
Japan Exlan	——	——	2.9
Others	0.3	2.6	4.1

(E) Electric Refrigerator Manufacturing

Name of company	1956	1957	1958
Hitachi	27.3	25.7	28.8
Tokyo Shibaura Electric	28.2	28.4	22.2
Matsushita Electric Industrial	24.2	28.5	20.4
Mitsubishi Electric	17.1	14.0	15.8
Nippon Electric (3)	——	0.4	2.5
Sanyo Electric (3)	——	0.8	5.2
Fuji Electric (6)	——	——	1.2
Hayakawa Electric (4)	——	1.1	0.5
Yaou Electric	——	1.1	0.4
Others	3.2	——	3.0

SOURCES: Up to 1958, Fair Trade Commission (ed.), *Shuyō sangyō ni okeru seisan shūchūdo* (Concentration of Production in Principal Industries), 1960. For 1960, 1962, and 1963, *Tōyō keizai tōkei geppō.*
* The numbers in parentheses following the names of companies refer to the *keiretsu* listed in the text.

seen in prewar Japan. These were the *zaibatsu*. The differences between the prewar *zaibatsu* and these *keiretsu* do not consist merely in the fact that the prewar *zaibatsu* had holding companies as their nuclei while the postwar *keiretsu* have certain principal banks at their centers. Each of the prewar *zaibatsu* had its own sphere of activity, the Mitsui *zaibatsu* in paper, synthetic dyes, coal, and foreign trade, the Mitsubishi *zaibatsu* in heavy industry centered on shipbuilding, in marine transportation and plate glass, and the Sumitomo *zaibatsu* in metal manufacturing industries centered on rolled copper and aluminum. They made their principal investments in these fields, each adopting a system which secured for it fairly stable markets, and each sought monopolistic control of the industries in which it was concerned.

The postwar situation, however, differs from this. A good example of this fact is provided by the moves made by large enterprises in relation to the oil-chemicals industry and the atomic energy industry. From the very first the giant financial *keiretsu*—Mitsui, Mitsubishi, Sumitomo, Fuji, and Dai-Ichi—lined up in competition in equipment investment.

Thus the immense sums of capital funds supplied through the city banks since the war were not invested selectively, as in the prewar period, in the principal industries in which the various *zaibatsu* had their interests. Investment has been carried out in such a way that each of the *keiretsu*, accepting the fact that it will come into rivalry with its fellows, contrives to get under its own control a complete set of all the new industries. This being so, why has investment behavior aiming at set control by each *keiretsu* appeared in the postwar Japanese economy? In this regard we can think of the following four circumstances:

1. It goes without saying that one important factor was the subdivision of undertakings occurring as a result of the application of the Economic Deconcentration Law, as in the cases of the Integrated Steel Manufacturers and the paper industry. The ability to maintain control over markets which until then had been more or less stable collapsed, and entry into new industries in the form of new enterprises was facilitated.

2. If *keiretsu* were not to fall behind in taking advantage of the recent wave of technical innovation, they could not afford to stand pat, each holding on to its own field of activity and relying only on its traditional "stable" markets. They were obliged to get under their control as many of the new industries as they could, enlarging the scope of their field, and strengthening the links between their industries in a multilateral and comprehensive manner.

3. The above two circumstances may be said to be typical of Japanese business in general, whether organized as a part of a *keiretsu* or not. Why, then, is it that, in spite of this, practically all the new enterprises which we have listed above are connected

with the financial *keiretsu* of some powerful bank? In the modern heavy and chemical industries, where sweeping technical innovation has occurred, enlargement of the scale of operations through the integration and diversification of production (as in the case of the oil-chemical refinery) is required, if only for technical reasons, and there is a strong tendency for the needed capital funds to assume immense proportions. Because of this it is only large enterprises which can accumulate or obtain elsewhere large sums of capital and which have the backing of big financing banks that can enter these industries. In sum, entry to these industries by new enterprises did in fact occur, but there was a great difference between this and the "free entry" spoken of in economics textbooks. The firms which entered these industries were no more than a very limited élite of large enterprises backed by powerful banks which could easily supply the immense sums needed for investment in equipment.

4. We cannot ignore what is known to the economics textbooks as "the internalization of the external economy." The term refers to those benefits accruing which are given to the enterprise in a fortuitous manner by changes in the whole body of the industry of which the enterprise is a part and in the national economy as a whole, as opposed to benefits accruing as a result of efforts made within the enterprise itself. For example:

Let us consider the case in which a new undeground line is opened and a new underground station built at an intersection in a city. There is no doubt that, thanks to this, the intersection will be twice as busy a place as before and the shops already established at the four corners of the street can be expected to receive a windfall in the form of a great increase in the number of customers. This is clearly thanks to the "external economy."

Similarly, as the motor industry is established and developed in the Japanese economy, the manufacturers of thin steel plate, tires, piston rings, ball bearings, electrical fittings, and other automobile parts will naturally benefit from it. The establishment of the motor industry has just the same effect as the "'underground station at the intersection." By its essential nature this kind of "external economy" produces effects on the generality of industries through the intermediacy of the element of complementary production, through the relations existing among the goods produced.

In the postwar Japanese economy, however, investment plans have been drawn up with the intention of blocking, as far as possible, the general effects produced by the "external economy" and of confining such effects within the bounds of one's own *keiretsu;* in other words, of aiming at the "internalization of the external economy." Good examples of this are the establishment of Mitsubishi Monsanto Chemicals as a market for the carbide produced by Mitsubishi Chemicals, the establishment of Aichi Steel for the purposes of manufacturing special steel for Toyota Motor, the establishment of Nippon Denso as an independent company for the specialized production of electrical parts for Toyota Motor, and the establishment of Toyota Motor Sales for the purposes of integrating the sales branch of Toyota Motor. Such plans to "internalize the external economy" are also one of the factors leading to the adoption of investment behavior aiming at set control of new industries by each of the *keiretsu*.

Once this principle of aiming at set control is adopted by all the *keiretsu* the result is that all *keiretsu* become rivals in each of the industries in which they are concerned. Competition is intensified. According to the usual economics textbooks, competition among the enterprises is developed in accordance with "the principle of the maximization of profits." But when we consider the competition among the *keiretsu* in postwar Japan we find it more appropriate to regard it as having been carried on in accordance with "the principle of maximizing sales" with the aim of enlarging the *keiretsu's* share of the market, rather than in accordance with "the principle of maximizing profits." That is to say, in order not to be left behind by the others, each *keiretsu* has taken steps to enlarge its share of markets in each industry whenever it can, and has frantically competed with its rivals in equipment investment. This kind of investment behavior aiming at set control has also been a driving force in the spectacular economic growth in Japan since the war. On the other hand, it has also been a cause of "excessive competition."

William J. Baumol gives the following six reasons for behavior aiming at maximization of sales on the part of enterprises in recent times:

a) There is reason to fear that consumers will shun a product if they feel it is declining in popularity, though their information on these matters is doubtless often spotty.

b) Banks and the money market will tend to be less receptive to the desires of a firm whose absolute or relative sales volume is declining.

c) Perhaps even more important in this connection is the very real danger that firms whose sales are declining will lose distributors—a major marketing setback.

d) Management also is not unmoved by the fact that in a declining firm personnel relations are made much more difficult when firing rather than hiring is the order of the day.

e) The firm which declines (or remains small when others expand) can lose monopoly power and the power to adopt an effective competitive counter-strategy when it is called for.

f) Executive salaries appear to be far more closely correlated with the scale of operations of the firm than with its profitability. And in the modern corporation, which is characterized so often by separation of ownership from management, many executives find it politic to avoid an absolute or relative decline in their operations. Here, management's concern with the volume of sales is compounded of its very conscientious concern with the responsibilities of its trusteeship and a desire to play good stockholder politics. In any event the effects are the same— volume of sales achieves the status of a prime business objective.

Among these, e and f would seem to be particularly important. In Japan's economy since the dissolution of the *zaibatsu* the principle of the maximization of sales has predominated, partly because of a general separation of ownership and management. The consistent application of this principle is also a characteristic of decision making regarding equipment investment.

The Economic Policies and Economic Institutions Which Sustained the Rapid Growth

Let us look into the policies adopted by the governments of postwar Japan. In the preceding sections we have directed our attention at the investment behavior aiming at set control adopted by the *keiretsu* as one thing in particular which sustained the type of growth pattern led by investment in private equipment and which produced the "excessive competition." However, such decisions to invest on the part of large enterprises were not the sole cause of the rapid economic growth led by investment in private equipment. Institutional mechanisms making possible such decisions already existed in law or in government policy. It was for this reason that subjective decisions to invest on the part of large enterprises were able to be translated into objective investment behavior. This being so, what were the institutional and policy elements which sustained the investment behavior aiming at set control adopted by the *keiretsu?*

As we have stated already, if we set aside the question of the labor force we are left with the questions of the conditions for the supply of capital funds and the conditions governing imports of technology, capital equipment, and raw materials.

Overloans Dependent on the Bank of Japan

First, on the capital funds side the pillar for capital funds which sustained investment behavior aiming at set control by the *keiretsu* was the special indirect financing known as "*keiretsu* financing." Without the support of immense sums in credit from the powerful banks we could never expect this type of investment behavior to have been possible. Again, without the investment behavior aiming at set control by the *keiretsu,* and without inter-*keiretsu* competition for the enlargement of shares of markets, there would probably have been no such immense equipment investment as there is at present, nor would the overloans by the city banks have been so great.

The fact, however, was the opposite of this. The city banks did not shrink from making overloans in supplying funds to the enterprises in their *keiretsu* and thus seeming to promote investment behavior aiming at set control by the *keiretsu*. To make up the sums which they could not supply, the city banks got loans from the Bank of Japan. Table 7 shows the fluctu-

Table 7. Movements of Deposits Rates Before and Since the War

	Year End	All Banks	City Banks	Local Banks
Prewar	1930	77.8	63.0	86.6
	1935	62.4	52.2	73.8
Postwar	1951	105.6	116.9	85.2
	1952	103.4	113.1	85.4
	1953	102.8	110.7	86.2
	1954	99.1	106.0	84.6
	1955	89.3	90.6	82.4
	1956	92.0	94.4	82.5
	1957	100.1	107.4	84.0
	1958	95.7	101.0	82.2
	1959	93.7	98.3	81.9
	1960	93.2	97.8	82.6
	1961	96.4	103.3	84.1
	1962	96.4	105.1	83.5

SOURCE: Calculated from *Hompō keizai tōkei.*

ation of deposits rates (the proportion of loans to deposits, including debentures) of all banks, city banks, and local banks.

From the table we see that overloans (an abnormally large volume of loans in comparison with deposits) are a special phenomenon of the postwar period. These appear principally in the city banks. In particular it should be noted that the deposits rates of the city banks, which maintained very healthy levels before the war, worsened sharply after the war. This was the result of the tendency of aiming at set control by the *keiretsu,* pushed forward with the financial backing from the powerful banks. For this reason the city banks' degree of dependence on the Bank of Japan (the ratio of loans from the Bank of Japan to deposits, including debentures) rose markedly. Table 8 shows this.

The overloans by the city banks accompanying this rise in their degree of dependence on the Bank of Japan produced notable characteristics in the formula for the supply of funds by the central bank of Japan.

There are three formulas for the supply of currency by a central bank. First, the central bank buys up gold or foreign exchange within the country and issues central bank notes at a certain rate in relation to this, and only insofar as is covered by it. Under this formula no increase in note issues

Table 8. City Banks' Degree of Dependence on the Bank of Japan

Year End	Percentage of dependence on the Bank of Japan
1930	0
1935	0
1953	16.9
1954	12.9
1955	1.4
1956	4.5
1957	18.3
1958	9.8
1959	7.2
1960	9.0
1961	22.7
1962	19.2

SOURCE: Calculated from *Hompō keizai tōkei*.

occurs except under conditions of a favorable international balance of payments. Second, the government issues bonds or securities and the central bank buys these up by means of a "buying operation" (on the open market) and supplies currency to the amount covered by them. Third, the central bank issues its notes by making loans to the city banks.

From Table 9, Breakdown of Principal Assets of Central Banks (for a central bank the issue of central bank notes represents an increase in debits, and the significance of the table is that of showing by what assets these are sustained) we see that West Germany has adopted the first formula, the United States, England, and Italy the second formula, and France and Japan the third formula. It is true, however, that as an accompaniment to a favorable turn in her international balance of payments France has recently

Table 9. Percentage Breakdown of Principal Assets of Central Banks (end of 1962)

	United States	England	West Germany	France	Italy	Japan
Gold and foreign exchange	29.1	0.01	64.6	34.2	21.2	13.8
To government credit	56.5	97.8	26.3	25.8	59.8	18.3
To private credit	0.3	2.1	8.0	36.0	17.7	62.2
Others	14.1	0	1.1	4.0	1.3	5.7
Formula	No. 2	No. 2	No. 1	No. 3	No. 2	No. 3

SOURCE: *Nippon keizai wo chūshin to suru kokusai hikaku tōkei*.

been making a fair increase in the proportion of funds supplied under the formula which depends on purchases of gold and foreign exchange. In Japan, in contrast to this, the proportion of loans to private credit has been extremely large. This is due to the increased loans to the city banks by the Bank of Japan.

Thus the formula under which funds are at present supplied by loans made by the Bank of Japan is a characteristic one, examples of which are not often found in other countries. There is some tendency to hold "that a high growth rate is accompanied by a corresponding withdrawal of deposits, that the city banks borrow cash reserves for this purpose, and that this result is inevitable in a growing economy." What the statistics show, however, is quite the opposite. In fact the loans made by the Bank of Japan vary with the increases and decreases in the loans made by the city banks. If these loans were made as cash reserves to meet the necessities of deposits withdrawals, we would expect the loans made by the Bank of Japan to vary with the increases and decreases in deposits.

In sum, the formula under which funds are supplied by loans made by the Bank of Japan is a mechanism by which investment funds are supplied at comparatively low rates of interest, principally to the city banks. Because of this mechanism the Japanese productive potential has been correspondingly nurtured and strengthened. The Bank of Japan usually gives the impression that it is critical of the policy of rapid economic growth, but the actual state of its business must be said to be a good deal at variance with this impression.

The lending of immense sums at low rates of interest by the Bank of Japan may, in itself, be a factor provoking over-investment. Along with the size of these loans from the Bank of Japan, what is important is the formula for the allocation of these loans among the city banks. What is at issue is the actual state of selective loans of the Bank of Japan. The selective loans of the Bank of Japan are one of the measures for financial control taken by the Bank of Japan as a result of a low-interest policy having been in effect consistently since the war, regardless of the demand for funds, and the fact that the demand-adjusting functions of interest rates have not been in operation. Practically nothing is known, however, about the actual state of the loans, and in particular about standards laid down by the Bank of Japan itself. For this reason, in the present study we are left no alternative but to infer the practices and standards of selection from the figures for loans from the Bank of Japan by the principal city banks as given in the Negotiable Securities Reports.

From Table 10 it is clear (1) that there has recently been a sharp rise in the degree of dependence on the Bank of Japan by the principal banks; (2) that on the whole these banks seem to receive loans from the Bank of Japan in proportion to their deposits, but that the Mitsui Bank and the Dai-Ichi Bank are exceptional throughout, and show a distinctly higher degree of dependence on the Bank of Japan; and (3) that if anything, at least as

Table 10. Borrowings from the Bank of Japan by Principal City Banks

	September 1960		March 1961		September 1961	
Banks	Borrowings from the Bank of Japan (million yen)	Degree of dependence * on the Bank of Japan (percent)	Borrowings from the Bank of Japan (million yen)	Degree of dependence on the Bank of Japan (percent)	Borrowings from the Bank of Japan (million yen)	Degree of dependence on the Bank of Japan (percent)
Fuji	32,791	4.86	48,424	6.32	97,657	12.39
Mitsubishi	30,882	4.78	53,524	7.31	84,570	11.05
Sanwa	34,993	5.62	57,235	8.11	97,488	13.48
Sumitomo	32,095	5.26	54,956	7.97	93,813	13.03
Mitsui	39,528	10.32	58,994	13.00	101,510	21.42
Dai-Ichi	34,646	8.59	50,762	11.08	86,277	18.44
All City Banks	392,176	7.51	573,049	9.64	965,218	15.69

SOURCE: Compiled from Negotiable Securities Reports and *Hompō keizai tōkei*.
*The degree of dependence on the Bank of Japan here means borrowings from the Bank of Japan over deposits.

far as the six great banks listed in the table are concerned, the absolute sums borrowed from the Bank of Japan by these banks, including those with comparatively few deposits, such as the Mitsui Bank and the Dai-Ichi Bank, are roughly of the same order in all cases, being balanced at around ¥30,000 million in September 1960, around ¥50,000 million in March 1961, and roughly ¥90,000 million in September 1961.

Thus, the standards of the selective loans of the Bank of Japan would appear to have been governed to a marked degree by a formula providing for fixed sum loans distributed on an equal basis among the principal banks, rather than providing for fixed levels proportionate to the ability of each of the city banks to comply with requests for funds. We may call this the principle of equality among the *keiretsu* as revealed in the loans made by the Bank of Japan.

In this way this principle of equality, linked with the pipe lines of the powerful banks, has become "built-in" as one of the principle institutional factors in investment behavior aiming at set control by the *keiretsu*.

The Formula for Foreign Exchange Control

It is not only the Bank of Japan's formula for the supply of funds that has been operating under the principle of equality among the *keiretsu,* a special policy aiming at nurturing Japan's productive potential. This has also been the case as regards the formula for foreign exchange control in Japan since the war.

In accordance with the Dodge Line, a policy arrived at in 1949 with the aim of arresting inflation, the multiple exchange rates hitherto in use were unified in a single rate of $1=¥360. Many people cried out that this was a revival of the laws of value. In fact, however, a revival of the laws of value in their complete form was not envisaged. The domestic price system was not directly tied up to the international price system. This was because at the end of 1949, the year in which the Dodge Line came into effect, a Foreign Exchange and Foreign Trade Control Law was passed, and under it powerful controls over trade and exchange were imposed.

1. As a general principle exports were free, but the foreign exchange obtained from exports had to be sold to a foreign exchange bank within 10 days. This restriction of foreign exchange holding was an indispensable condition for the implementation of the trade and exchange controls set out below.

2. In order to use effectively the limited ability to import, the foreign exchange budgeting system and the foreign exchange quota system were instituted and every effort was made to repress imports of finished goods, particularly imports of products which would threaten domestic production. On the other hand, an exchange control system based on the assumption that only indispensables should be imported was put into effect with a view to nurturing domestic productive capacity. As a result of these measures the principal articles imported were technology, machines, and raw materials.

There is no doubt that this exchange control system was clearly devised and operated with a view to protecting and nurturing domestic productive potential. Speaking generally, when work is to begin on a new undertaking reliance on technical research the outcome of which is uncertain involves many dangers for the success of the enterprise. Rather than doing this, the more use that can be made of technology which is already in a completed state and which also provides ample prospects from the point of view of paying its way, the more profitable it will be. Further, this new technology will be all the more profitable if the importation of finished goods from abroad is stopped until the technology is fully introduced in enterprises at home.

The postwar exchange control system had the target of catching up with international levels of technology at the earliest possible date, and, as we have seen above, was operated from the point of view of nurturing domestic productive potential. But a closer examination reveals that it was not merely a policy for nurturing domestic productive potential. Just as the Bank of Japan's formula for the supply of funds was a special policy aiming at nurturing domestic productive potential and strongly colored by the principle of equality among the *keiretsu,* so, too, did the exchange control system have its own special coloring.

As an example, let us consider the strip-mill revolution in Japan. In 1950, as a result of the First Rationalization and the Second Rationalization

Plan which followed it, Japan became the second-largest owner of strip mills (rolling mills) in the world, following only the United States. The firms to which licences were issued by the Ministry of International Trade and Industry when the technology was introduced included Yawata Iron & Steel, Fuji Iron & Steel, Nippon Kokan (Fuji Bank *keiretsu*), Kawasaki Steel (Dai-Ichi Bank *keiretsu*), Nakayama Steel (Sanwa Bank *keiretsu*), Nisshin Steel (former Nippon Iron & Steel *keiretsu*), as well as Tokai Iron & Steel (Fuji Iron & Steel *keiretsu*), Sumitomo Metal Industries (Sumitomo Bank *keiretsu*), Kobe Steel (Dai-Ichi Bank *keiretsu*), and so on—a large number of enterprises belonging to the various principal *keiretsu*.

Thus, in the case of the exchange control system operated from the point of view of nurturing domestic productive potential, too, we have strong evidence of the influence of the principle of equality among the *keiretsu*. This is found not only in the case of the strip mill. We can point out clear evidence of this "principle of equality among the *keiretsu*" in all the cases of the introduction of technology from abroad in the process of technical innovation which has taken place since the war.

If the policy of nurturing domestic productive potential in the capital technological aspects had not taken the form of "the principle of equality among the *keiretsu*" in this way and if funds had been manipulated so that investment was made selectively, synthetic fiber manufacture being attached mainly to the Mitsui *keiretsu,* the electronic industries mainly to the Mitsubishi *keiretsu,* thermo-electricity mainly to the Hitachi *keiretsu,* the ammonia industry mainly to the Sumitomo *keiretsu,* and the oil-chemicals and atomic energy industries being carried on under government management, the investment behavior aiming at set control by the *keiretsu* to which we have drawn attention above would, of course, not have taken place. Through this exchange control system, which was operated so that profitable investment opportunities were given to all the *keiretsu* indiscriminately, the system of set control by the *keiretsu* was strengthened still further.

What emerges from the above analysis would seem to be that the Bank of Japan's formula for the supply of funds and the Ministry of International Trade and Industry's exchange control formula were both operated with the target of nurturing domestic productive potential from the point of view of capital funds and technology, but that in substance they formed an integral part of the system for the strengthening of *keiretsu* control, deeply colored by "the principle of equality among the *keiretsu*."

The principal enjoyers of this equality of opportunity were the enterprises belonging to the *keiretsu,* and it need scarcely be noted that a fairly clearly defined difference could be observed between the enterprises which were members of *keiretsu* and those which were not. The fact that the Bank of Japan loans in particular were, on the whole, limited to the city banks would also seem to demonstrate this. Herein we may find the third characteristic of the postwar Japanese economy.

The Key to the Secret of the Rapid Economic Growth

Let us now summarize the argument which we have developed at some length above. We have made clear the following three points as constituting the key to the secret of the high growth rate of the Japanese economy since the war, particularly from 1955 to about 1960:

1. The establishment of special indirect financing possessing the attributes of "*keiretsu* financing" to a high degree.
2. The investment behavior by which each *keiretsu* sought to gain control of a complete set of the new industries.
3. The Bank of Japan's formula for the supply of funds and the formula for foreign exchange control which operated in such manner as to give profitable investment opportunities to all the *keiretsu* indiscriminately.

We cannot, of course, provide an all-embracing explanation of postwar Japan's economic growth with the help of these three characteristics alone. Nevertheless, we may say that at least insofar as we focus our attention on entrepreneurial behavior in postwar Japan these three characteristics constitute an important key to the secret of the high economic growth rate. As we have already made clear, what particularly excites our attention is the fact that these three characteristics are not discrete and unrelated factors but have mutually promoted the organization of enterprises in the *keiretsu* form in the postwar Japanese economy. We may describe the situation by saying that the process of rapid growth itself was nothing other than this organization in *keiretsu,* the form in which new groups of enterprises were organized.

Assuredly these groups of enterprises made frenzied efforts in equipment investment, intending to get practically all the principal new industries into their hands on the basis of funds collected from the pipe lines of the powerful financial *keiretsu,* so that they might strengthen their control. However, since this kind of investment activity was carried on simultaneously and in parallel form in a fair number of *keiretsu* it produced "excessive competition" with regard to the structure of the market in each industry, although it occasioned immense accumulations of capital in each of the *keiretsu.* If anything, the result produced was that the more capital concentration by the *keiretsu* advanced, the more the concentration of production declined. In this three-dimensional structure of the rapid economic growth, organization in *keiretsu,* and excessive competition, we may find the important characteristics of the postwar Japanese economy.

Finnish Regional Development Policy

PEKKA LAHIKAINEN

In comparison with most industrialized countries regional development policy is a relatively recent innovation in Finland. While there have been various government measures affecting some development regions dating back over several decades, a collection of unco-ordinated measures does not constitute a deliberate regional development policy. The legislation on development regions passed in 1966 and other suggestions of the advisory committee appointed to study these problems, above all those concerning the improvement of vocational training in the development regions, constituted the first efforts to create a genuine regional development policy. The legislation defined the borders of the development regions and divided them into two zones in addition to stipulating, with certain conditions, tax reliefs and interest subsidies to be granted to enterprises investing in these areas. At the same time the Regional Development Board was founded to formulate regional development policy. The Board includes representatives of the state and various development regions and interest groups. In May 1969 the Board completed its proposal for a new comprehensive plan for regional development policy. The measures suggested were divided according to their effects on three groups—manpower, enterprises, and the community. The measures in the last mentioned category were aimed at improving the level of services in the area and the operational prerequisites of enterprises. It also recommended that growth center policy be integrated with over-all regional development policy. The major part of the Board's proposals has already been embodied in legislation.

Low productivity is a major problem in the Finnish development regions; this is a result of the dominant role of primary production on the one hand and slow structural change on the other. As the rate of growth is slow the release of labor from agriculture results in unemployment and migration of the population to other areas. These problems are further reflected in a low income level and vastly unequal income distribution. The primary aim of the regional development policy is to accelerate structural change in the region's economy. Productive resources should be channeled into the fast growing and competitive industries, which are more capable of absorbing manpower released from the traditional sectors of the economy.

Apart from measures of fiscal and industrial policies, an active manpower policy is also being pursued to attain these targets. Efforts are being directed toward increasing inter-occupational and inter-regional mobility of labor. In addition steps must be taken to encourage the emergence of

Reprinted from the *Bank of Finland Monthly Bulletin,* February 1970, pp. 20–23, by permission of the publisher.

population centers for the acceleration of structural change necessitates that resources be channeled into population centers with an infrastructure sufficiently large and diversfied to support services. The expansion of the centers and the concentration of operations will result in substantial economies of scale. The bigger the center, the greater is the supply of labor and its degree of diversification and the larger is the market especially for consumer products, raw materials, and semi-finished products. In addition, the cost of creating and maintaining the infrastructure of a population center is relatively less expensive for a large center.

The new legislation divided the less-developed regions into two zones according to the degree of backwardness. Only the southern and southwestern parts of the country were left outside these zones (see map). The borders of the regions and zones were determined on the basis of a study measuring the stage of development of the area around the population center and using 34 variables.

Measures directed toward labor aim at improving the competitiveness of the population, especially the youth, of the development areas. Raising the level of education in development regions attracts enterprising activity and provides better opportunities for those moving from these regions to the other parts of the country.

The most important in this group of policy measures, and one of the most important in the whole regional development policy, is the improvement of vocational training in development regions. The new legislation provides for substantial allowances to the municipalities for the maintenance of vocational schools. A further need is for a more developed employment service and improved vocational guidance. Steps have already been taken to improve vocational course activity and to enlarge the migration subsidies for labor.

Measures affecting enterprises are intended to improve the regional distribution of productive activity. For this purpose tax reliefs are granted to manufacturing enterprises, small workshop businesses, peat industry, fish cultivation, nurseries, market gardening, and breeding animals for fur. For small workshop businesses to receive this type of support their production must exceed a stated minimum level. All these firms enjoy the right of free depreciation in the year of acquisition and for nine subsequent years as regards establishing, expanding or renewing productive capacity for the part of fixed assets. This concession, however, does not involve exemption from tax but only the postponement of tax liability to help the firm over the initial difficulties in getting established.

Apart from this, the above-mentioned enterprises situated in the first zone of development regions are in fact granted an extra 30 percent depreciation regarding the acquisition of fixed assets, which is to be effected by writing off an extra 3 percent over 10 years.

Fixed assets purchased for the establishment, expansion or renewal of an enterprise shall not be counted as property in either income or property

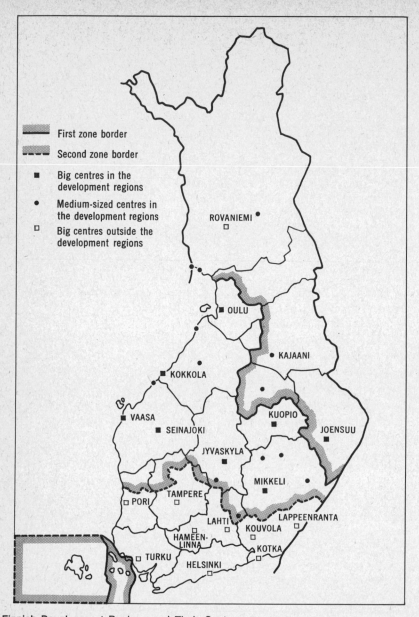

ROVANIEMI

OULU

KAJAANI

KOKKOLA

VAASA

SEINAJOKI

KUOPIO

JOENSUU

JYVASKYLA

MIKKELI

PORI

TAMPERE

LAHTI

LAPPEENRANTA

KOUVOLA

HAMEEN-LINNA

KOTKA

TURKU

HELSINKI

Finnish Development Regions and Their Centers.

taxation for a period of ten years following their adoption. Further, these firms cannot be subject to discretionary municipal taxation over the same period. New enterprises in development regions also enjoy certain reliefs in regard to stamp duties.

The most important of the direct measures applied is the special credit system for development regions. The state subsidizes interest payable on development region credits in order to aid firms immediately after their establishment, or for a short period subsequent to a major investment project. Thus the credit system, which is applied to the same group of enterprises which enjoy tax reliefs, complements the effects of the latter. In addition, these credits are available for tourist industry enterprises, for example, hotels, motels, holiday villages. Interest subsidies are paid on credit obtained from the regular money market. The subsidy is 100 percent and 80 percent in the first and second zones respectively of the interest charged by the credit institutions for two years subsequent to the investment. For the two following years the subsidies are 50 percent and 40 percent respectively.

The following example illustrates how the position of an entrepreneur is affected by the interest subsidies. Assume that a 1,000 mark credit is granted both in the first and second zone, with a loan period of 10 years, annual amortization of 100 marks, and an interest rate of 8 percent throughout the loan period. Of the total interest expenses of 440 marks in the first zone the state pays 212 marks, and in the second zone the corresponding subsidy is 169.6 marks. The entrepreneur thus has to defray 4.1 percent in the first zone and 4.9 percent in the second zone of the 8 percent interest charged by the credit institution.

There is a stipulation in the law that provides for a further differentiation of two development zones; development credit may total 60 percent of the total investment in the first zone and 50 percent in the second. The example did not take account of this stipulation. An issue of bonds or debentures may, according to the law, be included in development region credits as well as a direct loan from abroad.

It was proposed in the report of the Regional Development Board that the conditions for obtaining a state guarantee for the loans be made easier for the entrepreneurs. Because the diversification of productive activity in development regions is hampered by low entrepreneurial drive and inexperienced management, the Board also recommended improvements in the educational system and advisory services available to entrepreneurs.

As regards the Finnish growth center policy the following outlines may be given here. Policy measures affecting the development of the community are intended to increase the well-being of the population by providing more diversified services, creating employment, and improving the facilities for education. A concomitant development is a more favorable climate for enterprising activity. The suggestions of the Board, for example, town planning and the expansion of the telephone network. It was emphasized in the relevant government bill that infrastructure investment should be geared to creating sufficiently large and efficient operational units. This is possible only if investment is focused, as much as possible, in centers with adequate growth potential. Optimal-sized units and efficient investment will result in a decline in unit costs, and the consumers will benefit from this in the form of lower tariffs and tax rates.

The policy measures affecting the enterprises do not favor the population centers at the expense of rural areas, that is the tax reliefs and interest subsidies are the same for both. On the other hand, it is the intention to make the centers attractive for enterprises and manpower. The implementation of the growth center policy depends greatly on future investment decisions by the state and the cabinet. The growth of the population centers could be accelerated, for example, by granting them housing loans and by linking them to the automatic telephone network. The Regional Development Board has made a report on the prospects of the population centers serving as growth centers. The nine largest centers proved to have the best prospects for future growth and hence to form a counterbalance to the dominance of Helsinki (see map). A comparison between 13 medium-sized centers having reached the status of a town revealed that the aim of having the same level of services throughout the country has not yet been reached. Below this group there is a category of 47 smaller centers. Their development is also dependent on the improvement of services and their environment, and it is planned that they should form service centers only, to contribute to the aim of equalizing the level of services throughout the country.

Discussion Questions

1. What are the sources of Japan's "miraculous" postwar growth record?
2. The term "Japan, Inc." has been used to describe the total involvement of the Japanese in generating growth. Would you find such an economic philosophy appealing in the case of the United States?
3. What are the main features of regional economic policy in Finland?
4. If you were a U.S. policy maker, what would you recommend for the development of America's economically deprived regions, such as Appalachia?

2 MICROECONOMICS

Decision Making
by the Firm

In the United States, corporate decision making is confined to a small, well-defined group. This group is comprised of salaried managers, men who usually have degrees in business administration, engineering or law. They decide what the firm will produce, how much it will produce, how it will market its product, how much capital investment will be made, and so on. In short, a group of experts decides how the firm will allocate its resources. The decisions made by these managers are then executed by the firm's workers. The latter have no voice in the decision-making process. Thus American workers do not participate in the decisions that effect a very important part of their lives.

This manager-worker dichotomy does not exist everywhere. Several countries have legally embodied different forms of industrial democracy. The two selections below describe the decison-making process involving workers in Yugoslavia and West Germany. In the former, workers councils—involving management by workers—came into being in 1950, while the West German variation, known as codetermination, became law in 1951. It is important to note that the phenomenon of industrial democracy is not simply confined to socialist Yugoslavia, but is also part of the basic social fabric of capitalist West Germany.

Heinz Hartmann is Professor of Sociology at the University of Muenster. Aleksander Bajt is affiliated with the University of Ljubljana in Yugoslavia.

Codetermination in West Germany

HEINZ HARTMANN

Codetermination, West Germany's contribution to participatory democracy in industry, represents an elaborate and sturdy scheme. Legally enacted in the early fifties, codetermination has stood up to all kinds of tests and has become entrenched as a social institution. With the West German economy apparently unharmed by codetermination, this particular design for employee participation in management has attracted a great deal of attention from observers in similar economies who wondered whether perhaps the German case might hold some answers to their own problems.

It is unfortunate for such outsiders that codetermination has some paradoxical features which make it difficult to reach a balanced judgment. The very coexistence of a capitalist credo and extensive concessions to trade union influence confronts us with a basic paradox which is compounded by other, secondary contradictions. Some executives were instrumental in introducing codetermination, while many workers seemed fairly indifferent. The most recent paradox was added by the ascendancy to power of a coalition of Socialist and Free Democrats after the Parliamentary elections in September 1969. While everybody vainly expected the Social Democrats to expand on codetermination, it now appears that such initiative might well come from the ranks of the conservative opposition.

Why has codetermination succeeded as a social experiment? How radical is it? What makes it function? What are the frictions, tensions, and conflicts besetting codetermination in action? How do different groups feel about its consequences? Will codetermination spread? What is its promise for the future? This article will briefly set forth the mechanics of codetermination, its objectives, accomplishments, weaknesses, and prospects for the next three to five years. There is no room here, regrettably, to look into the comparative aspects of this peculiar German institution.

Mechanics

Codetermination in its most stringent form originated in an effort on the part of some top executives to resist the early dismantling drives of the occupation powers. These industrialists offered various plans for labor participation in management in order to win trade union support. The idea of industrial democracy, of course, had well-established roots in the history of the German labor movement. Steps toward a legal consolidation of informal gains and toward formal prescriptions beyond such advance led to the Codetermination Law of 1951. The Law applied to the coal, iron, and

Reprinted from *Industrial Relations,* February 1970, pp. 137–147, by permission of the publisher and author.

steel companies. Among other provisions it stipulated that half the seats on the supervisory board (roughly corresponding to the board of directors of a United States company) should be allocated to employee representatives and that the executive committees should include a "labor director." The supervisory boards were to be chaired by one "neutral," not party to either management or labor. In addition the Law gave new powers to works councils, including the right to participate in some major management decisions. (Work councils in Germany consist of representatives of blue-collar and white-collar workers. Usually these representatives are trade unionists, but they are not formally bound to follow union instructions. It is from the ranks of such councils that most of the employee members of the supervisory board are recruited.)

The labor director, often considered the symbol of codetermination, is appointed by the supervisory board from a trade union slate which, as a rule, is a product of joint deliberations between representatives of the employees of the specific company and representatives of the national trade unions (which in Germany, contrary to United States practice, are not officially organized on the company level). The labor director is a full-fledged member of the executive committee, that is, his responsibility and privileges are not limited to his prime functions of personnel administration and social services but extend to general management.

In 1952, one year after the passage of the Codetermination Law the West German Parliament passed a new law pertaining to industries other than coal, iron, and steel. Although this legislation, the Works Constitution Law, was intended by the trade unions to extend codetermination beyond its early confines, their new effort failed. The Law provided for increased powers of the works council and, among other things, required supervisory boards to reserve one-third of their seats for employee representatives. By comparison to the former state of affairs, organized labor had improved its position. But, if the Works Constitution Law produced codetermination outside of the coal and steel industries it was a highly diluted version of employee control, and the trade unions soon became dissatisfied with this much weaker form of employee participation.

Some observers felt that the 1952 Law contained elements of a Phyrric victory. Not only had political conservatives managed to keep these more recent demands well under the level of the Codetermination Law, but the unions also discovered that they had weakened their position by increasing the powers of nonunion agencies. In particular, the strengthening of the works councils without parallel re-enforcement of formal union controls worked against the trade unions. Now it was the councils rather than union officers which seemed to strive for and win concessions from management. Seeds were laid to rivalry between these two forms of employee representation, and some observers felt that the unions had pulled the rug out from under themselves.

The following years saw tenacious efforts by the trade unions to improve their legislative success of 1951. But progress has been an uphill struggle. In

1955, Parliament passed a Personnel Representation Law which introduced some employee participation into decision making in public administration. One year later, a new law subjected holding companies in the coal and steel industry to codetermination. But provisions here were less advantageous to organized labor than in operating companies. Then, many mergers in the coal and steel industries between 1952 and 1968 reduced the number of companies subject to codetermination by more than one-third. The union therefore fought for and managed to conclude an agreement with the respective employers' associations which allowed all supervisory boards and labor directors to continue to function in a minor form in spite of mergers. Finally, Parliament was induced to intervene in one crucial case where a very large firm under codetermination threatened to change its industrial classification because of diversification. For a transitional period of five years, this company continues to be treated as part of the coal and steel industries.

Most campaigns were in the nature of salvage operations; they were to rescue union influence from unfavorable developments in the economy. In the middle of 1969, however, one important event played into the hands of codetermination. The critical state of the German coal industry resulted in many mines being fused into one consolidated company which now includes 94 percent of the productive capacity in mining. Initially, this merger meant the displacement or rather functional demotion of 28 labor directors. However, since the coal miners' union had played an important role in the creation of the consolidated firm, its position was strengthened. Current plans call for establishing a hierarchy of labor directors from the holding company down to individual mines or smaller units of operation. Estimates are that there will be 50 or 60 such positions.

These new labor directors will have responsibility for a broad range of personnel and social problems. By contrast to former labor directors, who often relied on their own resources, this particular group will build on an elaborate system of staff support. Even more important for union influence, these labor directors may also win jurisdiction over management ranks. Instead of being subject to special personnel offices outside union control, members of management may now become subject to powerful labor directors.

German partisans of codetermination sought to extend these institutional arrangements in the mining industry to other industries. Small wonder that their efforts met with strong opposition. Yet before looking into the politics of codetermination tomorrow, brief comments are in order as to its present objectives.

Objectives

The idea of employee representation has extensive roots in history and strong affinities to Christian, Marxist, and corporate capitalist thought. Yet many societies have found other answers to this problem than the solution practiced in Germany, and some have not felt any strong need to establish employee representation at all. What are the forces then, conceptual and pragmatic, which created this peculiarly advanced system of participatory democracy in industry?

One strong argument emerged soon after World War II. At that time, German trade unions agreed with many other critics that "industry had helped Hitler into the saddle." They concluded that industry, especially the powerful enterprises in mining and steel, should be subjected to some form of popular control. If socialization was out of the question, at least representatives of democratic persuasion should exercise a watchdog function in managerial bodies. Never again should industrialists be allowed to support or subsidize a nationalist, let alone a Nazi, party.

Over the years, this argument waned and changed in character. Since the German party system offered no nationalist option, political surveillance proved unnecessary. But the trade unions increasingly made more of the argument that large enterprises should be open to public control, because of their general social relevance. Without launching a frontal attack on capitalism, owners were reminded of the social responsibilities inherent in private property; and in the eyes of the trade unions, codetermination presented a promising way of making certain that such responsibilities would not be shirked. The recent efforts of organized labor are directed toward extending codetermination to the 400 largest companies outside the coal and steel industries (which account for roughly 70 percent of total industrial sales).

A second major argument relates to industrial democracy. The concern here is for the position of the individual employee and his relationship to the company hierarchy and the society at large. Prior to World War II, authority patterns in the mining industry were paramilitary and worse, and several of the very large steel companies were controlled by notorious autocrats whose highhanded ways of dealing with underlings set the leadership style for the rest of management. Democratization here meant a showing of respect for employees and allowing them the opportunity to appeal decisions and exert influence.

Over time this program took on diffuse features. It was re-enforced by complaints about the alienation of modern man from the products of his labor and from himself. Recent socialist proposals have tended to treat the industrial firm as a formal political system, with employees representing their own constituency within a management-government. Other arguments related to society at large. Industry was to be attuned to the democratic patterns set in other sectors of society and vice versa. Plant democracy was seen as introducing employees to democracy in general.

Interestingly, at least in the early postwar period, the strongest ideological arguments did not come from trade unions or the Social Democratic Party. Rather, it was the Catholic wing of organized labor and its intellectual promoters who looked upon codetermination as a basic social issue of moral and philosophic consequence. According to one source, the ideo-logical underpinnings of codetermination were provided not by Karl Marx but by Wallraff and Nell-Breuning, two Catholic professors who are quick to quote papal encyclicals and Vatican pronouncements. To date, they are the driving force behind demands for more codetermination on the part of the Social Committees *(Sozialausschuesse)* of the Christian Democrats. Their reasoning revolves around the relative merits of labor and capital. Some Catholics consider these factors of production as ethically equal, other members of the Catholic labor movement argue that labor is of more value than capital. From these premises, they deduce organizational consequences. Nell-Breuning advocates reversing the distribution of power on the super-visory boards; this would mean "two-thirds of the seats for labor, one-third for capital."

Finally, codetermination is vested with the ultimate objective of safe-guarding socio-economic stability and growth. This pragmatic goal has been emphasized in response to recent crises, problems of adaptation, and changes in technology and economics. It has been claimed, for instance, that in the iron and steel industries codetermination prevented trouble during a 10 percent reduction in the labor force; at the time, 1964, the representa-tives of labor were able to convey to their electorate convincing reasons for this drastic cut-back and to forestall wildcat strikes and breaches of com-pany discipline. Similarly, codetermination is credited with a calming effect when the labor force was reduced in mining (a labor force which was de-pressed even further when many inefficient mines had to be closed). Naturally, employee representatives not only mediated in the name of tech-nical and economic rationality, but also asked for an achieved tangible concession to cushion the results of layoffs, firings, and displacement.

Achievements

To what extent can we prove the success of codetermination—if any? Attempts at objective evaluation will have to proceed through a thicket of claims and counterclaims, and there is no guarantee of a definite conclusion. The president of the mine workers' union recently maintained: "There would have been killings and assaults if, during the times of crisis of the coal industry, codetermination would have been missing from this industry. It was only because of codetermination that we were able to channel the emergent radicalism." Over four weeks later, however, extensive wildcat strikes occurred throughout Germany, and there were voices attributing these spontaneous demonstrations to the "procrastination" caused by the codetermination decision-making process.

Assessing the achievements of codetermination represents a problem of discouraging complexity and scope. Whether West Germany has been spared a class struggle because of codetermination, whether the individual worker has won or lost opportunities to make his influence felt, whether the competitive standing of the industries concerned has improved or declined are difficult questions. Not only do verdicts depend on who judges what; there also is the well-known problem of isolating causes and effects. And there are few data available comparing codetermination industries with other industries.

A few hard facts have been established. For one, authority relationships in the coal and steel industries have "softened," property rights have become less significant, and social services have been improved. Secondly, employees obviously feel satisfied with codetermination as an institution. These are no mean accomplishments, especially when balanced against the apparent failure of the Works Constitution Law. The latter contained such weak requirements, such loopholes, and lack of sanctions that unco-operative employers were able to escape with a minimum of concessions.

However, as soon as one approaches intricate questions and nuances of judgment, the answers become more subjective and highly controversial. What of the effects of codetermination on managerial decision making? Critics have often charged that the participation of employee representatives not only slows down the decision-making process, but also leads to a corruption of task orientation by political considerations (to horse-trading instead of optimal solutions). It is here that the specific effects of codetermination are hard to demonstrate. Under the sponsorship of the former German government, a commission of experts was put to work to determine, among other things, how decisions in fact evolve under codetermination. To date, no report has been published. But there is nothing in the commission's tentative conclusions to substantiate the criticisms. On the contrary, many observers quote instances where companies have profited by having employee representatives participate in decision making.

Employees are convinced that codetermination has been a success. Almost all respondents to a representative survey conducted in 1968 among employees in the coal and steel industries, reported that codetermination is providing them with advantages: better social services (51 percent), higher wages and salaries (22 percent), improved working conditions (8 percent), increased influence in personnel and business policies (6 percent), and job security (4 percent). Outside of this select group of supposed beneficiaries, positive opinions on codetermination are less frequent: only one in every five Germans and one in every three employees is impressed with codetermination.

Weaknesses

Opinion polls reveal that there are serious obstacles to the popular acceptance of codetermination. While many respondents, especially those in industries under codetermination, are satisfied with present arrangements, they are not exactly anxious to expand the system. In those large-scale enterprises which are the trade unions' next codetermination targets, employees are concerned with more urgent issues—primarily inflation. Next in rank are four other concerns (including the fairly "hopeless" item of German reunification), and it is only somewhere lower on this scale that respondents express a desire for the introduction of codetermination into their industries. Finally, a representative survey of all employees in West Germany showed even less popular support for the expansion of codetermination; the item dropped to eighth, trailing a series of more urgent preferences: full employment, improvement of pensions, higher wages, better education, and others. Incidentally, the question of codetermination was given equal weight by union and nonunion respondents.

Opponents of codetermination are quick to link this lagging support to what they consider another weakness: the social distance between employees and their representatives. As was indicated before, German trade unions are not organized on the company level; their administrative base is the district. Trade union officers, so the argument runs, are of necessity remote from problems in the plant, and their representatives in the company are spokesmen of an outside organization rather than of employees proper. It is true that the labor director in the coal and steel industries is a union candidate, that unions nominate more than half of the employee representatives on the supervisory board, and that other employee nominees for the board who are to be proposed by the works council must be cleared by the trade unions. This lopsided union influence appears to conflict with the fact that most employees think of codetermination as involving their own participation in managerial decision making, while only a very small percentage considers codetermination as a matter of trade unions standing in for those employed in the respective firm. On the other hand, these opinions may imply an argument against the alleged alienation of union representatives and employees.

Another alleged weakness has more complex ramifications: the divided loyalties of the labor directors who are pledged to protect employee interests but are at the same time, full-fledged members of management. Even if these labor directors could master the schizophrenic skills of keeping the two sets of interests separately, there are fears that labor directors will be torn by irreconcilable conflicts, will subconsciously accept management as their reference group, or will yield to the temptations of material privileges. The labor director's conflict is occasionally compounded by the fact that he is delegated to represent management in collective bargaining or is commissioned by his management colleagues to win the approval of his clientele to mass layoffs and shutdowns. Even if the large majority of labor directors has successfully met such stress, it is obvious that this dual allegiance does constitute a built-in weakness of codetermination.

A final shortcoming of codetermination is that the powers of the trade unions on the supra-company level are fairly limited. For decades, organized labor has vied for more influence at the level of the entire economy, seeking joint representation, for example, with employers and the government in a steering and planning body on the federal level. The absence of such a superstructure is a handicap when opposition at this higher level impedes the enforcement, let alone the expansion, of codetermination. German trade unions have had to accept such opposition for so long that they have hardly found it worthwhile to make it an issue. It was only recently, however, that this weakness was thrown into stark relief when the electoral success of the Social Democrats raised hopes for governmental support of codetermination but objections from the minority partner in the current coalition dashed these expectations.

Prospects

During the months preceding the September 1969 federal elections, the Social Democrats, along with the trade unions, made a number of legislative proposals to consolidate and extend codetermination as well as to strengthen and expand the procedures under the Works Constitution Law. While part of this was election propaganda, there is no doubt that these brothers-in-arms thought the time ripe for new advances in employee participation. They were responding to a pervasive mood in German society for more democracy in formal organizations. Not even the more conservative Christian Democrats (CDU) could remain immune from this general feeling. The CDU confirmed its acceptance of codetermination as currently enacted and declared itself willing to discuss limited additions.

The elections then turned the CDU out of power and made possible a coalition of SPD and Free Democrats (FDP), a liberal party left of center. Since the SPD needed the FDP to gain a precarious majority of 12 votes in Parliament, the Free Democrats found themselves with considerable bargaining power in shaping the platform of the new government (in spite of their almost fatal losses at the polls). One issue on which they felt strongly was codetermination, and they were able to make their views binding on the new coalition. The FDP backs a program of rather modest intent and proportions. It is opposed to any extension of codetermination as practiced in the coal and steel industries. In their eyes, this system offers too much power to outside functionaries and not enough opportunities for control by employees. In order to increase the exercise of such direct employee influence, they recommend reforming the Works Constitution Law, which on the whole is much more employee-oriented than the Codetermination Law. In particular, they intend to redesign and activate the economic committee, a group staffed by equal portions of managers and employees. To date, very few of these committees, which were meant to disseminate information, ever accomplished even this limited objective. The program of the FDP also includes the introduction of "youth representatives," awarding training time for those active in the interests of employees, and protecting minority groups in the company.

The acceptance of this fairly timid program by the SPD threw organized labor into this quandary: Should unions continue to sound their trumpets lest their cause be without voice or should they turn quiet to aid a new government which on the whole feels much more partial toward labor? There has been much wavering in the union camp. On some occasions, high ranking union officials affirmed that more codetermination would remain a high priority item on their agenda. The president of the single most powerful union, the metal workers' organization, late in 1969 maintained that the new government would expand codetermination. On balance, however, organized labor is unlikely to jeopardize the political wing of the labor movement now in power.

Ironically the present impasse may be broken by an initiative of the Parliamentary opposition. The social committees (*Sozialausschuesse*) of the CDU, largely staffed by ideologically minded Catholics ardently favoring codetermination, now may be released from the leash of the conservative majority of their own party and given leeway long enough to embarrass the coalition government. If they should propose advances in participatory democracy which would go beyond the FDP program, the SPD might be forced to renounce its coalition agreement. There is some evidence that the Social Democrats would welcome such a pretext to escape the restraining ties of their junior partner. But if the opposition remains satisfied to see extension of codetermination thwarted by the FDP, then the following four years will see nothing but some elaboration of the Works Constitution Law and the Personnel Representation Law.

Conclusion

Presently, the unions' optimal opportunities lie in the ongoing reorganization of the German mining industry now consolidated into one giant company. The mining union has had considerable influence on this process from the very beginning, and it has been able to secure privileges for itself and for the union representatives in this company which go significantly beyond the prerogatives so far available under codetermination. This holds true for the functional differentiation of the office of labor director, the hierarchical extension of this office over several levels, and the availability of expert staffs. If these achievements can be held and refined, then the next big campaign to spread codetermination can proceed at a much more advanced level than would be possible now. There is a good deal of hope among many partisans of codetermination that this campaign will be launched, at the latest, four years from now when the Social Democrats promise to do even better at the polls than last September.

Decentralized Decision-Making Structure in the Yugoslav Economy

ALEKSANDER BAJT

Development of Decision-Making Structure

The development and operation of any modern national economy is the result of a multitude of decisions constantly being made in the economy. There exists great variety among individual national economies as to the structure of this decision making. Three properties of decision making are particularly important: (1) the degree of centralization or decentralization, (2) the way in which central decisions are conceived, and (3) the manner in which central decisions are put into effect.

The first property gives us three models of decision making—the anarchic, the decentralized, and the centralized ones. In the anarchic decision model, there is no decision center on the level of national economy; all decisions are made by not consciously co-ordinated individual economic units, enterprises and households. In the centralized decision model there is only one decision center, individual economic units having only to execute what is stipulated by the decision center. In the decentralized decision model, there are central decision bodies, but they limit their decision activity to what is necessary for the co-ordination of private preferences.

The second property gives us two models of decision making, the democratic and the autocratic ones. In the first one, economic units (enterprises and households) are the sole original decision makers, central decision bodies having only derived or delegated decision making power. In the second one, central decision bodies appropriate autonomous rights in decision making, independent of individual economic units, and superimposed upon them.

The third property gives us two more models of decision making, the direct and the indirect ones. In the first model, the central decision bodies secure, with direct and *in concreto* decisions, the implementation of central decisions. In the indirect one, they induce or stimulate the implementation of central decisions by establishing and quantifying the so-called regulators. Individual economic units are free to choose between alternatives. They take regulators as factors of maximization of their income (profit). By choosing the maximum income path, they choose it on the basis of regulators, thus placing themselves in the course projected by central authorities. In this way, regulators act as endogeneous constraints to decentralized decision makers.

Reprinted from the *Economics of Planning,* Vol. 7, No. 1, 1967, pp. 73–85, by permission of the publisher.

The decision as to what is necessary for the co-ordination of private preferences is one of the basic decisions in any economy. Modern economies try to achieve rather ambitious goals like full employment, elimination of cyclical movements, high rate of growth, and similar. The extent and the character of central decision activity depends a good deal on these goals and their ambitiousness. Economic liberalism, for instance, does not establish any specific goals for national economies. The decentralized model changes in this case into the anarchic one; and the last two properties of decision making become irrelevant.

This fact and the enumerated three properties of a national decision-making structure allow for the construction of four decision-making models within national economies: (1) the decentralized anarchic model, (2) the decentralized, democratic and indicative model, (3) the decentralized, autocratic and indicative model, and (4) the centralized, autocratic and directive model. Of course, these are only the more important decision-making models. All three properties of decision-making model construction may assume rather different degrees of intensity and may apply to different numbers of sectors within the national economy. Thus a rather lengthy list of decision-making models may be constructed. However, since our aim is to give a general, and not a detailed picture of the Yugoslav postwar development of decision-making structure, we may content ourselves with the enumerated four main models.

To begin with, the Yugoslav path of development of the decision-making structure can be presented by the following sequence of the four main decision models. At the beginning, from 1947 on, the structure of Yugoslav decision making corresponded typically to the centralized, autocratic and directive model, the fourth one. In 1950 and the following years, the first elements of decentralization, and more or less during the same time the first indicative elements could be noted in the Yugoslav economy, thus approaching the third model with increasing rapidity. Later on, and particularly after 1960, autocratic and centralistic elements became even weaker (compare the theory of the dying out of the State), and the economy started to move toward the decentralized anarchic model, although important centralistic and even directive elements were preserved. Here, somewhere midway between the two models, the decision-making structure of the Yugoslav economy now lies. The main centralistic elements seem to be the centrally determined rate of saving and investment, the centrally determined level of business activity, administratively frozen prices, and some investment objects being financed by centralized resources. The last two items present at the same time elements of direct implementation of central decisions, while the implementation of the first two items is secured by indirect measures of fiscal and monetary policy. The decentralized anarchic elements of the model are presented primarily by the nearly complete independence of enterprises regarding the distribution of their incomes and the utilization of their resources, and the absence of efficient co-ordinating forces, particularly in the field of investment. By now, Yugoslav enterprises finance out of their proper resources (together with resources collected by, and borrowed from the banking system) over 70 percent of total investment in fixed capital. During the first three months of 1967, this figure increased to as high as 80 percent. Several years ago, the percentage was much lower, around 47 percent in 1964. In the 1947 model, there were practically no enterprise investment resources; depreciation allowances had even to be paid to budgets of socio-political communities.

The development of the Yugoslav decision-making structure during 1947–66 shows, therefore, a radical shift from the one extreme point toward (not to) the other. Presently, there are signs of a desire to move one step further, toward the decentralized, democratic and indicative model, presented under (2). The shift from the autocratic toward the democratic model is represented partly by the new planning ideology which stems from the belief that planning, just like all other decision making, belongs to the workers and not to the state, and partly by numerous attempts to create co-ordinating bodies outside the state, able to eliminate anarchic elements in the economy by the economy itself. Investment banks, financed and managed by enterprises, inter-firm loans and participation in management, technological co-operation between enterprises, increasing competence of chambers of commerce and of professional associations of enterprises, integration of vertically interdependent processes and similar are the main organizational forms. These tendencies toward more co-ordination, democratic and indirect this time, are not generated by central authorities primarily; it is the enterprises that feel themselves acting in somewhat of a vacuum. In an anarchic economy, the risk implied in investment decisions by individual enterprises increases enormously. Enterprises have insufficient information about the future development of the economy (plans are not regarded as reliable information), domestic and foreign, and of market conditions. No wonder, therefore, that the investment propensity of Yugoslav enterprises is declining (and this not only as the counterpart of an increasing propensity to consume), for the first time in the postwar period.

The described process of development of the Yugoslav decision-making structure, both as actually effectuated and expressed as tendency, can be presented schematically. This is done in Figure 1.

The inserted arrows show the course of development; the uninterrupted ones the really effectuated development, the interrupted ones the development expressed in the past or in the present as tendency. Figure 1 shows that the Yugoslav economy found itself in 1947 in the centralized autocratic and directive model, moved later to the decentralized autocratic and indicative model, started to move further toward the decentralized anarchic model, and now shows tendencies to move in the direction of the decentralized, democratic and indicative model.

As already mentioned, this presentation is very schematic indeed, omitting many important details. None the less it reveals, in my view,

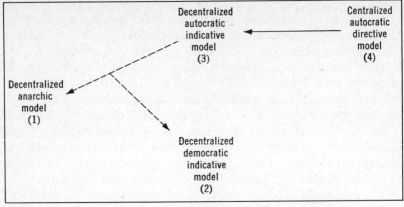

Figure 1. Development of the Yugoslav Decision-Making Structure.

what is essential in the development of the Yugoslav decision-making structure. In the following section, the most important elements of its present state will be discussed.

Workers' Management and the Economic System

The basic element of present Yugoslav decision-making structure is doubtless best presented by autonomous enterprises, linked one to another primarily, and in some respects exclusively, by the market, an institution introduced in 1950 and subsequently developed. If one disregards the fact that means of production are socially owned (as opposed to privately owned)—and there are a good many reasons in the present Yugoslav distribution of income for permitting such a disregard—autonomous enterprises, however peculiar from the viewpoint of other socialist economies, do not present any element of distinction as against capitalist economies. It is (1) the inner decision structure of Yugoslav enterprises and (2) their outer decision environment that presents a peculiarity of the Yugoslav economy from the viewpoint of both socialist and capitalist economies.

1) The inner decision structure of Yugoslav enterprises is characterized by workers' self-management. From 1950, when workers' self-management was established, it has evolved considerably to the present time. In the beginning, it was a type of indirect or delegated self-management. Two representative bodies of workers: a workers' council as the highest legislative body within the enterprise and a managing board, together with a director as the executive organ of the worker's council, all were empowered (elected by workers, excepting the director) to decide on general policy of the enterprise and on concrete questions of day-to-day management, each within its sphere of competence. By now, workers' self-management is direct self-management or, more precisely, the intention is to render it as direct as possible. The idea is that workers have the

right and duty to decide directly on any problem both of production and distribution, and that they must be educated to be able to do so. Representative bodies of workers, workers' councils, managing boards, and directors still exist (by now all elected, directors included). Their role, however, should be primarily that of co-ordination. In this way, the democracy of decision making in enterprises tends to become as direct as possible. In order to make it effective, enterprises, and particularly the large ones, are split into "working" or "economic" units, small enough to enable workers to have sufficient insight into production and realization problems and to decide upon them, collectively if possible. It is difficult to predict how these ideas will materialize. Besides some positive results, they have also, to date, produced negative ones, in particular a tendency to make working units within the same enterprise independent. Not infrequently, many independent enterprises get disaggregated in this manner. And the economy of labor, the number of workers, and the utilization of their working day, is not of the highest efficiency.

We stated at the beginning that a democratic decision-making structure implies autonomous enterprises and households as the original decision makers. Workers' self-management, and particularly the present direct one, provides the democratic decision-making structure of the Yugoslav economy with a new content. It is to the workers, or better, to workers' collectives that basic and autonomous decision making appertains, enterprises being only the form of their productive activity, and households only the form of their consumptive activity in a market economy. In the discussion concerning who is, or ought to be, the subject of economic activity in the Yugoslav economy, the view increasingly prevails that it is not the enterprise but workers, or workers' collectives. The existing Law on Labour Relations already makes use of this idea.

2) The outer decision environment of Yugoslav enterprises is represented by the so-called "economic system." This phrase has two interpretations in Yugoslavia, a broader and a narrower one. In its broader sense, the economic system includes all the basic institutions of the Yugoslav economy; social property of the means of production, self-management of workers in enterprises, and social management in socio-political communities. In this broader sense it is labeled also as the socio-economic system. In the narrower sense, the economic system is equivalent to the system of regulators, which in Yugoslavia are called "economic instruments." These are tools intended to create for enterprises an outer decision environment which will induce them to determine according to highest economic efficiency, private and, possibly, national. We may label these tools also "inducing regulators" or simply "inductors."

There are at least three fields where such inductors are needed if the economy is to operate at optimum without direct state interference in realization of plan preferences. The first field is the distribution of national income, the second its utilization and allocation, and the third the stability of growth movements. Inducing regulators can consequently be divided into distributors, allocators and stabilizers. The following main inductors are presently in use in the Yugoslav economy: interest on capital used by enterprises, depreciation allowances, excise tax together with import duties, personal income tax, interest premiums and investment contributions, social insurance contributions, bank reserves, interest on credits together with amortization periods (annuities), and other cruder forms of credit regulation.

Let us describe briefly these inductors. Any enterprise has to pay interest on capital, fixed and circulating, engaged in production. The rate of interest has been fixed at 3.5 percent; there are, however, numerous exceptions, sinking in some instances, to the zero level. Thus, the average rate for the whole economy does not exceed essentially 2 percent. Depreciation rates, only their lower limits, are set by Law. Excise tax rates are unified now at the level of 12 percent of the selling price (only federal; in addition republican and communal excises have to be paid at a rate of 8 percent approximately), and apply to ultimate consumption only. This is a major novelty introduced in 1965; prior to this year, excise tax rates were extremely differentiated. Important exceptions in both respects are the excise tax for tobacco, gasoline and related products, liquors, and some metals; and many necessities are free of excise tax. Personal income taxes and social insurance contributions are paid directly by enterprises at proportional rates (the progressive personal income tax, paid individually by income earners, does not, as yet, have any important economic function). Interest premiums, representing differentiated percentages of interest payments that investors (borrowers) must pay to banks, are offered by socio-political communities to investors in order to induce them to allocate their resources to desired activities. Essentially the same function is performed by the contributions of the socio-political communities in the financing of investment. Interest on credits (bank credits, inter-enterprise credits, credits of certain remaining funds) are generally very high for short-term credits and lower for investment credits. In general, short repayment periods go along with high interest rates, and vice versa. Both instruments are used *grosso modo* with the same intentions as in capitalist countries; so is the third monetary instrument, bank reserves. It is worthwhile to note that open market policy is unknown. In fact, there is no capital market as in capitalist countries. There are tendencies to improve the efficiency of these instruments in order to enable them to substitute for cruder forms of credit regulation.

Some of the enumerated inductors perform only one of the three main functions; some of them perform two or even all three functions. At the same time they act, in the latter case, as distributors, allocators, and stabilizers. In some cases, the activity of individual inductors is powerful and/or direct in one field but weak and indirect in another. In Table 1, the main inductors presently in use in Yugoslavia are arranged according to the function they perform in the economy. The use of bold-face indicates fields where the action of the corresponding inductors is strong and/or direct.

From Table 1 it is possible to conclude that there are especially numerous inductors dealing directly with distribution, and especially few dealing with stability of the economy. From their introduction to the present, the main interest has been on distribution; as a matter of fact, the history of the Yugoslav economic system (in the narrower sense) is a history of the development of instruments of distribution. The reason is obvious. In the past, investment resources were largely centralized in investment funds of socio-political communities, and there was therefore no particular need to build a system of allocators. The job had been done by planners. As for stabilizers, cycles in business activity have been discovered only recently, and the need for stabilized purchasing power of money is also of recent origin.

Table 1. Main Inductors in Yugoslavia

Distributors	Allocators	Stabilizers
Interest on capital	Interest on capital †	**Interest on capital** †
Interest on credit	Interest on credit †	**Interest on credits with**
Depreciation allowances	**Depreciation allowances** †	**other instruments of**
Excise and import taxes	Excise and import taxes *	**monetary policy**
Personal income tax	Personal income tax †	
Social insurance	**Social insurance**	
contributions	**contributions** †	
	Interest premiums and	
	investment contributions	

* Primarily via prices.
† Also via prices.

Since prices are determinants of real incomes, all inductors that affect relative prices also influence distribution via prices. And since prices also affect allocation and use of factors, all inductors affecting relative prices also influence utilization and allocation of resources. Particularly important in this respect are interest, both on capital and credits, and depreciation allowances. Excise taxes and import taxes act almost exclusively via prices.

Evaluation of the Present System of Inductors

As a rule, Yugoslav policy makers are most theoretically minded. The building of the Yugoslav economic system has been based upon, or at least accompanied by theoretical considerations such as the role of the law of value in socialist economy, the relation between the market and the plan, normal prices, and the withering away of the state, to name a few of the many examples. Practical solutions, not only in economy but also in social life in general, are applications of the corresponding theoretical models. The best known Yugoslav system of distributors, the so-called system of "the rate of accumulation and funds" in 1952, in which the contributions of enterprises for financing common social needs were proportional to wages, was based directly on the Marx' value model in which prices of products are proportional to the quantity of labor entailed in their production or, in a practical approximation, to wages. The present system of inductors does not emanate from any specific economic model. To some degree, it is a result of a desire to construct a system of distributors capable of a remuneration consistent with the principle "to everybody according to his work." Elimination of the progressive income tax in 1963 was undoubtedly a result of this desire. To a much higher degree, the present system of inductors seems to be the consequence of a philosophic model of a self-managing society in which there is no place for the state, and where all affairs, economic and noneconomic, are managed directly by the people themselves. The most interesting feature of this model is the independence of enterprises regarding production, distribution, and utilization of their incomes. Its main distributor is the proportional income tax and other contributions proportional to the personal incomes. These are the incomes of the socio-political communities and of special funds (social insurance, for instance) of workers' domiciles and have the function of providing financial resources for development of their social activities. All together they engage 20 percent of national income (1966), which is about one half of the net product engaged to cover common expenses (administration, instruction, health, centrally financed investment, and similar). All other distributors engage considerably lower parts of the national net product (excise tax 11.1 percent, interest on credits 4.1 percent, and interest on fixed and circulating capital of enterprises 2.5 percent—all in 1966).

Here I see the main deficiency of the present Yugoslav system of economic instruments. In an underdeveloped country with a great shortage of capital and rather abundant supply of labor, one should expect the price of capital to be high and price of labor to be low. While wages are low indeed, the cost of labor for enterprises, as a result of personal income taxes and other contributions dependent on personal incomes, is rather high. Some portion of unemployment can be explained in this way. Intensive capital investment is induced even in regions where there is great latent unemployment in the private agricultural sector. Similar is the influence of low interest rates on fixed and circulating capital. It is true that interest rates on credits are much higher and credit repayment periods very short. However, these credits primarily supply enterprises with additional capital, making the average price of capital none the less comparatively low. New enterprises with capital wholly financed by credits usually get them on better terms— the only important exception being manufacturing industry enterprises, particularly the small ones. Furthermore, because of low capital charges and high labor costs, prices in Yugoslavia are distorted; they do not express real costs of production that, from the point of view of the whole economy, consist only of capital engaged and labor consumed. As a result, the structure of production together with the foreign trade structure is misdirected. It is not possible to discover true comparative advantages and to participate organically in international divisions of labor. Inductors which possibly perform their distributional duty quite satisfactorily may act, therefore, as very poor and misleading allocators.

In fact, however, the present inductors act as well as very poor and misleading distributors. The desire to give enterprises as much independence as possible, inspires the belief that the market will be able to secure unaided the distribution "to everybody according to his work." This, of course, is not the case; large differences in capital intensity, technical level of capital equipment, land productivity, and monopoly power between individual enterprises lead, in fact, to results diametrically opposed to the expectation. Low capital charges, no technological and land rent tax, and the unified excise tax are unable to correct these results sufficiently.

Here, perhaps, is the right place for a word about the Yugoslav discussion on normal prices. Contrary to similar discussions in the Soviet Union and other socialist states, there were rather few advocates among Yugoslav economists of so-called "value prices," constructed proportionally to the quantity of work only; in practice to the wages. The system of "the rate of accumulation and funds" which, in fact, was a system of value prices, was created before any real discussion among economists began. A majority of economists have seen the normal price as some sort of "production price" (*Produktionspreis*). As is well known, this price is proportional partly to wages and partly to capital engaged, fixed and circulating, and the relation of the two parts is dependent on the organic composition of capital (capital per time unit of labor). Recently, a new formula of normal prices has been devised, the so-called "income price." According to its authors, normal prices in a socialist economy are proportional to the sum of the material cost of production plus depreciation plus value added. The argument for this construction is the belief that the material cost of production plus depreciation of capital equipment expresses the embodied, and the value added the present labor, the income price thus illuding as the most orthodox interpretation of Marx' theory of value. The idea of income price was heavily criticized by a multitude of economists at a symposium on problems of theory and policy of prices held in Sarajevo in 1964. The main point against it is that material costs of production are no primary factor either of product or of its value or price, and that from the point of view of the economy as a whole, they do not exist at all. If prices were shaped according to the formula of income price, their structure would be distorted just as it is now, only in another direction; prices of the final stages of production would be relatively high, and prices of the first stages of production (raw materials) relatively low; and all prices would be somewhat independent of the capital intensity of the corresponding processes.

In a decentralized economy like the Yugoslav, rather strong stabilizers seem to be necessary to prevent business activity from oscillating too much. Proportional income and excise taxes, together with import duties (more than 30 percent of the national net product), supply socio-political communities and special funds with high incomes when business activity, and consequently also wages and salaries, are high, and with low incomes, when business activity, and therefore also wages and salaries, are depressed. They act, therefore, as amplifiers of cyclical movements. To better understand this mechanism we must add that Yugoslav fiscal policy firmly adheres to the principle of a balanced budget. Higher budget incomes, therefore, necessarily result in higher expenses for the socio-political communities and special funds.

In addition, the proportional income and excise taxes bring instability to the finances of socio-political communities and to autonomous budgets of noneconomic activities (instruction, for instance). And they stimulate, during booms, hypertrophic enrollment in these noneconomic activities; no subsequent recession is able to do away with them. It is true that a cost-push inflation, built on the Yugoslav system of distribution shifts all these movements to an upward trend and may counteract, in periods of recession, as a stabilizer. However, the increased share of wages and salaries in net income of enterprises necessarily decreases the share of investment, and shifts therefore the amplifying function of proportional income taxes from consumer goods to capital goods industries. Proportionality of taxes to capital would, in my view, avoid or lighten many of these difficulties. The present low rate of interest on capital is too weak to prevent oscillations or even to compensate the amplifying function of the income and excise taxes. In addition, higher interest rates on fixed and circulating capital would induce enterprises to make better use of their capital equipment—an old problem of the Yugoslav economy, aggravated particularly during the recent recession. Let us add that while enterprises are paying a 2 percent interest rate on capital (on the average), people are given 6 to 8 percent interest for their savings deposits.

The following conclusion seems to be warranted on the basis of what has been briefly sketched above. The decentralized decision-making structure of the Yugoslav economy needs a thoroughly elaborated and internally consistent system of economic inductors if it is to operate satisfactorily, that is to produce a high and sustained rate of growth, a distribution of income consistent with the principle "to everybody according to his work," and a stable price level. The present system of inductors, although its intention is primarily to cope with requirements of distribution, cannot be regarded as successful even from this limited point of view, much less so from the point of view of allocation of resources. As for stabilizers, there is still no need felt for them. It is not surprising that many existing inductors act inconsistently from the point of view of their various functions. A system of internally consistent inductors, distributors, allocators, and stabilizers seems to be a task that still has to penetrate the consciousness of the Yugoslav economic policy.

Discussion Questions

1. Discuss the fundamentals of West German codetermination.
2. What are the principal features of decentralized decision making in Yugoslavia?
3. What do you view as the main advantages and disadvantages of worker participation in economic decision making?
4. Do you think "industrial democracy" will ever emerge on a significant scale in the United States?

Government and the Firm

In the United States the relationship between the power of the government and the corporation has evolved in a most extraordinary fashion. Buttressed by the philosophy of laissez-faire, corporations formed trusts to exercise monopoly power over price and output. It was not until 1890 that legislation emerged to cope with antisocial corporate activity. While the evidence suggests very mixed success on the part of existing antitrust legislation, it seems fair to say that government and business for a long time were regarded as natural enemies, with the latter viewing the former as unduly encroaching upon its activities.

While the rhetoric that goes back and forth between Washington and the headquarters of the corporate giants may even today smack of such an antagonistic relationship, it seems fair to say that government is more an ally than an enemy of business. The shaky courtship with its many broken engagements has turned into a blissful marriage and the arguments between the couple are not more than the normal disagreements between any two partners in a marriage. Job development credits, accelerated depreciation allowances, oil import quotas, agricultural subsidies, are all evidence that the marriage is here to stay. Furthermore, the 1946 Employment Act committed the United States to pursue a full-employment policy, that is, to create a more stable economic environment within which business could operate.

Unlike the best of marriages, the government does not fully trust its marriage partner. Hence, should business step beyond the bounds of propriety, the acts of Congress and the decisions of the federal courts are available for use in restoring marital harmony.

The articles which follow examine the two aspects of the relationship between government to which we have alluded. The second article looks at Great Britain's Monopolies Commission, set up to deal with essential aspects of the monopoly problem. The first article examines the effects that French economic planning has had on the behavior of business firms. The French experience should be given careful attention. The implementation of an incomes policy, with its attendant price and wage controls is a clear concession to the ineffectiveness of the market mechanism, and *the French planning variant may well provide a model for the U.S. economy in the future.*

Hans Schollhammer is a Professor in the School of Business Administration at the University of California–Los Angeles. C. K. Rowley is on the faculty at the University of Kent, England.

National Economic Planning and Business Decision Making: The French Experience

HANS SCHOLLHAMMER

In spite of the famous statement of the 1930s—"we are all planners now" —national economic planning (broadly meaning a method of organized social action designed to achieve certain specified overall objectives within a given period) versus individual or corporate freedom of decision making has remained the topic of many lengthy and inconclusive discussions. At the root of the debate is the conflict between the public authorities who are committed to a normative, official plan and the largely uncommitted individual decision makers of the business sector on whose co-operation the implementation of a national economic plan would depend. So far, this interrelationship between macro-economic planning and micro-decision making has been almost exclusively treated in a general, philosophical, and, to a certain extent, political manner.

It is perhaps natural that national planning is looked upon with mistrust in a free market economy. One reason for this is the association of national planning with the political and economic regime of the Soviet Union, which was the first country to develop a comprehensive and systematic five-year plan in 1928. Opponents of national economic planning claim that it is inevitably the first step on a "Road to Serfdom," because it always involves some form of intervention, manipulation, and coercion, even if the national plans are indicative rather than imperative. This unavoidable by-product of national planning, it is argued, tends to inhibit entrepreneurial initiative as well as organizational flexibility, which leads to a decline in economic productivity and ultimately to dictatorship "because it is the most effective instrument of coercion and, as such, essential if central planning on a large scale is to be possible."

The proponents of national planning generally emphasize the inherent weaknesses of the market mechanism which create the need for the elaboration of an over-all plan to provide the individual decision maker with

---

sufficient information to relate his decisions to those of the rest of the business community in the pursuit of a common preference function such as a high rate of growth or a high, stable rate of employment. A national plan, it is pointed out, is a kind of large-scale market survey which provides business executives with consistent information about future developments and anticipated governmental actions. It conveys not only what is probable but also what is desirable; it shows what the objectives are and specifies the means by which the public authorities intend to attain them. Consequently, business executives can make strategic decisions under reduced uncertainties, which results in less wastage, a higher economic efficiency, and increased freedom in the form of wider opportunities for growth of the individual firm in an expanding and co-ordinated economy.

In addition, proponents of planning point to three factors which have operated in recent years to increase the attractiveness of national economic planning:

1. The growing proportion of expenditures and investments controlled by the government.
2. An increasing planning consciousness, particularly among the larger business enterprises.
3. Improved means for collecting and processing large quantities of macroeconomic data quickly and efficiently.

This kind of deductive reasoning has not led to any satisfactory solution of the dispute between opponents and proponents of national economic planning mainly because it does not provide any specific, quantitatively oriented answers to some basic questions:

- To what extent are strategic and operational decisions of business firms actually affected by the existence of a national economic plan?
- How strong is the impact on the affected decision-making areas?
- Are there any factors by which the impact of the national plan is conditioned?
- What is the relative importance of these factors?
- What are the actual advantages and disadvantages of a national plan for the individual firm?
- Do the advantages outweigh the disadvantages or vice versa?

Answers to these questions must be found in order to come to a fair judgment about the desirability or nondesirability of national economic planning in a free market economy.

The French economy, basically a market economy, has been subject to planning for more than two decades, and the French system of planning has attracted considerable attention. Among the industrialized nonsocialist countries, France has gone furthest in planning its economic affairs. Its system has been in effect for more than 20 years and can be used as a model in attempting to find specific answers to the questions above by investigating the interrelationship between French national planning and the decision making of French business firms. This article presents the pertinent findings of such an investigation, based on in-depth interviews with more than two dozen business executives and on information obtained through questionnaires completed by executives of almost 400 French firms.

The Nature of French Planning

There has been a continuous planning evolution since the First Plan was drawn up in 1947. Methods and techniques have been improved, the emphasis of the plans changed, and their scope extended. The major evolutions have originated from the changing economic conditions to which the general objectives of the successive plans were geared. However, the broad lines of the system and the planning approach have changed little. There is always concern about achieving a maximum rate of growth, balanced regional and sectoral development, and an emphasis on investment activity. In addition, the planners aim to make the plan as comprehensive as possible and, most important of all, the plans have to be compatible with the democratic system and the concept of a free market economy. The methods used for reconciling the requirements of a general economic plan under the constraints of a free market system are described by the authors of the First French Plan as those of a "concerted economy." All those social and economic forces who later put the plan into practice are called upon to help prepare it. It is hoped that the plan, because it forecasts and influences their decisions, brings about enough consistency among individual decision makers and consensus among decentralized objectives to become substantially self-realizing.

Despite their evolutionary nature, French plans have always retained the following characteristics:

1. The plan is worked out in terms of branches of activity and not of companies or products. It does not dictate a course of action to private enterprise—it is not a control device—it simply states the general objectives fixed for economic and social development and the particular goal for each branch. Within this framework each firm is free to choose its own target. A firm can maintain its position within its branch, can enlarge it, or can diminish it. The firm acts on the basis of better information, but at its own risk. The plan is only an instrument "d'orientation de l'économie" and "should provide the individual investors with an idea about the expected economic development which can be used as basis for appropriate decisions." The public authorities intervene only where there is a danger of imbalance on an economy-wide or sectoral scale.

2. French planning seeks to draw on the expertise of all major decision-making centers in the nation. In the First Plan, Monnet was already using the expression "concerted economy." He realized that because of the

proverbial French individualism the plan would only be successful if it were a combined effort in which all French were associated, directly or indirectly. This spirit is reflected in the structural organization for the preparation of the plan, particularly in the "Planning Commissions" which are perhaps the most significant feature of the French planning system. Organized apart from the French Planning Commissariat which is basically the permanent administrative organ of the French planning system, these planning commissions are made up of representatives of the major social categories which have a determining influence on the economic life of the country: executives of private and public business enterprises, representatives of industrial associations, labor unions, and the civil service. The role of the commissions is threefold:

- They are a source of information about past activities and future prospects of their sectors, and the data which they supply provide the basis for the final synthesis of a national economic plan.
- They indicate measures which the public authorities and private decision makers should follow in order to accomplish the stated sectoral and national targets. They also formulate recommendations which, in their view, are likely to improve the conditions which are necessary for an effective achievement of the plan's objectives.
- They review the implementation of the plan, analyze deviations between plan targets and actual accomplishments, and come up with revisions or additional recommendations.

For the Fifth Plan, which covers the period from 1966 through 1970, 31 planning commissions with a total membership of over 2,000 persons exist. There are 25 vertical commissions which are organized on an industry basis, such as steel, chemicals, mining, energy, and transportation, and deal only with the sector entrusted to them. The six horizontal commissions deal with problems common to the whole economy and are responsible for synthesizing the data supplied by the vertical commissions and for preserving the fundamental equilibria: the production equilibrium, financial equilibrium, manpower equilibrium, and balanced regional development.

Table 1 shows the steady increase in the number of commissions and in the number of people involved in planning. Table 1 indicates that the employers and their associations play a major role in the commissions. The high percentage of civil servants within the planning commissions is explained by the relatively large size of the public sectors and the civil servants' active involvement in the supervision of the plan's implementation. Table 1 also reflects the increasing participation of the labor unions.

3. As far as the implementation of the national plans is concerned, the French planning authorities have at their disposal a large armory of instruments which can be used to put the plan into action and to enforce com-

	Business executives *	Professional organizations †	Farmers and farm managers	Labor union representatives	Civil servants and "ex-officio" representatives ‡	Other experts	Total
First Plan (8 commissions)							
Number of members	108	59	19	77	118	113	494
Percentage of total	22	12	4	15	24	23	100
Second Plan (22 commissions)							
Number of members	137	95	21	34	184 –126	133	730
Percentage of total	19	13	3	5	42	18	100
Third Plan (21 commissions)							
Number of members	119	140	22	52	201 –188	170	892
Percentage of total	13	16	2	6	44	19	100
Fourth Plan (26 commissions)							
Number of members	211	248	20	114	202 –330	254	1,370
Percentage of total	15	18	1	8	29	19	100
Fifth Plan (31 commissions)							
Number of members	406	430	67	291	457 –145	299	2,005
Percentage of total	19	21	3	14	29	14	100

* Including nationalized industries.
† Formal groupings based upon industry or occupation, for example, trade associations and industrial associations.
‡ Every commission has a certain number of ex-officio members (*membres de droit*) who are civil servants, such as the Director of the Budget, the Director of the Treasury, and the Director of the National Bureau of Statistics.

pliance with its prescriptions. Generally, a peculiar mixture of psychological, structural, institutional, legislative, and administrative arrangements make the plan work. The most important are the large public sector which accounts for almost half of the total fixed capital formation, the credit controls, and an array of fiscal incentives for those business endeavors supporting specific plan objectives.

In general, the French approach to implementation of the plan has been characterized as one that uses sticks and carrots, "where there are more carrots than sticks." Indeed, French government authorities have shown great readiness to make use of incentives to stimulate adherence to the plan's provisions. Where the incentives for implementing the plan are insufficient, they are supplemented by authoritarian regulations and direct interventions, such as the necessity for permission to build a plant, governmental approval of prices for certain products, or the stipulation of certain requirements for obtaining credit. However, French governmental officials, as well as planning authorities, regularly emphasize that they do not favor using their power of coercion to implement the plan. For instance, Valery Giscard d'Estaing, while Minister of Finance and Economic Affairs, stated in Parliament that all resources of persuasion should be exhausted before direct governmental interventions and pressures in favor of the realization of the plan are taken. He stated further that "if recourse to public resources should prove necessary in exceptional circumstances, the State would withdraw its participation as soon as the desired ends were reached. . . ."

The Impact of French Planning on Decision Making

Every business enterprise has certain functional decision-making areas to which top management pays relatively more attention than to others. In general these areas are those which are particularly critical for the attainment of the company's objectives. With respect to these areas the management is obliged to anticipate future developments and to plan appropriate actions more carefully than for noncritical areas. Empirical investigations have shown that, apart from purely technological production problems, the most critical issues with which business executives are confronted are generally the firm's investments and related financial commitments, marketing strategy decisions, and research and development (R&D) activities. Decisions related to these four areas are almost always interrelated, but they are frequently reached independently. An investigation of a representative sample of 371 French business executives' perception of the intensity with which their decisions and/or actions in the four mentioned critical areas are affected by the provisions and projections of the French national plan, led to the results shown in Table 2 and Figure 1.

Table 2 and Figure 1 show very clearly that the French national plans exert their greatest influence on business investment decisions, followed

Table 2. The Influence of the French National Plans on Business Decisions *

	The influence of the national plan is			
	Very important	*Important*	*Of little importance*	*Of no importance*
On investment decisions	31	33	15	21
On financial decisions	26	33	23	18
On marketing decisions	15	24	35	26
On R&D decisions (allocation of funds)	11	11	20	58

* Percentage of total number of answers provided by 371 French firms.

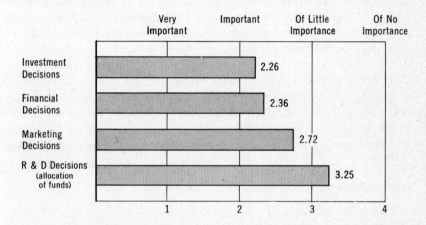

Figure 1. French Executives' Perceptions of the Influence of the National Plan in Four Decision-Making Areas.

closely by financial decisions. The influence on market strategy decisions is considerably lower, and it is relatively insignificant as far as R&D decisions are concerned, even though 39 firms stated that the national plans exert a very important influence on their R&D decisions.

An examination of those factors which French executives generally take into account when faced with investment decisions revealed four conditions. In order of diminishing returns these are:

• Market expectations.
• Access to the money or capital market.
• Technological developments.
• Fiscal privileges which the French planning authorities offer as incentives for certain decisions that are regarded as supporting the objectives of the national plan.

Except for technological developments, the French planning authorities have direct control over these conditions, and it is thus not surprising that in general the French national plan affects business investment decisions rather strongly.

First, the production and investment targets which the plan represents influence market expectations by providing a rather clear picture of what the market will be like. The company can determine its place in the co-ordinated growth of the economy and move in the direction indicated by the plan. The plan thus creates a climate of confidence that a certain growth target will be attained, which goes a long way toward the actual accomplishment.

The second powerful means is the government's control of the banking apparatus. The banking system is bound to take account of the planned targets and provide financial means, particularly for those operations which conform to the targets. Since the majority of the large enterprises, which mainly determine the level of economic activity, depend on outside finance, it is obvious that the national plan exerts a strong impact on them.

The third reason for the particular influence of the plan on investment and financial decisions can be found in the existing system of incentives which the planning authorities grant to those firms whose activities are in conformity with the objectives of the plan. This leads to the conclusion that the influence of the national plans is largely a function of the means which the planning authorities can bring to bear in implementing the plan.

Conditioning Effect of Company Characteristics

Obviously, French national plans do not affect all business enterprises in the same manner. Which factors other than those directly plan-related condition the impact of the plan on the strategic decisions of the individual firm? An empirical investigation of these factors provided evidence that the personal attitudes of executives (either in favor of or against planning per se) play a rather insignificant role in this regard. Much more important are certain company characteristics, such as:

- Size of the company.
- Ownership situation (whether the company is privately, publicly, or foreign owned).
- Type of business (whether it is in a capital- or labor-intensive industry).
- Marketing orientation (whether the firm supplies the domestic market only or foreign markets as well).

The conditioning effect of these four types of company characteristics can be seen in Table 3 and Figure 2. The influence profile in Figure 2 clearly shows to what extent the differences in intensity with which business executives take account of the plan are caused by the operational characteristics of their enterprise.

Table 3. Summary of the Perceived Impact of the French
National Plans on French Firms *

| | The plan's influence is | | | |
	Very important	Important	Of little importance	Of no importance
Size of enterprise				
Small	5	16	31	48
Medium	16	25	32	27
Large	31	31	23	14
Control of equity				
Private ownership:				
French control	22	28	26	24
Foreign control	14	21	38	27
Public ownership	51	31	12	4
Type of business				
Capital-intensive	24	27	25	24
Labor-intensive	18	28	31	23
Marketing orientation				
Exclusively domestic	26	25	23	26
Mainly domestic (limited				
export interest)	22	32	25	21
International orientation	20	21	35	24

* Percentage of total number of answers provided by 371 French firms.

The decisions of executives of large organizations are more strongly influenced by the plan than those of executives of small or medium-sized firms. For a majority of the large firms the influence of the plan is important, whereas for the small firms it is of little, if any, importance. Thus, it is a comparatively small but influential group of executives who take the plan seriously and who assure its relative success. Almost all of these executives are intimately familiar with the plan and contribute their expertise to its preparation. The findings of this investigation provide clear support of Andrew Shonfield's assertion "that the activity of planning, as it is practiced in France, has reinforced the systematic influence exerted by large-scale business on economic policy."

Particularly striking is the difference in impact on French-controlled versus foreign-controlled firms. The profile indicates that executives of foreign-controlled firms let their decisions be influenced by the French plan to a substantially lesser degree than the executives of private firms under French control. This fact reflects:

- The relatively greater independence of foreign-controlled firms
  from particular national environmental conditions of which
  economic planning is just one.
- The necessity for multi-national firms to make decisions which take

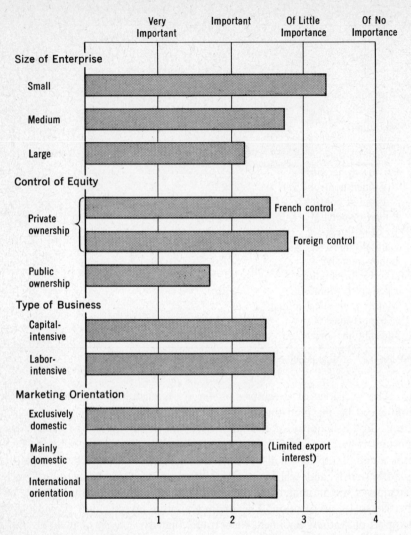

Figure 2. Conditioning Effects of Four Company Characteristics on the Influence of the French National Plan.

account of their particular international constraints and which subordinate, if necessary, nationally oriented considerations to their international aspirations.

• The relative newness of a large percentage of foreign-controlled enterprises in France whose management is either against "state planning" as a matter of management philosophy or whose management is "neutral" but hasn't yet had time or found it necessary to acquaint itself with French planning.

Even though differences in impact on capital-intensive versus labor-intensive firms are not spectacular, the profile shows that capital-intensive organizations are more strongly influenced than labor-intensive ones. This is mainly due to the pre-eminent position of investments in capital-intensive firms. Since investment decisions are more strongly influenced by the plan and since investments play a more important role in capital-intensive firms than in labor-intensive organizations, the former must necessarily be more strongly influenced by the national plan, a situation which is borne out by the findings.

Differences in the market orientation are not very significant as determining factors for the degree of influence which the national plan exerts. Firms which supply the domestic market only and those which have only limited export interest show practically no difference at all. However, multinational firms or firms which depend to a large extent on exports show that they take less account of the plan than the domestically oriented firms —obviously because their decisions are influenced by developments abroad.

The very existence of a national economic plan and the way in which it is prepared and implemented creates certain conditions. To the extent that these conditions are conducive to a better attainment of the firm's objectives, they have positive effects. Conversely, they have negative effects to the extent that they are detrimental to the attainment of the firm's objectives.

In general, a national economic plan can have positive effects on: the information available to the firm; the firm's level of business activity; the firm's relationships with various social groups; and the impact of competition. Other less direct positive effects can be seen in such areas as economic education and the co-ordination of government and business decisions and long-range planning.

The Information Effect

Business decision making requires a continuous flow of data, and many authors have emphasized the increasing demand for information in this era of accelerated changes. One advantage of the national economic plan for the individual firm is thus the fact that management is provided with an increasing amount of consistent information. The plan as a source of information has three major properties:

1. Since the government is committed to implement the plan, it represents a set of authoritative knowledge which can be relied upon to a large extent. This reduces uncertainties and consequently facilitates appropriate decisions in light of the anticipated development.
2. Using an input-output approach to national planning and taking account of certain balancing conditions such as financial

equilibrium and manpower equilibrium means that the plan is also a set of coherent, logical information which gives the decision makers in the individual economic units reassurance that it is safe to "play the game."

3. The plan not only provides an extension of the field of cognition of economic interrelationships, but also provides an increase in the length of foresight in time. In particular the long-term projections, such as the 20-year "plan horizon" of French national plans, indicate trends of developments or processes which are anticipated far in the future and are occurring so slowly that any single decision maker on the firm level could hardly be aware of their existence. Also in this respect the plan for the individual firm has the advantage of reducing uncertainties of future developments and provides a basis for timely adjustments to anticipated changes.

The Dynamism Effect

Built into any form of planning is the drive for achievement. The French national plans are no exception. In fact, they are noted for consistently stating targets which at the outset seem hardly attainable, taking into account such constraints as monetary stability and external equilibrium. But for the individual businessman who is striving to retain the firm's relative competitive position and who is told what the expansion of his sector must be in order to achieve the over-all target growth, this acts as an incentive for expansion and consequently has a dynamic effect on the level of business activity.

However, the stipulation of a high-growth target alone is not sufficient for injecting dynamism into an economy. In addition, it is necessary that the business community be confident that the growth target will actually be achieved. In France, where public authorities control about one-half of the total investment activity and where there exists a large armory of other means to insure the implementation of the plan, there has thus far been little widespread doubt or distrust that the growth target could be attained.

In this connection the plan is a vehicle to make those on whom the level of economic activity largely depends growth-conscious and thus more dynamic. Comparing the presently prevailing business attitudes of executives of large organizations with the somewhat complacent well-documented attitudes of their predecessors in the first half of this century, one cannot fail to notice the change in pace; French businessmen credit the plan with being at least partially responsible for this inspiring dynamism and vigor.

The Harmonization Effect

It can be hypothesized that the French planning system, which calls for representation of the various social groups in the planning commissions, reduces social and industrial conflicts by creating a "social dialogue" which leads to a better understanding of each other's problems. In this way the plan becomes the basis for arbitration between the interests of wage earners and those of employers. This point of view emphasizes the democratic content of French planning procedures and regards the plan as a useful common denominator of policy making among various social groups and classes.

However, the plan or national arbitration force between employers and unionists seems up to now to have been only an ideal and not a reflection of the actual situation. In the words of François Perroux,

> To argue today that the Plan is an organ of social dialogue and collective creativity would be saying far too much. But to assert that it could not become this would be to deprive it of its most powerful source of energy and to refuse it its finest flight.

The Positive Impact on Competition

It has been repeatedly pointed out that the unique feature in the institutional setup of French planning is the planning commission, which includes representatives of the major firms of each individual industry sector; representatives of industrial associations; and civil servants, trade unionists, and other experts. French planners have frequently stressed the advantages of the "dialogue" which this system enables and its co-ordinating and interpreting effect. For instance, Pierre Massé pointed out that French industry, by avoiding the buildup of excess capacity, has achieved the same production with a lower level of investment than that necessary for the same results in other countries, and consequently, this has resulted in the aggregate in a higher return on investment in France.

The dialogue in the commissions has been interpreted, especially by American commentators, as a euphemism for collusive agreements, an activity which is regarded with suspicion. It has been frequently stated that the commissions' meetings provide an opportunity for restrictive business practices, such as sharing out investment or production quotas, particularly among oligopolistic units. The work of the planning commissions does indeed appear to imply that some agreement is reached between firms on planned investments, production, exports, and other important variables. "Here," David Granick states, "it seems to me we have the essence of French planning. It is the planning of each industry by its own members, acting as a great cartel, with the civil service sitting in on the game and sweetening the pot." S. Wickham, a French economist, phrases it this way:

> If, for instance, iron and steel industrials meet in a restaurant to discuss production of various types of steel plates with a view to agree on their respective productive capacity, this is cartelization. But, one will say, if they meet exactly for the same purpose in a conference room supplied to them by the Government, with a civil servant acting as secretary, then everyone

will praise this practice as avoiding duplications in the productive apparatus of the country and promoting full employment of fixed capacity.

In short, the planning commissions are regarded by some as the most useful part of the French planning machinery and by others as the potentially most dangerous part, because company representatives who work together in a commission may agree to share new markets and consequently may refrain from struggling too hard to alter their share of existing markets, and price competition may become extremely gentlemanly.

Two statements summarize very appropriately the effect of the planning system on interfirm competition. When asked how he feels about the planning procedure which leads to "ententes" and a reduction of competition, Massé replied that ententes between firms are not new and would happen even if there were no plan. However, "if they are going to happen anyhow, it is better that they should happen in the context of economic growth, and within the range of planning authorities."

Granick expresses explicitly what Massé implied with his statement. "A cartel can plan for expansion—indeed this is the most profitable type of programming when conditions are appropriate—and this is what the great combination of French cartels called 'the Plan' has in fact done."

Other Positive Effects

There are other effects which are not widely recognized among the business community because their influence is less direct and because they have only a long-range payoff. The two most important effects of this kind can be termed education and co-ordination effects.

Officials associated with the Planning Commissariat have pointed out that the national plan itself as well as the procedure for its development serve a useful educational function. The plan is an instrument of economic education for government officials, business executives, and, to a certain extent, labor leaders, opening their eyes to the economic interdependencies in a complex situation.

Ideally, the plan is a co-ordinated set of anticipated developments related to decisions to attain the envisaged objectives. In recent years the plan has become more and more the framework within which the various decisions as related to governmental economic policy are taken. This co-ordinating effect of the plan, which refers primarily to governmental economic decisions, has an important secondary effect on the business community in the sense that it increases the degree to which business executives can rely on the plan and thus is another factor in reducing uncertainties over future developments.

There can also be negative effects on an individual firm. To the extent that the intentions of individual companies in a certain sector correspond with the development as planned by the planning authorities, there is little occasion for conflict, and the plan will be implemented without resort to "corrective" or coercive means. But, if the plan advocates appreciable changes which individual firms have not anticipated or for which their motivation to comply is low, it creates difficulties for both the planning authorities and the individual firms. In general, the plan can have adverse effects on traditional behavior; investment schedules; the firm's profit-making capacity; the firm's competitive situation domestically as well as internationally; and the firm's or the sector's relative importance in the economy.

Adverse Impact on Traditional Behavior

Economic historians have repeatedly pointed out particular value standards and behavioral characteristics which are typical of the majority of small family-owned French enterprises. The preoccupation of the typical French firm with security and its concern with staying independent of outside influence is in direct conflict with some of the explicit or implicit objectives of the plan, which emphasizes industrial expansion and efficiency in the utilization of resources. For instance, in the directives for a selective lending policy which were issued in 1963 and are still in force, the banks were asked to respect the aims of the plan and to favor certain types of operations, such as regroupings of firms, which would lead to greater concentration and specialization.

Obviously, the plan's emphasis on efficiency, economies of scale, and industrial expansion is in direct conflict with the traditional conservative behavior of a majority of small family-owned firms. Since the governmental authorities provide inducements for compliance with the plan's objectives in the form of access to credit, differential tax rates, or subsidies, the firm that doesn't let itself be "induced" may soon find itself at an impossible competitive disadvantage.

This means that ultimately most French firms are forced either to sacrifice their traditional objectives or security, financial independence, and family control, and adopt the more dynamic objectives which the plan advocates—such as growth and efficiency—or to continue to cling to an outdated but time-honored mode of behavior and be faced with a high probability of losing out competitively.

Adverse Effect on Intrasectoral Competition

The impact of the plan on the competitive situation of an individual firm can be twofold. It can increase as well as reduce interfirm competition, and either situation can have negative consequences for individual firms in the sector.

First, the French plan states the investment and output targets for a sector, and obviously there are instances where most of the firms in the sector try to secure the largest share of the planned expansion for themselves. The attempt to grab the lion's share of the market leads to systematic over-investment and the buildup of excess capacity. This in turn leads to keen competition among firms, which generally has an adverse impact on the companies' profitability and eventually on some companies' survival particularly if their financial backing is not very strong.

From a macroeconomic point of view such a situation seems quite beneficial since it increases efficiency, reduces excess profits, and guarantees an optimum allocation of scarce resources. But, for the individual firm— or even for a majority of firms in a particular sector—the situation created by the existence of a national plan clearly has serious negative effects on the achievement of the firms' general objectives.

Second, one of the major concerns of the French planning authorities has been and still is that of gaining the co-operation of the various economic and social forces which can make the plan's objectives become reality. In this regard particular attention has been paid to the strategic sectors of the economy (the so-called basic industries) and the large corporations, which can be used for co-ordinating or coercing the actions of the smaller firms in the same branch. In most cases the representatives of the enterprise sector in the various planning commissions come from large firms.

It is obvious that the planning machinery can also be used for the self-interest of the industry, particularly by the larger firms to enhance their economic and financial power over the smaller firms. The larger firms generally can gain relatively more from the plan than the smaller ones because they can more readily gain special concessions for their co-operation with the plan in the form of differential tax rates or special depreciation allowances, and because they can more easily get access to the sources which provide working capital and long-term capital for development. In this regard, Chamberlain points out that "a kind of 'unholy alliance' may grow up between government and the major private power centers." This indicates that the plan provides a basis for changing the competitive situation between small and large firms in the sector in favor of the latter. Therefore, from the point of view of many small enterprises, the plan has an adverse impact on their relative competitive positions.

Adverse Impact on Intersectoral Competition

Criticism of the French national plan as "not neutral" has a long tradition and is not surprising in view of the fact that each of the successive plans favored certain sectors or economic activities. For instance, it can be shown that the emphasis of the national plan on the basic industry—the agricultural sector, the export-oriented industry—has been detrimental to the equal development of other industries and therefore the various "priorities" which successive plans pursued were justly criticized by those who did not belong to the preferred sector. The national plans' intersectoral discrimination effect means disadvantages for individual enterprises in nonpriority sectors as, for instance, when they cannot get the loans they would like to have for expansion. Obviously, preferential treatment of certain sectors over others is a sensible approach to using scarce resources in order to assure the attainment of certain primary targets. From the point of view of the economic system as a whole, there is thus little justification in classifying type of intersectoral discrimination as a negative effect, but it does create disadvantages for firms which are not in a priority sector.

Negative Consequences of Governmental Enforcement of the Plan

It has been pointed out that the planning authorities have direct or indirect control over a large arsenal of means for influencing the activities of the business community in the plan's direction. Among the most powerful means are selective controls over capital issues, over long-term borrowing from credit institutions, over medium-term borrowing from banks, over the selective distribution of bank credit, and over the various forms of tax privileges. The individual firm which must rely on outside finance and whose intended activities are limited by lack of the necessary financial means because of some plan-related considerations, rightly blames "the plan" for having a negative effect on its operations.

Obviously, the financial strings are potentially the most powerful to enforce compliance with the plan, and thus from the point of view of the business community the most negative effects of the plan are related to the financial considerations. However, it cannot be overlooked that other means which are employed to achieve the targets of the plan, to the extent that they are of a restrictive nature, have negative effects also. It can easily be seen how administrative, authoritarian controls, such as price controls, requirements for construction permits, special approval before a net business above a certain size can be established in the Paris area, and required permits to establish refining and distillation plants, are constraints on the free development of business activity and thus exert a negative influence.

Relative Importance of Positive and Negative Effects

French national planning offers a variety of advantages but also has negative effects. The utilization of the positive effects and the realization of the negative effects are largely conditioned by the firm's operational characteristics and the general orientation of the plan. Executives of the multitude of firms show great differences in their responsiveness to and co-operation with the plan. There are those who can afford to ignore it. There are those who cannot afford to ignore it but do so nevertheless and pay a certain price for it, and there are those who are more or less familiar with the plan and cognitive of its favorable and unfavorable implications.

French business executives who claimed to have a high degree of familiarity with the plan and related information were asked to evaluate the various effects of the plan. A total of 158 executives responded to this request; 14 of them were executives of small firms, 19 of medium-sized firms, and 125 of large firms. This somewhat unusual distribution reflects precisely the differences in plan-consciousness among executives of the various categories of firms. A surprising result—at least at first sight—is the fact that the separate tabulation of the evaluation of the various effects of the plan on the three sizes of firms showed practically no differences. This indicates that executives, to the extent that they are familiar with the plan and take account of its provisions, have largely the same perception of the importance of the various effects.

The results of evaluation are summarized in Table 4, Figure 3, and Figure 4, which provide a clear picture of the French executives' appreciation of the positive factors of the national plan and also shows their apprehension with regard to the more disagreeable aspects of planning. It indicates that a large majority of those French executives who stated that

Table 4. Effects of the National Plan and Their Relative Importance *

	Perception of the effect as			
	Very important	*Important*	*Of little importance*	*Of no importance*
Positive effects				
Information effect	34	61	5	0
Dynamism effect	38	35	16	11
Harmonization effect	0	8	43	49
Effect on competition	4	14	47	35
Education effect	0	5	20	75
Co-ordination effect	26	47	18	9
Negative effects				
Discrimination effect (intersectoral)	3	10	40	37
Discrimination effect (intrasectoral)	11	10	37	42
Financial means used to enforce compliance as inhibitors of company operations	31	43	20	6
Administrative means used to enforce compliance with the plan as inhibitors of company operations	6	21	53	20

* Percentage of total number of answers provided by a representative sample of 158 French business executives.

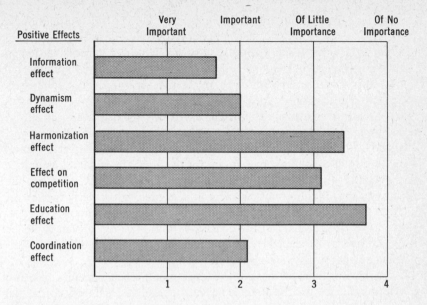

Figure 3. Perception of the Positive Effects of the French National Plan.

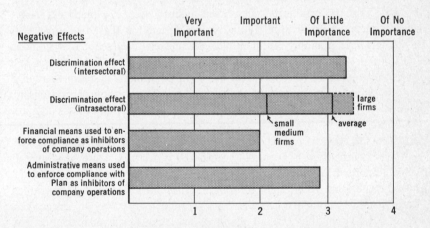

Figure 4. Perception of the Negative Effects of the French National Plan.

they take account of the national plan when reaching strategic decisions perceive that the most noticeable advantage is derived from the fact that the plan supplies them with a large amount of consistent information, at practically no cost, about anticipated developments in the economy as a whole and in the various sectors. It is especially with regard to investment and financial decisions and to a lesser degree with respect to marketing decisions that the information effect of the French plan facilitates appropriate decisions so that they are consistent with the anticipated over-all development.

The magnitude of the information effect of the plan can be questioned, especially in view of the fact that a majority of the executives of small and medium-sized firms make no use of it at all. However, it must be recognized that effective utilization of the potentially available information requires competent persons who can relate the general information which the plan offers to a firm's specific situation. But in small firms one seldom finds executives who make competent use of the plan, and almost always these firms either do not have the resources for or are prejudiced against qualified staff services that could analyze a complex set of aggregate data in order to extract what might be relevant for the firm. The apparent ignorance of the plan among executives of smaller firms cannot, however, lead to the conclusion that the information effect is negligible, particularly in view of the fact that executives of the large firms attach so much importance to it. Instead, we are led again to the conclusion that the French plan could be better utilized if the channels of communication between planning authorities and smaller firms were improved.

The investigation of the positive effects of French planning has also provided evidence for the French business executives' perception that the plans and the ways they are put into action are conducive to a high level of business activity and economic dynamism. From this evidence one can conclude that the traditional accusation against economic planning as being detrimental to individual initiative is a fallacy, at least in the context of French-style planning. Influential French executives seem to recognize that the growth orientation of the French plans generally supports the growth objectives of the individual firms. In addition, they seem to realize that the Plan is an important instrument for a co-ordinated, systematic application of economic policy means, which further enhances its "dynamism effect."

From the point of view of the individual firm, a reduction in intercompany competition is generally considered a desirable state of affairs. It has been argued that the French planning system, which invites competitors to elaborate jointly on their future decisions, is an officially sanctioned mechanism for collusive agreements. A majority of French executives, however, disclaim that French planning has such consequences. For any outsider, particularly someone who believes in the benefits and efficiency of antitrust regulations as they exist in the United States or Germany, this seems rather unbelievable. But it must be recognized that the majority of French business executives traditionally subscribe to a maxim of "live and let live," and they are thoroughly organized in professional associations. Seen in this light, it seems true that the French planning system itself is of little consequence with respect to interfirm competition, and there is little empirical evidence for claiming that it fosters collusive agreements among competitors.

Still another potentially positive effect of the French planning system has not materialized to the extent that was expected. It was hoped that the French approach to planning would provide a basis for a harmonious resolution of problems between the social classes. However, the empirical evidence so far allows only the conclusion that this expectation remains an ideal. But it should not be overlooked that the plan could indeed be a national arbitration force, and it must necessarily become so if income planning and planning in monetary terms are to have any meaning.

With respect to the potentially negative effects, the investigation led to the conclusion that in general French business executives feel most severely hampered by the planning authorities' control over external financing. The French banks' lending policy, that is, the extension of loans primarily for activities which are in conformity with the plan, is the single most powerful factor in making a large segment of business executives "plan-conscious."

From the point of view of smaller firms a negative effect of the French plan is its alleged discrimination in favor of large enterprises. Executives of the small and medium-sized firms on the one hand feel that the plan fosters intrasectoral discrimination, whereas on the other hand the executives of large firms seem to be quite unaware of this effect. There is evidence for both points of view. However, a careful analysis of the situation leads to the conclusion that what the executives of smaller firms perceive subjectively as the plan's discrimination in favor of large firms is in reality an outgrowth of the small firms' ignorance in plan matters. As a result, the smaller firms do not make use of the various advantages and positive effects which the plan offers in the same manner as the larger firms do.

Alleviation of the intrasectoral discrimination effect of the plan among executives of smaller firms can only be achieved by increasing their cognition of it and by making them aware also of the gradual change in managerial attitudes among executives of the larger firms. The executives of the larger firms have become more aggressive and efficiency-minded, whereas a majority of the executives of small French firms still adhere to a more traditional, complacent, "live and let live" management concept.

From the analysis of the positive and negative effects of French planning on company operations, two general conclusions can be drawn:

1. To secure the positive effects and advantages of French-style planning generally requires an active endeavor on the part of the firm's management, whereas the negative effects materialize much more "automatically" and can hardly be avoided, particularly if the firm has to rely on external sources of finance.

2. In total, the positive effects of French planning outweigh the real or imagined negative effects. This is certainly the major reason for the rather favorable attitudes toward French planning and the institutional setup among the majority of those business

executives who are cognitive about their country's planning effort. As a result, French executives either laud or ignore but rarely oppose their country's planning system.

This situation does not prevent the executives from voicing strong disapproval of certain plan-related innovations or changes which they feel would create more difficulties and disadvantages than benefits. Numerically, those executives who actively support French planning may be relatively small in comparison with the total number of business executives, but there is no doubt that they represent mainly the large firms, and their attitudes therefore carry considerably more weight than the rather neutral or ignorant attitudes of the others.

The Relevance of the French Experience to the United States

There are some who believe that national planning will never play more than a rudimentary role in our free enterprise system. On the other hand, many people see a growing planning-consciousness in the United States. For instance, in specific large-scale projects by federal, state, and local governments, a good deal of program planning as well as some form of national economic policy planning, more for the purpose of direction than for promotion of development of certain industrial sectors toward explicitly stated national aims, can be observed. Those who believe that a free market system in our age will be successful only if it is supported by substantial elements of long-range forecasting and planning, see a promising development in this increasing planning consciousness at the national level.

In fact, considering the complexity and interdependence of such large-scale programs as the space program, the development of water resources, the construction of the interstate highway system, programs for urban renewal, and the necessary expansion of the ground facilities for air transportation, it becomes obvious that some form of co-ordinated, long-range national plan is necessary. It seems untenable that the decisions with respect to such far-reaching programs should be made largely in response to external pressures or by sheer drifting. There is ample justification for some form of systematic long-range national planning which would lead to an elaboration of national goals, targets, and the means which are necessary to accomplish them within a given time period. Otherwise we will only perpetuate what Secretary of Labor W. Willard Wirtz has characterized in these terms:

> . . . what we are doing really right now is flying the most powerful economic machine in the history of mankind, and I mean to include all of our scientific and technological developments, and we are flying it by luck, by instinct, with almost no instruments at all in the cockpit. . . .

The periodic development of long-range national plans could provide a very suitable instrument panel in the cockpit of our economic "flying machine." The question is: Can we learn anything from the French planning experience? Obviously, since any national planning system must be tailored to the specific economic, social, and political conditions of a country, a duplicate of the French system is quite out of the question. However, certain principles which have proven their worth should be considered:

- The repeated extension of the so-called plan horizon for the successive French plans has shown the value of systematic long-range projections for a period of up to 20 years. These projections are synchronized with the conceptualization and design of a broad spectrum of choices so that decisions conditioning the future can be made in a coherent manner and do not risk involvement in contradictory situations.

- Jean Monnet's idea that a national plan must be derived by a national consensus is certainly a relevant one, although not easy to implement, as the French experience has shown. Nevertheless, a continuous effort has to be made to guarantee that national planning is a collective endeavor, which means that all those who are instrumental in implementation of the plan should also be involved in its preparation. This calls for a particularly active participation by the business community which can provide essential data and information for sectoral projections. A synthesis and harmonization of the various sectoral projections would then lead to a national plan which would become the framework for a co-ordinated application of our economic policy instruments and would provide a basis for effective corporate planning and decision making. This form of national planning, which results from an extensive and organized exchange of information among all the social forces and decision-making centers in the economy, constitutes neither an intrusion into the freedom of private enterprise nor a reduction of competition between the individual firms; competition will only take place at a more enlightened level.

- The French planning system has demonstrated its viability because of its built-in flexibility which has enabled it to respond quickly to new conditions and problems as they arise. Flexibility must certainly be a major characteristic of any national planning system in a free market economy, and it refers particularly to the administrative apparatus, the selection of targets, and the means which have to be applied in order to accomplish the desired goals. One must always keep in mind that there is nothing sacred about national planning; it is only a tool designed to achieve certain specified national objectives in an optimal way. As a tool, national planning can be extended or limited in scope, used for various purposes, and applied under different economic systems.

In addition to these considerations, it is important to recognize—regardless of one's own opinion about the relative merits of national planning —that the methods and procedures which have been developed and tested for national planning purposes can make a significant contribution to increasing the effectiveness of business planning. These methods and procedures can play an important role in devising effective planning systems, particularly for large and conglomerate enterprises. This too is a facet of the interrelationship between national and business planning.

Mergers and Public Policy in Great Britain

C. K. ROWLEY

Introduction

The 1965 Monopolies and Mergers Act will be viewed by many Americans as a logical development in British antitrust policy. The history of British antitrust is brief by comparison with that of the United States. Indeed, prior to 1948 there was no general legislation in Britain concerned with the freedom of companies to create or to abuse positions of market power. Public intervention was limited to specific legislation regulating the activities of public utilities. Private citizens were provided with limited safeguards against damage issuing from the abuse of market power, at common law both in contract (restraint of trade) and in tort (conspiracy).

In 1948, the first rudimentary machinery for the implementation of antitrust in Britain was provided by the Monopolies and Restrictive Practices Act. An administrative tribunal, the Monopolies Commission, was created and was empowered to investigate certain areas of market power at the behest of the appropriate department of government, the Board of Trade. Responsibility for implementing the Commission's recommendations rested with the government. The 1948 legislation established British antitrust policy within the framework of the civil and not the criminal law.

For a period of eight years, the Monopolies Commission was responsible for all investigations into the economic and social effects of private enterprise market power, whether founded upon single firm dominance or upon a network of restrictive agreements operating within the framework

Reprinted from *The Journal of Law and Economics,* Vol. *11,* April 1968, pp. 75–84, by permission of the publisher.

of a trade association or other cartel-like organization. The 1956 Restrictive Trade Practices Act reduced the Commission's area of responsibility and at the same time revitalized British antitrust policy.

The 1956 Act created a judicial body, the Restrictive Practices Court composed of judges and of lay "experts," which was required to adjudicate within the framework of civil law upon restrictive agreements referred to it by the Registrar of Restrictive Trading Agreements. The 1956 Act—in contrast to the 1948 Act—established the onus of proof firmly against the parties to restrictive agreements. To succeed before the Court, it was necessary to negotiate an agreement successfully, through one of seven carefully defined public interest "gateways" and to satisfy the Court in addition that any benefit from the agreement was not outweighed by corresponding detriments. Meanwhile, the Monopolies Commission, in a suitably abbreviated form, retained its jurisdiction over agreements concerning export markets (largely because secrecy was considered important) and over the affairs of the dominant firm.

The combined incidence of the 1948 and the 1956 legislation offered considerable protection to the general public against the abuse of market power. A number of loopholes remained, it is true, but with a relatively simple extension of the existing legislation they could be eliminated. However, the merger path to market power remained unimpeded. During the 1950s, despite a rising trend in the volume of mergers affecting British companies, there was little public concern about such activity.

From 1960 onward, however, public awareness of the merger problem as viewed from an antitrust standpoint, gathered momentum. The politicians of all parties sensed the change in public opinion and responded during the 1964 General Election campaign with promises of merger legislation. In 1965, the newly-elected Labor Government, despite a crowded Parliamentary program, honored its political pledge on the merger issue.

The Legislative Framework

The necessary machinery for the regulation of mergers in Britain was created by the Monopolies and Mergers Act 1965. The pattern of intervention was to be essentially administrative. The judicial machinery, approved since 1956 for the control of restrictive practices, was by-passed. The government through the Board of Trade was to be responsible for the selection of merger references. The Monopolies Commission, in a suitably expanded form, was to direct inquiries and to report in an advisory capacity to the government. The government was to retain full prerogative for the execution of policy, within the limits laid down by the Act.

The 1965 Act affected mergers likely to create or to extend market power. The minimum requirements to be met before a merger could be referred for investigation were clearly established:

. . . either (i) as a result, the following conditions prevail, or do so to a greater extent, as respects the supply of goods or services of any description, that is to say as respects the supply of goods of any description, at least one-third of the goods of that description which are supplied in the United Kingdom or any substantial part thereof are supplied by or to any one per-son, or by or to the persons by whom the enterprises (so far as they continue to be carried on) are carried on, or, as respects the supply of services of that description in the United Kingdom or any substantial part thereof is, to the extent of at least one-third, by or for any one person, or by or for the persons by whom the enterprises (so far as they continue to be carried on) are carried on; or (ii) the value of the assets taken over exceeds five million pounds.

The minimum market share criterion was widely anticipated, although the precise share adopted had been criticized within and without Parliament since its initial introduction in the 1948 legislation. Any attempt at evaluating market power by reference to market share must be arbitrary, not least because of the difficulty of delimiting markets. The one-third minimum share established in 1965 was no exception. At least, however, the measure constituted no more than a threshold requirement for merger investigations. The Monopolies Commission was free to refer to other yardsticks of market power when conducting specific merger inquiries. Few critics could legitimately contend that the threshold of market power determined by the 1965 Act was pitched too high.

The second criterion is more questionable. The President of the Board of Trade was quite specific, during the debate on the second reading of the Bill, that the "value of assets" criterion was designed to deal with market power:

One obvious case . . . is where competition in a vital industry might be markedly reduced. That is why we have provided, as an alternative to the criterion of monopoly, a size of assets test, so that what are called vertical or diversifying mergers could be investigated if the public interest required.

The logic of this analysis is difficult to follow. In what manner conglomerate mergers might provide companies with power in specific markets was not explained. And if the President was concerned lest in due course the conglomerate company might extend its share of specific markets through the medium of subsidized competition a safeguard already existed in the form of the 1948 legislation. It is possible that the President of the Board of Trade was confused between company size and economic power, a confusion not at all uncommon among members of the Parliamentary Labour Party. For the most part the value of assets criterion appears to be irrelevant when evaluating mergers in terms of antitrust policy. It is not without interest, therefore, that five out of the first six non-newspaper mergers to be investigated under the Act were referred to the Commission on the value of assets criterion.

Upon receipt of a merger reference the Monopolies Commission was first to report whether the merger satisfied the criteria established by Section 6(1)(b) and if so to investigate and to report whether the merger operated, or might be expected to operate, against the public interest:

> . . . and if the Commission so find, the Commission shall consider whether any and if so what action (whether under this Act or otherwise and whether by a Minister of the Crown, government department or other authority or by the parties concerned themselves) should be taken to remedy or prevent any mischiefs which result or may be expected to result, and may, if they think fit, include recommendations as to such action in their report.

The 1965 Act laid down a time-limit within which each merger inquiry should be completed. The Monopolies Commission was to report upon a reference within such time-period as was specified by the Board of Trade or within such further time, not exceeding three months, as the Board of Trade might allow. If a report was made outside the established limit it was not to be published and no proceedings were to be taken upon it. The Act established a maximum period of six months (nine months with the extension) within which each merger report was to be completed.

The reason for the time-limit on merger investigations is clear. The government was empowered to refer merger proposals before they were acted upon; if necessary a "stand still" order to prevent the premature completion of a merger might be made. In such circumstances, speed of inquiry might be of paramount importance. The shares of the companies concerned might well be the subject of speculation; share prices might then fluctuate considerably. Speculation of this kind might weaken the ability of affected companies to raise new capital at times when investment opportunities were otherwise attractive. Moreover, any movement in share prices during the investigation period might affect existing shareholders' decisions as to the attractiveness of the merger proposal. Counter bids might take place during the "stand still" period for the control of either or of both parties under investigation. If such bids were to fall outside the scope of the 1965 Act, they might well succeed before the Monopolies Commission was able to complete its inquiries.

A speedy inquiry is little less important in the case of completed mergers. Lengthy investigations might delay the desired reorganization of management and the rationalization of production. In the meantime, enthusiasm for reform within the combine might be dissipated and vested interests in the maintenance of the existing order might be allowed to strengthen their position. If, on the other hand, reorganization and rationalization should proceed apace, prior to the completion of the investigations, a recommendation that the acquisition be divested might prove very difficult to implement. However undesirable the merger, the cost of divestment might even outweigh the benefits which would ensue.

Nevertheless, the six-month time limit on merger inquiries was received with some surprise, and not a little concern. The Monopolies Commission had been criticized consistently since 1948 for slowness in completing its inquiries. A number of its dominant firm inquiries had taken six years to complete. Was it possible, asked the skeptics, for the Commission to report authoritatively within six months of receiving a merger reference? And if it could not report authoritatively, should it be required to report at all, on matters of considerable economic importance?

> In certain respects the provisions of the Bill in relation to mergers give rise to anxiety. It is difficult to see how the Commission could produce an authoritative report in the time allotted. . . . The Monopolies Commission could easily mar its reputation in other fields by poor work on merger references.

By empowering the Board of Trade to delay proposed mergers, the Labour Government exceeded the proposals of the 1965 Conservative White Paper. The "stand still" provision acknowledged the complexity of implementing divestment recommendations. On the one hand, it might prove extremely difficult to unscramble assets once rationalization had occurred. On the other hand, the divestment of an acquisition might have to proceed slowly to avoid inflicting hardship upon existing shareholders. It is not an easy task to unload large blocks of voting stock on a market accustomed to dealing in marginal share transfers, without affecting stock values adversely. It is true, that institutional investors might be persuaded on occasion to take up large "placings" of stocks; this was achieved, for example, in the denationalization of British steel during the mid-1950s. But circumstances might not always be suitable.

"Stand still" orders prohibiting the completion of referred merger proposals could be annulled by resolution of either House of Parliament. In any event, they became invalid forty days after the Commission's report was published, unless subsequent action was taken by the government. Despite their limited scope, the "stand still" orders aroused resentment within the business sector. Many businessmen considered that the existence of such powers were irreconcilable with the pragmatic approach to market power which was supposed to underlie British legislation. More extreme critics viewed the "stand still" provision as a further stage in the inexorable extension of authoritarian government in Britain. "Stand still" powers have been used by the Board of Trade in two of the first six non-newspaper mergers referred to the Monopolies Commission.

The 1965 Act did not lay down public interest "guidelines" to assist the Monopolies Commission in its inquiries. The lack of direction in the merger legislation contrasts markedly with the precise public interest "gateways" determined in 1956 for the Restrictive Practices Court:

> In considering . . . whether the fact of enterprises having ceased to be distinct enterprises operates or may be expected to operate against the public interest, the Commission shall take into account all matters which appear in the particular circumstances to be relevant and have regard (amongst other things) to any matters to which the Board may from time to time direct them to have regard; and the Board shall publish any direction under this subsection in such manner as they think fit.

The unwillingness of the Labour Government to prescribe public interest "guidelines" for merger inquiries conflicted with the policy of the previous Conservative Government as outlined in its 1964 White Paper:

> The Government contemplate directing the Commission's attention to certain considerations. . . . They have in mind such considerations as efficiency, technical and technological advance, industrial growth and competitive power in international trade.

In part, the omission of public interest criteria from the 1965 Act reflected widespread scepticism about the usefulness of broadly defined "guidelines" and concern lest a more precise wording of the statute should introduce undesirable rigidity into the Monopolies Commission's inquiries. Undoubtedly, there was a genuine desire to allow the Commission considerable flexibility, at least during the initial merger inquiries. Fundamentally, the philosophy of the government on mergers was one of pragmatism.

With the extension of British antitrust to encompass mergers, a corresponding need arose for new statutory powers to enforce contrary decisions of the Monopolies Commission. The appropriate powers were provided by Section 3 of the 1965 Act:

> (5) The Board may prohibit or restrict the acquisition by any person of the whole or part of the undertaking or assets of another person's trade or business, or the doing of anything which will or may result in any bodies corporate becoming interconnected bodies corporate, or may require that, if such an acquisition is made or anything is done which has that result, the persons concerned or any of them shall thereafter observe any prohibitions or restrictions imposed by or under the order. (6) The Board may provide for the division of any trade or business by the sale of any part of the undertaking or assets or otherwise (for which purpose all the activities carried on by way of trade or business by any one person or by any two or more interconnected bodies corporate may be treated as a single trade or business), or for the division of any group of interconnected bodies corporate, and for all such matters as may be necessary to effect or take account of the division. . . .

These extensive powers of intervention were exercisable by the making of an appropriate statutory instrument. Retrospective Parliamentary sanction for an order was possible where immediate intervention was deemed necessary. The Board of Trade was able to prohibit acquisitions, to lay down conditions, and to order their dissolution. Perhaps the most important postwar extension of the power of the executive in the affairs of the private sector was legislated with scarce a suspicion of public anxiety. Thus far has the climate of opinion shifted in recent years in Britain in favor of executive intervention in the affairs of private enterprise.

The 1965 Act established the framework for the public supervision of mergers. Those most intimately affected by the new legislation awaited with some concern the early reports of the Monopolies Commission. For the most part, however, the legislation was received with considerable satisfaction and not a little complacency.

Public Interest Issues

Since the 1965 Act failed to establish precise public interest "guidelines" for merger inquiries, the responsibility for so doing rested with the Monopolies Commission. In many respects, this was not undesirable. The Monopolies Commission had paved the way between 1948 and 1955 for the public interest "gateways" which were laid down in the 1956 Restrictive Trade Practices Act. Moreover, from the Commission's dominant firm reports after 1956 public interest criteria had emerged which might be relied upon by companies anxious to comply with the current philosophy of antitrust in Britain. It was not unreasonable to presume that the Commission might conduct a similar exercise in the field of mergers.

The task facing the Monopolies Commission should not be underestimated. Comparatively little is known about the economic effects of mergers. By its nature, a merger investigation puts considerable emphasis upon the predictive powers of the Commission. Any conclusion must inevitably be the more susceptible to public criticism. Nevertheless, the Commission has set about its task in a positive—some would say a cavalier—fashion.

At the time of writing six non-newspaper merger investigations have been completed by the Monopolies Commission. In three instances, the mergers were allowed to proceed prior to the completion of the Monopolies Commission's investigations. (The British Motor Corporation Limited and the Pressed Steel Company Limited; Guest Keen and Nettlefolds Limited and Birfield Limited; British Insulated Callender's Cables Limited and Pyrotenax Limited.) In each of these, the Commission reported favorably upon the merger. In one instance the merger was not completed, although the Board of Trade had not exercised its "stand still" powers. (United Drapery Stores Limited and Montague Burton Limited.) In this case, the Commission recorded a contrary decision. On two occasions, the Board of

Trade made use of its "stand still" powers. (Ross Group Limited and Associated Fisheries Limited; The Dental Manufacturing Company Limited or The Dentists' Supply Company of New York and the Amalgamated Dental Company Limited.) In the former case, the Commission recorded a contrary decision. In the latter, it reported favorably upon each proposal. The Board of Trade has conscientiously supported the Commission's conclusions.

Discussion Questions

1. How does economic planning in France affect the decision making of the individual French firm?
2. Does the French experience suggest that a similar policy of national planning in the United States could be compatible with America's traditional ties to a free enterprise economy?
3. What policies have the British followed in dealing with corporate mergers?
4. Compare British and U.S. anti-monopoly policies.

Income Distribution and Wage Determination

The highly related issues of income distribution and wage determination are important concerns for economic society. The issues are related to the extent that one society will, for example, reward certain occupations much more than another country relative to some other set of job skills, for example, doctors' and lawyers' incomes relative to the income of semi-skilled manual workers. They are also interrelated in so far as a society makes a choice as to how capital will be rewarded relative to labor. In the aggregate, the degree of inequality between various groups reflects these societal decisions and is often a measure of the degree to which a country is attempting to pursue the ephemeral concept of economic justice.

There are a variety of causes for occupational differentials as well as for the differences which arise between large groups of individuals. Such factors as skills, whether innate or acquired, the structure of demand for certain kinds of job skills, discrimination, the raw market power of individual corporations, as well as the clout of powerful labor unions, all enter in the scenario.

The article by Berislav Šefer is a comprehensive description and analysis of how Yugoslavia, coping with the dual problem of harnessing a socialist ideology to market forces, and wedded to the concept of worker control, pursues income distribution policies. Berndt Öhman's analysis of the behavior of Sweden's most powerful labor organization, the LO, calls attention to the way in which the union exercises its strength within the Swedish economy. He shows that the LO (Federation of Swedish Trade Unions) has moved from a position of trying to maximize its own vested interests to one of consideration of the impact of its actions on the economy as a whole.

Berislav Šefer was formerly Head of the Federal Bureau for Economic Planning in Yugoslavia. He is now Professor at the Political Science College in Belgrade and Scientific Associate of the Economic Institute in Zagreb. Berndt Öhman is associated with The Institute for Labour Studies in Stockholm.

Income Distribution in Yugoslavia

Income distribution policy is a topical issue in all countries, regardless of their economic and social systems or levels of development. On the other hand, a country's level of development and its economic and social system do determine the nature of the problems to which it gives rise and the methods adopted by society to deal with them. In this sense, Yugoslavia has its own approach and its own procedures, and Yugoslav society has an entirely individual way of bringing its influence to bear.

Income Distribution in the Context of a Market Economy and a Self-Management Scheme

In Yugoslavia undertakings act as the basis and mainspring of economic development. This is because of the three fundamental tenets of the country's socio-economic system:

1. the social ownership of the means of production throughout most of the economy and the consequent exclusion of private ownership as a basis for appropriating the fruits of other people's labor;
2. the existence of a market economy, subject to the operation of economic laws, above all, the law of values;
3. the workers' self-management scheme, which is a concrete manifestation of socialist relationships and entitles the workers, through their self-management bodies, to decide how part of the revenue of undertakings should be used.

Workers in Yugoslavia do not "earn wages." What are known as their "personal incomes" consist of a share in the total revenue available for distribution by the undertakings in the productive sphere or institutions in the non-productive sphere [1] in which they are employed. Undertakings derive this revenue from their work and the marketing of their products or services. After discharging their obligations toward society in the form of taxes and contributions, they are free to use the remainder for the payment of personal incomes, the maintenance of "common consumption

Reprinted from the *International Labour Review*, Vol. *97*, No. 4, April 1968, pp. 371–389, by permission of the publisher.

[1] The productive sphere comprises industry, mining, agriculture, forestry, construction, communications, trade, catering, and handicrafts, that is, fields in which new commodities are produced. The non-productive sphere comprises education, health, social insurance, government, social protection, and other, similar social activities where no new commodities are produced. The division is based on the Marxist approach to productive and non-productive work.

funds" (catering for certain collective social needs), or for capital investment. Institutions in the non-productive sphere enjoy similar freedom but do not derive their revenue in the same way; most of it comes from budgetary or other public funds, depending on the social significance of their work and their specific programs and results. Consequently, personal incomes are not fixed by society on the basis of general regulations, wage scales or wage agreements; society's main concern is to provide uniform conditions in which incomes can be earned.

Undertakings are thus free to make many economic decisions affecting the volume and pattern of production (and, by extension, the income they will earn), as well as the distribution of their income. This process, of course, is subject not only to the normal laws of the market itself but also to certain constraints imposed by the community (and especially the state).

In the first place, an undertaking must produce in order to earn a share in the distribution of income. Since it is exposed to market forces, moreover, it has to operate efficiently, making the best possible use of all factors of production (labor, equipment, raw materials, and power); otherwise it will not be competitive. It earns its income by marketing its goods, and the size of its income depends on how far it meets demand and how efficiently it operates.[2] For objective economic reasons as well as in its own interest, it must avoid distributing its entire revenue in the form of personal incomes for its workers and must set aside a proportion for investment; otherwise, both production and consumption will subsequently stagnate.[3] Its aim is thus to expand production, thereby increasing its own revenue and the funds available for personal income, that is for raising living standards. A mechanism is thus built into the system itself to ensure that the immediate objective of economic activity is to promote the wel-

---

[2] Price increases can also be a source of revenue, of course, but the fact that revenue is derived in this way does not necessarily imply a departure from the principle of distribution in proportion to the work done. (In accordance with the law of values, goods are marketed at prices that take account not only of their individual production cost but of the average cost as recognized by society. The more efficient manufacturer accordingly earns more on each new product: conversely, the more expensive manufacturer earns less. This, however, does not mean that the principle of distribution according to the work done has been abandoned. It merely means that distribution is subject to the laws of a market economy.) It is specifically to prevent prices from becoming an unjustified source of revenue that one of the major aims of social policy and development planning is to achieve stability and combat inflation. Most prices are still state-controlled or subject to supervision.

[3] Yugoslav experience over a period of 10 years or so of progressive decentralization of funds and economic decision making has shown that undertakings are acutely aware of this. Even undertakings with relatively low levels of personal income have earmarked large sums for investment. In this connection see Savka Dabčević-Kučar, Miladin Korać, Miloša Samardjija, Jakov Sirotković, Rikard Štajner, and Tihomir Vlaškalić: *Problemi teorije i prakse socijalističke robne proizvodnje u Jugoslaviji* [Problems of the theory and practice of socialist commodity production in Yugoslavia] (Zagreb: Ekonomska biblioteka, Informator, 1965), especially pp. 53–95.

fare of the people and that the wealth so created is distributed solely on the basis of the results of work, as measured by the market.[4]

Within the socio-economic structure described above the state has a specific part to play, primarily in securing uniform conditions for the operation of undertakings and in insuring that the income of each group of workers increases in proportion to the results produced by its members. This is achieved by planning and the operation of various economic controls such as taxation, price and credit policies, import and export regulations, and the allocation of long-term credits (which influence investment and industrial expansion). These controls constitute the second form of constraint within which undertakings and institutions operate.

The aim of government action, however, is not to usurp the functions of the undertakings but to create conditions in which self-management can operate effectively. The state—that is to say the Federation and the individual republics and communes—also appropriates part of the income of undertakings in the form of taxes, which are then devoted to various common purposes such as administration and defense; to certain social activities[5] such as social and health insurance, education and the arts, and to economic development projects, where the money is used for investment, to offset customs tariffs, to assist economically backward areas, and so on.

From what has been said above, it should be clear that in the Yugoslav system the problem of income distribution arises in a quite specific form. Individual, sectoral, regional or other income differentials are primarily a reflection of differences in the results of work; they act as an incentive to economic development, increased production and higher earnings, an incentive which, it may be hoped, will ultimately lead to the elimination of differences in general. If the incomes earned by certain groups or in certain areas are low, this is mainly due to their low level of economic development and limited resources and not to the actual system, which is based on equality.[6] This being so, the main emphasis in income distribution policy and in society's efforts to influence income distribution and development must be directed toward creating uniform eco-

---

[4] See Berislav Šefer: *Životni standard i privredni razvoj Jugoslavije* [Living standard and economic development of Yugoslavia] (Zagreb: Ekonomska biblioteka, Informator, 1965), pp. 10–19.

[5] These activities have not been completely organized along self-management lines and are still economically separate; even here, however, it is hoped to reduce the role of the state as an intermediary in the course of time and to integrate these activities within the self-management economy.

[6] All underdeveloped countries with limited basic resources face the problem of how far poverty should be reduced by a redistribution of income and how far a solution should be sought in economic expansion and a higher general level of earnings. While society's efforts must be directed toward establishing equitable criteria for income distribution, the main emphasis must be on laying a proper foundation for the eradication of poverty in general. A policy of redistribution according to the results of work provides the necessary economic incentives while respecting the principle of social justice.

nomic and social conditions, so that differences in income are the closest possible reflection of differences in the results of work and are not caused by other factors such as monopoly or privilege, or by inequalities in the level of economic development or of education and other social conditions affecting the workers' opportunities. This is where action by society is needed—which is not by any means the same as action by the state; as the economy and society develop, such action can and indeed must be organized along self-management lines.[7]

The government has many ways of achieving its objective of uniform conditions. The most important is its prices policy, which is pursued both by means of price fixing and through society's supervision of price levels. This provides the economic basis for the initial distribution of revenue as between undertakings. Another method is the distribution of revenue within the undertaking: interest is levied on fixed and circulating assets, contributions are payable to various budgets and toward such purposes as education and the social health insurance schemes; there is also a legal definition of what is to be regarded as revenue. Legislation has been passed fixing a minimum percentage for depreciation, although undertakings are at liberty to raise this figure. Business conditions are also influenced by foreign exchange controls and the machinery of international trade (how far and in what ways commercial dealings with other countries should be liberalized or domestic industry protected, and so on). Credit policies and the bank rate are other factors. Finally, investment programs are affected by the funds available in the central banks, whose policy is to a large extent determined by the Federation.

The self-management system was introduced in Yugoslavia 17 years ago, but it is still, in a sense, in its initial stages. At that time the country was at a very low level of development, and even after the system was introduced the government had to play a very active part in all spheres of social and economic life, including income distribution policy. As the economy developed, the material basis came to be laid for a change in policy; this is the process that is now underway and in some senses is only beginning. Hence, although Yugoslavia is now undoubtedly moving toward less government intervention and greater freedom for undertakings and the other agencies of the self-management system in matters of income distribution, it must be remembered that the movement started from a point where all decisions in such matters lay with government.

---

[7] It would be impossible within the limits of an article to give an account of all the premises on which the Yugoslav economic and social system is based. For a more thorough treatment of the subject the reader is referred to Mijalko Todorović: *Oslobodjenje rada* [The freeing of work] (Belgrade: Kultura, 1965); Milentije Popović: *Društveno ekonomski sistem* [The social and economic system] (Belgrade: Kultura, 1964), pp. 259–400; *idem: Neposredna socijalistička demokratija* [Direct social democracy] (Belgrade: Kultura, 1966), pp. 172–199; Miladin Korač-Tihomir Vlaškalić: *Politička ekonomija* [Political economy] (Belgrade: Rad, 1966), pp. 185–215 and 301–349.

Basic Features of Income Distribution

Trends Up to 1964

Fundamental changes were made in the distribution of national income immediately after World War II.

First, the ratio between capital accumulation and consumption in the over-all distribution of national income was radically altered. It has been estimated that the rate of capital accumulation between the wars was between 5 and 8 percent, giving an average annual growth rate of national income of about 2.2 percent.[8] Immediately after World War II the rate of accumulation rose to about 20 percent (or a little over); this figure has been maintained and has even tended to increase throughout the 20-odd years since the war. For the level of economic development attained at that time it represented a very high rate of capital accumulation, involving a deliberate restriction of consumption.

Secondly, the available consumer goods were redistributed to benefit the workers and small farmers at the expense of the capitalists and middle classes, whose level of consumption was high. This redistribution, which is estimated to have affected about 40 percent of the total volume of such goods, substantially improved the living standards of the recipients in the immediate postwar period.[9]

Thirdly, the entire system of business enterprise was reorganized on the basis of direct management by the state, and in consequence income distribution policy was wholly determined by government decision. From 1950 this system was gradually replaced by the self-management scheme and the whole economic and social structure was reformed accordingly.

In spite of the radical changes that resulted, the proportion of total net income available to undertakings remained at the unsatisfactorily low level of about 40 percent.[10] Undertakings normally had sufficient revenue to maintain the standard of living of their workers (that is through the payment of personal incomes and the establishment of "common consumption funds"), but they had relatively little money left over for new capital projects, and most of the surplus devoted to investment came from outside sources in the form of credits from the Federation and the individual republics and communes. This did not provide the self-management scheme with a particularly broad base on which to operate; hence the constant tendency to spread the burden of investment by a steadily increasing recourse to taxation. In addition, the state assumed responsibility for financing and developing all non-productive activities; many benefits in the field

---

[8] Ivo Vinski: *Nacionalni dohodak i fiksni fondovi na području Jugoslavije 1904–1959* [National income and fixed assets in Yugoslavia, 1904–1959] (Zagreb: Ekonomski Institut, 1963).

[9] Šefer, *op. cit*, p. 59.

[10] *Komuna i standard* (Belgrade: Rad, 1960), p. 64.

of social health insurance, education, and so on, were progressively extended in this way, and it is not surprising that there was no substantial change in the proportion of the gross social product available to undertakings until 1963, when it amounted to about 48 percent, rising further to around 50 percent in 1964.[11]

It is precisely because of these features of income distribution up to 1964 that there was no significant change in the over-all distribution of gross social product. The share of consumption, and especially personal consumption, in fact diminished over that period, while the share of investment increased.

In defining its economic policy the government has stated that this trend has been one of the basic flaws in income distribution in the past and must be progressively corrected with the help of the reforms undertaken in the last two years (about which more will be said later).

The very rapid expansion of the national economy over recent years has meant a considerable increase in all forms of income affecting the standard of living—especially those devoted to personal consumption, such as personal incomes, pensions, children's allowances, and the private earnings of self-employed farmers and handicraft workers. There has been a similar increase in the volume of revenue allocated to various social purposes of major importance for the workers, such as education and health. Real national income over the period 1956–1964 increased by about 118 percent, or 10.2 percent per year. The real volume of personal consumption rose by 98 percent and public consumption by 284 percent, representing annual averages of 9 and 18.3 percent respectively. Measured in terms of these last two items the money available out of current income for the improvement of living standards increased by 122 percent, or 10.5 percent per year.[12]

This high rate of growth has been a contributory factor in the very rapid improvement in the standard of living of the population. Even so, it is typical that personal consumption has risen more slowly than national income—despite the fact that any improvement in the latter, as was mentioned earlier, was obtained at the cost of a depressed level of personal consumption—and that the volume of revenue available for public consumption has been expanding very much more rapidly. This is undesirable; it has meant that personal incomes, which are directly related to the results of work and to business generally, have not kept pace with the rising trend of national income. They have admittedly improved with the rapid

---

[11] Author's estimates.

[12] The figures for national income are based on *Statistički godišnjak FNRJ*, 1966, p. 110, and those for personal consumption and social expenditure are an estimate made by the Federal Bureau for Economic Planning. Social expenditure covers material outlay on social projects and capital investment (including housing) in the same sphere, that is, only expenditure directly serving to improve the standard of living; it excludes the cost of administration and national defense.

over-all expansion of the economy, but the disparity has reduced the effect of several factors in the standard of living that act as a direct incentive to business and economic development, while greater prominence has been given to other factors unrelated to the results of work as far as the individual is concerned. Through the use of public funds there has in fact been a steady increase in expenditure not only on activities such as education and health services that naturally have to be financed in this way but also on other activities that should normally be paid for out of personal incomes and as part of personal expenditure, on condition that society contributes to their development in other ways.[13]

The building of houses and flats has been a typical example; over the past few years housing schemes have relied exclusively on public sources of credit, while private individuals have played little or no part in solving housing problems. In addition, with the level of personal incomes as low as it has been, some types of consumer goods have had to be subsidized, with the result that income rates have become even less meaningful than before and the criteria for income distribution have become increasingly distorted.[14] When it is remembered that education, health, and other social services are financed entirely out of budgetary funds (or in some similar way out of special public credits), that housing has been the exclusive concern of the public authorities, and that many consumer goods and services have been subsidized, one is forced to conclude that the economic conditions required to establish a direct link between standards of living and the results of work and business generally have not been fulfilled in practice and that the economic foundations for a distribution "to each according to his work" has not been laid.

As the data quoted earlier have shown, the past few years have been remarkable for the high rate of economic growth and the accompanying expansion of personal consumption and all types of income for the improvement of living standards. Further evidence can be found in the fact that real personal incomes increased by 80 percent, or 7.5 percent per year, between 1956 and 1964.[15] But it is also clear that there has not been an adequate policy for distribution either as between personal and public consumption or even in the single sphere of personal consumption, on account of the grants and subsidies that have been paid. By weakening the control of the workers over income distribution and enlarging the role of the state in this sphere, this has been instrumental in slowing down the economic and social processes based on the workers' self-management scheme and in reducing the benefits of development as a whole. An over-

---

[13] The result has been a very heavy burden of taxes and contributions on personal incomes, amounting in 1964 to 73.2 percent of net income.

[14] In 1964 subsidies and grants represented about 7 percent of net personal incomes. See Šefer, op. cit., p. 84.

[15] *Statistički godišnjak FNRJ, 1966*, p. 272.

haul of the system, or rather of the machinery through which it operated, was evidently necessary, and in mid-1965 far-reaching economic reforms began to be introduced.

The Reforms of 1965

The aims of these reforms, which are still under way, are briefly as follows. It is hoped to lay the foundation for a consolidation of the workers' self-management scheme in all sectors of the economy and society, to relieve the state of responsibility for the distribution of total income (including the funds necessary for economic growth), to make further progress in the international division of labor, to effect a transition from labor-intensive to capital-intensive industry, and to increase the general efficiency of business. Once this last aim has been achieved, it will be financially possible to increase the proportion of revenue devoted to personal consumption, to reduce that devoted to investment and other forms of public expenditure, and to link the individual worker's standard of living more directly with the results of his work.

The reforms began with changes in price levels and price structures. Subsidies on consumer goods were slashed and, to offset the increased cost of living, undertakings and institutions scaled up their workers' personal incomes as far as their available resources allowed. In this way earnings were brought into a more realistic relationship with prices and were more directly geared to economic performance, thus establishing a consistent link between the standard of living and the results of work, with a built-in guarantee that greater efficiency would mean higher total revenues for undertakings and hence more money for the workers in the form of personal income. Since all non-productive activities—including social services, such as education and health—are financed from taxes on personal incomes, the system provides automatic machinery for increasing the revenue in the non-productive sphere, in line with trends in the productive sphere.

Simultaneous changes were introduced in connection with housing. Rents were fixed at a realistic level that would cover maintenance and depreciation and allow a reasonable margin for new building. Certain public funds that had previously been raised by special taxation were made over to undertakings. Rent subsidies will continue to be paid by undertakings as a temporary measure until 1970 when the degressive annual rate will lapse and rents will be paid entirely out of the workers' own pockets. In principle, housing has been made to pay its way, any necessary credits being provided by the banks.

Sweeping changes were also made in the non-productive sphere. Social insurance contributions and taxes were reduced, and expenditure was accordingly scaled down to what was financially possible; hitherto it had had a tendency to snowball out of all proportion to the real capabilities of the economy, as was seen above.

The reforms now under way should integrate productive and non-productive activities more closely, consolidate the position of the workers' self-management scheme and gradually reduce the function of the state as an intermediary and organizer.[16] In principle, this should pave the way for an increasing recognition of higher living standards as the motive force in economic and social progress in a system where the distribution of purchasing power among the different sectors of the population is more consistently linked with the results of work, and where public consumption and the corresponding funds are kept separate from personal consumption and earned income.

From the results so far achieved these objectives are clearly being attained, in spite of certain difficulties. Undertakings now have about 60 percent of total net revenue at their disposal. In the initial stages there was a temporary drop in living standards, because the adjustment of personal incomes was not completed until six months later. Even so, the drop in real terms had not merely been checked by 1966—the trend had actually been reversed; real personal consumption had risen by between 4.5 and 5 percent and average real earnings per employed person by about 11 percent. The appreciable difference between the two growth rates is chiefly attributable to a major increase in savings and a contraction of consumer credit, both of which occurred around the same time. This marks the opening of a new phase in income distribution policy in general and in the realm of living standards in particular; it should lead to a further improvement in welfare, based essentially on economic performance, and a gradual reduction in the redistribution of income by the state.[17]

Problems of Personal Incomes

From the foregoing it will be readily appreciated that the problem of personal incomes in Yugoslavia is an extremely complicated one.

The Basis of Personal Income

One constant preoccupation is to co-ordinate real personal income trends with changes in the productivity of labor. This in its turn raises the basic question of how productivity should be measured.

In a market economy where the means of production are managed directly by the workers, and where the workers decide how most of the revenue should be employed, personal incomes cannot be determined solely on the basis of physical output per worker; this could in fact rise considerably, while all the other indicators of business efficiency were on

---

[16] The various charges on personal incomes in the form of social insurance contributions taxes, etc., have been reduced to 51.7 percent of net income.

[17] All figures for 1966 are provisional estimates.

the wane. The capacities of the market, for example, may have been miscalculated; products may have met with sales resistance; the cost of raw materials and supplies may have increased; and other operating expenses may have risen. Any of these circumstances would inevitably lead to financial inconsistencies and even to actual losses. Under a workers' self-management scheme, these have to be borne by those responsible for the unsatisfactory conduct of affairs and for the mistakes of economic planning. Otherwise the state would have to assume responsibility for redistributing revenue among undertakings, which would naturally imply a different social basis for economic enterprise.

The revenue earned by undertakings is therefore the basic criterion of labor productivity, because it reflects society's assessment of the market value of the work performed (due allowance being made, of course, for expenditure on raw materials, power, and other production and operating costs). However, since business conditions vary depending on the market and the workings of the economic system, total revenue and personal incomes roughly follow the same trends as the average social productivity of labor in the broadest sense of the term.

Income is not distributed, therefore, on the basis of individual performance alone; a corrective is applied not only by the market but also by society in different ways. It nevertheless remains true that an undertaking doing more than average business always has a chance of earning more than average revenue (with commensurate earnings for the workers), which is in itself an incentive to economic efficiency.

Mention was made earlier of the various ways in which society brings its influence to bear—through prices, credit policies, taxes and contributions, long-term credit arrangements for industrial expansion programs, foreign trade policies, and so on. All these forms of economic pressure can indirectly affect the earning power of undertakings and hence the personal incomes of their workers.

Income Differentials

It is against this background that personal incomes are determined in the different economic sectors, subsectors, and individual undertakings (and also in institutions in the non-productive sphere in the light of the proportion earmarked for the purpose in the distribution of total revenue). It is likewise on this basis that personal income differentials arise as between different sectors and subsectors and different undertakings and institutions, and also between and within occupations.

Average personal incomes per worker obviously vary quite considerably from one sector of the productive or non-productive sphere to another; in fact they can only serve as a very rough guide, because the average for a given sector or subsector covers widely different skills and hence widely different incomes (which are society's recognition of results). Taking the average personal income of all employed persons in 1966 as 100, the highest average rate (187) was earned in design of organizations, and the lowest (77) in the timber industry. The inter-sectoral differential was therefore in the region of 100:240. The industries with the best averages were petroleum, electrical equipment, shipbuilding, chemicals, air and sea transport, foreign trade, and banking.[18] A comparison with the position in other countries shows that, broadly speaking, the same range of average incomes occurs as between the different sectors. Industries obviously develop at different rates according to the country, and it would be difficult to lay down any hard and fast rules or standards regarding differentials throughout the world. It is clear, even so, that average personal incomes in some sectors of the Yugoslav economy are comparatively low because of the depressed level of their total revenue. Coal mining is one example. The collieries' difficulties, however, have wider economic implications than the limited problem of the miners' earnings and are different in nature. The entire coal mining industry needs modernizing: a number of pits are uneconomic and will have to be shut down, the pattern of fuel consumption is changing, and so on. As far as their incomes are concerned teachers are also at a disadvantage. Here the problem is connected with the very rapid growth of education and the unsystematic distribution and structure of the school network; any solution to income problems will therefore have to be sought in a more rational organization of the educational system.

Depending on training, average personal incomes in the economy as a whole may vary from an index number of 100 for unskilled laborers to 247 for persons with a university-level education. The gap is narrower in the productive sphere (100:244) and wider in the non-productive sphere (100:287).

The skill differentials are not large and may even be considered inadequate to reflect the real differences in work performed. This is due to the earlier policy of wage equality, with its fixed rates for each occupation and level of skill—a tradition that still lingers. The differential between the lowest-paid 5 percent of the labor force (semi-skilled and unskilled workers in public services and government) and the best-paid 5 percent (persons with a university-level or other advanced form of education) in both the productive and the non-productive spheres is about 100:260, or a little above the over-all figure. Given that the skill structure of the labor force is still not homogeneous enough, skill differentials must be expected to widen to some extent in the changed conditions of economic life; this is regarded as desirable at this stage in the country's development.[19]

---

[18] *Savezni Zavod za statistiku: Indeks, 1967,* No. 4.

[19] The present differentials are still relatively modest and do not provide sufficient incentives, as may be seen from the following example. Before World War II the ratio between an unskilled worker's wage and the salary of a factory manager varied between 1:14 and 1:20. It is now about 1:6 or 1:7 and may be even further reduced if the family budget is swollen by children's allowances.

Differentials in average personal income also exist within a given skill group, depending on the activity, sector or subsector in which the worker is employed. These vary from group to group and are smallest for persons with a secondary education (where the ratio between the lowest and highest averages for persons of equal skill engaged in different activities was (100:121), unskilled workers (100:126) and skilled workers (100:119). They are highest for university-level specialists (100:143), highly skilled workers (100:140) and specialists with an advanced level of education (100:135). Although these figures in principle relate to persons in the same skill categories, they obviously mask the differentials due to occupation; unfortunately there is no up-to-date information for average personal income on an occupational basis. It is also a fact that differences in average personal incomes can be found in the same related occupations. This encourages labor mobility, which in turn makes for greater uniformity of income rates. It also argues an economic need for investment and better working conditions, which would tend to iron out differences in the total revenue of undertakings.

It has already been observed that personal income differentials are unsatisfactory from the economic point of view. About 70 percent of all employed persons fall in an income bracket ranging from 20 percent above to 20 percent below the general average. If this situation were plotted as a Lorenz curve, it would be obvious how far the pattern of income rate is affected by the earlier policy of wage equality. Further evidence can be found in the coefficient of inequality, which over the past few years has been appreciably less than 20 percent.[20] In an economy where personal income acts as the fundamental and direct incentive to economic development this fact, when viewed in the light of the nature of the economic and social system, presents a problem, because differentials of this order do not afford an adequate incentive.

Cost of Living

A further point that needs to be stressed in connection with personal incomes is that a great many problems have arisen in recent years on account of the increased cost of living. The reforms in the economic system were based on sweeping changes in price levels and price relationships, and the cost of living has risen fairly sharply since 1965, when the changes began to be made.[21] Real incomes have not kept pace with increases in nominal

---

[20] The coefficient of inequality indicates how much of the money available for the payment of personal incomes would have to be redistributed for all workers to have the same average earnings. It is quoted only as an illustration of the present situation and not in any way as a yardstick for attempting to achieve greater equality. In view of the data available to the author the figure should be regarded as an approximation; it is based on the distribution of personal incomes by level of income (see *Indeks*, 1967, No. 4, op. cit.).

rates and this has reduced their effectiveness as an incentive.[22] One of the purposes of the reforms was to lay a foundation for stable prices and a stable cost of living, without which there could be no hope of applying the principle that the workers' real personal incomes should depend on the results of their work and be distributed on that basis. Signs of an improvement have been visible in recent months, mainly because economic policy measures have succeeded in bringing the purchasing power of money into line with the available funds. Otherwise, personal incomes are adjusted to the cost of living by the undertakings themselves, bearing in mind the revenue at their disposal. Provision has been made by law for pensions to be scaled up if the cost of living rises by more than 3 percent.

Minimum and Maximum Rates of Income

One final problem in connection with personal incomes is that of maximum and minimum rates. The reader will by now have realized that personal incomes are determined freely in the light of the financial position of the undertaking. In this sense there is no set maximum or minimum. Provision has nevertheless been made for a minimum personal income to be paid to all workers if their undertaking is in difficulties and cannot itself pay a sufficient income.

As regards higher incomes, in addition to the general taxes payable by all workers on a pro rata basis, a progressive tax is also levied on personal incomes above 20,000 dinars[23] at the rates shown in Table 1.

It is not the aim of social policy in Yugoslavia to guarantee a minimum standard or to prevent those who wish to from earning more and more; all incomes are a reflection of the worker's job and the results of his work, and differentials are consequently attributable to differences in work per-

---

[21] There is no system for the automatic adjustment of personal incomes to the cost of living. Basically, personal incomes reflect the total revenue available to undertakings, which, in their distribution of revenue, also decide what the rate of personal incomes is to be. If the cost of living rises, the undertaking itself decides in the light of total revenue whether personal incomes are to be increased. This explains why the changes in the cost of living in 1965 (when the economic reforms began to be applied) did not automatically result in higher incomes; a corresponding rise did not in fact take place until a few months later. Nor is there any automatic system of adjustment in the non-productive sphere, where revenue is derived from contributions paid out of workers' personal incomes. If, therefore, an increase in the cost of living leads to higher personal incomes in the productive sphere, there will automatically be more money available for the non-productive sphere, and hence for the payment of higher incomes there as well. Certain suggestions have been put forward for introducing an adjustment system that would in principle be the same for all undertakings, but no more than preliminary discussions have been held as yet.

[22] The cost of living has risen faster over recent years than labor productivity; this negative trend is obviously not desirable over a long period.

[23] This figure is rising slowly in step with personal incomes generally, and the progressive tax becomes due when the worker's personal income reaches about twice the overall average.

Table 1. Progressive Income Tax Rates

Portion of income in excess of 20,000 dinars per year	Progressive income tax rate (in percent)
Up to 10,000 dinars	3
10,000–15,000	6
15,000–20,000	9
20,000–25,000	12
25,000–30,000	15
30,000–35,000	20
35,000–40,000	25
40,000–50,000	35
50,000–60,000	45
60,000–70,000	55
Over 70,000	65

formed. Basically it is in the interests of society to develop in the country's economic potential and to encourage workers to earn more, rather than to safeguard the lowest income rates by a protective policy of redistribution.[24] A policy of this kind is actually unnecessary in Yugoslavia, because the general level of personal incomes is well above what might be regarded as the minimum. Furthermore, it is felt that at this stage the lowest prevailing rates of income are not merely undesirable; they should be eliminated because they point to a low standard of efficiency and productivity, and undue social concern for them might in fact have the effect of shielding unproductive methods. It is estimated that the income levels of about 10 to 12 percent of the labor force are still unsatisfactory, when compared with the standard of living enjoyed by the general population. Hence the need—which the reforms are designed to meet by economic methods—to change the whole pattern of production and so lay the foundation for higher incomes generally and the disappearance of the lowest incomes in particular.

Income Distribution Policy Until 1970

The income distribution policy to be followed in the next few years has been laid down in the development plan for 1966–70,[25] which defines the nation's development policies and programs including those required for

---

[24] Various measures have been taken to standardize earnings on the basis of general economic progress, primarily through long-term investment policies and the planning of investment. The low earnings in the underdeveloped areas are a problem apart, but a special federal fund has been set up to provide such areas with development credits. Various other measures have been taken in this connection: money has been made available for the modernization of existing industries, easy terms have been arranged and so on. Action has been taken in many different ways, but every possible effort is being made to apply a progressive economic policy.

income distribution as a result of the reforms begun in 1965.

The plan takes as its point of departure the economic conditions created by the reforms (in the field of prices, taxes influencing the distribution of income between the productive and non-productive spheres, tariff and credit policies, and so on) and the other consequential changes that will be made in the course of the 5-year period, and on this basis lays down the main lines of future income distribution policy, which are as follows.

Over the 5-year period income will be redistributed to the advantage of undertakings, which will thus have money to finance industrial expansion. It is estimated that by the end of the period undertakings will have at their disposal more than 65 percent of total revenue and, together with credits available through the banks, about 70 percent of the available investment capital.

This is expected to encourage more efficient business management and so, in practice, to provide a greater margin for the redistribution of national income to the workers in the form of personal incomes. The rate of accumulation is expected to decline by 1970, while that of consumption will increase, thereby, restoring the necessary balance. With national income rising by about 7.5 to 8.5 percent per year, it is hoped that personal consumption will increase by 8.5 to 9.5 percent and saving by 6 to 7 percent. There will also be a slackening in the growth of expenditure on administration and defense (that is excluding the social services, the cost of which will have to rise in line with increasing personal consumption).

This process of redistribution will, of course, be gradual. The forecast in the plan is that most of the changes will take place in the latter half of the five-year period, since the first step will have to be to increase the efficiency of business.

The plan also lays down the action to be taken in the coming years to implement this policy. All the proposed measures respect the principle of guided development, while recognizing the independence of self-managed undertakings. Programs have been drawn up for social taxation; the foundations of a credit policy have been laid down; legislation has been passed providing for the Federation to contribute to the financing of investment; gradual changes are being made to the currency regulations and the system of foreign trade (with a tendency toward liberalization); a policy has been approved for the accumulation of reserves, especially reserves of foreign currency, and so on. The aim of all these different measures is to pave the way for the income distribution policy described above.

In practice, of course, there are still many problems to be solved. The most important are certainly those connected with the reorganization of

---

[25] *Društveni plan razvoja Jugoslavije 1966–70* [Social plan for the development of Yugoslavia, 1966–70], Biblioteka Savezne Skupštine, Series III, Vol. *7–8* (Belgrade, 1966).

the economic and social structure along self-management lines. The old system of direction and organization by the state has almost completely disappeared, but there is still a need for co-ordination and co-operation between undertakings not only in matters of development policy and planning but also in such spheres as income distribution, where future developments cannot be determined solely by the workings of the market. At present consultations on development policy and income distribution take place in the economic chambers and in the associations formed by certain groups of undertakings and also in the trade unions. Even closer consultation and co-ordination has been achieved between integrated undertakings. Even so, the idea is gaining ground that the self-management scheme will need a far more ramified and comprehensive organization if the functions hitherto (and, frequently enough, even now) performed by the state in matters of economic development are to be adequately discharged. The first steps along these lines are being taken at the moment and a great deal more can be expected in the years to come, given the exceptional importance of the problem at the present stage of national development.

In general, income distribution policy has great potentialities as an instrument for promoting economic and social development, consolidating the material basis of society, and solving the many problems of living standards created by limited resources. The coming years will reveal new ways of generating wealth to improve the living standards of the workers in their threefold capacity of producers, managers, and beneficiaries of their own efforts.

A Note on the "Solidarity Wage Policy" of the Swedish Labor Movement

BERNDT ÖHMAN

The concept of the perfect market plays a central role in economic theory. It is utilized primarily as a norm for comparison, no one ever maintaining that such a market ever existed. The labor market tends especially to be characterized as "less adequate than any other type of factor or product market in the economy." The difficulty of applying traditional economic theory to the labor market is one of the greatest problems of

Reprinted from *The Swedish Journal of Economics,* September 1969, pp. 198–205, by permission of the publisher.

"labor economics" and has led to a situation where, as Dunlop points out, "general economic model builders are not familiar with labor market developments and in which labor market specialists are inadequately familiar with central theoretical developments."

One of the most important deviations from the perfect market is the presence of trade union organizations on the labor market. They can impede the mobility of the labor force and, among other things, create restrictions on free price formation for labor.

The impact of trade unionism on wage determination is a matter of controversy, it is true, but it constitutes a formal and very likely, a real deviation from market price determination.

Trade unions are treated as monopolies in labor economics. This does not necessarily imply that they act as profit maximizing enterprises in a strict economic sense. It is also not clear what is to be meant by profit in this case. One can imagine either that trade union members' total wage bill be maximized, or that the wage level be increased as fast as possible, but these goals are identical only when employment is independent of the wage level. Trade unions can also have certain objectives regarding the level of employment, membership, and so on. They are, however, considered to be a disturbance to the perfect market.

Even if the trade unions can thus be considered as monopolies, it is not clear that they behave as in the typical monopoly case of economic theory.

There is special reason for a labor movement such as the Federation of Swedish Trade Unions (LO), comprising the vast majority of Swedish workers, not to pursue a narrow monopolistic policy. Such a labor movement must also consider the total social and economic consequences of its wage policy, because these consequences will affect its own members to a very great extent. Thus, the Swedish labor movement has greater reason to see its wage policy from a social-economic point of view than, for example, the American trade unions which almost all can disregard these consequences. It can also be put this way: there is less incompatibility between the private and socio-economic aspects of the Swedish trade union movement's policy than, for example, the American trade unions.

It was not until the 1930s that the Swedish labor movement gave final shape to something that might be termed an ideology and strategy concerning wage policy. It was then that the so-called "solidariska lönepolitiken" (here termed *solidarity wage policy*) was introduced and which has become the wage policy doctrine pursued by the Swedish LO since then. The import of this doctrine has not always been clear, but it is associated among other things with the idea of equalization of wages.

During World War II and the transition from the unemployment of the thirties to the postwar full-employment situation, there occurred a certain degree of wage equalization.

But at the same time new difficulties appeared for the labor movement. A rapidly increasing inflation led to demands for wage political restraint on their part. One development was that the labor movement was forced to agree to a wage freeze toward the end of the forties. This treatened to rob the labor movement of its function. Because of the inflation, there were also claims for pursuing a less ambitious employment policy, that is for a more moderate full employment.

It was during this difficult period that the LO in 1951 published a congress report, *Fackföreningsrörelsen och den fulla sysselsättningen* (The Trade Unions and Full Employment) which is its fundamental wage policy document. An outline of a program for full employment without inflation through stabilization policy was presented there and within this outline was a wage policy program for the labor movement. The import of this stabilization policy program was, in short, to lessen demand and thereby also inflationary tendencies through a strict monetary and fiscal policy. Through selective employment stimuli and measures for facilitating a better functioning labor market unemployment was to be met without creating new inflation.

A very active labor market policy would thus make a high degree of employment possible without inflation.

In this stabilization program the authorities were given the main responsibility for preserving the value of money. No longer were any unreasonable demands for wage freezes to be made on the labor movement. The labor movement thereby freed itself from its previous wage-policy dilemma.

But even with a strict economic policy preventing demand inflation, there remained a risk of inflation due to monopolistic price formation on product and labor markets. The basic idea was that a labor market policy stimulating mobility could to some extent prevent the appearance of bottlenecks due to shortage of labor, and thus reduce the presence of monopolies. It was also thought possible to prevent the exploitation of newly arisen monopoly positions on the product market by initiating price controls.

On the other hand, the labor movement rejected a public regulation of wage determination, but it was well aware of its possibilities for creating wage inflation. Trade union wage policy had therefore to be formed in such a way that it could not become an independent factor causing inflation. As an objective of the wage policy therefore a money wage development was outlined which on the whole was to be consistent with productivity developments (after profits of enterprise have been forced down as much as possible considering employment).

The labor movement would then forgo further possible inflationary wage increases. It therefore does not place the *entire* responsibility for the value of money on the government—as is commonly believed—but rather clearly asserts that the trade unions have their own share of the responsibility also now demonstrating a certain restraint.

The prerequisite for such a wage policy was that the government pursued a full-employment policy which did not lead to inflation and wage drift. In other words the labor movement regarded itself as having the possibility of affecting wage developments in accordance with its intentions only under conditions of stable, non-inflationary full employment.

A further prerequisite for a stable wage development of this kind, was for the wage structure not to be such as to create strong feelings of resentment respecting an unjust evaluation between different internal earner groups. The wage policy had to create a reasonable valuation of the wage relationships between different groups from a social-economic and equity point of view—it had to be a solidarity policy. Fulfillment of this demand was a precondition for the LO's co-operation in restraining wage developments to a certain extent; otherwise different groups would have been expected to compete for the greatest wage increases. In the long run the solidarity policy was a condition for general wage stability.

The labor movement's wage policy therefore was to combine two objectives: one, of securing a wage development in accordance with productivity gains and two, of establishing a just wage structure. The LO's intentions on the first point were quite clear, but on the second, what was a "just" wage structure? An objective answer to that question is of course not feasible. It is most interesting, however, to consider how the labor movement conceives of it.

The solidarity wage policy is first contrasted with the so-called "ability-to-pay principle" which implies that the financial differentials in ability to pay between different branches of the economy are to be utilized in attempts to obtain as large a wage increase as possible.

The labor movement has two arguments for such a policy. It quickly provides workers with a portion of developing productivity gains and it creates wage differentials which stimulate the flow of labor to expanding high-wage industries.

This policy is however totally rejected. It is true that in practice it is natural to expect differences in wage movements to develop reflecting differences in ability to pay but "such a principle cannot be established as a norm for wage policy." Stabilization considerations themselves motivate against it since it leads to a "harmful race between different wages and between wages and prices." The solidarity wage policy must instead work with "a kind of equal-wage principle as a goal." Here consideration is taken for special demands for occupational training, accident risks, working conditions, conditions of hiring, and so on.

An additional argument against the ability-to-pay principle is that it does not make work of the same type equally expensive for all employers (it therefore reflects an imperfect market). Low wages imply a form of wage subsidy. But subsidies to less profitable industries ought to be avoided. Instead they should be compelled to rationalize. This reasoning clearly presupposes "that the most profitable enterprises are also the best paying ones and at the same time the most efficient from the point of view of the whole economy." Over and beyond the stabilization argument therefore, there is a clearly stated growth policy argument for the solidarity wage policy in *Fackföreningsrörelsen och den fulla sysselsättningen.*

The practical application of this solidarity wage policy can take place, it is said, according to two methods: firstly, by a systematic work evaluation and secondly by an evaluation "according to the possibilities of recruiting and retaining labor force in the different sectors." The latter method implies that wages shall be evaluated in view of long-term market tendencies which according to a common conception in labor economies very well coincides with the economic theory of the perfect market. "The competitive hypothesis is useful in explaining general, long-term trends in wage relationships," F. C. Pierson writes.

The work evaluation method is discussed in some detail. It amounts to an attempt at obtaining more objective wage structure criteria, but it is admitted that the method is imperfect, necessarily involving arbitrary elements. One interesting criterion for successful work evaluation is however presented. The ultimately most tenable evidence for the success of labor evaluation, it is written, can be said to be that the movement between different groups "goes just as much in the one direction as in the other, that is that those who work for the lower wage abstain from seeking their way to the higher paid employments to such extent that shortages of labor arise within their previous areas of work. Constant shortage of labor in one area implies that wages are too low there unless this shortage depends on other discernible conditions creating a hindrance to recruitment of new labor." Hence a good work evaluation ought to be in agreement with the long-run tendencies of the market itself.

The two different methods therefore lead to one and the same result: a realization of the wage structure of the perfect market.

The consequences of the solidarity wage policy for the spread of wages depends on whether the perfect market has greater or lesser differentials than the actually existing one, something which is difficult to determine a priori. In *Fackföreningsrörelsen och den fulla sysselsättningen* it is stated that "from the general viewpoint of solidarity, priority must be given to groups which in spite of strong increases are still at a low level while on the other hand groups with higher wages should not expect the same because of previous low rates of increase." Practically every wage equalization was previously "reasonable and equitable" but, the document continues, "the strong equalization which has occurred during and after the war has however brought the question in many aspects into another light."

The prevailing conception of reality was therefore that a wage equalization was still in order but that it was less urgent than before. It can be of interest to note the aspects of this equalization relating to stabilization policy. In an article in 1948 Rehn writes that an equalization of this type would involve especially large wage increases for the low wage groups. He therefore finds a general period of price increase to be unavoidable in connection with such an equalization. One would therefore have to accept a "once-and-for-all inflation," but later after the equitable wage structure was established he thinks that a solidarity wage policy would be a condition for wage stability.

Wage equalization was the central thought in the solidarity policy as it was conceived during the 1930s. In the theoretically more sophisticated version in *Fackföreningsrörelsen och den fulla sysselsättningen* the equalization principle is still to be found but the central point is now establishment of a just and rational wage structure. Consideration is taken here to the character of work in different aspects. What appears to be compared is not only the wages of work, but its total "net advantages," which ought to be the equalization target for all work.

It is apparent that the labor movement chooses to abstract from the considerable individual differences in labor capacity. Wage differentials reflect not only differences in requirements for different types of work, but also differences in individual productive ability. This aspect of the problem is not discussed in *Fackföreningsrörelsen och den fulla sysselsättningen*.

It can also be maintained that all relevant factors are not included in the concept of "net advantages." Some essential factors are, for example, the geographical situation of the place of work and its distance from the home. Variations in these factors can lead to significantly different wage demands (for the same work) from the side of the employee precisely because he follows the principle of equal net advantages. The general rule that the same type of work shall be equally expensive for all employers cannot therefore be applicable in a truly general sense.

Here we find an important aspect of the solidarity policy: wage differentiation between different types of *work* is discussed, but not between different *individuals*. It is thereby maintained that wage differences which are based on the characteristics of *enterprises* are unjust and irrational, whereas those reflecting the varying productive ability of *labor* (that is its marginal product) are not rejected. It is not discussed as a problem. For this reason those factors are included in the concept of "net advantages" which are directly related to conditions at the place of work (as they are experienced by workers), but not other factors of relevance to the individual (such as preferences concerning geographical position or distance to the work place).

The usual interpretation of the solidarity wage policy is presumably that it means wage equalization. According to the beliefs expressed in *Fackföreningsrörelsen och den fulla sysselsättningen*, the application of this policy should lead to just such an equalization. But in principle also the opposite could result. The central problem involves namely the determination of certain criteria for wage structure—criteria which stand in agreement with the perfect market—and the resulting wage spread among earners is hence strictly speaking not an object for policy consideration. From this point of view the term solidarity wage policy can be regarded as somewhat misleading.

The solidarity wage policy is of great interest from an economic-theoretical viewpoint. The Swedish labor movement is in a certain sense a clear monopoly—but it does not have a monopolistic goal structure. It applies a social-economic perspective to total demands for wage increases and advances the perfect market as a norm for wage structure. It ought therefore to "improve" a free (from government intervention) but imperfect market. As Clark Kerr has pointed out, the labor market can exercise an influence toward increased uniformity, that is equal wages for equal work independent of person and firm. "Unionization, instead of 'distorting' the interfirm wage structure, may act instead as a substitute for greater mobility."

Reynolds, in similar manner maintains that "the doctrinaire view that trade unions, being 'monopolies,' must by definition have an adverse effect on the wage structure, does not stand up well in the light of empirical studies, for one can make at least as good a case for the contrary opinion."

The solidarity wage policy was furthermore built into a greater socio-economic context in which labor market policy occupied a key position. But the government as well, through its labor market policy, took measures to establish a smoothly functioning labor market of the more perfect type. The policy of the authorities facilitated therefore—and was an outright prerequisite for—the implementation of the solidarity wage policy: labor market policy was to create that mobility of labor which one surrendered to create through wage differentials (between the same types of work in different enterprises). The common theory behind this conception was that wage differentials constituted a weak stimulus toward labor mobility.

In conclusion, the solidarity wage policy is intimately entwined with a more general economic-political ideology. One had little confidence in the free market. It functioned unsatisfactorily and government and union corrective measures were necessary. At the same time the nature of these corrections implied high estimation for the rationality and justice of the perfect market's results. The interesting implication which follows is that this "monopolized" labor market ought to exhibit some of the characteristics of the perfectly competitive market of economic theory.

Discussion Questions

1. How do the Yugoslavs determine their patterns of income distribution?
2. Would you consider Yugoslav income distribution policies to be more "equitable" than U.S. policies?
3. Discuss the role of Sweden's main labor union in wage determination and overall national goals?
4. How would you compare the goals and national outlook of Swedish unions with those of American labor unions?

International Trade

No single problem is more enigmatic to the student than the subject of international trade and finance. Yet, if one is to come to grips with the major problems of the U.S. economy in the late sixties and early seventies, an understanding of international finance is essential. The basic question is: How did our chronic balance of payments problem arise, and what is the rationale for choosing devaluation as the solution, as the U.S. did in 1972?

After World War II there was a so-called "dollar shortage." That is, the dollar was undervalued to the extent that other countries wanted to buy more from us than we wanted to buy from them. This shortage ended after the Marshall Plan, our massive-level defense spending, and West European and Japanese recovery placed dollars in foreigners hands.

The result was a persistent disequilibrium in the U.S. balance of payments position; or to put it another way, there was a glut of dollars causing an outflow of gold and an increasing loss of faith in the dollar, relative to other currencies. This problem was further aggravated by a balance of trade deficit in 1971, the first time this had occurred in the twentieth century.

A number of remedies are possible when there is a chronic balance of payments disequilibrium. The U.S. could seek a sharing in the burden which we bear in NATO; we could push for increased efficiency in domestic industry to improve the price competitiveness of our export industries; and we could obviously move to distasteful protectionist-type measures designed to purposively insulate American industry from the competition of foreign imports.

But all of these measures fail to get at the basic problem: namely, that the U.S. dollar was overvalued and therefore had to be devalued. Such a measure means that the rate of exchange between the U.S. dollar and all other currencies will be altered so that the dollar will now exchange for less of any other foreign currency and vice versa. Therefore, foreign goods now become relatively more expensive to Americans and conversely, American goods become relatively cheaper for foreigners. This would tend to decrease U.S. imports and increase our exports.

The two articles in this section deal with two devaluations—the 1967 British devaluation and the 1957 Finnish devaluation. Both articles evaluate the effects of devaluation on international trade and thereby provide an insight into what the U.S. may expect from its own devaluation policy.

Nils Meinander is Professor of Economics at the Swedish School of Economics in Helsinki. Michael Bromwich is a Lecturer in accounting at the London School of Economics.

The Finnmark Devaluation—Implications and Follow-Up Measures

NILS MEINANDER

When the authorities responsible for devaluation claim to have been acting under pressure this explanation may be construed in two different ways; either the country found itself insufficiently adapted to the rest of the world, with a consequent rapid depletion of the foreign exchange reserve unless direct control over foreign exchange payments was introduced, or equilibrium could have been restored rapidly enough using the traditional fiscal, monetary, and wage policy measures, but only at the expense of such objectionable encroachments that it was considered easier politically to endure the pressure of devaluation. Unfortunately, the nature of this pressure has not been clearly defined, so that we do not know whether devaluation was the result of bad planning or of loose political conduct.

Rather than develop these distinctions further, we should try to analyze the implications of what has occurred. When the previous devaluation was effected on September 15, 1957, the intention was to lay the foundations for the country's final adaptation to its natural international economic milieu, where, after the war, payments in foreign exchange had already to a great extent been freed from restrictions. Therefore, the bold step was taken of rescinding import licensing as well as the special rates applicable to certain types of foreign exchange transactions, and this necessitated the lowering of the external value of the Finnmark. The intention then, of course, was to maintain equilibrium in the balance of payments on current account using only price relations as a regulator, but in practice this was not possible. Figure 1 shows the development of the balance of payments on current account during the period between the two devaluations. In the past few years some kind of stabilization seems to have taken place in that

Reprinted from *Unitas*, Vol. *39*, No. 4, 1967, pp. 179–187, by permission of the publisher.

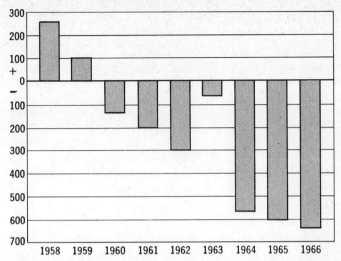

Figure 1. Balance of Payments: Surplus or Deficit for the Period 1958–1966.

the deficit has remained around a half milliard marks. It no longer appeared pertinent or even possible to cover this deficit by means of foreign loans.

Are the Causes of the Fundamental Disequilibrium Due to Time Factors?

The failure may be explained in many ways. It is always possible to develop the guiding principles for another type of economic policy. Had the domestic demand been kept at a lower level, it would have been possible to stimulate exports and check imports sufficiently to ensure equilibrium. If we are to avoid a new devaluation we must now succeed where we failed before.

In order not to exaggerate the difficulties that may be expected, it would appear appropriate to record here some features that may well be said to have rendered adaptation difficult between the two devaluations.

1. The basic situation was unfavorable since war damage compensation and the resettlement activity, neither of which had any direct connection with the international economic development to which the country was ultimately to be adapted, had tied resources to such a large degree during the first decade of reconstruction.

2. The transfer of labor from agriculture, which had previously happened rather slowly, was speeded up during the period between the two devaluations.

3. Customs duties in respect of EFTA countries were removed.

4. The increase in real income caused a shift in demand toward goods which promoted the propensity to import.
5. A weakening in the general economic situation took place, particularly in respect of forest industry products which still hold a predominant position in our exports.

In the years ahead, these features will make themselves felt to a lesser degree than hitherto. Our industry, which was built up to cope with the war damage reparations, must now, at last, be capable of ensuring its adaptation to the markets in the West also, with due regard to the selection of products and to charges. The internal migration from agriculture may, on the other hand, be expected to continue, perhaps even at an increasing rate of progress. Employment policy as well as the attempt to give state support to investment in less favored areas may also be expected to continue to tie resources in the public sector. The continued integration in Western Europe may well result in still keener foreign competition beyond the demands already made by the adaptation to EFTA. The obviously rising standard of living will cause a further shift in demand with a consequent pronounced propensity toward imports. As for the general economic climate abroad, hardly anything may be said at this juncture except that the prospects of a comparatively early improvement seem greater than the risks of a continued deterioration.

To sum up, the features hampering adaptation are not likely to be felt as much as before, but on the other hand no new trends have emerged in the general economic outlook that would render possible an automatic adaptation without strenuous efforts in the field of economic policy.

Will Inflation Consume the Devaluation Profit?

Devaluation as such provided no long-term solution to the balance problem, since in many ways it freed inflationary forces making adaptation more difficult. Compensation will be demanded by various pressure groups.

Wages are to a great extent tied by the prevailing agreements which provide automatic adjustments up to the beginning of 1969. At the turn of the year 1967/1968 a wage increase compensation of a good 2 percent is anticipated as compensation for the rise in the cost of living during 1967. In 1968 two automatic wage increases of 3 and 3.5 percent respectively will take place. Thus, at the end of next year, wages may be expected to be at least 8.5 percent higher than they are at present. It is difficult to predict the general improvement in productivity but if something like 3–4 percent can be achieved there is every reason to be satisfied. Unfortunately, it is scarcely an exaggeration to estimate that the effect of the wage adjustments on prices will be a good 5 percent if, at the same time, allowance is made for the automatic compensation on the agricultural income.

Moreover, there is the inflationary effect of the devaluation itself.

Luckily, certain prices of raw materials continue to show a downward tendency and EFTA tariffs are reduced further. It seems possible that the rise in prices caused by devaluation will not equal the full devaluation percentage, but will perhaps average only 25 percent. As the share of imported goods in the wholesale price index is one fifth, this index is not likely to rise by more than 5 percent, as far as this calculation is applicable. However, we also know that as a result of the devaluation, autonomous upward pressure will be exerted on prices, the effect of which is difficult to calculate. In all probability, the wholesale price index will rise by at least 6 percent but may easily go up a further 1 or 2 percent as a result of devaluation. The total increase will then be at least 11 percent, possibly as much as 14 percent, by the end of 1968. The cost of living will follow suit, although at a slower rate, but a total increase next year of 10 percent is hardly an over-estimation.

Even if it is possible, despite the continued inflation during next spring and summer, to maintain the main wage policy front in accordance with the prevailing agreements, it will none-the-less be necessary to grant compensation from the beginning of 1969 for that portion of the rise in the cost of living which from November 1967 to November 1968 exceeds 4 percent. This compensation may be expected to amount to around 6 percent which will be additional to the 8.5 percent previously recorded. Thus, even before the next round of agreements, the wage level will be about 15 percent higher than at the time of devaluation. At the negotiations to be held next autumn, demands on the employers seem inevitable and these are expected to bring about a rise in wages from the beginning of 1969, slightly above the figure already determined by the compensation mechanism. Unless a tangible change can be achieved in the labor market policy, an appreciable increase in the wage level will thus have to be fused into the price structure during 1969. A calculation in figures, which, of course, may unfortunately differ from reality in its schematism, seems to point clearly to a continued inflationary spiral.

Unless something can be done to avert this development, the authorities will soon have to face demands for a new devaluation. What can we do to avoid this? What is the real meaning of devaluation in this connection?

One possibility would, of course, be to pursue a more realistic and stringent incomes policy. It is comparatively easy to suggest the general principles for a pattern for such a policy. The trade unions would then be denied the possibility of obtaining full compensation for price increases. Both Parliament and the government would be compelled to adopt a policy of restraint when it comes to overstepping the limits laid down for public finance in the budget for 1968. To expect that this disquietingly broad framework will be made narrower during the next discussions in Parliament would be tantamount to placing confidence in a highly improbable course of events.

The hopes of continued possibilities under the current economic administration to curb sufficiently the increases in subsidies that may be justified by the inflation are based on more realistic foundations. It is easier to check an increase in appropriations than to reduce amounts already allocated. It can only be hoped that the compensation demands that become topical in public finance as a result of devaluation have already been essentially allowed for in the budget for 1968.

In the event that the agreements prevailing in 1969 contain no automatic wage compensations beyond those warranted by the improvement in productivity, it should be possible at the beginning of 1970 to judge whether devaluation and the follow-up measures have come up to expectations.

A mechanical analysis with purchasing power parities will at least facilitate the outlining of further discussions on the problem. To indicate the exact percentage by which the Finnmark was over-valued at the moment of devaluation is in itself problematical, but the figure of 20 percent that has occasionally been quoted appears realistic. If, until the price-increasing effects of devaluation have ceased, internal inflation could be confined to the difference between the resultant rise in the rates of exchange and this over-rating percentage, that is, a good 10 percent, then a final stabilization of our currency at a lower level would become discernible. However, to this percentage can be added a margin for additional price increases created by the simultaneous foreign inflationary cycle. According to our calculations, in which wholesale prices are expected to rise by considerably more than 10 percent and the cost of living by about 10 percent, this margin will be approached already in 1968. Thus in 1969 there will remain no more than the margin within the framework of the price increases abroad. To say that this margin is disquietingly narrow is not to paint a somber picture, particularly as no further inflationary impulses are forecast from public finance. On the contrary, the heavily expanded budget amounts for next year are supposed to have been adjusted to the new price level, to which devaluation is expected to lead.

Devaluation as an Incitement to Structural Changes

Estimates show that unless the situation is used to damp down income expansion, we shall soon find ourselves back where we started. So far, however, the inflation calculation has only included the effect of certain changes, assuming that many things will remain unaltered. The technical conditions for production, the standard demands and consumption habits of people in general, the general public's savings volume, dynamics in commercial and industrial life abroad, all this and a number of other factors are subject to change, so that the forecast will differ from reality. It has rightly been said that the express purpose of devaluation was to bring about a far-reaching economic structural change within the country's economy.

The structural change entails the continuance of intensified industrialization which will create new domestic production, capable of competing on world markets. It is totally unrealistic to imagine that the marketing of our industrial products could be ensured merely on the strength of bilateral agreements, at prices in excess of the world market level. Nor is it necessary to complicate the argument by trying to guess which countries would like and which countries will achieve association with the EEC and what may happen to those remaining outside. In any case, we must prepare to develop an industry capable of holding its ground on a market where technical development is rapid and competition is becoming increasingly keen.

In what way and, above all, how rapidly will devaluation facilitate this structural change?

In the export business, profitability is strengthened when prices quoted in foreign currencies are converted at a higher rate of exchange. It is true that the export charges detract from this but, if the government makes proper use of its powers, then the effect will not be entirely lost. For industry selling on the home market, the increase in import prices will likewise create ample scope for remunerative production. Increasing income will tend to consolidate the basis for self-financing. Thus a moderate impulse to creative new investments may already be expected.

For the structural change to become evident, however, the financing of industry must be facilitated to a far greater extent. The government's growth package is a contribution to this change but unfortunately only a too moderate one. Unless credit-granting can be stimulated on a considerably broader front no really far-reaching structural change can be anticipated.

Devaluation has created certain conditions for invigorating credit expansion. The foreign exchange reserve, the most important barrier to credit expansion so far, will grow. A forecast of the development of the balance of payments on current account over the next few years does not preclude the possibility of the 400 million mark deficit expected for 1967 being transformed into surplus of 100–200 million marks in 1968, which surplus will grow to 600–700 million in 1969 at best. The main point is that devaluation will thus tend to strengthen the basis for a credit policy more favorable toward investment.

This does not, however, give a sufficiently clear picture of the development of the financing possibilities.

The volume of public finance and commercial credits are connected. The higher one is allowed to rise, the smaller the volume left for the other if inflation is to be checked and the external liquidity ensured. As a rough schematizing of the expansive effects of the government budget within the national economy, we may take its sum total to indicate the extent to which resources are utilized. If the balance of public finance is to be ensured by means of loans raised on the market or loans from the central bank, through increased company taxation or through increased private taxation there will in any case remain less for the financing of the desired structural changes.

Thus, a general restraint in public finance is important not only in respect of inflation's rate of progress for which income compensation will be demanded. There also exists a significant connection between the size of the government budget and the possibility of financing the structural change, without which it would be impossible to maintain even the present standard of living on a long-term basis.

The Connections Between the Inflationary Round and the Structural Change

When discussing the experiences and promises of devaluation, it is tempting to place the inflationary cycle and the structural change side by side, in terms of time, when considering the speed with which things are happening. Should it be possible to bring about a radical structural change already before the end of 1969—during which those inflationary impulses should reasonably be depleted—then the combating of inflation would be materially facilitated.

The following are the initial prerequisites for a rapid structural change:

1. Completed technical plans for new industrial activity which have hitherto been checked by doubts as to profitability and/or by inadequate financing.
2. A system for the allocation of capital capable of selecting and evaluating such new industrial projects as may survive international competition.
3. Readiness to stake quickly on marketing to an extent large enough to ensure sufficient sales at home and/or abroad.

It would be sanguine to assume that quick results will be achieved from the change-over, since even under more favorable circumstances it takes time to create and adapt new industrial activity. Only where unused capacity is available and where, owing to the small volume of orders in hand or to profitability difficulties, the organization has run idle, can production be speeded up comparatively rapidly. A considerable time is usually required from the moment the financing possibilities have improved until the investment decisions, with all their relevant details, have been properly developed, the plants built and the machinery installed. This interval is obviously much longer than the estimate of the inflationary round given here.

Thus the belief that structural change tends to damp down inflationary pressure is not firmly based. It is more realistic to presuppose a state of affairs where the inflationary round first has to be endured and stabilization at the new and lower level of the money value brought about, before the effects of the structural change become more apparent.

This makes very heavy demands on the economic policy. Unless the inflationary spiral can be broken within a reasonable period of time with the help of a realistic incomes policy, it cannot be expected that an improvement would come sufficiently quickly from the quarter of productive activity. Neither will it be easy, in the face of incessant internal inflation, to create either real or psychological conditions for new investments, which frequently involve so many risks, since their profitability is determined on a larger market, where the general rate of inflation is more moderate. Unless there is confidence in the monetary stability the investment rush may easily break down. It is hardly an exaggeration, therefore, to regard the length of the inevitable inflationary round as being the period of grace given to our authorities for the follow-up measures of devaluation.

The Effects of Sterling Devaluation on International Trade

MICHAEL BROMWICH

Devaluation is the most controversial of all the tools that could be used to solve the British balance of payments crisis. The highly technical language in use makes the heated argument over devaluation no easier to understand.

However, the debate is a complex one and a few technical terms are necessary to follow it. The earlier part of this article explains these in simple language but does not take long before plunging into the heart of the discussion.

Balance of Payments

The United Kingdom's balance of payments tells about Britain's receipts and payments of foreign exchange resulting from transactions with other countries. It charts the movements in British reserves of gold and foreign exchange. Exports of goods and services ("invisibles") increase these reserves. Spending on imports, overseas defense commitments and aid, reduce them. Overseas investment by United Kingdom nationals not offset by foreign investment in Britain also reduces the reserves.

The Deficit

A deficit results when the foreign exchange needed to pay for imports and meet government expenditure overseas is greater than that earned from British trade abroad plus other inflows of foreign exchange. The demand

Reprinted from the *Canadian Chartered Accountant*, November 1967, pp. 354–358, by permission of the publisher.

for sterling, by people who hold foreign currencies, is then less than the supply of sterling created by those who hold pounds and wish to exchange them for other currencies. If the money market was free to respond to the forces of supply and demand, then the price of sterling in terms of foreign exchange would fall. A pound would be traded for fewer dollars or francs.

This would result in the sterling prices of British imports rising, while goods from the United Kingdom would become cheaper in terms of foreign exchange. Thus fewer francs would be needed to buy a British car whose price in sterling had not changed. More British goods would be exported and less foreign goods imported by the United Kingdom. In time, the excess demand for foreign exchange in place of sterling would be reversed, and the British balance of payments would return to equilibrium. A flexible exchange rate would therefore automatically solve a balance of payments crisis.

Unfortunately, members of the International Monetary Fund are required to stabilize the rate at which their currency exchanges for other monetary units. Variations in the parity value of the pound are not allowed by the rules of the game, except that devaluation is permissible to cure fundamental difficulties in the balance of payments. To maintain sterling's value when threatened, the British authorities buy pounds in the market by selling foreign exchange from the United Kingdom's reserves. This creates an artificial demand for sterling and, provided sufficient pounds are purchased, the sterling exchange rate remains constant. A deficit on the British balance of payments therefore cannot be allowed to continue as the reserves of foreign currency would soon run out.

Britain's difficulties are aggravated by sterling's role in the international monetary system. Many countries hold part of their reserves in sterling. Moreover, many foreigners keep a stock of pounds to finance their trading activities.

A British deficit, giving rise to a threat of devaluation, would cause some of these holdings to be liquidated. Britain's situation can thus be likened to that of a man who runs both a bank and a business and whose business has a bad trading year. His business misfortunes can generate doubts about his bank's credit-worthiness, and perhaps start a run by depositors. Such runs by overseas sterling holders have been a persistent feature in recent British crises.

The Remedies to Deficits

The United Kingdom's deficits of the last 15 years do not mean that the British people have been living beyond their means, except in some special sense. In most recent years, indeed, Britain's exports of goods and services have exceeded her imports. These surpluses, however, have been insufficient to pay for Britain's world role. To bring the balance of payments into equilibrium either this outflow must be reduced or the trade surplus increased.

The British government is trying, with some success, to reduce its expenses overseas. This could, however, have adverse effects on the trade balance because much of the outflow generates British exports. To reduce government expenditure overseas, in contrast to insuring that such money is efficiently spent, involves much more than the balance of payments. It is essentially a political decision with vast repercussions throughout the world.

Thus, Britain must try to improve her import/export balance if she is to remedy the deficit. The possible tools that can be used are: deflation at home (which would depress imports); devaluation; international loans (to finance the deficit); import controls and export subsidies.

The controls and subsidies are contrary to international agreements, though import surcharges have been used temporarily at the price of noisy criticism from abroad. If such measures were used permanently, in spite of their illegality, retaliation by others would swiftly follow. This would destory any gains achieved.

International loans are effective short-term aids which should not be used as substitutes for action by the United Kingdom government.

Thus, the choice narrows to either deflation or devaluation or some combination of the two. Both would have considerable effect on world trade and neither can be discussed in isolation.

Deflation works by causing British employment and aggregate demand to fall, reducing the demand for imports from overseas. It does little to increase exports; there seems little evidence that lower profits on the home market force manufacturers to try to recoup these abroad. Deflation releases the resources for exports but gives no incentive for these to be used. The cost of such a policy is severe unemployment (in present day Britain, this means average unemployment of over 2 percent) and reduced economic growth. This is a heavy cost, both to the United Kingdom and to the world, as lower economic growth reduces the role Britain can play overseas. But the weightiest argument against deflation is that it is a *temporary* solution. As soon as the squeeze is relaxed, up shoot imports and the crisis reappears.

Trade and Devaluation

The Theory

It will be recalled that, with a free foreign exchange market, a British deficit would cause the price of sterling to fall, and thus set off a process which would bring the balance of payments back to equilibrium. Devaluation, by lowering sterling's parity rate, acts on exports and imports in the same manner.

At the moment, a pound exchanges for $2.80 American. Assume a 50 percent devaluation. After this, the price of the same pound would be $1.40. This results in the sterling price of American goods in Britain rising, and the dollar price of British goods falling. More goods from the United Kingdom will be demanded in the United States and fewer American goods will be wanted in Britain.

There is considerable evidence that British goods are too highly priced in the world market. To the extent that this is so, devaluation would be helpful. Moreover, lower prices would offset some of the non-price weaknesses of British exports about which complaints are legendary.

The mere creation of demand for exports is not enough. These exports must be profitable. Devaluation creates the needed incentive; for instance, with a 50 percent devaluation the dollar price of British goods in America could be halved without reducing profits earned on them. If the price is reduced by less than half, the profit margin can be increased. Moreover, some of this extra profit could be used to improve after-sales service, and so on.

The Trading Effects of Devaluation

Most experts, including those opposed to devaluation, agree that the British trade balance would respond favorably to devaluation. Devaluation would have two effects on both imports and exports. First, lower export prices in foreign currency would increase the volume of sales abroad, thus increasing the flow of foreign exchange into Britain. Second, the exports would sell at lower prices, thus reducing the amount of foreign currency obtained by the United Kingdom.

For imports the reasoning is reversed. Here, higher prices would reduce imports in volume but increase their unit price.

A successful sterling devaluation depends, in the case of both imports and exports, on the volume effect outweighing the unit price effect. There is little empirical evidence on this point. Most of the evidence in existence, notably that of Canada and France, suggests that the conditions do exist for a successful sterling devaluation. If the pound responds to devaluation, as well as did the franc, a surplus on trading of £600 million per year should be obtained. The special conditions affecting sterling, however, militate against so successful an outcome.

If other countries retaliate against a sterling devaluation, this would lessen the chances of its success. However, as no devaluation in recent history has ever been completely matched, some net gain to the United Kingdom is likely. Indeed, there is reason to think that this gain would be sufficient to remedy the British deficit.

It is difficult to forecast which other countries, of those who compete with Britain for world trade, would follow the pound. Their decision would depend on the degree of British devaluation, the strength of their balance of payments and the way in which the devaluation was carried out.

Other Countries Might Devalue

Assume a 10 to 15 percent devaluation, as recommended by many experts, processed through the International Monetary Fund and aimed at returning the British balance of payments to equilibrium. Most of the United Kingdom's competitors (the majority of whom are substantially in surplus) are unlikely to see this as an attack on their trade balances. The hope is that the benefits of a strong Britain, able to afford its world role, are sufficient to ensure that most countries would be willing to bear some loss in their trading positions.

Thus, the crucial question is whether other important countries have problems which would force them to devalue with the pound. In the early sixties the United States was possibly in this situation, but the recent picture appears more hopeful; there now seems little risk of the dollar having to follow a 10 to 15 percent sterling devaluation. Further, because those countries (for example, Germany) who have gained from the rapid growth of manufactured exports to the United Kingdom are unlikely to devalue, these exports should fall considerably.

On the other hand, some of the countries which supply imports to the United Kingdom would match a sterling devaluation. Most of the sterling area countries and the majority of other primary producers, would follow the pound as they have done previously. These countries supply Britain mainly with food and raw materials, and compensatory actions by them would reduce the inflationary impact of devaluation (of which more later).

If sterling devaluation was nullified by retaliation, Britain would be forced to use deflation or direct controls. This is another reason for supposing retaliation to be unlikely, because these alternatives would press more severely than devaluation on other countries. For instance, if Britain deflated she would suffer a loss of economic growth. This reduced growth would mean that other countries would have to shoulder part of her future world responsibilities. By devaluation, on the other hand, Britain might regain equilibrium while maintaining economic growth; this should enable her, in the long run, to support a higher level of imports, to the benefit of other countries.

Further, the British government is not the only one to believe in the sacred position of its currency. Many competitors, for prestige reasons, would be reluctant to devalue, and most do not have a deficit forcing them to abandon their god.

Another type of retaliation has been suggested as a possibility. Some countries might try to gain trading advantages over other nations by devaluing more than necessary to match sterling. This might initiate a second round of devaluations, aimed at recouping trade losses due to this aggressive devaluation. Thus it is frequently argued that if sterling is devalued, the world would be plunged into a spiral of retaliatory actions similar to those of the thirties. There seems little evidence to support this; the sixties are not the thirties and international monetary co-operation has greatly improved. In 1949, about 30 countries devalued without causing any second round of retaliatory action.

Devaluation and Inflation

Devaluation makes the production of exports and import substitutes more attractive to British manufacturers. If devaluation occurred at the wrong time, namely when the economy was fully stretched, then the resultant additional demand for resources would cause inflation. This could quickly wipe out the gains from devaluation. The government therefore would have to depress the home market to free resources. Thus, devaluation is not necessarily a soft option.

A sterling devaluation in 1967 would not encounter this problem, as there is spare capacity in the British economy. This "slack" has been generated by the recent deflationary policies aimed at resolving the sterling crisis. If the United Kingdom was forced, by a sterling crisis, to devalue at the peak of a "go" period, on the other hand, the difficulty would be acute. This strengthens the case for action now, as the government seems to be about to press the "go" button.

However, despite the existence of spare capacity, the government would still have to be on the alert as an inflationary situation could quickly arise because devaluation does not, by itself, depress economic activity. Thus, Britain would need a strict prices and incomes policy, with the emphasis on counter-inflationary measures. Again, devaluation is not a soft option.

Devaluation could lead to inflation in yet another way. Given rising import prices there would be demands for higher wages and prices. However, import prices might not rise very much, as most of Britain's supplies of food and raw materials would devalue in sympathy with the pound. In addition, the most rapidly growing sector of imports—manufactures— should be severely reduced by devaluation. However, the need for a strict prices and incomes policy to guard against inflation is underlined.

The Long View

Most measures acting on the balance of payments itself—international loans, deflation, and devaluation—usually give short-term solutions. In particular, inflation (not shared by other countries) can quickly erode the gains from devaluation. On the other hand, devaluation may have some long-term advantages, not shared by other short-term measures, in that it provides incentives for the production of export and import substitutes.

If the poor export performance of the United Kingdom is not due to uncompetitive prices, devaluation would only partially remedy the situation. Poor salesmanship, bad design, and the like must be remedied by other means, though devaluation would help here by making exports more profitable.

Wealth Effects of Devaluation

Is Sterling Devaluation Immoral?

It will be remembered that sterling devaluation causes foreign holdings of sterling to lose value. Many people, especially bankers, regard this outcome as immoral, involving a breach of confidence with those who hold sterling. This they equate with an abdication of Britain's monetary world role and a severe blow to its world prestige. Therefore, they maintain that a sterling devaluation must never be countenanced or even mentioned.

There seems little sense, but much emotion, in the arguments. Their advocates consider a high rate of unemployment and little economic growth a small cost for the maintenance of a fixed exchange rate. And this view is seemingly shared by the British government, judging by the past record.

The ordinary British voter probably regards unemployment and stagnation as too high a price to pay for a fixed exchange rate. There seems good sense in this view which is supported by a recent study of the dollar. This suggested that any benefits which did accrue to the United States, from the international monetary role of the dollar, were outweighed by the damage done by the anti-speculative measures necessarily associated with a key currency.

Further, it should be noted that no agreement exists which guarantees sterling holdings against devaluation. Speculative runs on the pound are evidence that foreign nationals know this. In addition, because of the greater risk of devaluation a higher rate of interest is paid on sterling holdings than on dollar holdings. This higher rate of interest would partially offset any loss resulting from a 10 to 15 percent devaluation.

The World Monetary System and Devaluation

A more serious question concerns the world monetary repercussions of a British devaluation. There are two unpleasant possibilities. First, that enough people might turn from sterling to gold and dollars to force a dollar devaluation; followed in turn by the rest of the world. Past history and the size of the American reserves make such wholesale devaluation unlikely. Even if the worst did happen, though the short-term consequences would be serious, in the long run the world economy would merely be back at square one, with perhaps the world liquidity problem solved as a bonus.

Second, one British devaluation may soon be followed by another, initiating an unstoppable depreciation of the pound, monetary chaos, the destruction of the sterling area, and a severe reduction in world trade.

However, the sensible time to leave sterling is prior to devaluation. To sell pounds after the event would be a vain attempt to bolt the stable door. Only if another horse was thought to be inside would a run on the pound be justified. Past experiences suggest the opposite would occur. More people would wish to hold the strong sterling which results from devaluation.

Any devaluation would need to be sufficient to convince holders that a second is unlikely. So the degree of devaluation required may be greater than that needed to right the balance of payments. This might provoke retaliation. There might be advantages, particularly to prevent retaliation, in allowing the pound to "float" and, after devaluation, rise to its natural rate.

All likelihood of chaos could be avoided by guaranteeing all official and trade holdings of sterling against further devaluations. However, Britain does not have the reserves to back such a guarantee. Some international co-operation would be needed, and this might be a step toward the solution to the world's liquidity problems.

Conclusion

Finally, the cost of the $2.80 parity rate should not be forgotten: to Britain, a series of "stop/go" cycles of increasing severity, reducing economic growth to a snail's pace; to the world, a Britain that constantly has to be propped up and which cannot afford to make a worthwhile contribution to international welfare.

The only way to cure the fundamental weaknesses of the British economy is to attack them at their roots. A reduction in the ratio of imports to national income is essential. British costs and prices must be held down relative to those of other countries. All restrictive attitudes on both sides of industry must be abandoned and the emphasis put on technological efficiency.

These aims are easy to list, as the British Prime Minister is fond of doing, but difficult to achieve. Many doubt whether the British government really has effective policies working toward these ends. By devaluing, the government cannot escape the need for a successful incomes policy nor avoid unpopular actions to improve the long-term position. This is where Britain must be successful.

Discussion Questions

1. Discuss the impact of the devaluations in Finland and Great Britain.
2. Would you expect the United States to have similar results with devaluation of the dollar?
3. What problems does the United States have which could make its experience with devaluation more difficult to predict?

3 DOMESTIC ECONOMIC ISSUES

Pollution

Economics is more closely associated with the quantitative dimension of life than with the quality of life. As such, industrial societies give far greater attention to Gross National Product than to gross national quality. One factor of the quality of life, or the lack of it, is environmental pollution. Pollution is an inescapable phenomenon of production. The very act of converting inputs into output generates pollution. If you produce cellophane wrappers, they have to be disposed of in some fashion. If you produce paper, it too must ultimately disappear into the environment as a waste product. The residual substances emanating from the process of production enter into the environment and disrupt its natural workings. Waterways become industrial sewers, the sky becomes an atmospheric cesspool, and the consumers of affluence leave a growing legacy of environmental disruption.

But pollution is a two-edged sword. For the very existence of people is a factor in the pollution problem. Where there are people, there is human waste. The more people, the greater is the amount of waste material. It is a tautology: people equal pollution.

The two most obvious solutions to the duality of environmental disruption are to reduce total GNP and the birth rate. The first is not likely to occur as a result of either governmental policy or citizen demand. The second is occurring in the United States and is likely to continue in the foreseeable future.

Beyond these simplistic solutions lie even more complicated policy mixes. For example, the composition of GNP could be altered to include a greater proportion of durable goods and these commodities could be produced to last a longer period of time. A second technological solution is to recover certain materials such as paper, glass, and aluminum and to recycle them for reuse as inputs. A third possibility is developing processes which convert presently harmful effluents into harmless materials before they reach the environment.

Government can enter by imposing strict regulations on the amount of pollutants permitted to enter the water and air—and enforce these regulations. Others suggest that pollution rights be sold to producers and *the revenues collected be used to maintain the environment in a fit condition. Another position is that producers pay the costs of cleaning up their discharges, or their prevention in the first place, passing on the costs to consumers. That is, anti-pollution devices should be viewed as part of the cost of doing business.*

The article by Harland Manchester is a study of European disposal facilities which have converted garbage into heat and electric power. His article provides one concrete example of the possibilities for a technological solution to the pollution dilemma.

The second article is an excellent overview of the problem of environmental disruption from the perspective of different economic systems. Professor Dahmén first looks at some of the basic facts of pollution in different economic systems and then gives attention to the potential approaches for solving the environmental problem under different systems.

Harland Manchester is a roving editor for Reader's Digest. *Erik Dahmén teaches at the Stockholm School of Economics.*

Refuse Is Reusable

HARLAND MANCHESTER

Near the center of the pleasant small city of Rosenheim in southern Bavaria stands the municipal incinerator. All too often, such plants are smelly, smoke-belching eyesores that stir the wrath of their neighbors. This windowless, brightly painted, new concrete building is immaculate, dustless, and noiseless. Every day, about 75 tons of kitchen, household, and commercial refuse disappear through its steel doors and make no more trouble. Instead, they are transformed by fire into steam to heat houses and electric power to run lights and machines. And the vapor from its stack is so clean you can hardly see it.

This is one city's solution to a problem of mounting urgency throughout the world. Since trash production increases with income, it is particularly crucial in the United States. Every day, U.S. families throw out an estimated 480,000 tons of paper, cartons, tin cans, bottles, plastic bags, kitchen garbage, old furniture, worn-out clothing, molting mattresses, and broken appliances. This is a new high, not only because there are more people, but because per capita production of trash is steadily increasing. For one thing, we use more canned and packaged foods and drinks and return fewer bottles. Trends show that about 165,000 more daily tons will

Reprinted from the *National Civic Review,* February 1968, pp. 81–87, by permission of the *Reader's Digest* which published the article in condensed form under the title "Better Ways to Deal With Waste." © 1968 by the Reader's Digest Assn., Inc.

be added to this national trash pile in another decade, and that the curve will still climb. More than half the country's cities and towns still cart the stuff to malodorous, rat-infested dumps. These can be found everywhere, from the smoldering dumps of Hackensack Meadows, within view from New York City's Empire State Building, to the unsightly deposits in San Francisco Bay. And, as cities and suburbs expand, we are running out of dumping space and producing new kinds of pollution that foul up the air and the streams and spread disease.

Because of our vast land area, we have long been spared the worst results of indiscriminate trash disposal, but this relative immunity is now exhausted. Our slovenly habits have caught up with us, and the smell of rotting garbage has become a national stench. Government agencies from Washington down to the councils of the smallest towns are aroused to the need for action. Two years ago, the solid waste disposal act was passed by Congress, and more than a hundred research and demonstration projects are now under way to demonstrate new and improved techniques for the utilization and disposal of our refuse.

Leading sanitation experts are turning to Europe for guidance. Because of greater population density and a long tradition of neatness, most European communities are far ahead of us in safe and inoffensive refuse disposal. Last spring, the disposal systems of a dozen continental cities were investigated.

Methods vary widely; no single plan will work everywhere. Rosenheim's refuse-burning power plant was tailored to fit the needs of the city of 32,000 and the surrounding towns. Five years ago, Mayor Albert Steinbeisser explained, safe refuse disposal areas were hard to find. The result was "wild dumping" on unused land, and the situation became a scandal. Meanwhile, the city's demand for electric power was doubling every seven years. The small city power plant was forced to buy extra power from outside at high prices to meet rising needs. There was also a potential demand for central steam heat, if an acceptable plant could be located near the city's center. The city itself could not supply enough refuse to fuel a plant of the needed size, but 44 neighboring towns, all with disposal problems, were glad to find an outlet for their trash.

The new plant opened three years ago and has fulfilled all promises. It is now producing an annual 35,000,000 kilowatt-hours of electricity, nearly enough to supply Rosenheim, which is no longer at the mercy of outside electric plants. Steam heat is delivered economically through 5 miles of buried pipes to about 90 stores, banks, schools, factories, and office buildings, and to 458 private dwellings. Steam delivery has a boot-strap-lifting effect, explains Mayor Steinbeisser. "When you sell heat to homes, they have no fires to burn garbage, so they send it to us and we make more steam." Householders pay the city for collecting their trash.

All the newest advances in power-making incineration can be seen in the Rosenheim plant. Every day, collection trucks from the city and from towns within a radius of 22 miles bring about 75 tons of trash and dump them in the plant's enclosed concrete bins. Clamshell "grabbers" mounted on cranes dump big loads into the inclined burners. Heat is piped from the flaming section to dry out the incoming trash, and about 10 quarts of furnace oil are used in burning every ton of refuse. At the end of the burning process, metal objects are removed by shakers or by magnetic belts and are sold for scrap, and clinkers are ground into pellets for use in road-building. As the smoke goes up the stack, 98 percent of all dust particles are removed by filters. Just across the street is a large dairy—a type of plant unusually fussy about dust and odors. Its owners not only give the incinerator a clean bill of health, they use its live steam for sterilization.

Bookkeeping is complicated for such a dual-purpose plant, designed both to get rid of a nuisance and to make power, but Mayor Steinbeisser reports that sales of steam and power pay the operation costs, plus a little profit. Since the plant opened, both the volume of refuse and the demand for electric power have increased, and the new system has worked so well that next year Rosenheim plans to build a second plant to convert junk into kilowatts.

At Munich, 40 miles away, a quite different type of trash-burning power plant is attracting engineers from all over the world. It was built to cope with a double pollution problem. On the one hand, prosperity had spurred the usual boom in trash production, and the city was running out of suitable dumping space. At the same time, a rising demand for electric power had brought a sharp increase in sulphur-bearing smoke from the city's coal-burning power plant. Almost no sulphur is produced by the combustion of household refuse, so the city decided to reduce both nuisances by burning trash to make steam to run electric generators and provide heat for homes.

The new incinerator-power plant, which has been running for nearly three years, can burn about 45,000 tons of refuse a month, and disposes of about 80 percent of the household and commercial debris created by the 1,300,000 inhabitants. The energy in the trash is converted into power which comes back over the wires to run lights and appliances. This is a hybrid plant which burns both coal and refuse in different burners. Refuse produces about a fifth as much heat per pound as coal, and garbage truck delivery is more subject to interruptions than coal shipments, so this dual system ensures even power output.

Roughly speaking, this plant is now taking an annual mountain of over 500,000 tons of smelly, disease-breeding junk and reducing it to a sterile residue about 15 percent of its former volume, composed mostly of scrap metal, slag, and ashes. This is shipped by train to scrap dealers and landfill sites. While the use of two fuels makes cost analysis difficult, Munich officials report that power and steam sales and garbage collection fees pay for the cost of plant operation. Other bonuses hard to list in a balance sheet are cleaner air and streams, aesthetic betterment, and a consequent increase in real estate values.

Heartened by the success of the pioneer, Munich is now building a new refuse-power plant in the downtown area from which steam can be piped for office and home heating. The combined plants should take care of all the city's refuse in a clean and odorless manner for several years to come.

Several other European cities are now burning refuse to make power and heat. One of the largest units is at Essen, which burns the trash and sewage produced by 1,400,000 people in four cities to make electric power for peak use. A giant plant using the latest techniques opened in Rotterdam about three years ago, and all efficiency records may be broken by a plant now under construction in Amsterdam. In 1966 an elegant small plant, with sleeping and dining quarters for the staff, was opened on the bank of the Rhone river eight miles outside Geneva. A fleet of barges brings the debris of the entire canton to be burned to produce electric power. There are five other plants of this type in Switzerland, and more are being built. The city of Milan is building a chain of incinerators to convert refuse into kilowatts to run street lights and the tram network. All these plants have technical refinements and standards of cleanliness virtually unknown in the United States.

Another ingenious method of getting value from refuse is now being tested in a small pioneer plant at Kolding, a Danish provincial town of 37,000. Household refuse is being "cooked" to make commercial gas, which is piped back to houses for domestic use. This method was designed by Georg Borggreen, manager of the town gasworks, as an answer to a familiar crises. Kolding was running out of dumping space, dumps were fouling up the water and attracting disease-spreading rats, and refuse was being hauled several miles at high cost. Mr. Borggreen knew there was gas in the stuff, and built a small pilot plant where he cooked batches of debris. City fathers saw the gas burn with a bright flame, and advanced funds for further tests. Now, about 18 tons of refuse a day—half of Kolding's output —are being heated in four tall metal retorts to make gas. As a by-product, the water squeezed from the refuse, heated to a high temperature, is piped to heat buildings. The plant is located in the center of town, and gives off no fumes or smoke. Mr. Borggreen has plans for expanding the plant to process all Kolding's refuse and sewage, thus freeing the town from importing expensive coal. A private company has been formed to build other refuse-gas plants, and the process has been patented in 11 countries.

Such operations are small compared to the big system in Paris, which leads the world in the conversion of refuse to power and heat. The city's truck fleet collects 1,600,000 tons of junk a year from Paris proper and 50 suburbs, and three quarters of it is burned in four big plants to make steam to run generators and heat buildings. The city began turning garbage into kilowatts more than 50 years ago and has been enlarging and modernizing its plants ever since. It now sells enough power to the national electric grid to serve a city of about 50,000 inhabitants, and its steam heats hundreds of Paris apartment houses, hotels, and official buildings. These sales recover about a third of the cost of financing and operating the plants.

The newest and biggest plant, at Issy-les-Moulineaux, rebuilt two years ago, burns 450,000 tons of refuse a year and is hailed as a model of efficiency. The clean, white concrete building is a good neighbor of a residential area, emitting no dust or visible smoke, and is virtually noiseless. On the collection bunker a long line of power-operated steel doors enables some 20 trucks to dump their loads without waiting. Its four furnaces produce steam which does double duty, first spinning the turbines of the power plant, then, at lower pressure, passing through pipes to heat buildings. An even bigger power-from-refuse plant is now under construction, for like everyone else, Parisians are producing more trash every year.

Not all Paris' refuse is burned. Every year, trains haul 200,000 tons to landfill sites, mostly northeast of the city, where, in several areas, it has been tamped down and covered with dirt to make new farmland, parks, and athletic fields. This disposal method, used for many years all over the world, can handle only a fraction of modern municipal refuse. Most cities are running out of landfill sites near enough for practical use. Another fraction of Paris' refuse is sifted and ground into raw agricultural compost and shipped to farm areas and sold for about the cost of transport.

The return of refuse to the land is of limited value to metropolitan centers. Its fertilizer value is low, handling costs are high, and, since the introduction of concentrated commercial fertilizers, few farmers will use it. At the new plant at Schweinfurt, Germany, all household refuse and sewage from the city of 58,000 is converted into top-grade compost by a unique process. A few years ago, Schweinfurt faced a crisis. Sewage was dumped on the banks of the river Main, and seepage from the increasing volume of sludge polluted the water and raised a stench. Refuse was dumped into sandpits, menacing the safety of ground water. Heinrich Meyer, a leading European sanitation expert, and Fritz Caspari, a biologist and chemist, tackled the problem.

Schweinfurt is surrounded by vineyards which have a special need for mulch, and the two men devised the so-called "Brikollare process." Sewage and refuse are combined and compressed into bricks. Piled in a curing shed, they generate heat, and fungi develop which weld them into compact blocks. Germs and weed spores are killed, and the result is a brownish, sterile compost, inoffensive to the nose. The bricks are stored and reground when needed by the farmers. When the plant opened in 1965, conservative Bavarian farmers were slow to accept the material, for they had had bad luck with raw compost that damaged their vines. The treated material caught on quickly, however, and the plant now has more orders than it can fill. The plant was built for twice its present capacity, and Mr.

Meyer, its manager, plans to process more and more refuse from neighboring towns. Mr. Meyer told me:

> Tremendous amounts of high-grade compost could be used to advantage on German farms, but we must accept the fact that compost plants do not pay except in terms of refuse disposal. Today our compost sales cover about 40 percent of plant operation costs, and we hope to boost that to 50 percent. This does not discourage us, for we are not in the compost business, but in the waste disposal business. We have to build disposal plants, just as we have to build hospitals, to protect public health. I am tired of hearing of new methods that will convert garbage into money. It is about time people stopped daydreaming. Garbage is a nuisance, and we have to get rid of it in the safest and most efficient ways possible without robbing the taxpayer blind.

Other European communities are fighting the battle of refuse with mechanical monsters which shatter the stuff to bits so that it will take up less room. Wiesbaden, Germany, blessed with the "biggest pit in Europe" —a vast cavern made by a cement plant just out of town—thought of the future and built four concrete towers 120 feet high. Conveyor belts carry the stuff up and dump it, and power-driven hammers smash up old furniture, barrels, cartons, tin cans, and kitchen waste into a granular compact pulp which is tipped into the big pit. This reduces its volume by half, and city mathematicians estimate that they will have no garbage worries for 300 years. Smaller electrical pulverizers, both stationary and portable, built by a British firm, are used by about 20 towns in Britain and on the Continent. They sort out large hunks of metal which can be sold as scrap, and even electrocute flies to prevent their breeding. There is still the residue to dispose of, but the problem has been cut in half.

U.S. study groups have been beating a path to European disposal plants, and have returned with new ideas for coping with our grim pollution crisis. A team from New York City, composed of city officials and engineers from the Consolidated Edison Company, has proposed the construction of a giant modern incinerator in Brooklyn which would convert city refuse into salable steam and, at the same time, reduce New York's notorious smog. Elmer R. Kaiser of the New York University School of Engineering and Science, a leading authority in refuse disposal, estimates that about half of the city's 6,000,000 tons of refuse a year may be usable fuel. Burned under boilers to displace coal and oil, it would greatly reduce the emission of noxious sulphur which is becoming a serious health problem. Under the plan outlined by Austin N. Heller, commission of air pollution control, the city would build and operate the incinerator and sell the steam to the utility, which would dispatch it through its network of heating pipes.

Since most U.S. incinerators are obsolete, air-fouling nuisances, voters often oppose them, but, as European cities have demonstrated, there is no technical reason why an incinerator cannot be as clean as a bank.

The first modern, European-type incinerator in this country opened last April at the Norfolk, Virginia, Naval Base. The incinerator consists of two units, each capable of burning 180 tons of refuse per day, and makes steam to supply berthed vessels. The designers, Metcalf & Eddy of Boston, are now drawing up plans for a plant more than four times as big for Chicago.

Meanwhile, a variety of ingenious techniques for pulling the country out of the muck are being explored with the aid of more than a hundred grants from the solid wastes program of the U.S. public health service. To list a few: Harvard's department of industrial hygiene is designing an experimental "incinerator ship" which will burn refuse at sea to avoid city air pollution, and dump the ashes in designated areas of the ocean. The University of Pennsylvania is exploring the use of pipelines for the transportation of refuse from homes and industries to remote disposal sites. (Such a system is now operating in a suburb of Stockholm, serving blocks of apartments housing some 1,500 families.) The city of Chicago is working on a plan to pipe processed sewage 90 miles into the country for use as fertilizer. The American Public Works Association is exploring the economics of operating "trash trains" to rid Chicago and Westchester County (New York) cities, among others, of their debris. The Maryland Department of Health is testing the feasibility of shipping refuse to fill abandoned strip coal mines. There are 2,400 such mines in western Maryland alone, and the program might restore it to farming or recreational use.

Nearly two-thirds of U.S. household refuse is composed of paper and paper products, which may take several months to disintegrate in a town dump. At the sanitary engineering research laboratory of Manhattan College, John Jeris and his associates are working on a plan to speed up the biological process to three days. By slowly aerating waste paper in a rotating bin under carefully controlled conditions, they encourage cellulose-hungry bacteria to do their work faster and produce well-digested compost suitable for farm use. Despite the small demand for commercial compost, many scientists believe that eventually we must return to the soil much of the organic matter we harvest from field and forests.

The budget for the solid waste program is only $12,195,000—about six cents per capita. A serious handicap is a shortage of trained engineers and other scientific personnel, for garbage lacks the glamour enjoyed by space and cybernetics. The program has awarded grants totaling $500,000 to eight universities for training graduates in waste disposal.

"Waste disposal is one of the richest and most neglected fields for tomorrow's scientists and inventors," says Richard D. Vaughan, chief of the program. "We welcome new ideas from any source, at home or abroad. At least we are beginning to move American waste disposal into the second half of the 20th Century."

Meanwhile, as population mounts and per-capita production of trash steadily increases, we must seek out and put to use the best methods available to rescue ourselves from the tidal wave of debris.

Environmental Control and Economic Systems

ERIK DAHMÉN

Aims and Limitations

There are three important limitations. First, only those forms of environmental damage which influence human well-being will be discussed. The economics of natural resources will only be included indirectly. Second, only industrialized countries will be dealt with. Third, two rather refined economic systems will be in focus: *private capitalism* characterized by a market economy, that is freedom for separate entities to buy and sell competitively in a climate ruled by free price information and profit maximization, and *socialism* without this freedom but characterized instead by centralized decisions on resource allocation and prices, including the setting of production goals for separate production units an, to a varying degree, incentives to attain various specific goals, such as minimization of production costs.

Historic Facts

The first question to be answered is: Has the pace of environmental deterioration been different under various economic systems? The answer appears to be no. Differences in the degree of environmental disruption exist between countries of different levels of development with different population densities, different degrees of urbanization, different geographical conditions, and different climates. But there is no evidence whatsoever that the economic systems have been of any importance in this connection. It should be added—without discussing the point in detail—that neither the political organization, whether democratic or totalitarian, nor the political color of the government, appear to have been significant. Moreover, state-owned companies have been no different from privately owned companies in the extent to which they have damaged the environment.

The fact that so far there has not been any connection between various

Reprinted from Peter Bohm and Allen Kneese, *The Economics of Environment,* St. Martin's Press, Inc., Macmillan & Co., Ltd., 1971. The article first appeared in *The Swedish Journal of Economics,* Vol. *73,* No. 1, March, 1971.

economic systems and the rate of environmental deterioration, does not exclude the possibility that different systems might have different means of pursuing a successful environmental policy. This is because development, essentially similar, up to now, may have been due to inadequate knowledge. This in fact seems to be the main explanation for the absence of any connection between economic system and environmental deterioration. An additional explanation could be that the same comparatively low value has been placed on environmental conditions in both economic systems. Consumption has perhaps been given universal priority at the expense of the environment, particularly in countries which lag behind with respect to consumption, that is the socialist ones that started out on a low consumption level. But in most instances the damage has no doubt been tacitly accepted. Discussions leading to explicit decisions on the order of priorities have been the exception.

Causes of Environmental Deterioration

An analysis of the causes of environmental deterioration could serve as a useful basis for examining environmental control problems in various economic systems.

Attention could be drawn to technological and industrial progress, population development, urbanization, geographical conditions, and climate. But technology, industralization, and urbanization themselves are the results of more basic factors. Geographical conditions and climate can, at most, be regarded as contributory causes, but never sufficient in themselves to cause environmental degradation. However, if we take a step backward in the causal chain, we find that certain characteristic conditions have played a determining role everywhere.

One condition is organizational in nature, that is a highly developed disintegration of economic activities into discrete stages that was unknown in old agrarian societies. Different stages of decision making have arisen to take charge of different parts of the production process and very often decisions within separate producing units have today far-reaching consequences for the general public which can have very little influence on the decisions. This organizational structure has been created by the process of industrialization in both main types of economic system. In the capitalistic system, no production goals for separate producers are set by a central authority. On the whole, no central directives are given with respect to the organization of production, the choice of a production process, financing measures, and so on—or to questions of pollution and waste treatment. In socialistic systems, central authorities set production goals and decide on questions of resource allocation and financing, but producers have approximately the same freedom as in a capitalistic system in the area of technological and other types of measures affecting the environment.

This disintegration has been accompanied by the creation of a growth-promoting network of continuous contacts among producers and between producers and consumers. These contacts have been established either through the medium of a price mechanism acting on a free market or have been organized by special institutions allocating real and financial resources as well as final products among the separate entities. The first method has been developing gradually in private capitalistic countries, whereas the second was established by means of political decisions in socialistic countries.

Besides these two types of contact networks disintegration has had numerous other effects some of which are of great importance not only from a theoretical point of view but also with respect to environmental developments.

One important effect is referred to in the literature dealing with market economies as "externalities," defined as effects of production and consumption on other producers and consumers without corresponding payments. These externalities can be either positive or negative. The negative ones include environmental damages which imply a use of scarce resources and, consequently, should be regarded as socio-economic costs. Such damages represent externalities partly because environmental utilities often are so-called "public goods," that is goods which if available to one are equally available to all others and therefore cannot be sold and bought on a market. Thus in market economies no "bills" are sent to producers and consumers through the market mechanism for this kind of socio-economic costs. Moreover, particularly under strong competitive conditions, considerations of the profit-and-loss-account sharply limit the producers' possibilities of calculating, voluntarily, the negative externalities as costs. So far governments have corrected this "market failure" only in very limited ways and to a slight extent.

In socialistic systems characterized by the same kind of disintegrated activities, environmental damages, being "external" from the viewpoint of the separate entities, have generally been neglected in the same way as in the private capitalistic market economies. In other words, externalities which by definition cannot possibly be taken care of by the market mechanism have not been taken care of by any other mechanism in the non-market economies. In the latter case there has been a "planning failure."

Under both systems, a number of remarkable consequences of this failure of the market and/or the authorities to react have appeared.

One consequence has been that producers have regarded production methods and products which damage the environment as the least expensive alternatives. If there had been no possibility of omitting the socio-economic costs represented by environmental damages from the cost calculations, these alternatives would instead have often appeared to be the most expensive. Thus cost calculations that are too narrow have eliminated economic incentives to choose non-damaging production methods and products as long as the damaging ones are cheaper.

As a result of the choices made by producers, prices of goods whose production, distribution or use involved environmental degradation have been too low with respect to socio-economic costs. Consequently, consumption and production of goods such as these have been stimulated in a way which damages the environment, as compared with the production and consumption of goods whose production, distribution or use has not damaged the environment. Indirect effects have thus been added to the direct ones.

These two immediate consequences have in turn had another effect, the importance of which has been considerably underestimated not only by non-economists but also by many economists who are primarily occupied with theories applicable to stationary economies or who regard technological progress as an exogenous variable in the process of industrial development. Since technological research is often influenced by business considerations, this type of research has shown comparatively little interest in finding and developing new techniques and new products with less damaging effects on the environment. This lack of incentives to *innovate* methods and products beneficial to the environment is one of the most important, but very much neglected, causes behind long-run environmental deterioration. Furthermore, there are reasons to believe that a misallocation of scarce resources for research has implied lost opportunities of limiting environmental degradation at a considerably lower cost than has so far proved possible.

These factors, all of which are not basically related to the ownership of productive means nor to the market or non-market organization but to a great extent to the disintegration of activities and thus to the existence of externalities, have formed the basis for the environmental deterioration that has occurred everywhere. In both economic systems certain additional technological elements have entered the picture, that is those leading to numerous *large* production units. Therefore, environmental damage has quantitatively become very significant and has been spread over vast geographical areas. As a result, legal redress for damages has proved increasingly difficult to obtain. Environmental disruption has appeared instead as a general welfare problem for society as a whole.

Goals and Means of an Environmental Policy: A Theoretical Approach

Starting from this sketchy analysis of the factors behind environmental disruption let us first deal with the problems related to the way environmental policy *goals* may be set. Considering the fact that something (*inter alia* consumption) has to be sacrificed in order to achieve an environmental improvement, a basic question becomes *who* should decide on the goals, that is *how much* is it desirable to sacrifice in favor of a better environment? The question is whether different economic systems have essentially different characteristics, that is whether they face different difficulties with respect to the setting of the goals.

I have difficulty in seeing any difference worth mentioning between the two economic systems in this respect. A possible desire to accept consumer preferences would make it necessary in both cases to rely on some sort of opinion poll. If there is no free market, this is self-evident. But a free market which in a sense is usually a mechanism functioning continuously as an "opinion poll" does not solve the problem either. Many vital environmental values cannot be registered by the price-system revealing consumer preferences, since they are "public goods." However, opinion polls on environmental problems would be difficult to carry out, regardless of the economic system. There are obvious reasons for this.

Whenever the question of environmental improvement comes up a position must be taken on the goals of income distribution or, rather, on distribution of welfare. The benefits of a measure that improves the environment will by no means always be enjoyed in equal measure by those who have to pay for it. This question of welfare distribution also has an intertemporal aspect in that several generations are affected. This is especially important in the area of the environment and it renders the idea of building on "general opinion" rather suspect. This is particularly because many forms of environmental damage may be irreversible.

In addition policies to improve the environment may sometimes give rise to problems with respect to the balance of payments. Although problems such as these could always be solved by using a package of policy means it is easy to imagine the difficulties in having people take a stand with regard to matters that are often highly complicated and "technical."

Even quite apart from this type of problem, it should be pointed out that public opinion could seldom be based on sufficient information of a generally understandable nature. Questions of fact are often subject even to scientific controversy—for example, in reference to the forms and magnitudes of risks in environmental deterioration.

The general conclusion seems unescapable that the goals of environmental control must on the whole be based on a factual basis, preferably by means of some sort of cost-benefit-analysis, available only to central decision-making bodies. Very often it will be a question of making investment calculations under great uncertainties. In this respect there are no significant differences between capitalistic market and socialistic non-market systems.

Let us then turn to *means* of improving the environment in the different economic systems. The first observation is as follows: In view of the fact that environmental deterioration is basically caused by the externalities characteristic of all systems of disintegrated activities one way of attaining environmental control in both systems stands out fairly clearly in relation to the "resource allocation approach" to the problem of environmental degradation. It would involve having decision makers within the separate entities weigh damage to the environment as a cost just like any other cost of doing business.

One question concerns whether this problem can be solved through centralization of the *decision-making process* as regards choices of production methods, product design, pollution, waste treatment, and so on. It is possible, assuming retention of the disintegration of activities, to establish one or relatively few decision-making instances where some of the units' externalities can be "internalized," that is made to enter into their cost calculations?

In a private capitalistic system, such a strong centralization of decisions is not conceivable. Producers cannot be guided in every separate instance by detailed central directives on all technical points involved in production methods and products. Both the legal and the administrative difficulties would be too great.

Establishing one or more large centralized decision-making bodies may appear more practicable in a socialistic system, inasmuch as ownership itself is already centralized. But this kind of centralized authority is not practicable here either. The legal aspects offer no problems, but the administrative side does. Even here producers cannot be given instructions on every aspect of the problems on a case-to-case basis.

This leaves us with two more conceivable ways of attacking the environmental policy problem. There are two main approaches worth discussing.

One group of means (usually preferred by legal experts, administrators, and other laymen in the field of economics) consists of prohibitions or agreements which are referred to here simply as *regulations*. These regulations mean that the socio-economic costs represented by the damages to the environment are not permitted to exceed certain limits, which are determined from case to case. The rules can be unspecific so that the producer in question can, himself, attempt to discover how to limit the damage. But the rules can also give instructions on how the delimitations should occur.

One result of this approach is that producers' costs are raised. They may be forced to invest, for example in waste treatment plants. Or they may shift to more expensive production or distribution methods. In both cases the environment is improved not only directly but also indirectly. The price increases which producers can be presumed to try are likely to reduce demand and therefore lead to a reduction of production that still damages the environment, though to a smaller degree than earlier.

Such regulations, based on intermittent administrative initiatives from instances outside the producer circles, can be used in both economic systems. The question is whether the method might be expected to be equally effective in both systems.

In a market economy a desire arises on the part of producers to bring down the costs of a waste treatment plant or a new production process in order to reduce the strain on the profit-and-loss account. In non-market economies regulations can first of all be presumed to make it more difficult to reach a prescribed production goal. Therefore a similar incentive would also appear here, if the production goals set by the central planners are maintained and no sufficiently increased supply of resources is made available, such as additional financing. The question is whether the incentives in such a case can be expected to function with as much force as when profits are threatened in a private capitalistic market system. The answer depends on the effectiveness of the incentives for managements to minimize production costs. Therefore one crucial question is how *inter alia* bonuses used in such a system really function in this respect. In my opinion there is not much evidence of effective functioning so far. But this does not exclude the possibilities of introducing appropriate bonuses for attaining specific goals with respect to environment quality.

One characteristic of all regulations in both economic systems is that they are rather inflexible and not very well suited for reducing the damages to an optimum level from a general resource allocation point of view. Furthermore there is no incentive among producers to find *new* production methods and products more beneficial to the environment but not prescribed by the regulation. This incentive to innovate would be limited to firms offering various abatement and purification equipment and alternate processing techniques and possibly co-operating with those who have directly or indirectly the regulative power. The incentive for the other producers can be assumed to be directed at just minimizing the extra costs brought about by the regulation. Even this limited incentive would disappear if the authorities choose to subsidize away the marginal cost increases resulting from the regulative prescription. Furthermore, in such a case there would be no corrections of the price relations between various products and thus no indirect beneficial effects on the environment. This would be irrational from the point of view of environmental policy.

Owing to the limitations and weaknesses of the regulation method there are reasons to look for another method which, at least with respect to the points touched on so far, would be superior to the regulation method. And, if so, how useful might it be in different economic systems?

The approach which is most immediately apparent to an economist is that which involves *charging a fee* for environmental damages. This method would not set any strict limitations for the damages inflicted on the environment. Instead, a bill would be presented. Its amount would be reduced or increased proportional to the reduction or increase in environmental damage. This can be assumed to help reduce the damages to an optimum level from a general resource allocation point of view in a more effective way than the regulation method. The fact that a stronger incentive to bring down the damage would be given is of particular importance. Even if the initial effect in the form of, for example, investment in waste treatment equipment or other technical solutions might not be the same in the fee method as in the regulation method (that is in the case of rather small fees) there is a great probability that the effect in terms of environmental improvement over a *period of time* would be greater. Above all it could be hoped that *technological progress* in the field of environmental control would receive a powerful and continuous stimulus. In theories of economic development, insufficient attention is usually paid to the fact that impulses go out from company managements and from potential founders of enterprises to technicians, product designers, and indirectly to researchers. It would be of great benefit, particularly in a discussion of environmental policy means, if we could include this fact in the picture. I would launch the hypothesis that through innovation in various abatement and treatment techniques, in processing and in the form of new products, consumers' sacrifices in terms of consumption could be reduced considerably, possibly in the short run but certainly over the *long term,* by the use of fees as an important complement to regulations. It seems quite possible that the marginal returns on research and development investments on the environmental front could be large. It is even likely that basic research, which is not stimulated by industrial activity but develops by reason of "pure curiosity," has long possessed a store of potentially valuable technology to offer in the environmental area but that it has not yet been of special interest for producers to find and develop these possibilities.

Now the question is how strong the incentives provided by the fee method would be in a market economy compared to a non-market economy.

In a private capitalistic market economy the incentives no doubt would prove strong because of the strain on profit and loss-accounts. In the other economic systems, the fees are likely to give comparatively weak incentives and to be less effective than regulations. This is because the fees cannot usually make attainment of a prescribed production goal more difficult in the same way as regulations. The effects of a fee could be absorbed more easily, for example by cutting outlays in some other areas in a way that would not immediately disturb the factory's production to the same degree. This conclusion should be modified only insofar as there is an effective "profit" incentive even in the non-market system, that is to the extent that a factory's possible cost reductions are generally fully rewarded. So far, this does not seem to have occurred. Here again, however, future improvements *inter alia* in the bonus system might change the picture.

Before arriving at some summary conclusions it should be kept in mind that comparisons here have been made between rather refined types of economic systems and equally refined alternatives for environmental control. This has been done exclusively in the interest of simplification. Such a method may be acceptable as a basis for an analytically more ambitious and more detailed discussion of various "mixed" economic systems and various combinations of policy means.

Summary Conclusions

1. Since severe environmental deterioration has been going on for a long time regardless of economic system, measures are now discussed both in capitalistic market economies and in socialistic non-market economies to bring about a shift in direction. If we draw up a static picture of today's situation and that of the future, there is reason for pessimism, especially since all countries have a costly bill to settle for many years of sins. But if we take a more dynamic view of the matter and if we succeed in working out rational methods for environment policies, then there are grounds for optimism. There is no natural law saying that present environmental disruption is unavoidable, and the costs for correcting damages might not, over the long term, prove to be as enormous as they may seem today.

2. Environmental policy measures are surely available in both economic systems which I have here dealt with. The central problem does not lie in the conditions of ownership nor in the market or non-market organization but in the disintegration of activities which has been an element in industrialization and therefore in economic growth everywhere. This disintegration has resulted in calculations of socio-economic costs that are too narrow and therefore in a misallocation of resources and environmental deterioration. The main task of environmental control should be to enforce more accurate cost calculations.

3. More accurate cost calculations would make producers inclined to choose technical alternatives more favorable to preserving the environment. Some such technical possibilities already exist although it has not been attractive to use them. More accurate cost calculations would also influence future technology in the right direction. Therefore there is in both economic systems a hitherto neglected opportunity to stimulate technology in a way more beneficial to the human environment than we have experienced so far.

4. In capitalistic market economies the most effective way of enforcing changed cost calculations and, in particular, of promoting new technologies would very likely be to *charge* producers for the damage done to the environment. This is because charges such as these would create more or less strong business incentives to act in compliance with the environmental policy goals set up by authorities. In a socialistic non-market system the impact of charges for environmental damage would be dependent on the extent to which separate units are under pressure not only to reach prescribed production goals but also to minimize production

costs and maximize "profits." Insofar as such pressures are comparatively weak, *regulations* of various kinds instead of charges would seem more appropriate.

Discussion Questions

1. How would you evaluate the relative merits of using the market system to solve the problems of pollution?
2. Is it necessary to introduce economic planning to combat environmental deterioration?
3. Discuss the European use of trash for heat and power in the light of America's growing solid waste problem.

Health

Americans spend about $60 billion a year for health services, or more than $300 for every man, woman, and child, in an industry which lags behind only agriculture and construction in size. Despite the enormity of these expenditures, Americans have increasingly questioned the widening gap between our potential to provide adequate health care for all and the failure to deliver such care. Many have even described the situation as a crisis. Critics point to the fact that we have an estimated shortage of 50,000 physicians in the United States. Furthermore, prices in the health services industry have risen at a rate far exceeding the overall Consumer Price Index (CPI). During the period 1950–70, the price of medical care rose twice as much as the CPI for all items. Thus, not only are the poor being priced out of consuming adequate health care, but the resources of the middle class are also being severely strained. Another major problem is that health services are, from a geographic perspective, distributed quite unevenly. For example, in relative terms, there are more than twice as many physicians in private practice in the states of New York, California, Colorado, Massachusetts, and Connecticut than there are in states such as South Carolina, Alaska, and Mississippi. An examination of this disparity between smaller geographic units would produce even greater perversities, such as between ghetto and suburb.

In the articles offered for consideration in this section, the reader is presented with an overview of the Soviet health system—its philosophy, growth, and results. The second article, dealing with Norwegian dentists, addresses itself to the specific question of the distribution of health services within a country. Here the crucial question is whether the individual health professional should have the right to decide his place of employment, or whether the public weal should receive a higher priority.

Progress of Public Health in the USSR, 1917–1967

BORIS PETROVSKY

The health of the people has been proclaimed as one of the basic concerns and duties of the Soviet state. Medical assistance in the USSR is qualified, free, and accessible. The health service is based on centralized guidance, planning, and financing; its main features are as follows: it is state-run, there are close connections between medical science and practice, emphasis is placed on the prevention of disease and the active participation of the population in measures to protect their own health and that of all members of society.

The achievements of the Soviet health service are well-known. They have been made possible, among other things, by a constant rise in the material and cultural level of Soviet life, the establishment of a ramified network of medical institutions, the provision of ample hospital accommodation and medical personnel, and successful development of medical science and the medical industry.

Free Medical Assistance

All medical institutions in the USSR (whether a small village hospital, an out-patient clinic, or a large city hospital) give medical aid free of charge irrespective of how long the patient stays in the hospital, what operation he has, or what medicines he receives. There is no charge for measures to prevent or treat diseases, for medical advice, all kinds of laboratory tests, obstetric aid in childbirth or treatment in children's sanatoria (there are over 1,000 such sanatoria in the USSR with a total of 135,000 beds) and in tuberculosis sanatoria. Many industrial and office workers go to holiday homes either completely free of charge or at 30 percent of the cost, the difference coming from social insurance funds. In 1965 over 8 million people spent their vacations at holiday homes and received treatment at sanatoria or health resorts polyclinics; of them, over seven million did so either partly or wholly at the expense of these funds.

All expenditures on public health and physical culture comes out of the state budget and the funds of state bodies or co-operative, trade union, and other mass organizations as well as of the funds of collective farms. In 1965, the state allocations for these purposes amounted to 6,700 million rubles, or 28.9 rubles per head of the population.

Reprinted from *Population Review*, Vol. *11*, No. 2, 1967, pp. 17–24, by permission of the publisher.

From the Social Security Funds

Big sums are also allocated for social maintenance and social insurance. Social security needs are fully covered by the state (it is an all-embracing, non-contributory scheme). Temporarily incapacitated workers receive allowances of up to 90 percent of their pay, depending on their length of service. All expectant mothers get paid maternity leave. The old and disabled receive pensions. Contributions toward the cost of sanatorium treatment and vacations at holiday and rest homes are also made from social security funds.

Facilities for the encouragement of open-air holidays, including mountaineering, and the organization of various camps for school children and students are also financed from these funds, and subsidies provided for dietetic canteens in factories.

Thanks to free medical aid and a ramified network of hospitals, polyclinics, sanatoria, and other medical institutions, the most qualified and costly medical aid has become available to every citizen of the USSR, no matter where he lives—in the densely populated Ukraine, or sparsely populated Yakutia, in sunny Turkmenia, or in Karelia with its severe climate, in town or country, in large industrial centers or distant hamlets. When necessary, anyone may call a doctor to his home and receive qualified medical aid. Medical assistance is available to every one, in all cases—from that of the common cold to the complex heart operation which requires consultations with eminent specialists and the use of expensive, sometimes unique, apparatus.

Prevention—the Main Principle of the Soviet Health Service

Prevention of disease is the main principle of the Soviet health service. All social, economic, and public health measures are aimed at preventing and eradicating disease, and further improving the environment, and working and living conditions.

The Soviet government generously subsidizes all measures to protect air, water, and soil from contamination, improve living conditions of millions of people, and further develop the network of therapeutic, prophylactic, and children's institutions. Of late, a number of important measures were carried out in the USSR to raise the general well-being and to meet cultural requirements of working people. There are ample sports facilities of all kinds, which are of great value in maintaining and improving the general health of the population.

Everything for Man

Public health in the USSR is not only the concern of purely medical institutions. The whole socialist system, and its legislation and institutions are designed to serve man. Concern for people is clearly seen in all branches of socialist construction; everything that is done for man serves to maintain and strengthen his health and prolong his life. The health service is not confined to medical aid in hospitals and polyclinics. It also involves labor protection, improvement of working conditions at industrial enterprises, construction of sanatoria and holiday homes, and reduction of the working day which will become shorter and shorter as the country makes progress.

Achievements in the control of tuberculosis in the USSR are primarily the result of improved working and living conditions and of better nutrition and catering.

The liquidation of unemployment and the eradication of prostitution resulted in the sharp reduction in incidence of venereal disease.

Successful control of malaria is associated with planned drainage of marshland and other reclamation work on tens of thousands of square kilometers.

The policy of the Soviet state is one of satisfying the growing requirements of the Soviet people, and of solving major social problems, the ultimate aim of which is the maintenance of health and satisfaction of the people's material and spiritual welfare. The foundations of the health service were laid in decrees and resolutions of the Soviet government adopted shortly after the Great October Socialist Revolution (on social insurance, free medical aid, nationalization of medical institutions, sanatoria, pharmacies, and so on).

Written Down in the Constitution

The rights of citizens as regards health service are embodied in the Constitution of the USSR, the basic law of the socialist state.

Article 120 of the Constitution reads: "Citizens of the USSR have the right to maintenance in old age and also in case of sickness or disability." It says further: "This right is ensured by the extensive development of social insurance of industrial, office, and professional workers at state expense, free medical service for the working people, and the provision of a wide network of health resorts for the use of the working people."

There are no private clinics in the USSR, all therapeutic and health establishments are financed by the state. Doctors receive salaries from the state. The state character of the health service ensures the over-all planning of all measures taken in the field of public health.

The entire health services come under the control of the USSR Minister of Health, who is a member of the Council of Ministers of the USSR. Among the tasks of his Ministry are the planning, co-ordination, control, and guidance of all the work carried out by the ramified network of public health bodies and medical institutions, as well as of the medical supplies and pharmaceutical industries.

Each of the 15 union republics of the USSR has its own Ministry of

Health which is in charge of health services within the republic. The central Ministry of Health comes under the Council of Ministers of the USSR, and the ministries of union republics under the councils of ministers of their republics. There are regional, territorial, and city public health departments of local Soviets of Working People's Deputies. They are subordinated both to the local Soviet of Working People's Deputies and to the higher public health body.

All these public health bodies are headed by doctors. In town and country health questions are dealt with by heads of town or urban district health departments, or by chief physicians of rural district hospitals. They are responsible for all aspects of medical and public health work within a district or a town.

One Overall Plan

The Soviet public health system functions according to an overall state plan and is therefore very flexible and effective. With planning on a general scale it is possible to expand the network of medical institutions and increase the number of medical personnel with proper consideration for the requirements and specific features of each area of the country. The Soviets of Working People's Deputies—from village Soviets to the Supreme Soviet of the USSR—have permanent public health committees consisting of deputies, doctors, and representatives of the public.

An overall system of training doctors, nurses, midwives, and so on, the planned development of therapeutic, and prophylactic institutions, and the co-ordination of research insure the constant advance of Soviet medical science and practice.

The democratic character of the health system enables wide sections of the public to take an active part in the work of public health bodies. Each polyclinic, hospital or any other medical institution has a public council formed of representatives of the population served by the given institution. Industrial enterprises, collective farms, schools, and residential sections have health posts whose task is to carry out health education work. These health posts come under the Red Cross and Red Crescent Societies.

Thus, in the Soviet Union health protection and promotion is the responsibility and concern both of the local authorities and the public.

Treatment and Prophylaxis for Adults

Medical aid in numerous in- and out-patient therapeutic and prophylactic institutions is available to the entire population of the country.

Out-patient treatment is available at out-patient departments of hospitals, polyclinics, specialized clinics, consultation centers, and first aid posts. The majority of them are attached to hospitals, but some are independent.

Such institutions provide a service in surgery, gynecology, neurology, ear, nose and throat diseases, ophthalmology, stomatology, and in many other fields of medicine. Larger polyclinics have specialized casualty, cardio-rheumatological, endocrinological, urological, infectious diseases, and other departments. In addition polyclinics also carry out checks on healthy people in order to detect initial signs of disease in its early stages. Systematic prophylactic examinations and screening are among the most important tasks of polyclinics.

Out-patient institutions also have laboratories, X-ray rooms, various facilities for diagnosis, physiotherapy, and so on. Particular attention is paid to the early detection of gynecologic diseases, and women are therefore inspected regularly at special gynecological departments. Attached to the polyclinic are emergency services provided with cars to give urgent medical aid when needed in patients' homes.

The work of the polyclinic and similar institutions is based on the territorial principle, that is, all the work of a particular sector of a given district is organized and co-ordinated by the district physician, who is thus the local family doctor.

The district physician receives patients in his office and visits them in their homes. If necessary, laboratory workers also go to patients' homes to take samples for analysis or to make electrocardiograms (for which purpose they take with them portable electrocardiographs), and so on.

Besides attending to his patients, the district physician also keeps an eye on their living conditions. In-patient treatment is given in general hospitals, specialized clinics, hospitals of factory medical and public health units and some kinds of prophylactic clinics. Age factor is not a restriction in hospitalization.

2,225,500 Hospital Beds

In 1965, there were 2,225,500 beds in hospitals, maternity homes, and specialized clinics, or 96 beds per 10,000 of the population. In 1913, Russia had only 13 beds per 10,000. Characteristic of the rate of growth is the fact that under the last 7-year plan the number of hospital beds in the USSR increased by 693,000.

In general hospitals in the towns, medical aid is given in all the main branches of medicine. Specialized hospitals—cancer, tuberculosis, psychiatric, infectious diseases, physiotherapeutic, ophthalmological, and so on —exist for the treatment of particular diseases. There are also separate children's hospitals.

First Aid

The emergency medical service is designed to deal with urgent calls.

This service works 24 hours a day. First aid is given when some one is suddenly taken ill or is injured in an accident (severe injuries, burns, poisonings, sunstroke), and so on, wherever the emergency arises—at home, in the street, or at an enterprise. These services and the transportation of patients to hospitals are also free of charge.

On an average, the emergency service deals with 30 million calls a year. A tendency to specialized emergency services has been increasing over the past few years.

For specialized aid a team of one or two medical doctors and two or three nurses or other auxiliary personnel is organized. This team has at its disposal the necessary apparatus to give aid in cases of myocardial infarction or any other acute heart disease, as well as in severe injuries, poisoning, burns, or cerebrospinal affections.

To remote, sparsely-populated areas of the country medical specialists are taken by ambulance transport—planes, helicopters or aerosleighs.

Medical Aid in Industry

Industrial enterprises where the number of workers exceeds 800 (at enterprises of coal, oil, mining, and chemical industries the number of workers must be over 500) have medical posts. Enterprises where there are 300 or more workers and certain shops at large factories have first aid posts headed by a feldsher (medical assistant). The primary task of these health posts is to carry out prevention measures and gives first aid in cases of a sudden illness or injury at work.

In addition to this, the staff of these posts carry on systematic observation of the sanitary conditions of the enterprise, study working conditions, and see that people who need sanatorium treatment or rest, a special diet, and so on get it.

Through these posts, public health boards and institutions carry out sanitary, prophylactic, and health-promoting measures in industrial enterprises.

Practically all large industrial enterprises have their own medical and public health units providing all the workers with medical care and carrying out prophylactic measures. These units, which not infrequently extend their services to the families of the workers, and sometimes even to the rest of the population in the locality, consist of a hospital, a polyclinic, a number of first aid posts in the various shops, and an overnight sanatorium, as well as crèches, kindergartens, dietetic dining rooms, and so on.

The overnight sanatorium, generally built either in the factory grounds or nearby, is for workers who need special treatment, diet, and additional rest as a preventive measure but are not sick in the sense that they need to stay away from work. They go to the sanatorium after work is over each day and spend the night there—usually for a period of a month at a time.

Medical work is usually closely linked with the general work of an enterprise, helping to improve working conditions and reduce incidence of disease among the workers.

Factory polyclinics function on the same territorial principle as ordinary polyclinics. One general practitioner usually attends 2,000 workers, while at enterprises of the chemical, coal mining, and oil-processing industries he serves 1,000.

Health Service in the Countryside

The organizational principle of medical service in the countryside is the same as in the towns. But because some country areas are sparsely populated and working and living conditions on farms differ from those in the towns, therapeutic and prophylactic work takes different forms in some respects.

The whole of a country district is divided into areas. One of the largest villages in the area has a hospital with 25–100 beds and an out-patient department, or an out-patient clinic.

Midwifery centers, collective farm maternity homes, crèches, and other similar public health institutions, staffed mainly by medical assistants, midwives, and nurses, are located in different villages of a health area (on state or collective farms, at forestry or peat-extraction enterprises, and so on). The medical staff of these institutions work under the chief physician of an area hospital (or outpatient clinic). Midwifery centers give emergency assistance in urgent cases before the arrival of a specialist (either at home or at the center) and also deliver babies. In addition, they carry out a great deal of sanitary and prophylactic work, detect infectious diseases and isolate patients, give inoculations, publicize health and hygienic rules, and so on.

If necessary, they send patients to an area hospital.

Country Hospitals

An area hospital, which is in charge of all the medical institutions of a country health area is in turn responsible to a regional hospital.

The district hospital is the center for specialized medical aid in the countryside. It usually consists of an inpatient department (150–400 beds) an outpatient department staffed with all the main medical specialists, a laboratory, an X-ray room and other facilities for treatment and diagnosis, a dental department, a chemists's shop, and so on.

Patients are admitted to the district hospital at the order of the area doctor, who refers them there in all cases when specialist's medical aid, or advice is needed, or complicated tests or other kinds of investigations which cannot be done in an area hospital or outpatient clinic are necessary.

All specialists at a district hospital regularly visit area hospitals and give consultations there.

They also help area medical personnel with out-patient treatment and systematic observation of the health of the local population.

Highly specialized medical aid—whether for treatment or diagnosis, especially in the fields of chest surgery, urology, oncology, tuberculosis for which facilities are not available in district hospitals, are obtainable at big regional or republican hospitals, specialized clinics, and so on.

Elimination of Causes of Diseases

The prophylactic principle of the Soviet health service is reflected in the wide application of what is known here as the dispensary method. This is a system of keeping patients under observation, constantly checking on their state of health. Its use means that active prophylactic measures can be taken, can be detected in the early stages, treatment can be given in good time, and the causes of diseases eliminated.

It is not only patients suffering from chronic illnesses such as vascular hypertension, gastro-intestinal diseases, diabetes, cancer, and tuberculosis who are subject to dispensary observation. Certain groups of healthy people —children of all ages, expectant mothers, and adolescents, as well as certain categories of workers and office employees at industrial enterprises—are also kept under review. If dispensary observation shows it to be necessary, the patient is transferred to other, easier, work, put on a special diet, or sent to a sanatorium.

Prophylactic examinations can bring to light signs of diseases hitherto unsuspected by patients who consider themselves absolutely healthy and so do not go to a doctor. The doctor himself looks for the patient.

This is especially important in cases of such insidious diseases as malignant tumors, tuberculosis, and vascular hypertension. People showing signs of these diseases are kept under dispensary observation.

The dispensary service has saved the life, health, and working ability of many thousands of people (especially in cases of cancer).

Many specialists, including oncologists, tuberculosis specialists, general practitioners, obstetricians, and gynecologists, participate in mass prophylactic examinations and screenings at industrial enterprises, on state and collective farms, and at colleges and universities.

The following figures are characteristic of this work: in 1965 alone, over 80 million people were involved in prophylactic examinations. Millions of people are inspected yearly with a view to the early detection of malignant tumors and tuberculosis. People suspected of having one of these diseases are directed to special medical institutions for treatment.

A total of 30,896 oncological, anti-tuberculosis, anti-venereal, and other dispensaries, departments, and centers were established by 1965.

Mortality Rate Decreases

The incidence of disease has decreased considerably. Average life expectancy in the USSR is more than twice what it was in Tzarist Russia before the Revolution and has been as high as 70 years over the past few years. The USSR has become the country with the lowest mortality rate—in 1965 it was 7.3 per 1,000 population.

Infant mortality rate decreased 34 percent during the last 7-year period, and in 1965 was 27 per 1,000 live births.

At the same time, there are still a number of unsolved problems in public health. One of them is the specialization of medical workers.

Every patient has an attending physician, the one who "treats" the patient. The attending physician must not only be a good specialist; he should be a good psychologist who can understand and take into account all the special characteristics of the patient, of his environment, and his family. If need be the attending physician calls for assistance from other specialists who have a deep knowledge of some particular branch of medicine. There is still a shortage of such specialists, and efforts are being made to increase their number. To this end, the system of medical training is to be reorganized. During the seven years at medical institute the student will have to become a qualified specialist with a thorough knowledge in one aspect of medicine.

The Problems of Medical Institutions in the Countryside

The problem of what to do about the small hospitals which are widespread in the countryside has not yet been completely solved. There are still quite a lot of them. As a rule, they are situated in areas with a low population density and where it would not be worth building large specialized hospitals. Small country hospitals will either be amalgamated or abolished. Instead, outpatient clinics will be opened in the larger villages.

To solve the problem of small hospitals, it is proposed to build modern medical institutions with many special departments in towns and centers of rural localities. Large hospitals of this kind, where rural population can receive highly-qualified medical assistance, are already being built.

During the five-year period 1966–70 the number of hospital beds will be increased by 456,000 and will have reached 2,680,000 by 1970, which will amount to 10.9 hospital beds per 1,000 population. Every two years the number of hospital beds increases by about 200,000, that is, by the number of beds Tzarist Russia had in 1913. Moreover, the increase in hospital accommodation is to be seen predominantly in such specialized medical institutions as neurosurgical, traumatological, urological, stomatological, pediatric, and tuberculosis hospitals and departments.

Especially rapid is the construction of medical institutions in the republics previously known as the backward outskirts of pre-revolutionary Russia. New large hospitals will have cardiological, gasteroenterological, and hematological departments, departments of children's surgery, chemotherapy of cancer and leucosis, and many other departments. Only large hospitals (300–400 beds) will be built in the countryside.

The problem of organization in hospitals of special recuperation departments for patients who have survived myocardial infarction or injuries, or who are paralyzed, has not yet been completely solved either.

Among other problems to be solved, there are also problems of modern hospital construction in various zones of the USSR with due account for climatic and geographic conditions. Further development and perfection of the Soviet health system are closely connected with such problems as scientific organization of work, mechanization of the work of personnel in therapeutic and prophylactic institutions, and many others.

Mother and Child Care

In the USSR special attention is paid to maternity and child welfare. Mother and child care in this country is not simply a narrow medical problem limited to the organization of a network of maternity welfare centers, maternity homes, polyclinics, and hospitals. It is the consequence and expression of the new role played by emancipated women, possessing equal rights with men, in all spheres of the economic, social, political, and cultural life of the country. Equal rights with men to work, rest and leisure, education and social insurance are not merely laid down in the Constitution of the USSR, the material basis necessary for the realization of this equality is provided.

The primary aim of maternity and child welfare in the USSR is the prevention of disease.

Care of a child commences long before the child is born and is expressed in labor protection legislation, particularly that relating to expectant mothers.

112 Days Maternity Leave

During pregnancy, on a doctor's recommendation, women are freed from night work and if necessary are transferred to easier work on the same average monthly pay. They are granted 112 days of maternity leave (56 days before and 56 days after confinement). Post-natal leave with full pay is extended to 70 days after the birth of twins or in case of complicated childbirth.

Working mothers are entitled to time off to nurse the baby.

Baby food centers organized by children's polyclinics provide babies with milk and supplementary foods. Bottlebabies and infants in need of supplementary food receive supplies free of charge.

19,000 Maternity and Child Welfare Centers and Polyclinics

Women and children are kept under observation by special medical institutions. In 1965, there were 19,333 of these institutions—maternity and child welfare centers and polyclinics. This figure shows a great advance in mother and child care, especially if one realizes that the corresponding figure for 1913 was only nine.

Among the tasks of maternity welfare centers are the prevention and treatment of specifically women's diseases, the propagation of information about sexual matters and birth control, and observation of pregnant women. Obstetricians and gynecologists keep prospective mothers under constant observation and take all measures necessary to prevent complications that might arise during childbirth.

There are now 227,000 beds in maternity homes. All babies are in fact provided with skilled medical assistance, and in the towns all births take place in maternity homes, which drastically reduces mother and child mortality.

Following the discharge of mother and child from the maternity home they are visited by pediatricians and special district children's nurses.

Pregnant women, mothers of first children, and even members of their families are taught the rules of child care.

The number of children's institutions—crèches, nursery schools, and kindergartens—has greatly increased. In 1913, in pre-revolutionary Russia, there were 4,600 children in such institutions, while in 1965 the figure was 7,700,000. The extensive network of children's institutions helps in the bringing up of children and makes it possible for their parents to take an active part in the social, cultural, and political life of the country.

Parents have to pay only 18 percent of the cost of the child's accommodation in a crèche or nursery school, the rest being covered by the state.

70,000 Pediatricians

Numerous Young Pioneer camps, tourist camps, stadiums, swimming pools, and other sports facilities have been built especially for children. Child health is taken care of by over 70,000 pediatricians specially trained for this purpose.

There is a network of children's specialized sanatoria where treatment is given to children suffering from rheumatism, tuberculosis, and certain other diseases. To study the physiological and pathological features of childhood, scientific research institutes concerned with maternity and child welfare have been set up by the Academy of Medical Sciences of the USSR and in the Union Republics. Specially-appointed pediatricians keep all children attending school and preschool institutions under observation. Each child is examined by many specialists before he is admitted to school. There are special instructions for compulsory vaccination of children against diptheria, whooping cough, smallpox, tuberculosis, and poliomyelitis.

Mothers of large families and unmarried mothers receive monthly allowances.

Thanks to the constant concern of the Soviet state the physical development of children and adolescents has greatly improved, their weight and height have increased, while mortality among children of all age-groups is decreasing.

Diseases Recede

For the last seven years (1958–1965) the incidence of poliomyelitis has decreased 98.8 percent, diptheria 96.6 percent, and whooping cough 78.7 percent.

The state provides children with full-calorie and varied food. Baby foods, the standard norms of which have been evolved with the help of pediatricians, are manufactured by the food industry in ever increasing variety. The prices of these foods are lower than those of usual foodstuffs.

The dominating trend in the child health program is prophylaxis. Prophylaxis is the guiding principle of all the measures taken to protect the health of children.

Hygienists control the manufacture of children's clothes and toys and see to it that they correspond to special hygienic standards.

The Soviet state is sparing no efforts to raise a healthy generation of young people able to start out in life with a good all-round development, both mentally and physically.

Freedom of Employment and Maintenance of Public Services:

A Study of Obligatory Service for Dentists in Norway

JON RUD

The problem of securing an adequate supply of trained manpower to practice in various professions is one encountered in most countries, industrialized as well as developing. In the latter the difficulty arises from inadequate education and training resulting in a general shortage of qualified manpower, from lack of co-ordination between training and high-level manpower requirements, and at times also from the loss of trained staff through emigration. Although in industrialized countries the shortage of

Reprinted from the *International Labour Review,* Vol. *95,* Nos. 1–2, January/February 1967, pp. 78–94, by permission of the International Labour Office.

professional staff may be less acute in absolute terms, these countries are faced with the need to meet the ever-increasing demands of a variety of professions (and occasionally also the attraction of employment opportunities abroad).

Apart from these general problems there is also the question of distribution of the available manpower within the country. It is often found difficult to attract qualified persons in professions such as medicine, dentistry, teaching, and so on, to rural areas or to remote regions.

In these circumstances, certain countries have placed limits on the free choice of employment in some professions in the interests of maintaining public services in such fields as health and education. The question has thus arisen in what circumstances and under what conditions a limitation of the basic human right of free choice of employment may be acceptable in the wider interests of the community as a whole.

It may therefore be of interest to review the problems that have arisen in Norway in providing adequate facilities for dental care for the population in remote regions and the solutions so far adopted or envisaged. In spite of the fact that Norway (together with Sweden) has, according to the latest statistics available on the number of inhabitants, per dentist,[1] the best coverage of dentists in the world, it has been judged necessary by the authorities, as a temporary solution, to introduce legislation providing for a period of compulsory service for dentists in order to overcome the acute shortage in certain regions. This legislation has been the subject of proceedings in the Norwegian courts to test its compatibility with the Constitution and the international instruments ratified by Norway. One of these cases was also brought before the European Commission on Human Rights.

The Introduction of a Public Dental Care Scheme

The development of a system of public dental care started in Norway in the early part of this century. In 1917 Norway was the first country to legislate the principle of free dental care in the primary schools, although in the beginning this statutory provision applied only to urban areas and in certain cases a nominal fee was charged. By 1949 almost three-quarters of all children in primary schools were guaranteed free dental care. In addition, some of the more wealthy municipalities had made provision for dental care for young persons up to the age of 18 years. However, the possibility of receiving dental treatment varied considerably from one area to another.

At that time approximately 70 percent of the population lived in rural

---

[1] W.H.O.: *Annual epidemiological and vital statistics, 1961,* Part III: *Statistics of health personnel and hospital establishments* (Geneva, 1964).

areas and 30 percent in urban areas, whereas for the dentists the proportions were exactly the reverse. There were also considerable differences between the relatively densely populated areas in the southern part of the country and the sparsely populated ones in the north and on the west coast. The three northern counties situated north of the Arctic Circle comprise 30 percent of the national territory but only 10 percent of the population, the population density being approximately four persons per square kilometer. Whereas in 1946 there were 650 inhabitants per dentist in the capital, Oslo, the corresponding figure in the northernmost county, Finnmark, was 13,440; and it must also be realized that inhabitants in such sparsely populated areas often have to travel long distances to receive dental treatment.

In the face of problems such as these, the Norwegian Dentists' Association in 1945 called for the appointment of a committee to examine the question of establishing a public dental care scheme. This led to the enactment on July 28, 1949 of an Act providing for a public dental service, which came into force on July 1, 1950. Under the Act, all children and young persons between 6 and 18 years of age are to receive free dental care and all other persons treatment at rates to be fixed by the Ministry of Social Affairs (section 1). For the purpose of implementing the Act, the country has been divided into districts (normally corresponding to the municipalities). In each district there is to be at least one district dentist (section 5), responsible to a county dentist who is the head of the public dental service in his particular county (section 4). The legislators did not aim at the immediate introduction of public dental care throughout the country, but were in particular concerned with providing services to the regions which had so far been behind in this regard. It was symptomatic that the first county to introduce this scheme was Finnmark (a county with an area of nearly 49,000 square kilometers but with only 70,000 inhabitants), where the number of inhabitants per dentist, as mentioned above, was 13,440 in 1946. According to section 20 of the Act, the public dental service was to be fully established in all of the 20 counties of Norway by 1965, but this has not been possible.

It was realized at the time when the Act was adopted that it would be difficult to fill all the positions of district dentists which were to be established, especially in northern Norway. Already, in 1946, before the introduction of the scheme was contemplated, it was estimated that during a ten-year period 450 dentists would have to be trained over and above the normal annual supply of 50 from the Norwegian Dental College. In fact, however, during the period in question, the normal annual supply was somewhat smaller than planned, and only 145 additional dentists were trained. The number of children covered by the school dental service also increased considerably, and the need for dental care among children became greater because the increased consumption of such commodities as chocolate and sugar led to considerable tooth decay. Thus, whereas in the period 1945–46 an average of 178 fillings per 100 children was made, this figure went up to 369 by 1952–53.

Measures to Facilitate Recruitment Before 1956

In 1950 the Ministry of Social Affairs, with a view to increasing the supply of dentists to the public dental service, proposed that students should be admitted to the Norwegian Dental College on condition that they signed a declaration undertaking to work for two years, on completing their studies, in the public dental service in any district to which they might be assigned. In addition, students meeting certain conditions might study at approved universities and colleges abroad; but they were also to be required to sign a declaration. Students studying abroad without the authorization of the Norwegian authorities would likewise be required to sign a declaration before being admitted to the supplementary courses to obtain a license to practice in Norway. This system, with which the Norwegian Dentists' Association agreed in view of the serious situation, was brought into effect as from 1951, and in December 1954 a Royal Decree amended the regulations for admission to the Norwegian Dental College accordingly.

Early in 1955, however, the legal validity of the undertakings given prior to the adoption of the Royal Decree was questioned. The students who were about to graduate in the spring of 1955 submitted this question to the Legal Office of the Ministry of Justice, which in July 1955 answered that assignment to a post in the public dental service fell within the scope of the declaration signed by the students at the time of admission to the Dental College. On the other hand, it indicated that there might be doubts as to whether this condition for admission could be imposed under the existing legislation relating to the Dental College and whether it was lawful having regard to general principles of administrative law.

One of the graduates of 1955 refused to accept an assignment and others indicated that in their view they were not legally bound to accept such assignments. The students who were about to graduate in 1956 stated in a letter to the Ministry of Social Affairs, dated March 2, 1956, that as the agreements entered into with the Ministry were not legally binding, they could be disregarded.

Legislative Measures Since 1956 Providing for
Compulsory Service for Newly Qualified Dentists

The staffing of the public dental service had in fact been precarious for some years, and the Ministry of Social Affairs feared that if the possibility of posting new graduates were suddenly to cease, the whole dental welfare service might collapse. The government therefore tabled a Bill, the basic provision of which (section 1) was as follows:

Persons who in 1955 or later have passed the examination in dentistry in this Kingdom, or have obtained approval of a foreign examination in dentistry giving it the same effect as the Norwegian examination in dentistry . . . may . . . be required for a period of up to two years to take a position in the public dental service which, though having been advertised, remains vacant.

Unless the dentist concerned agrees to some other arrangement, the assignment shall be made in such a manner that the service can be commenced at latest three months after the conclusion of his academic studies or after the termination of such military service as is immediately subsequent to his examination. . . .

Assignments may not be made for service which extends beyond June 30, 1963.

Assignments might be made for service in the municipal dental service for schools or in the public dental service established under the Act of July 28, 1949.

The Norwegian Dentists' Association, in commenting on the Bill, expressed its regret at the proposal but also indicated that it fully understood the need for this measure, particularly in view of the refusal by one dentist to accept an assignment. The Norwegian Academic Union expressed doubts whether such legislation, in peacetime, "would be in conformity with the Constitution and with the general legal principles on which our democratic society is built." On the other hand, the Ministry of Justice (Legal Office) considered that the Bill was not contrary to any provision of the Constitution.

The Bill aroused strong opposition in Parliament. The arguments advanced by the Opposition may be summarized as follows: the Bill was the first step on a road which might have the most serious repercussions on democracy; compulsory direction of manpower was not permissible in normal circumstances; the Bill was contrary to Article 4 of the European Convention on Human Rights, ratified by Norway; the lack of dentists was the result of the State's negligence in providing educational facilities; if today the principle involved were admitted, compulsory direction of labor in many other branches of activity might have to be accepted tomorrow.

The Minister of Social Affairs, in answering these objections, stated, *inter alia,* that the government regretted having to introduce the Bill, but in the circumstances this was the least harmful solution. It was not only the principle of individual liberty that was involved; there was a conflict between this principle and that of providing adequate health protection for all citizens, wherever they might live. Moreover, there were certain modifications to the former principle: it was not regarded as objectionable to impose a period of compulsory service in connection with training in several branches of the health sector. Similar systems existed in other sectors, for example, in the armed forces. The government had considered other possible solutions, for example, further economic inducements, but it was felt that the salaries of dentists in the public dental service were already considerably above those offered to other public servants with academic education.[2] In the circumstances, therefore, the need for adequate health protection among the population in the remote regions would have to take precedence over the dentists' demands to be able to choose their place of employment freely.

The Temporary Act concerning Compulsory Service for Dentists was passed on June 21, 1956, and came into force immediately.

In March 1962 the government proposed that the Act of 1956 should be prolonged for a further period of three years, that is to June 30, 1966, and the period of service reduced to 18 months. Prolongation was considered necessary for two main reasons: the supply of graduates had been smaller than expected in 1956, and the increased standard of living had created a greater demand for dental services. In the government's view it was not possible to fill all posts in the public dental service without compulsion.

The parliamentary Committee on Social Affairs agreed that in view of the continued shortage of dentists it was necessary to prolong the Act. However, one political party insisted that since the Act was temporary it should be prolonged for as short a period as possible, and it accordingly recommended that the Act be prolonged for only two years. Certain measures that ought to be taken to overcome the difficulties were also suggested: special scholarships to be made available to students who agreed to work for a certain period in the public dental service; pension rights to be acquired after a shorter period of service than normally required; favorable loans to be granted after a certain period of service to enable a dentist to establish his own private practice.

The Committee on Social Affairs made certain unanimous recommendations as to other measures which should be taken, particularly with a view to expanding training facilities.

When the Bill was debated in the Lower House itself, several members of the Opposition parties, while agreeing in the circumstances with a prolongation until 1966, expressly stated that this was the last occasion on which they would vote for prolongation of the Act.

In April 1965 the government again proposed a prolongation of the Act of 1956 for the period up to June 30, 1969, while reducing the period

---

[2] See footnote 13.

of service to 12 months. The reason for this proposal was the difficult personnel situation in the public dental service, particularly in northern Norway and certain areas of western Norway.

In considering this proposal, the majority of the parliamentary Committee on Social Affairs agreed that the Act should be prolonged as proposed but recommended that the period of service should be maintained at 18 months. The minority of the committee declared that compulsory service was wrong in principle and that measures should be taken without delay to get away from the present situation; sufficiently energetic efforts would not be made as long as the authorities could rely on the Compulsory Service Act. The minority was of the opinion that by granting scholarships, collaboration with the students and other measures not involving compulsion, it would be possible to fill the vacant posts. In view of the situation, however, these members recommended that the Act should be prolonged only until June 30, 1967 and that the period of service (as proposed by the government) should be reduced to 12 months.

During the debate in the Lower House the Minister of Social Affairs, commenting on the recommendations of the minority of the Committee on Social Affairs, stated that a prolongation for one year only would have no effect. As far as economic incentives were concerned, the government had gone as far as it reasonably could; young dentists being compulsorily posted were in a privileged position as compared with other academic professions. Training facilities could obviously not be extended greatly in the course of one year, and in any case the problem of distribution would always remain. "This problem is particularly accentuated in a country such as ours, with large distances and a scattered population," said the Minister, "but it also exists in more densely populated countries in Europe."

The majority proposal was adopted by both Houses of Parliament (by 50 to 45, and 17 to 16 votes, respectively).

During the parliamentary debate, one member referred to the possibility of introducing compulsory service in other professions. He said: "Today we have a compulsory Act applicable to dentists only, and it is one of the main arguments against the Act that it applies only to one academic group. . . . I wish to request the Ministry of Church and Education to consider the introduction of a general obligation, imposed upon admission to our universities and colleges, to carry out a certain period of compulsory service after graduation, if this is deemed necessary in the public interest."

In its report for the period 1963–65 on the Forced Labor Convention of 1930, commenting on the Act of 1956 and the fears expressed by some academic associations that the Act might become a permanent solution and that the same system might be adopted with regard to other professions, the government, however, underlined the fact that "at present there is absolutely no question of introducing a general system of compulsory service for graduates." [3]

The Iversen Case Before the Norwegian Courts

In 1959 a Mr. Iversen, who had recently qualified as a dentist, was assigned in accordance with the provisions of the Act of 1956 to take up a post in January 1960. In May 1960 he left this post. Criminal proceedings were then instituted for failure to comply with the Act and a local court in February 1961 found him guilty and imposed a fine of 2,000 crowns. He appealed against this judgment to the Supreme Court, submitting that the Act was: (i) invalid as contrary to the Constitution; (ii) invalid as contrary to the European Convention for the Protection of Human Rights; (iii) only applicable to students having made a declaration undertaking to serve in the public dental service (which he had not done).

The Supreme Court, in December 1961, dismissed the appeal. Three of the five judges held that none of the three objections was valid, whereas two judges accepted the third objection. The majority finding held, with regard to the first objection, that while it was possible that in extreme cases a law might be invalid because it was contrary to certain general principles of law of a constitutional nature, even if (as in this case) it did not violate any specific provision in the Constitution, the Act of 1956 could not be ruled out on such grounds. The majority also held that Article 4 of the European Human Rights Convention,[4] prohibiting forced or compulsory labor, was not applicable in the present case. On this point, the presiding judge stated: "The work in question is in the person's own profession, of short duration, well paid and in immediate continuation of his completed studies. Even if, at the time, such an assignment may in many cases be contrary to the interests of the individual concerned, it is clear to me that it cannot be considered as an infringement, let alone a violation, of any Human Rights."

The Iversen Case Before the European
Commission on Human Rights

On June 8, 1962 Mr. Iversen lodged an application to the European Commission on Human Rights requesting the Commission to state that the Act

---

[3] Cf. I.L.O.: *Summary of reports on ratified Conventions,* Report III (Part I), International Labour Conference, 50th Session, 1966 (Geneva, 1966), p. 92.

[4] Paragraph 2 of this Article reads as follows: "2. No one shall be required to perform forced or compulsory labour."

Paragraph 3 of this Article provides for certain exceptions: (a) prison labour; (b) military service, (c) service exacted "in case of emergency or calamity threatening the life or well being of the community"; as well as (d) "any work or service which forms part of normal civic obligations."

of 1956, as applied to him, was contrary to Article 4 of the European Human Rights Convention.

Apart from certain formal objections to the application, which were rejected by the Commission, the government's observations on the substance of the matter (that is whether the service required from the applicant was "forced or compulsory labor" within the meaning of the Human Rights Convention) may be summarized as follows:

The term "forced or compulsory labor" should be given "a reasonable and working interpretation so as not to prevent a democratic government from enacting measures necessary for extending social benefits to its citizens." Account had to be taken of the "exceptional geographical problems, . . . the enormous distances, the difficulties of communication and the arctic weather conditions prevailing during the winter months." The unequal distribution of various social services seriously affected the social and health conditions of the outlying communities, and the Acts of 1949 and 1956 were an attempt to overcome these difficulties; they should therefore be considered "in the light of their humanitarian and social purpose." The government considered that, viewed in its historic context, the European Human Rights Convention envisaged the suppression of concentration and labor camps. The background of the Slavery Convention of 1926 and the I.L.O.s Forced Labor Convention, 1930, dealing with conditions in colonial territories, showed that "forced labor" was regarded as not far from "slavery." The definition of "forced or compulsory labor" in the latter Convention [5] had to be seen against the background of the adoption of that Convention.

The government also referred to the practice of I.L.O. bodies (that is in particular the Committee of Experts on the Application of Conventions and Recommendations), and suggested that the criticism of various systems of direction of labor in certain countries, which constituted a general channeling of labor and involved very long, often indefinite, periods of compulsion to work did not apply to this case. The I.L.O. "had no objection to the practice that certain work was required as a condition for admission to universities for scholarships or for state-financed studies, or as a condition for the exercise of a profession.[6] If any such scheme had

---

[5] Article 2, paragraph 1, of the Forced Labour Convention, 1930, reads as follows:

"For the purposes of this Convention the term 'forced or compulsory labour' shall mean all work or service which is exacted from any person under the menace of any penalty and for which the said person has not offered himself voluntarily."

Paragraph 2 of this Article contains certain exceptions in respect of military service, prison labor, work in cases of emergency, minor communal services and normal civic obligations. See footnote 9.

[6] In 1962 the I.L.O. Committee of Experts on the Application of Conventions and Recommendations in a general survey concerning forced or compulsory labor had stated: "In most countries students wishing to obtain a diploma or a permanent position in certain professions are bound to serve a limited preparatory or probationary period in the profession concerned. This kind of obligation, whose non-fulfill-

been operative in Norway, the Applicant would have been faced with the same obligation as he now had. . . ."

In a decision dated December 17, 1963 [7] the European Commission on Human Rights (by a majority of six of its ten members) found that Mr. Iversen's application was "manifestly ill-founded." The reasoning of the majority was split, so that there were in fact three different views in the Commission.

Four members of the majority held that the service in question was "manifestly not forced or compulsory labor." They noted that the term "forced or compulsory labor" was not defined in the European Human Rights Convention and "no authoritative description of what it comprises is to be found elsewhere." In their view, however, the term could not be understood "solely in terms of the literal meaning of the words, and has in fact come to be regarded in international law and practice, as evidenced in part by the provisions and application of I.L.O. Conventions and resolutions on Forced Labour, as having certain elements . . . ; these elements . . . are, first, that the work or service is performed by the worker against his will and, secondly, that the requirement that the work or service be performed is unjust or oppressive or the work or service itself involves avoidable hardship." [8] These members pointed to the fact that

---

ment is generally sanctioned only by the refusal of the diploma or position desired, cannot be regarded as constituting forced labour. This is also the case where, before undertaking certain lengthy and expensive studies financed by the State or by other public or private bodies, students must agree to be employed for a specific period in certain positions, when they have completed their studies, subject to the repayment of the costs of their education on their failure to do so. It likewise seems unobjectionable, when admission to higher forms of education is gained by competition, that a number of the places available should be reserved for students who have not been successful in previous competitions and who have accepted certain forms of employment during a specific period. In some countries, on the other hand, all students who have completed their studies, including often young workers who have finished their vocational training may, on pain of various punishments, be compulsorily impressed—sometimes for periods which may be as long as three years—into forms of employment which need not necessarily bear any relation to the technical or professional training which they have received. Such a system appears to constitute forced or compulsory labour within the meaning of the international labour Conventions." (*Forced Labour:* Part III of the Report of the Committee of Experts on the Application of Conventions and Recommendations (Geneva: I.L.O., 1962) para. 81.)

[7] *Yearbook of the European Convention on Human Rights, 1963,* pp. 278–332 (The Hague: Martinus Nijhoff, 1965).

[8] The two criteria referred to—the involuntary nature of the work and the fact that it would be unjust or oppressive or involve avoidable hardship—may be compared with the elements contained in the definition of "forced or compulsory labor" in the Forced Labour Convention, 1930, namely the involuntary nature of the work and its performance under the menace of a penalty. While the latter definition does not refer to considerations of hardship or injustice, these factors were reflected in the conditions and guarantees which the 1930 Convention required to be observed when forced labor for public purposes was used exceptionally in the transitional period pending its complete abolition.

while service under the Act of 1956 was obligatory, it was "for a short period, provided favourable remuneration, did not involve any diversion from chosen professional work, was only applied in the case of posts not filled after being duly advertised, and did not involve any discriminatory, arbitrary or punitive application." The requirement to perform such service was therefore not "unjust or oppressive."

The two other members of the majority considered that the situation in 1956 and 1960 of the public dental service was properly regarded by the Norwegian government as "an emergency threatening the well-being of the community in northern Norway," [9] because there was "the threat of a breakdown in the supply of volunteers from among whom the public dental service in northern Norway had hitherto been maintained." The government was confronted with the task of protecting public health, recognized in the European Human Rights Convention,[10] and with "the inherent difficulties of administering the service caused by the scattered character of towns and settlements and the severe climate and intractable terrain; and a regional shortage of qualified dentists." The Commission could not, in their view, question the judgment of the government (and Parliament) as to the existence of an emergency because there was evidence before it "showing reasonable grounds for such judgment."

The minority of four members was of the opinion that the conditions of service (for example, salary, time-limit, professional facilities) did not as such exclude the applicability of the Convention, since the work in question "was imposed upon the Applicant subject to penal sanctions." These members considered that, in view of the complexity of the legal problems involved and the number of opinions held on the subject, the application could not be regarded as "*manifestly* ill-founded." In their view, the question of the existence of a state of emergency within the meaning of the exception provided for in Article 4, paragraph 3 (*c*), of the European Human Rights Convention required further examination.

---

[9] As noted above, Article 4, paragraph 3, of the European Human Rights Convention provides that the term "forced or compulsory labor" shall not include "(c) any service exacted in case of an emergency or calamity threatening the well-being of the community." Compare this provision with the corresponding saving clause in Article 2, paragraph 2 (d) of the I.L.O.s Forced Labour Convention, 1930: "any work or service exacted in cases of emergency, that is to say, in the event of war or of a calamity or threatened calamity, such as fire, flood, famine, earthquake, violent epidemic or epizootic diseases, invasion by animal, insect or vegetable pests, and in general any circumstance that would endanger the existence or the well-being of the whole or part of the population."

[10] Under Articles 8 to 11 of the Convention, which guarantee the respect for private and family life and the right to freedom of thought, conscience and religion, to freedom of expression and to freedom of peaceful assembly and of association, restrictions may be imposed on the enjoyment of these rights, *inter alia,* for the protection of public health. Other international instruments contain positive provisions for the protection of health—see footnote 16.

The Norwegian Dentists' Association Case

In December 1962 the Norwegian Dentists' Association brought an action against the State, moving that the Act of 1962 prolonging the provisional Act of 1956 be declared null and void in regard to the members of the Association, because it was contrary to the Constitution and to international Conventions ratified by Norway. The City Court of Oslo on June 30, 1964 gave judgment for the state, and upon appeal to the Court of Appeal and subsequently to the Supreme Court this decision was upheld (judgments of March 8, 1965 and March 28, 1966, respectively). All judgments referred to the pleadings and judgment in the Iversen case and to the fact that the written Constitution did not contain any specific provision prohibiting the legislature from infringing the individual liberty through orders to perform public service. On the other hand, it was stated that "it is generally assumed that the Constitution is based on certain principles of liberty and justice which, although not explicitly stated in the Constitution, impose a limit on the legislature."

On the facts of the case it was found, however, that the Act was not contrary to any such principles of liberty and equality. The Court of Appeal put special emphasis on the fact that the Act was passed for the purpose of overcoming an acute difficulty in one sector of the public health service, was of limited duration and limited the period of service as far as possible, while ensuring reasonable financial remuneration. The Supreme Court also emphasized that the Act was "a temporary solution of urgent humanitarian and social needs." Both courts expressly reserved their position were the Act to become a means of compulsorily recruiting dentists for the public dental service on a permanent basis.

Finally, as regards the compatibility of the Act with the European Convention for the Protection of Human Rights and Fundamental Freedoms, reference was made by all courts to the decision by the European Commission on Human Rights and in particular to the opinion of the four members of the majority, with which they expressed agreement.

The Problem Brought to the Attention of the I.L.O. Committee of Experts

In May 1965 the Norwegian Dentists' Association submitted certain comments concerning the Act of 1956, as amended, with regard to the application by Norway of the I.L.O.s forced labor Conventions and requested that the compatibility of this legislation with the Conventions in question be examined by the I.L.O.

The Association's position in the matter was supported by the Norwegian Academic Union and by other Scandinavian academic professional associations. The Norwegian Government in its report on the Forced Labour Convention, 1930, for the period ending June 30, 1965, submitted detailed replies to these observations and referred in particular to the legislative history of the Act of 1956 as well as to the judicial proceedings which had taken place.

The Committee of Experts on the Application of Conventions and Recommendations, in its report of 1966, took note of the statements made by the various professional organizations as well as the government's comments. It noted that the government had emphasized "the temporary nature of the Act, which is intended to deal with an exceptional situation involving the well-being of the populations in remote regions, . . . [and] that various means of finding a long-term solution to these problems are being studied." [11] While not stating any conclusions on the matter at this stage, the Committee requested the government "to supply information in its reports on further developments in this regard."

The Search for Alternative Solutions

The government's policy, as stated on numerous occasions before Parliament, has been to do away with the present system of compulsory assignment of dentists to the public dental service. Problems of recruiting persons for certain posts in the public service in remote regions, and in particular for jobs requiring academic qualifications, have existed and still exist in many fields. There are particular difficulties in the public health sector (doctors for hospitals and district services, and qualified nurses), but it has also been found difficult to find enough primary and secondary school teachers as well as clergymen.

Among the measures taken to secure an adequate supply of teachers to the northern regions are special post adjustments, increased compensation for removal costs and special grants (the so-called northern Norway scholarships) awarded to pupils at teacher-training schools and to university students who undertake to serve in schools in northern Norway for a certain period. In 1963, 343 pupils and students applied for such grants. Nevertheless, a report of 1962 showed that in the whole country altogether 1,145 posts in primary and secondary schools remained vacant; a considerable part of these vacancies were presumably in the remote regions. Moreover, a very substantial part of such posts in remote regions has been filled by teachers who are not fully qualified. With regard to clergymen (who in Norway are public servants), inducements include additional increments for service in northern Norway and increased compensation for removal costs. Public servants residing in the area north of the Arctic Circle (that is almost one-third of the total area of the country) also receive special contributions toward heating costs. The authorities

---

[11] I.L.O. *Report of the Committee of Experts on the Application of Conventions and Recommendations,* Report III (Part IV), International Labour Conference, 50th Session, 1966 (Geneva, 1966), p. 63.

are on the whole satisfied with the effect of these measures and a system of compulsory service has not been envisaged for these categories.

With respect to doctors, there was in fact compulsory service for the entire public health sector during World War II and for some years after it. On April 19, 1940, ten days after the invasion of Norway, a provisional order was issued giving the authorities wide powers to requisition health personnel. In November 1946 the government proposed to replace this order by legislation of more limited scope, with a view to gradual transition to normal conditions. The Act, which on the government's proposal was to remain in force until May 1, 1948, was passed unanimously on April 18, 1947; it was, again unanimously, prolonged by Act of April 30, 1948, for a further period of one year. Under the Act, doctors, dentists, and pharmacists could be required "when necessary owing to a shortage of personnel" to serve for a period of one year. Nurses and midwives could, under the same conditions, be called up for six months. In 1949, in view of the continued shortage of personnel in the public health sector, the government requested a further prolongation of the Act until 1952. However, two associations of doctors protested, stating that the Act, according to its terms and spirit, was an exceptional measure, justified in time of war or similar situations, but not in a normal, peacetime situation; instead, economic and other conditions of work should be improved so as to make posts in remote regions more attractive. The parliamentary Committee on Social Affairs proposed that the Act be prolonged, but only until July 1, 1950, and this proposal was unanimously adopted by Parliament.

Since 1950 there has thus been no compulsory service for doctors. Although the question of reintroducing a compulsory service Act has been brought up on some occasions in Parliament,[12] the Ministry of Social Affairs has considered that the incentives that have been introduced are sufficient. While certain posts in the public medical service (district doctors) and public hospitals have remained vacant for varying periods, provisional arrangements have been reached voluntarily to fill such posts in urgent cases. The situation is also eased by the existing system of medical education, which involves a final period of one-and-a-half years' practical training as a condition for being admitted to the final examination. In addition, medical students who agree to serve in the public health service after graduating are granted a special scholarship.

As far as the public dental service is concerned, the authorities have been aware since 1950 of the difficulties of recruitment. At first an attempt was made to attract dentists to posts in the dental service by offering favorable salaries and working conditions. In fact, dentists have been placed quite favorably in the state pay scale, and the authorities have even considered their remuneration unduly high as compared with other persons

---

[12] See, for example, the statement by a Member of Parliament on p. 277.

with academic qualifications in the public service.[13]

In June 1964 further measures were introduced to stimulate applications for district dentist posts: district dentists on fixed salaries were allowed to increase their working hours (normally 39 per week) by up to 400 hours yearly in return for a substantial increase in their salaries; the percentage of fees allocated to district dentists on alternative salaries (that is dentists who have opted to receive a lower fixed salary but in return are entitled to receive part of the fees for treatment given to adult persons) was raised from 20 to 25; a supplement was made payable for administrative duties; and posts of chief district dentist were introduced in certain big districts.

Certain special conditions were made applicable to service in northern Norway in 1964. Dentists serving in the same district in northern Norway for a period of between three and five years were to double their seniority ranking for purposes of promotion. The special contributions toward heating costs for public servants were granted to district dentists and removal and transportation costs were made payable even for short-term assignments. Apart from these special conditions and benefits there is no salary differential for service in remote areas.

The various measures mentioned above seem to have had some effect: whereas 80 percent of the posts were filled by compulsory assignment in 1958, this proportion had been reduced to 40 by 1965, and this in spite of an increasing number of posts (in the northernmost county, Finnmark, where the number of inhabitants per dentist was, as previously mentioned, 13,440 in 1946, this figure had decreased to 2,190 by 1965).

With a view to working out long-term proposals to solve the problems of supply and distribution of personnel in the public health sector as a whole, a committee was appointed by the government in November 1963. According to its terms of reference this committee is to propose measures to insure a sufficient supply and appropriate distribution of health personnel, a more rational use of qualified medical manpower and a greater stability in occupations where the turnover rate at present is particularly high; and to evaluate the demand for doctors, dentists, midwives, nurses, and other types of qualified health personnel and make an estimate as to the net supply needed to cover adequately the needs within these various groups of occupations up to 1985.

---

[13] The basic salary of a district dentist is the same as that of a chief of division in the civil service, a counsellor of embassy, a chief of police, a lieutenant-colonel or a headmaster of a lower secondary school. By availing himself of the possibility of increasing his working hours (see the following paragraph) a district dentist will receive the same basic salary as a permanent secretary, a professor, a Court of Appeal judge, or an ambassador of the intermediate category. A comparison with the incomes of dentists in private practice would be more difficult; it was, however, claimed by a Member of Parliament in the course of the discussions in the Lower House in 1965 that, according to pubic income tax records, more than half of all private dentists in Oslo earned less than a district dentist.

In addition, another committee was appointed by the government in October 1964 to consider the demand for assistant personnel in the dental service, to propose the various categories of such personnel that may be used, the type of work which may be carried out, and the education and training to be demanded.

These committees have not so far completed their work, which involves extensive research into the whole situation with regard to the extension of education facilities at the university level, and so on. However, the Ministry of Social Affairs has expressed the hope that the former committee will be able to present some positive proposals which may be carried out fairly soon. The proposals to be made by the second committee are expected to have only long-term effects.

In December 1964 the Ministry of Social Affairs organized a meeting with representatives of students' organizations, the two training institutes and the Norwegian Dentists' Association. Among the remedial measures discussed were: voluntary promises by students to serve for a specified period (this in reality would be a return to the situation obtaining before 1956); practical service for a certain period as a condition for obtaining a license to practice (for which statutory provision already existed); [14] efforts to attract foreign dentists; admitting a certain number of students to the Norwegian dental training schools who would not otherwise be admitted because their secondary school marks were not sufficiently high, on the condition that they would serve in the school or public dental service; agreements with foreign universities to admit a certain number of Norwegian students; continued efforts to improve salaries and working conditions; and increased opportunity for private practitioners to undertake treatment of children and young persons. Consultations are still continuing on these matters.

In a statement to Parliament in May 1966 the Minister of Church and Education indicated that the number of dentists graduating would be doubled in 1966 as compared with the normal annual output in previous years, and that by 1975 the education capacity would be 150 dentists per year, that is three times as many as the average figure during the last 40 years. The Minister expressed the hope that the country would have come a long way toward a satisfactory supply of dentists by 1975.

Conclusion

In a situation such as that described above one is faced with a conflict of interest. On the one hand there is the individual's basic right, recog-

---

[14] Under section 2 (1) of the Act of 1927 concerning the rights and duties of dentists, the King-in-Council may at any time make it a condition for granting a license that the dentist has completed a period of practical training. A corresponding clause is contained in the Act of July 8, 1949 concerning recognition of foreign diplomas. These provisions have never been applied.

nized by international instruments,[15] to choose his place of employment and residence freely. Thus the Dentists' Association, in pleading before the Supreme Court, asked: "Is there any conceivably greater interference in the individual's liberty, penal sanctions apart, than deprivation of the right of free choice of the place of work and residence?"

On the other hand it is also a recognized human right [16] to be afforded necessary social services, including medical care, and increasing importance has been attached in the postwar period to the improvement of the material and physical well-being of all populations.

It is accordingly important to seek ways of reconciling these two claims —the claim of the individual and the claim of the community—whenever they risk coming into conflict, and to determine in what circumstances, and to what extent, it is proper to give precedence to one or the other.

The case studied in the present article is of special interest because —in spite of violent disagreements on certain aspects—a number of basic considerations appear to have found recognition from all the parties concerned. Thus, initially the situation was regarded as constituting an emergency, since, without compulsory service, the dental services in remote regions were expected to collapse. Both parties have likewise stressed that the measures taken to deal with this emergency were necessarily of an exceptional and temporary nature, pending the time when alternative, long-term remedies had been adopted and had taken effect. It has also been common ground that the long-term measures should rely on positive inducements and not on compulsion.

It is indeed clear that the solution to a problem of the kind described in this article is not confined to a choice between measures of compulsion (backed by penalties) and passive acquiescence in the existing situation. Between these extremes a whole series of administrative and educational improvments, of material and other stimulants, can be brought into play. As has been indicated above, in the current discussions between the Norwegian government and the organizations concerned various proposals have been made for greater inducements, through improved terms of service and the like, as well as for contractual or other arrangements

---

[15] Apart from the Conventions already mentioned in this article, reference may be made to Articles 13 (1) and 23 (1) of the Universal Declaration of Human Rights, which provide for the rights of everyone "to freedom of movement and residence within the borders of each State" and "to free choice of employment."

[16] Article 25 (1) of the Universal Declaration of Human Rights states: "Everyone has the right to a standard of living adequate for the health and well-being of himself and of his family, including, food, clothing, housing and medical care and necessary social services. . . ."

Article 13 of the Draft Covenant on Economic, Social and Cultural Rights (an article upon which agreement has been reached) also recognizes the right to "the enjoyment of the highest attainable standard of physical and mental health." The Declaration of Philadelphia—the constitutional definition of the aims and purposes of the I.L.O.—calls, *i.a.*, for provision of "comprehensive medical care" (Part III (*f*)).

whereby a certain period of service would be rendered in return for financial advantages during training in public institutions.[17]

It thus seems likely that in this case a formula will ultimately be found which will avoid all conflict concerning its compatibility with international instruments and the principle of individual liberty, while safeguarding the public interest in maintaining and improving social services for all groups of the population.

Discussion Questions

1. Discuss the workings of the Soviet system of health care.
2. Do you think such a system can fruitfully be implemented in the United States?
3. Discuss the Norwegian system of obligatory service for dentists.
4. Given the geographical mal-distribution of physicians in the United States, do you think that doctors should be obligated to serve in an assigned post for a certain length of time? If so, do you think it should be done without remuneration?

---

[17] Compare the conclusions by the I.L.O. Committee of Experts quoted in footnote 6. It should be noted in this connection that university studies are completely free in Norway and that substantial scholarships are granted by the state in addition to loans being made available on favorable conditions.

Women

In the late 1960s women emerged as the new force demanding freedom in this society. The term "sexist society" was added to America's list of sins. Basically, the women's liberation movement has three goals: (1) equal pay for equal work; (2) access to occupations which have traditionally been closed to them and concomitantly the elimination of the stereotyping of those occupations which are suitable to women; and (3) a reduction in the time spent in unpaid labor.

The evidence strongly supports the women's liberation movement. Income data for 1968 show that the median income of a woman was about 58 percent of the average male wage earner. Furthermore, the evidence shows that about 50 percent of all working women can be found in 21 occupations and a fourth in five occupations; namely, secretary-stenographer, household worker, bookkeeper, elementary school teacher, and waitress. Male workers were far less occupationally concentrated with 50 percent in 65 occupations. Beyond this is the demand that women should not be tied to housework by virtue of accident of birth, and that a nuclear family imposes responsibilities which should be shared by men on a more equitable basis than is now approved in our society.

The two selections in this section are hardly radical in tone. Norton Dodge's evaluation of the place of women in the Soviet Union demonstrates that Soviet women have much greater access to the professional positions than women do in America. In addition, the choice of a career is much less guided by societal prohibitions on what is "proper" for a woman. To be sure, demographic factors, such as the dramatic shift in the male-female ratio after World War II, have had their place in Soviet policy. Nevertheless, the Soviet woman participates in the professional life of her country to a much greater extent than her American counterpart.

The article which follows examines an experiment in the Netherlands. Like the United States, the Netherlands has a fairly rigid perception of the appropriate male-female roles. This industrial experiment accepts the traditional view of the main household role of woman, but allows women to choose, within certain limits, what days they wish to work as well as *the hours during the day which suit them. As something of a compromise between the traditional notion of full-time employment and the demand for full female liberation, it is worth considering whether this program has merit as potentially applicable to the U.S. case.*

Norton T. Dodge is Professor of Economics at the University of Maryland. J.L.J.M. van der Does de Willebois is an industrial sociologist at the N.V. Philips Works at Eindhoven in the Netherlands.

Women in the Soviet Economy

NORTON D. DODGE

Although the focus of this study has been on the role of women in Soviet science and technology, it has been necessary to discuss women in a much broader context. The complexity of the interrelationship of the roles of women, as wife, mother, consumer, and producer, makes it difficult simply to summarize or to characterize Soviet policy toward women in the Russian economy as a whole or in any part of it. These varied roles so interact that Soviet policy in one area may have unintended repercussions on the way in which women perform in other areas. There is still little evidence that Soviet planners have managed to achieve a single, coherent, overall policy with respect to the economic utilization of women but, rather, that they have several imperfectly co-ordinated and sometimes contradictory policies. An attempt will now be made, nevertheless, to summarize, interpret, and evaluate Soviet experience in the utilization of women in the economy, particularly in the fields of science and technology.

To begin with war, revolution, and political repression over the past five decades drastically altered the sex ratio in the Soviet Union in favor of women. In 1897, with a sex ratio of 99 males per 100 females, there was near balance between the sexes in the Russian population. But in 1926, as a result of World War I and the Civil War, there were 5 million fewer males than females, and the sex ratio was 94. The census of 1939 reported 7 million fewer males than females and a further decline in the sex ratio to 92. These changes reflected the impact of collectivization and the purges, in which more men than women were killed. But by far the most drastic change came with World War II, which decimated the adult male population. The 1959 census reported 114.8 million females and 94 million males, a deficit of 20.8 million males. By estimating backward, with published birth rates and certain assumptions about the distribution

Reprinted from *Women in the Soviet Economy* by Norton T. Dodge, © 1966, Baltimore: The Johns Hopkins Press, pp. 238–247, by permission of the publisher.

of mortality by sex, it can be estimated that in 1946 there were 26 million fewer males than females in the adult population and that the sex ratio for the entire population was only 74 males per 100 females. The tremendous imbalance of the late 1940s and early 1950s was moderated by time, and by 1959 the sex ratio had risen to 83. At the present time the imbalance in the sexes is confined to the age groups over 35, but it is estimated that not until 1980 will the sex ratio be 92, or at the level prior to the outbreak of World War II.

Irregularities in the Soviet population pyramid caused by war and other vicissitudes are so great that many decades will be required to moderate them. Although the male deficit is now confined to the low age groups, the manpower shortage continues for other reasons. Most important, the birth rate during and immediately after the war was unusually low. As a result, during the past half dozen years additions to the labor force have been small and the pressure to utilize women, which was so insistent in the decade following the war, has continued up to the present. Furthermore, the shrunken generation of war babies is now entering the childbearing age, and, therefore, the annual number of births is significantly reduced in another generation, these small numbers will in turn keep additions to the labor force and to the population below the normal level. Thus, irregularities in the population pyramid will be perpetuated through several generations.

The present population policy of the government is aimed at maintaining or increasing the rate of growth in population, because a large and rapidly growing population is viewed as an asset rather than a liability. Certain programs, such as family allowances and medals for mothers of large families, are designed to increase the birth rate. On the other hand, in 1955, the government felt obliged once again to legalize abortion because of pressures from women and from the medical profession which was concerned with the large number of illegal abortions performed under unsafe circumstances. Continuing concern over the high rate of abortion has led to increased efforts to develop and distribute effective contraceptive devices. The combined effect of legalized abortions and more effective contraception will be, of course, to reduce the birth rate at the same time other measures are being taken to increase it. Nevertheless, in spite of these contradictions in Soviet population policy, the intent of the government is to increase fertility. Thus far, however, the results are not impressive.

Demographic factors have played, and will continue to play, an important part in determining the role of women in the Soviet economy. The present high rate of participation of women in the Soviet labor force is not without precedent, however. In 1926, when the country was largely agricultural, almost every woman participated in economic activity outside the home for a part of the year. What is unique in the Soviet situation today is the very high rate of participation by women in the economy of a country so industrially advanced. At the present time, the Soviet participation rate of close to 70 percent in the working ages is almost twice as high as the rate in the United States. This high rate has been maintained despite a major structural shift in the population away from rural areas, where the participation rate has always been very high, into urban areas where the participation rate initially was much lower. Since 1926, however, the participation rate of urban women age 16 to 59 has increased from 40 to 67 percent. This increase has almost completely offset the decline in the average participation rate which would otherwise have occurred as the industrialization process proceeded.

Although rates of female participation in the labor force are high in all regions of the USSR, variations occur which are usually related to the degree of urbanization, the influence of Moslem traditions, and the size of the male deficit. Since urbanization and Moslem traditions tend to lower the rate, while the shortage of men tends to raise it, the rate reaches its extreme high in largely rural and traditionally Christian republics which were badly hit by the war, such as Belorussia, and its extreme low in the more urbanized of the traditionally Moslem republics, such as Azerbaidzhan. Another factor which affects the local rates of female participation, but about which little statistical information is available, is the lack of employment opportunity near women's homes or in particular specialties.

The continuance of a high rate of female participation at all ages, even through the childbearing and child-rearing ages, is another distinctive Soviet characteristic. In the age group 20 to 39, which encompasses the most important childbearing and child-rearing ages, approximately 80 percent of the women are employed, a remarkably high rate for a country as advanced industrially as the Soviet Union. Women begin to withdraw from employment in the socialized sector of the economy as they approach the retirement age, but many older women continue to work on private agricultural plots.

In the United States and other highly developed countries the pattern is quite different. Although in the United States 45 percent of the women in their early twenties are employed, many of these women withdraw from the labor force when they begin to have children. Only 33 percent remain employed in their later twenties. The participation rate then climbs to a second peak for women in their forties and early fifties when their children are able to fend for themselves. In the age groups under 40 and over 65, the participation rate of Soviet women is approximately double that of American women. In the age group 40 to 65 it exceeds the American rate by a little more than 50 percent.

The male population deficit in the older age groups, coupled with high female participation rates, has resulted in a substantial majority of women in the Soviet labor force age 35 and older. This is a crucial age group for any economy, since it is from this group that the leadership of an economy and of a society is normally drawn. This special circumstance has made the effective utilization of women since World War II even more vital for the Soviet Union than numbers alone would suggest.

If the present high proportion of working women in the Soviet Union is examined in terms of the gradual restoration of a normal male-female ratio in the population, the share of women in the total employment of the future is not likely to increase above the present 52 percent. In the United States and other developed countries, on the other hand, there is still ample room for growth in the employment of women. The President's Commission on the Status of Women projects a level of 34 percent for the United States in 1970. Given circumstances more favorable to working women, still further increases would be a possibility.

In the Soviet Union economic pressures compelling women to work to make ends meet play a major role in keeping women in the labor force. The shortage of men has left many women without husbands, and they must work to support themselves and their families. Furthermore, for many families a single pay check provides only a bare subsistence, and many married women feel they must work in order to maintain an acceptable standard of living. Also, government and party action has altered social custom and public attitudes toward the employment of women. At the present time, few fields are considered inaccessible, and a woman is actually likely to feel defensive if she does not have a job. The regime has been particularly successful in opening the fields of science and technology to women. Attitudes toward women participating in these fields have so radically changed that they are freely accepted everywhere—except in work considered detrimental to their health.

The policies of the Soviet regime on the employment of women, protection on the job, and maternity benefits have been embodied in extensive legislation and executive orders issued since the Revolution. Often the legislation has not been enforced, particularly during the war emergency when women were in fact employed in many occupations from which by the existing law they were excluded for reasons of health. At the present time, however, the legal provisions concerning Soviet women are generally enforced, and in this respect the Soviet Union is among the more enlightened countries of the world.

Another factor affecting the participation of women in the labor force is the burden of family responsibilities. Although adequate data are lacking, the participation rate of Soviet women appears to decline, as is normally the case everywhere, as the number of their children increases. We have seen, however, that the Soviet participation rate holds up remarkably well, even in the face of this burden, throughout the childbearing and child-rearing ages. This is possible partly because the varied child-care facilities provided in the Soviet Union free several million women with young children for employment outside the home. As has been pointed out, the demand for the services of these institutions continues to outrun the supply. According to estimates, approximately 12 percent of the children of nursery age and 20 percent of the children of kindergarten age can be accommodated in permanent child-care facilities. Substantially more can be accommodated in seasonal summer facilities. Most of the permanent facilities are concentrated in urban centers, and the seasonal facilities in the countryside. In a major city such as Moscow, almost half the children of nursery and kindergarten age are cared for in child-care centers, but in most communities there are long lists of children waiting to be admitted.

Although the government has allocated substantial investment funds over the years to the expansion of child-care facilities, it has been unwilling to assign to this program sufficient resources to satisfy demand. On the contrary, it has chosen to compel most working women to make their own arrangements—with members of their families or outside help—for the care of their young children. This policy can hardly be considered beneficial to the working mothers. From the standpoint of the regime's overriding goal of economic growth, however, the imposition of hardship on the working mother and a slightly lower rate of participation of women in the labor force have apparently been considered preferable to the diversion of investment funds and other resources to additional child-care facilities.

More information than is presently available would be required to judge whether the government's policy has struck the correct balance, given its schedule of priorities. It is equally difficult to pass judgment on party and governmental thinking with respect to housing, consumers' goods, and the provision of services to relieve women of some of the burden of housework. Such a judgment would require an assessment of whether or not a larger investment in labor-saving devices for the home would encourage a sufficiently larger number of women to enter the labor force, or would sufficiently increase the productivity of those already in the labor force, to offset the negative effect on the rate of growth which a diversion of resources to the consumer sector would entail. One would also need to assess the effect of such improvements on fertility rates and the long-run supply of labor. Until more data are available, these questions cannot be conclusively answered.

As the Soviet economy has passed through successive stages of development, there have, of course, been changes in the pattern of priorities. What was conceived as correct strategy during the period of forced industrialization under Stalin does not appear applicable today, at a higher stage of economic development when emphasis on producers' goods production is no longer so important. As a result, conditions in the Soviet Union are now favorable to greater investments in housing, production of consumers' goods, and child-care facilities with the aim of lightening the burden on women. Apparently the government expects to sustain or to increase the participation rate of women in this fashion rather than through the more Draconic policies pursued in the past.

Education was the first step by which Soviet women were enabled to equip themselves for a broader and more productive participation in the Soviet economy. Dramatic progress has been made in raising the educational levels of the population, and women have been, perhaps, the principal beneficiaries of this process. For all practical purposes, illiteracy among women has been wiped out except among the older generation and in some of the more stubbornly backward areas of the country. The most striking improvements have been realized by women in rural areas and in some of the less developed republics where, in the past, Moslem traditions barred women from acquiring an education. It should not be overlooked, however, that a third of the persons in prime working ages still have less than a four-year education, and that two-thirds of this group are women. It appears that the government has never intended to provide the bulk of the older female population with more than the minimal educational requirements for "functional" literacy. These older women apparently were written off at the start as prospects for the development of special skills.

By concentrating its efforts on the younger age groups during the past four decades, the Soviet government has succeeded in raising substantially the level of educational attainment of millions of young men and women in those occupational fields critical for economic growth and development. Great numbers of younger women have been given on-the-job training in industry and have become an important element in the industrial labor force. Similarly, many young women have been afforded a specialized secondary or higher educational training in science and technology and in other key fields for economic development. Girls have been as well prepared as boys for admission to the scientific or technical faculties of specialized secondary and higher educational institutions because the curricula at the lower educational levels were made uniform for both sexes. Initially, minimum quotas were set for women to encourage their enrollment, and other efforts were made to increase female matriculation, especially in scientific and technical disciplines. As a result, women have had opened to them many of the more interesting and attractive occupations from which they had previously been excluded. This has been a major positive accomplishment of the Soviet regime.

The remarkable success of the Soviet Union in attracting women to the fields of science and technology is apparent from the statistics on education which we have surveyed. The great demand for women with scientific and technological training which arose in the 1930s initiated the impressive increase in the proportion of women enrolled in these fields. Although comprehensive statistics on the proportion of women enrolled in specific fields of science and technology are not available, such data as we do have show that women make up approximately three-quarters of the enrollment in courses in the technology of food and consumers' goods production and approximately three-fifths of those studying chemical engineering, hydrology, meteorology, geodesy, and cartography. In fields such as mining engineering, transportation, and machine building, on the other hand, only a fifth to a sixth of the students are women. But 53 percent of the medical students and 25 percent of the agricultural students are women, both percentages having dropped sharply in recent years. It is estimated that at Soviet universities three fourths to four fifths of the students enrolled in biology, more than two thirds of those in chemistry, two fifths to a half in mathematics, and a quarter to two fifths in physics, geology, and the agriculture sciences are women. In comparison with other countries of the world, these are strikingly high percentages.

It should be emphasized that the choice of a specific field of study by young Soviet men and women is not decided by the state. The percentage of men and women enrolled in each discipline is a fairly faithful reflection of the relative attraction of a field. Initially, the proportion of women grew in all fields, but by no means to the same degree. Certain disciplines, such as medicine, came to be dominated by women; others, such as architecture, by men. In recent years, however, more men have been attracted to medicine—a tendency which has been reinforced by the fact that today men seem to be given admission preference. There have, then, been shifts in the attitudes of young men and women toward certain fields, with resulting shifts over the years in the proportion of women enrolled. To what extent these shifts are a function of altered admission policies and to what extent they depend on changes in individual preferences are matters for conjecture.

There has been a major shift in the over-all proportion of women enrolled in specialized secondary and higher education since World War II. During and immediately after the war, the proportion of women enrolled reached its peak. In the past decade, however, the proportion of women has declined—slightly in specialized secondary education and sharply in higher education. This decline has occurred in every field, but is particularly pronounced in medicine, agriculture, and the socio-economic disciplines. The immediate causes limiting the proportion of women in higher education have been changes in the organization of the secondary school system and more especially in the regulations governing admission to higher educational institutions. Although equality of the sexes remains the stated policy of the Soviet regime, actual admission policies indicate an increasing departure from this principle. Although we cannot be certain that the reduction in the proportion of female enrollment has in fact stemmed from considerations of efficiency, such a reduction does admit of justification on economic grounds. In fields such as medicine, an excessively high proportion of women (from the standpoint of efficient utilization) was permitted to receive training. The government is now eager to restore a more desirable balance of the sexes. In other fields also, where the proportion of women was always lower, the proportion is being further reduced in the interest of efficiency, since the productivity of professional women in most fields tends to be less than that of men.

Even though education has prepared many Soviet women for professional careers, most Soviet women are still engaged in heavy, unskilled work. According to 1959 census data, four fifths of the total 56 million women employed in the labor force were engaged in what is officially termed "physical" labor, and of these the majority were employed in agricultural occupations. Nonspecialized agricultural work alone accounts for one-third of the women engaged in physical labor. Typically, women are the field workers, and livestock tenders, while men handle the skilled mechanical and construction work and serve as administrators. When the other more skilled agricultural occupations are included, agriculture accounts for 63 percent of all women employed in physical labor. The large number of women still working in the fields, in spite of Soviet industrial advances, is one of the distinctive features of the Soviet economy.

Women have also come to play an important role in the nonagricultural sectors of the economy—particularly in industry and in the service sector. Throughout a wide range of occupations the percentage of women is substantially higher than that in the United States. Only in such traditional areas of female employment as secretarial, sales, and clerical work and nursing are the American percentages equally high. A high percentage of women is employed in communal and household services and in public dining, and women are relatively well represented in the garment trades and in various occupations in the textile and food industries. Large numbers of women may also be found in metalwork, construction, and transportation. Although most of the industrial and unskilled occupations have little intrinsic appeal for women, for those who lack training or talent for professional work they offer an opportunity to supplement the family income. Also, the high percentage of Soviet women in such occupations dramatically reflects the shortage of males of working age and the determination of the regime to maintain high rates of economic growth at the cost, if necessary, of individual welfare.

Perhaps even more distinctive than the high over-all participation rate of Soviet women, and the vital role they play in the older age groups of the labor force, is their heavy representation in white-collar occupations and the professions. This is the bright side of the employment picture for Soviet women. The role of women in white-collar occupations has increased greatly since the Revolution and has assumed proportions unequaled elsewhere in the world. Today, women comprise more than half the labor force employed in "mental" work. About half of the 11 million women in this category have had a specialized secondary or higher education. The proportion of women among specialists with a specialized secondary education is very high, amounting to 63 percent in recent years. Among professionals with a higher education, the proportion is 53 percent. Thus, women form a clear majority of the semiprofessional and professional labor force in the Soviet Union. The woman physician, engineer, research worker, or technician is a commonplace. American women, in contrast, make up very small minorities in most professions, the only exception being teaching; and in such fields as engineering, physics, and medicine, the professional woman is a rarity. For example, while women comprise only 7 percent of the physicians in the United States, they make up 75 percent of the total in the Soviet Union. In engineering, the contrast is even more striking; over a quarter of a million Soviet women are engineers, and make up a third of the profession, while in the United States, female engineers account for less than 1 percent of the total. The number of women in the natural sciences in the Soviet Union is also substantial, although the proportion of women varies considerably from field to field, tending to be higher in the biological sciences and chemistry and lower in a field such as physics.

In 1947, the only year for which data are available, women made up 35 percent of the staffs of Soviet higher educational institutions, while in the United States they constituted 22 percent in 1954–55. In the Soviet Union, 68 percent of the philologists were women, 48 percent of the teachers of medicine and biology, 45 percent of the chemists, and 40 percent of the education teachers. In the remaining fields, the proportion of women lay below the average of 35 percent for all fields combined. For example, 34 percent of the staffs in the arts were women, 30 percent of the historians, 29 percent of the geographers, 23 percent of the geologists, 21 percent of the physicists and mathematicians, 16 percent of the economists, and 11 percent of the engineers. U.S. statistics, while they do not follow exactly the Soviet classification of occupations, nevertheless present interesting comparisons. In 1954–55, 40 percent of education teachers in colleges and universities were women; 28 percent of those in English, journalism, and foreign languages; 27 percent in the fine arts; 20 percent in business and commerce; 14 percent in mathematics; 11 percent in the social sciences; 10 percent in agriculture and the biological sciences; 6 percent in the physical sciences; and less than 1 percent in engineering and architecture. As these figures reveal, only in education, and to a lesser degree in the arts, are the percentages of women at all comparable in the two countries. In all other corresponding fields, the Soviet percentages are substantially higher, evincing the success of the Soviets in utilizing the talents of women in fields which in the United States and other Western countries remain almost exclusively male domains.

Although the prospects for a woman's embarking upon a professional career in the Soviet Union are much more favorable than in the United States or other Western countries, the prospects for her professional advancement are not so happy; for the proportion of Soviet women in the higher professional echelons tends to decrease as the rank advances. This phenomenon can be observed even in fields, such as education and health, where women predominate. In the former, the proportion of women primary school directors in the Soviet Union is almost identical to the percentage of women teachers, but the percentage declines sharply from 72 percent for primary school directors to 24 percent for 8-year school directors and 20 percent for secondary school directors. A similar attrition occurs in higher education, where in 1960 women comprised 41 percent of the assistant professors and other lower-level professionals, 24 percent of the associate professors, 11 percent of the professors, 12 percent of the department heads, 9 percent of the deans, and only 5 percent of the deputy directors and directors. In medicine and health, although women make up 75 percent of the medical profession, they account for only 57 percent of the directors, deputy directors, and chief physicians of medical establishments. In research institutions where women make up half the scientific workers (*nauchnye rabotniki*), they account for about a third of heads and deputy heads of branches, 21 percent of the division heads and their deputies, and 16 percent of the directors and their deputies and other top administrative personnel. This pattern of declining representation of women as rank increases is repeated in all other fields for which data are available.

The lodging of a disproportionate share of women in the lower and intermediate professional levels suggests that the Soviet government is not receiving so high a return on its educational investment in women as in men, since Soviet professional women with comparable educational training show, on the whole, a lower level of achievement than men. Further evidence of this is provided by various indexes of scholarly productivity. For example, among the top Soviet scientists—full and corresponding members of the Academies of Sciences—very few women are to be found. Women also make up a very small proportion of the recipients of Lenin prizes. An extensive survey of scholarly publications gives further unmistakable evidence that the scholarly productivity of women is lower than that of men. In a comparison of the proportion of women in various specialties on the staffs of higher educational institutions with the proportion of scholarly articles contributed in each field by women, it was found that on the average women contributed about half as many articles as would be expected from their numbers.

The Soviets have done little or no research on the possible effects of various social or environmental factors on the achievement of women. To what extent their lower productivity and their small proportions at the higher administrative and professional levels may be due to innate rather than to socially or culturally determined factors is a question that cannot be easily answered. Unlike the woman farmer or factory worker doing a routine job, the Soviet professional woman is likely to derive considerable satisfaction from her work and to be seriously interested in it. But even though her motivation is high, the obstacles to achievement are considerable. Some of the important factors inhibiting a woman's productivity are lost work time and distractions due to family responsibilities, the interruption of a career because of childbearing, and job assignment difficulties. Such factors cannot, of course, readily be eradicated. Other conditions which involve the intellectual development of girls and their career motivations can perhaps be improved. Great progress has already been made in altering the image of a woman's role in society. The intellectual, career-oriented girl in the Soviet Union today can find much support and social approval compared with the girl of only a few decades ago. It appears, however, that conflicts between career and marriage and motherhood will remain for some time to come, since the greater involvement of a woman with her family is not susceptible of drastic change even in Soviet society. If the regime should choose to divert a greater proportion of its investment funds toward the provision of child-care facilities and consumers' goods to lighten the burden of housework, women would be thereby relieved of some of the drain on their creative energies caused by family responsibilities, and their productivity should increase accordingly.

It is evident from this survey that the Soviet regime has a very different attitude toward women from that of a largely unplanned, individualistic society such as our own. Reflecting a philosophy which conceives of the individual's welfare as the basic social goal, our society views the education of women, as well as that of men, to be desirable as an end in itself. Although much of our education is career-oriented, the failure of a young woman after her marriage to pursue a career for which she has been trained does not mean that her education is considered wasted. The raising of a family is considered in itself a sufficient contribution to the welfare of society and is not normally viewed as a distraction from which a woman should, if possible, be relieved so that she can pursue a "productive" career. In contrast, the Soviets see women as an economic asset or resource, to be developed and exploited as effectively as possible. This attitude reflects, of course, the regime's overriding goal of promoting economic development, a goal which has governed Soviet economic policies since the late 1920s. Concurrently, the regime has been concerned with the enlargement of women's rights and with freeing women from all forms of repression and discrimination. This idealistic motif in Soviet policy cannot be denied, but it must be viewed in the proper perspective.

As we have seen, Soviet policy toward women is complex and sometimes contradictory. However, if the predominance of the economic motive in determining Soviet policies toward women is recognized and borne in mind, many of the apparent contradictions can be better understood. It is true that, on occasion, policies inspired by idealism have coincided with those motivated by strictly material considerations, but wherever they diverge, the Soviets have consistently chosen to pursue the economic rather than the idealistic goal. In the first years following the Revolution, for example, the regime was altruistically concerned with securing women's rights and bringing about a greater equality of the sexes. A great deal of legislation was passed to these ends, and the percentage of women in specialized secondary and higher education institutions, as well as the percentage employed in industry and other branches of the economy, increased significantly during the 1920s and 1930s. But women were perhaps too successful in securing "equality." Too much equality can become a burden to women whose physiological function of motherhood makes impossible their avoidance of heavy responsibilities over and above those imposed by their work. Soviet time-use studies show clearly that the total burden of employment in the labor force and in the home falls much more heavily upon women than upon men. Although Soviet legislation recognizes that physiological differences necessitate certain safeguards to a woman's health and welfare, the laxity of enforcement and even the suspension of some of these safeguards during various periods of Soviet history suggest that the goal of greater production has more often than not overridden the altruistic concern for protection. Naturally, even under the most extreme pressures, the regime cannot afford a complete abandonment of safeguards and protective measures, since the effective utilization of women as producers depends to a considerable degree upon the reduction of the conflicts which arise from the woman's competing role as wife and mother. But if the regime had consistently placed women's welfare ahead of production in its scale of priorities, there would be concrete evidence of this in a greater abundance of child-care facilities and a more conscientious enforcement of protective legislation. Similarly, if equality of educational opportunity between the sexes had been of primary concern, admissions regulations and other factors which have contributed to the decline over the past decade in the proportion of women among students in higher education would have been altered when the decline first became evident. Failure to alter them until recently is evidence that the regime in fact preferred the efficient use of its limited higher educational facilities to the social ideal of equality. Apparently realizing that a woman is not likely to be so economically productive as a man in the course of a lifetime, Soviet planners opted for productivity as a social goal and chose accordingly to restrict access to higher education to a smaller proportion of women. It remains to be seen whether the recent modifications in admission requirements are sufficient to redress the balance between the sexes and to permit the percentage of women in higher education to rise to a level proportionate with the percentage of women in the college-age population as a whole.

In a totalitarian society such as the Soviet Union, many options are open to the regime in pursuing its policies which are not available to a government responsive to the public will. The party, both directly and through the government, exercises a decisive influence on almost every aspect of economic and social behavior. As we have seen, certain of the policies adopted may be mutually counter-productive—as are, for instance, those aimed simultaneously at the achievement of a higher birth rate and a greater participation of women in the labor force. Others may be in conflict with deep-seated beliefs and customs and may make slow headway—as, for example, the higher education of women in Central Asia, where the traditional subservience of women leads to the early withdrawal of girls from school. For the most part, however, through its control of the means of mass communication and education, the regime has succeeded in achieving acceptance of the new attitudes toward female participation in the labor force, particularly in sectors and occupations which had previously been all but closed to women.

To a society such as our own, which does not tap more than a fraction of the full economic potential of its women, both a lesson and a challenge are implied in the success of the Soviets in developing skilled and capable professional women, particularly in the fields of science and technology. Indeed, Soviet numerical superiority in certain scientific and technological fields is due entirely to the employment of a large number of women in these fields. Although it has been pointed out that the achievement of Soviet women, on the average, falls short of that of men, there can be no doubt that many talents and skills which would have been neglected in another society have been developed and utilized in the Soviet Union and that Soviet policies have made of women one of the major sources of economic strength. Indeed, the imbalance of the sexes in the Soviet population, particularly in the mature age groups, has made the effective participation of women in all sectors of the economy essential to its development. In other, more advanced, societies, this urgent need for the services of women does not arise. The Soviet example proves, however, that a large reservoir of female talent in the United States and other Western countries remains untapped or undeveloped. Although the tools and mechanisms required to exploit this potential may not be so readily available to our governments, nor the motivation to exploit it so pressing, it is clear that our own society could go much farther than it presently does toward a full utilization of its womanpower. Indeed, the question might be raised whether we can really afford—not only from the standpoint of the national interest, but also from that of the welfare of women as individuals—to neglect their potential contribution of talent and intellect and to leave them so largely at the margin of our economic life.

A Workshop for Married Women in Part-Time Employment: Implications of an Experiment in the Netherlands

J.L.J.M. VAN DER DOES DE WILLEBOIS

"The domestic and industrial issues are two aspects of a whole." [1]

There can be no doubt about it—the relations between the parties on the labor market reflect their relative strength. When jobs are hard to get, when there is substantial unemployment, poverty and a low level of development in general, then what is traditionally known as the demand side,

---

Reprinted from the *International Labour Review,* Vol. *96,* No. 6, December 1967, pp. 609–629, by permission of the International Labour Office.
[1] P. Jephcott *et al., Married Women Working* (London: George Allen & Unwin, 1962), p. 176.

that is, industrial undertakings and other employing units, dominates the situation; while what is traditionally called the supply side—workers of various classes and occupations—is under economic coercion, since the people concerned must earn a regular wage, wherever they can find it, in order to keep going. If workers so placed have any choice, it is not between one job and another but between "this job" and no job at all; in other words, when they seek employment their position of weakness prevents them from taking any but economic considerations into account.

During the past 15 years that kind of situation has largely ceased to exist in many countries and areas of Western Europe and North America. Instead—one may say, for the first time in history—not only is employment available for all, but there is a structural manpower shortage, an expanding economy, with rising levels of income and consumption, of well-being and general development. As a result large groups of workers have for the first time been able to choose between one job and another, one employer and another, and have thus been in a position to take non-economic considerations into account in their choice of work.

Industrial undertakings and other employing units—the demand side of the labor market—thus find themselves in a much more complex position. Not only are they faced by stronger and more fastidious supply groups; they also find themselves in competition with one another for the available work force. This situation obliges them to adjust their internal technical and organizational structure and their personnel policy; indeed, in the new situation continuity in recruitment has become a cause of concern and requires specific planning.

As yet the possibly revolutionary significance of the above-mentioned structural changes, both for the management of industrial undertakings and for public social, economic, and general policy, is hardly suspected, still less translated into clear-sighted proposals for future action.[2] Local, pragmatic experiments with new kinds of organization, working conditions, management, planning, and control are still exceptional. However, some of the results of such experiments can be offered for the construction of future policy.

The present article describes a particular experiment, made because of such a changed situation. Though neither dramatic nor revolutionary, it may be considered, against the background sketched in the preceding paragraphs, as not without significance. But before the scheme itself is depicted, a review of the relevant conditions must be given.

---

[2] Valuable data and suggestions in this regard may be found in the following: W. G. Bennis, *Changing Organizations* (New York: McGraw-Hill, 1966); J. F. Fourastier, *Les quarante mille heures* (Paris: Robert Laffont, 1965); E. Jacques, *The Changing Culture of a Factory* (London: Tavistock Publications, 1951); R. Likert, *New Patterns of Management* (New York: McGraw-Hill, 1961); D. Lockwood, "The Affluent Worker," in *Sociology*, Vol. *1*, No. 1, 1967; and H. J. van Zuthem, *Arbeid en arbeidsbeleid in de onderneming* (Assen, 1967).

National Background

The above-mentioned structural changes began to be felt in the Netherlands in the middle of the 1950s and became increasingly pronounced in the years 1959 to 1965. The growing shortage of personnel was experienced everywhere and stimulated a more deliberate search for means of tapping non-traditional sources of labor. In addition to foreign workers,[3] active interest was taken in the employment of women.

In the Netherlands in 1960 working women made up 23 percent of the gainfully occupied population and 26 percent of the total female population over 14 years of age. In both France and the Federal Republic of Germany the corresponding figures were about 34 and 40 percent. In Britain and the United States working women made up about 34 percent of the gainfully occupied population, in Sweden and Switzerland about 30 percent, in Italy 27 percent.[4] So the percentage of women working in the Netherlands could be regarded as low.

But, as in other developed countries, substantial shifts have been taking place within the general category of gainfully occupied women. While their number and proportion have remained approximately constant, there has been a steady fall in the proportion of women who help in their husbands' businesses, and a sharp rise in the number and proportion working in non-agricultural, non-domestic activities. In general, the number of unmarried women decreased between 1947 and 1960, absolutely and relatively, as a result of the fall in the average age of marriage and of the declining surplus of women over men in the age groups under 35 years. Yet, despite the absolute and relative decline in the same period the proportion of unmarried women going out to work increased by three points—from 55 to 58 percent of all unmarried women between 14 and 64 years of age.[5]

It is more interesting, having regard to the growing shortage of labor, to examine the position of married women and to compare this with the position in neighboring countries.

Again in the period 1947–60, the proportion of married women going out to work in the Netherlands increased sharply—from 2.5 to 4.7 percent of all married women. If wives helping husbands' businesses are included, we reach a total proportion, for 1960, of 7 percent of all married women. In Belgium 15.4 percent of all married women were working in 1947 and the number has greatly increased since. In the Federal Republic of Ger-

---

[3] On this point, see R. Wentholt, *Buitenlandse arbeiders in Nederland* (1966).

[4] See International Labour Conference, 48th Session, Geneva, 1964, Report VI (1) *Women Workers in a Changing World* (Geneva: I.L.O., 1963), and the figures from the (Netherlands) Central Statistical Office, reproduced in Sociaal Economische Raad, *Advies over de arbeid van vrouwen in Nederland, 1966,* p. 11. This report gives a good review of recent inquiries and publications on the subject in the Netherlands.

[5] Figures from the national census of 1960 provided by the Central Statistical Office, The Hague.

many, and in France, Great Britain, and the United States, about 33 percent of all married women went out to work in 1960.[6]

There is thus a striking difference between the position in the Netherlands and in the neighboring countries, where the married woman worker is a much more usual phenomenon.

This is due to various factors. For one thing, in the Netherlands industrialization and urbanization did not develop in real earnest until after World War II. For another, opinions and attitudes toward the employment of married women outside their homes changed slowly; the view that a married woman should look after the household, and nothing else, while the husband earns the family's living, is still strong and widespread in the Netherlands; it reflects the long-standing conception of the role of man and wife in the traditional Dutch family.

An inquiry on this subject [7] among a representative sample of women with family responsibilities revealed that 56 percent were more or less opposed to work outside the household, while only 20 percent were positively disposed toward such work. According to these women, the great majority of breadwinning husbands objected to their wives going out to work; so their attitude was apparently much more negative than that of the wives themselves. This generally unfavorable opinion is found in all groups of the population—rather more strongly among those with religious affiliations and less so among people with more money and higher educational levels.

However, there are indications [8] that the number of married women seeking employment is likely to rise further as a result of increasing urbanization, the fall in the birth rate and the average age of marriage, the mechanization of household work, and the rise in the level of education. The proportion of unmarried working women in the lower age groups will, however, probably decline as a result of the extension of the period devoted to education and training, the disappearance of the surplus of women over men, and (once again) the fall in the average age of marriage.

Probably, therefore, there will not be any marked change in the proportion of women in the total gainfully occupied population; it is likely to remain around 23 percent.[9]

Shortage of labor was very acute in large parts of the Netherlands in the period 1960–65 and the demand for women was even greater than that for

---

[6] See *Women Workers in a Changing World, op. cit.,* pp. 15ff.; and Viola Klein, *Women Workers, Working Hours and Services: A Survey in 21 Countries* (Paris: O.E.C.D., 1965).

[7] See Instituut voor Psychologisch Markt-en Motievenonderzoek (I.P.M.). *Arbeid buitenshuis door vrouwen met gezinsverantwoordelijkheid* (1962); and a report with very much the same title by the Family Council, published by the Minister of Culture, Recreation and Social Work in March 1966.

[8] See *Advies over de arbeid van vrouwen in Nederland, 1966, op. cit.,* pp. 12ff.

[9] Ibid., p. 14.

men. The shortages of men and women alike were greatest in industry.[10] However, there were considerable differences between the various sectors of the economy and the various regions.

Local Situation

Eindhoven is a highly industrial city in the south of the Netherlands, with some 180,000 inhabitants. Of the gainfully employed population, 61 percent work in industry, 38 percent in the services sector, and 0.9 percent in agriculture.

In the industrial sector the metal industry is predominant (employing 82 percent of the industrial workers), and its share of the gainfully occupied population has increased most rapidly. Far the greatest proportion of the work force—both men and women—in this industry are employed by Philips, which has its headquarters in Eindhoven.

Between 1960 and 1964 the demand on the local labor market so much exceeded the supply that departures from Philips' operative work force could not be counterbalanced by recruitment of new personnel. Contrary to the needs of the firm the numbers of male and female manual workers declined in those years by 8.3 and 14.1 percent respectively, while the population of Eindhoven increased by 7.4 percent.

It is thought that the decline at Philips was due to the attraction of the services sector, which until 1960 had been relatively underdeveloped for a town of Eindhoven's size and then expanded rapidly. This process, together with the decrease in "daily migration"—particularly of women and girls from the neighboring parts of Belgium, which were rapidly being industralized—largely accounts for the fall in the supply of female manual workers.

Besides such local phenomena there was the fact that the shortage of unskilled workers was also a national problem at the time. Whereas in 1936, 53 percent of boys leaving primary school went straight to work, in 1952 the proportion was 27 percent and in 1961 only 9 percent. In Eindhoven itself only about 6 percent of primary school leavers became immediately available for employment in 1960. So, apart from the various short-term causes, the decrease in manpower and the resulting shortage have also a clear long-term, structural element; it is this structural element that requires undertakings to adjust their policies so that recruitment may be kept going at a time of rising standards of living.

Accordingly, it was clear that the time had come at Philips to devote more systematic thought to rendering methods of operation more attractive, having regard to the human motivations of potential employees. New ideas in the social sciences were studied and shaped into a new concept of work organization, specifically adjusted to the Philips concern.

---

10 As in the United States, most working women (73 percent of the total) are in commerce and the services.

Small groups of workers and group autonomy, broadening the job and individual responsibility, shortening the "line," participation and consultation—these are the main starting points that led to the new concept that has become familiar in the Netherlands under the name of "job structuring."

The situation was certainly ripe for experiment. The decrease in the number of manual workers, particularly of the female sex, at Philips, Eindhoven, occurred at the very moment when activity in electro-technical manufacture was greatly expanding and the demand for women who could do precision assembly work was therefore also increasing fast. Sales departments were making plans which the production departments could not carry out for lack of personnel. No more women workers could be recruited from traditional sources. The only way out was to recruit married women—still a non-traditional source of labor in the Netherlands, as pointed out above.

A special committee at Philips, Eindhoven, had already worked out proposals for a personnel policy aimed specifically at that objective. Having applied these proposals, the Philips telecommunications works at The Hague—also struggling against a chronic labor shortage—had had encouraging experiences with an unusual scheme of working hours, specifically devised to provide part-time employment for married women; the scheme was advertised and the interest shown exceeded all expectations. Thereupon it was decided to begin a similar experiment in the much less urbanized neighborhood of Eindhoven and—in connection with it—to put ideas on "job structuring" into practice.

In the immediate vicinity of Eindhoven lies the satellite town of Veldhoven, a typical dormitory area of about 25,000 inhabitants including a comparatively large number of young families. Most of its working population consists of manual workers and clerks employed in Eindhoven. A small workshop for precision assembly of hearing aids, which was intended exclusively for the employment of married women and arranged—as regards lay-out, equipment, and organization—specially to suit them, opened at Veldhoven in 1964.

Hours of Work

One of the practical reasons why more married women do not go out to work, in the Netherlands and elsewhere, is of course the fact that a full working week of 45 hours is in many cases very hard to combine with the duties of a housewife. It can be assumed that a good many more married women would be disposed to take jobs, so as to earn something extra, if there were an appropriate opportunity not too far from home and suited to their requirements. So the first two important requirements are proximity and convenient hours of work.

As regards the first, a basic reason for choosing Veldhoven was to bring the jobs close to married women and indeed to put them not more than 15 minutes, on foot or bicycle, from their homes. Another basic reason may be expressed as negative: not to begin in the middle of Eindhoven's huge complex of factories, which might have scared off many women in advance. The opportunity of doing part-time work close to their homes, it may be assumed, reduces the preliminary obstacles, both physical and psychological, which married women must surmount before going out to work. A still better adjustment of working conditions to their situation can be obtained if the women themselves are enabled to fix the distribution of their own hours of work over the day and week. If so, they can arrange, for instance, for their working hours to coincide with the children's hours at school. Moreover, some may prefer to work in the morning, others in the afternoon. The Philips telecommunications works at The Hague had been the first, in 1961, to introduce this special freedom for married women to choose their own hours of work.

For reasons of economy in operation, however, it is necessary to lay down a lower limit for the number of weekly working hours, because part-time work inevitably involves higher costs for the establishment. (The question of costs will be discussed below.) At the works in The Hague the minimum number of weekly working hours for married women was fixed at 30. When taking up employment there, women can indicate their preference regarding distribution over the day and week. An agreement is then made, which—if desired—can be modified later. Time off, without pay, can be taken in case of unforeseen occurrences—for instance if the husband or a child falls ill. The system turned out to be a success; absenteeism and turnover figures in the department concerned were clearly favorable in comparison with the other parts of the same establishment.

In the light of this success, the following scheme was worked out for Veldhoven. Working hours range from a minimum of 25 to a maximum of 45 in a week. An individual contract is made with each employee, stipulating the number of hours she is to work and their distribution over the day and week. Distribution over the week must be such that the employee is present for several hours on not less than four days. This is regarded as a necessary condition, both for the employer, so that the workshop can be efficiently organized, and for the worker, so that she may keep up reliable, uniform standards of speed and skill. Women with children can split their daily hours, doing some in the morning and some in the afternoon; those with no children may complete their hours of work without a break, either in the morning or in the afternoon.

The agreement can be reviewed every three months if the employee so wishes; but experience has shown that a well-conceived agreement seldom needs modification. Time off, without pay, can be taken for a good reason, such as the husband's or children's sickness or holidays.

In March 1967, 60 women were employed at the Veldhoven workshop. Forty-one (68 percent) do the minimum working week of 25 hours; 12 of these are mothers who have chosen their children's school hours as their own hours of work, so they attend for a certain time in the morning and a certain time in the afternoon. The other women do more than 25 hours a week, but only 3 work a full week of 45 hours. Morning work predominates; the average number of women at the workshop in the afternoon is about 28, but toward the end of the afternoon only about 4 are left. None needs more than 10 minutes to go from home to work.

Recruitment, Selection, Engagement

In all its planning, and particularly in its plans for recruitment, Philips had to make due allowance for the prevailing view that a married woman's primary job and responsibility lie in her family, and to ensure that any woman recruited could remain a housewife first and foremost and regard her career in part-time employment as merely a chance to earn additional income. A form of part-time service that would interfere with this primary responsibility had to be avoided—by the employer as much as anyone; this was realized from the outset. The widespread Dutch opposition to the employment of married women thus called for a careful policy of "mutually recognized different responsibilities," including due social sense on the employer's part. The hours-of-work arrangement is one aspect of this; the methods of recruiting, selecting, and engaging the married women are another.

The consequence was clear: if proximity to the woman's home was to be an objective, recruitment would have to be restricted, so as to preclude travel over long distances. Furthermore, contact had to be personal, even at the stage of recruitment, if a real mutual adjustment of responsibilities was to be brought about. For these reasons an original approach was chosen: married women in Veldhoven and the immediate neighborhood received a letter presenting to them a workshop intended exclusively for married women; it referred to the attractive opportunity of earning extra income, close to one's home, at times chosen by oneself, and in comfortable surroundings; and, so that these various points might be explained and the working hours and other conditions discussed with those interested, the letter offered a personal visit by the future female personnel officer of the workshop.

A reply-card was enclosed in the letter, on which name and address and the times preferred for the visit could be indicated. About 1,500 copies were sent out; some 120 replies were received. That was only about 8 percent, but, even so, much more than had been expected. All those who replied were visited at their homes.

In the course of the interview—for the above-mentioned reasons of policy—the prospective employee's family situation was discussed in detail and there was joint consideration of the extent to which it would be proper, in the particular case, for the woman to accept part-time work and for the undertaking to employ her. Mothers with children up to the "toddler" age were strongly advised not to apply, because their family responsibilities would be hard to combine with a job outside the home. (There were no collective nurseries, and no plans to establish any.) Consequently, part-time employment away from home would be appropriate mainly *either* for married women who had no children yet *or* for those whose children were at school or even at work. In terms of age, the job would be appropriate for women between 20 and 30 and for those over 36.[11]

As a result of the visits to their homes, about half the respondents had to be dropped because their domestic situation seemed, on closer examination, to be hard to combine with part-time employment.

The remainder, about 60 in all, were invited to come to Eindhoven for a test and a medical examination. Testing was necessary because special standards of vision, intelligence, accuracy, and dexterity must be met for employment in precision assembly work on hearing aids. The workshop was started gradually, in small groups. At the end of 1964 about 85 married women were working here. By March 1967 the number had been reduced, according to plan, to about 60—simply by not making up the natural wastage. But rising sales are now obliging the management to think once more of a substantial increase in the number of workers.

Conditions of Employment

Apart from the special system of hours of work, conditions of employment at the Veldhoven workshop are very much the same as at other Philips establishments in the Netherlands. The workers on part-time are entitled to sick pay, holiday allowance, and so on, in accordance with the number of hours worked by each. A woman on a 25-hour week receives 15 days' paid leave a year (10 days of collective workshop holidays and five days to be taken individually). Where necessary, an individual arrangement for regular leave can be made, by the hour if need be.

In addition, as already stated, it is always possible to take time off without pay, for instance during the school holidays. In practice, however, at those times some arrangement can often be made at home—perhaps with the aid of the child's grandparents—in order to keep down the loss of earnings. Similarly, in the case of special circumstances or difficulties in the household or family, arrangements for absence can be made after personal consultation.

Penalties are not imposed at the workshop. In serious cases of fraud or abuse—which seldom occur—the person responsible is confronted with

---

[11] See Viola Klein, *Employing Married Women* (London: 1961), pp. 11–13; *Women Workers in a Changing World, op. cit.,* p. 93; *Advies over de arbeid van vrouwen in Nederland, 1966, op. cit.,* pp. 19 and 35, and M. Dublin-Keyserling, *"Gehuwde arbeidskrachten in de Verenigde Staten,"* in *Sociaal Maandblad Arbeid* (Alphen aan den Rijn), 5 November 1966, pp. 7 and 11.

her record. This is discussed with her, and she may be advised to leave. If so, she herself resigns.

Membership in the pension fund is voluntary, except for widows, who are obliged to join. Like all other Philips employees, each woman receives a "personnel card," with which she can obtain all Philips products at the same reduced prices as apply to anyone working with Philips.

Like the working hours, however, two features more peculiar to this workshop are the "structure" of the work and its organization. Before these are described, it will be useful to give further information about the married women employed at the workshop.

Who Comes to Work and Why?

The married women employed at the workshop are all wives of manual workers and junior office personnel. Though some of the women worked in factories before their marriage, according to the chief of personnel, surprisingly many have never done so but were formerly typists in offices, salesgirls in shops, or domestic workers.

The same was found in the case of the above-mentioned experiment at the telecommunications works in The Hague, where 150 married women are employed and fuller data are available. Of the 150, only 9 percent had had factory experience, 7 percent had been typists and 11.5 percent saleswomen, 17 percent had worked in households, and 39 percent had had no previous occupation. As regards education, 60 percent had been to primary school only and 40 percent had had some further education or training thereafter (17.5 percent at domestic science schools, 13 percent at junior secondary schools,[12] and 9 percent at training courses for hospital nurses, teachers, children's nurses and educators, dressmakers, or at girls' trade schools). The average age of the married women at The Hague factory is relatively high: 39 percent are between 30 and 40 years, 45 percent are between 40 and 50. Nearly 90 percent have children over 6. The additional earnings are presumably intended, in the first place, to enable the cost of the children's education to be more easily borne, a second motive being to permit more expenditure on "luxuries" such as cars or holidays.

At Veldhoven the average age is lower: the age groups above and below 35 years are more or less equally represented. Forty-four percent of the married women have no children; the other 56 percent have children over 6 (22 percent have only one, 24 percent have two, 8 percent have three, and two percent have four). The additional earnings seem to be intended

---

[12] Schools offering courses lasting three or four years, leading *either* to employment or to further specialized training in domestic science (in the case of girls) or in technical colleges (in the case of boys).

for purposes different from those mentioned in connection with The Hague —more to purchase durable consumer goods for comfort in the home (refrigerators, washing machines, television). But these data are subject to modification, since an average age can fluctuate over the years.

An important reason why married women go out to work is to earn extra money without any sacrifice on the part of their families.[13] This emerges clearly from their recruitment interviews. Conditions of work specially adjusted to their personal situation, as well as the proximity, the external appearance and equipment of the workshop, the kind of work, the presence of other women in similar circumstances, are then factors that make it easier for them to decide on part-time employment.

Other non-economic motives also play a part. In the inquiry among women with family responsibilities, to which reference is made above,[14] it was found that readiness to go out to work does not coincide with objectively ascertainable differences of income, indeed the inhibitions seem rather less serious in the case of people with higher incomes and more education: this fact indicates the existence of other important motivational components, such as an objection to being confined to domestic tasks, dislike of the relatively isolated position of many housewives, and the attraction of being able to engage in some useful and creative work besides one's household duties.[15]

With a view to further study, it would be interesting to know what other women or classes or groups of women are considered as points of reference when a person is deciding whether she will take on part-time or other work in addition to her duties in the home.

Work, Organization, Remuneration

The work of assembling hearing aids is particularly suitable for women: it is light, and it requires dexterity, care, and precision. Such assembly work can be organized in various ways. The production process includes seven distinct phases: mechanical assembly, electrical assembly, electrical checking, casing, acoustic checking, packing, and preparation for dispatch.

Before 1960, at Eindhoven, all hearing aids were made on the production belt, so that each worker had only one short cycle of operations to perform, lasting a few minutes. The small sets passed through a great many hands, with every chance of error, damage, and so on. Consequently, in 1960 the Eindhoven factory changed its method and began to organize

---

[13] See Jephcott, *op. cit.,* pp. 87 and 100, Elisabeth Pfeil, *Die Berufstätigkeit von Muttern* (Tübingen: J.C.B. Mohr, 1961), pp. 304ff.; Klein, *Employing Married Women, op. cit.,* p. 11; and F. Zweig, *The Worker in an Affluent Society* (London: Heinemann, 1962), Ch. VIII.

[14] I.P.M., *op. cit.*

[15] See also R. O. Blood and R. L. Hamblin, *A Modern Introduction to the Family* (London, 1961), particularly pp. 137–143.

production on the basis of small groups of workers, with broader jobs for the individuals. Each woman now carried out several operations, used several tools, and was thereby responsible for a definite phase of production. Between adjacent workers, space for "provisional stocks" of material was provided, so that a woman had greater freedom to work at her own speed. This method required a longer induction period and made greater demands on the worker's intelligence; but it also rendered the job more attractive.

From the employer's point of view, the new method of organization meant less waste. There were fewer waits, fewer disruptions due to delay, a rather larger output, and a rather higher level of quality. Individual tempo and productivity remains the same; the improvements were due to better organization and were obtained not by obliging the employees individually to work harder in an unchanged setting, but by providing a different setting —a more varied job content, greater responsibility and the possibility, within limits, of working regularly at one's own preferred tempo.

Production in the Veldhoven workshop is organized on the same lines. The women work mostly in groups of 10 to 12. Each group takes care of a particular kind of hearing aid and is responsible for all the phases of its assembly. Each member of a group performs several operations, which together make up a phase. Via the "provisional stock," the article then goes on to the next member of the group, who puts it through the following phase. In this way the whole hearing aid comes visibly into existence within the group. Each worker's individual place in the group and in the process is also physically emphasized by providing her with her own assembly table, which remains unoccupied while she is absent. The assembly tables are so arranged that the particular groups can be clearly distinguished.

There is one group which only makes the wires and packs the hearing aids. A small group of six makes self-contained elements which have to be fitted into the apparatus. For purely technical operations (repair of machines, fault-finding, acoustic checking) and for certain others requiring more physical effort, three men are employed.

As an experiment, the married women in the workshop are paid a fixed wage on the basis of the hourly rate laid down by collective agreement. A certain minimum level of output, which can comfortably be reached, is agreed on, and this entitles each woman to her starting wage, which is laid down in the terms of the agreement. If she produces more, her wage is raised after a certain time to an agreed higher rate. The running-in period lasts rather longer in the case of such part-time work than otherwise, but after four or five months almost everyone reaches the usual level of output without difficulty.

The jobs are analyzed and classified by degree of difficulty. Each class has its own wage scale, which offers the possibility of financial advancement through promotion from the initial (adaptation) level to "good" and "very good." The classes are entitled "second assembler," "first assembler," and "general assembler." A newcomer starts as second assembler. If she learns her job fast and seems able to take on more difficult work she becomes a first assembler and so enters a higher wage class. If she masters other production phases inside and beyond the range of her own group, so that she is outstanding as an assembler and at times of stagnation or peak can come in as a replacement in any phase, she is promoted to "general assembler" in a still higher wage class. There are only a few of these at the workshop. Half the remainder are second and half are first assemblers.

It is the *average* level of output which determines earnings; the worker is thus free to work a little faster for a time, and then a little slower, without any fluctuations in her earnings. This freedom is ensured also by the system of "provisional stocks," which lie between adjacent workers. Evaluation is based on criteria relating to tempo, quality, degree of difficulty, and conduct.

The system of financial advancement is an experimental move to introduce, even in the case of manual work, a fixed wage that can be adjusted after periodical review, as is done with salaried employees. It is an attempt to escape from the unit system. An account of the results and experience obtained under the new system will be found below.

As already stated, the broadening of the individual's job does not lead to any increase in individual productivity, because each person's task becomes more complex. Apart from the increased productivity of the establishment as a whole, due to system improvements, a clear advantage lies in the pleasant working atmosphere, the absence of nervous tensions, and the spirit of consultation, co-operation, and comradeship that characterizes relations among the personnel.

All this probably means more to the married women concerned than just a convenient opportunity of earning something on the side.

Group Leaders

As already stated, the married women work in small groups of 10 to 12 persons. Each group has a leader. A significant detail of the preparatory work for the Veldhoven experiment was the plan to allow the groups to choose their own leaders. However, this idea was subsequently dropped because of the demands that would have to be made on the holders of such posts, particularly in the initial phase: apart from authority, impartiality, patience, and tact, the leader must also have a thorough knowledge of all operations done in the group and be able to teach and co-ordinate these operations. Until the married women had acquired some industrial experience, the chance that their choice of leaders would be determined exclusively by personal sympathies and antipathies was too great. So was the risk that the chosen leaders would not meet the functional requirements that had to be attached to the role of leader in this particular workshop. The results of inappropriate choice would have been extremely harmful for the persons concerned, the groups, and the workshop as a whole.

So the group leaders are selected by the management and the woman personnel officer, who knows the women and is aware of relations within the groups. The leader is always drawn from the particular group itself, so that in principle every member of the group has the same chance of becoming leader.

But the leader remains an assembler and spends part of her time at assembly work. She is a working group leader and only leads when the situation requires her to (for an estimated 60 percent of her working hours). She gives help and advice in difficulties, arranges for supplies of material in good time, instructs, regulates, co-ordinates and sees to it that the others can work on steadily without being disturbed. She arranges the contacts with other groups, with the chief of department and the manager, and looks after the interests of her members. The leader is the central point for communications in and concerning her group. Every day there is a short discussion between the foreman-assembler and all the group leaders. The chief of department meets them twice a week to discuss any matters affecting work and relations in the workshop as a whole.

The group leaders earn, on average, only 8 percent more than a second assembler and 4 percent more than a first assembler. They wear no distinguishing uniform or insignia. All these points help to keep the personal distinction between leaders and members of groups as small as possible and to facilitate informal, friendly co-operation.

Unlike other Philips establishments, the Veldhoven workshop has no works council. This is because, organizationally and administratively, it forms a department of an undertaking at Eindhoven. Moreover, according to the personnel officer, the need for a separate representative body at the workshop has not shown itself—no doubt, among other reasons, because of its small extent, the frequency of consultation along the "line" and the part-time presence of most of the people concerned.

As already pointed out, recruitment is carried out by means of a personal approach; this same approach is characteristic of relations within the workshop. We have seen that, when unexpected situations and difficulties arise, they are examined and a reasonable solution is sought through personal consultation. The attitudes and speech that are current also differ from those of an ordinary factory: whereas most women factory workers are addressed in the familiar form of speech [16] and by their first names, the married women at the Veldhoven workshop are addressed as "Mrs." with their surnames and in the more formal style. This practice endorses their independent, responsible status. It may be a detail, but it is a significant departure from customary factory manners.

---

[16] In Dutch there are two words for "you," one more familiar, the other more formal.

Results

The workshop for married women at Veldhoven has now been in existence for three years. What have been the results of this experiment, for the employer and for the workers?

Results for the Employer

The average output per worker per hour is approximately the same as in the comparable department at Eindhoven, working full time. Nor is unwarranted absence any more frequent at Veldhoven than elsewhere.[17] On the other hand, the possibility of taking time off without pay during the school holidays is widely exploited at the Veldhoven workshop, which often finds itself 25–30 percent understaffed at such times; but leave of this kind is often voluntarily made good, at least to some extent.

The induction period is longer, that is, more expensive, than in the case of full-time work. Self-determined time schedules and an individual workbench for each married woman involve additional expense, because the available workplaces are occupied, on average, not for 45 hours but for only 28 hours a week. Consequently fixed costs per workplace per hour are 60 percent higher in the Veldhoven workshop than in other establishments; but as these overheads (rent, light, heating, and so on) amount to only 5 percent of total costs, the increase is balanced by advantages at the social and psychological levels.

These and other cost-increasing factors are accepted and regarded as the price that must be paid for a workshop specifically arranged and made attractive for married women workers. The net result, the productivity, is judged by the workshop and the general management to be clearly favorable. After The Hague and Veldhoven, special workshops for married women have been opened in two other places, Oss and Woensel; and further plans are ready for future action. This is proof that, all things considered, Philips regard the experiment as conclusive and as a success.

Results for the Married Women

The following features are important to the employees as human beings within the organization: each woman has her own place at the workshop—in the material, the organizational, and the social and psychological sense. She makes a distinct contribution, in freedom and independence, to the manufacture of a final product, which she can see growing within her own working group; she does so as a member of a small group of similarly situated women; she receives a fixed rate of pay and can be promoted in rank and wage; the group leader is chosen from the group and differs little

---

[17] See Viviane Isambert-Jamati, "Absenteeism Among Women Workers," in *International Labour Review,* Vol. *LXXXV,* No. 3, March 1962, pp. 248–261.

from the other members. Lastly, all questions affecting the woman's position and activity at the workshop are settled by consultation.

How is this situation viewed by the married woman worker herself?

Unless there are exceptional circumstances, the staff turnover will normally give a first answer to that question, particularly at an establishment like this one where the employees are mainly seeking a *supplementary* income. It may be assumed that a decision to leave will be more easily taken in such a case than if the worker has to live on her earnings alone.

Owing to the special circumstances of the initial or induction phase, the turnover in the first few years compared quite unfavorably with the normal level at Eindhoven. The average annual turnover for women working at the Philips establishments is 23 percent. At the Veldhoven workshop, the turnover of married women was 30 percent in the first year, 29 percent in the second, and 26 percent in the third (1966).

Analysis shows that the difference was partly due to the difficulties of the initial phase and partly to the specific character of the personnel. Some of the turnover in the first few years resulted from the many changes and regroupings in the work and its organization, the teething troubles from which new establishments inevitably suffer. (When a person's work is altered he often loses touch with it and may prefer to leave.) Secondly, it turned out that despite careful selection some women had been taken on in the early years who found great difficulty in doing precision assembly work even after an induction period. Of those who were evidently falling behind, some left, while it was possible to transfer others to Philips establishments at Eindhoven. Both these groups of cases increased the workshop's turnover.

However, a great deal of the turnover was due to household or personal circumstances—sickness or death in the family, pregnancy, change of residence, and so on. As at The Hague, such reasons have accounted for about 65 percent of all departures. This part of the turnover may be regarded as inherent in the employment of married women, whereas the two kinds of separations mentioned above are characteristic of initial difficulties in a newly established workshop of any kind.

A more stable situation is at last being established. Technical and organizational problems are settled, the three years' experience has contributed to a better understanding of the subject, and more wisdom is applied in the prospection and selection of personnel. The expectation for 1967, based on results for the first five months, is that the turnover will be very much lower than hitherto and will not even exceed 12 percent.

As to the opinions of the married women workers themselves, no direct and systematic investigation has been made. So far no such investigation has been necessary at the Veldhoven workshop; the staff consists of a relatively small number of persons, about whom, on the whole, more is discovered by the personal approach than is usually known in larger factories with a more impersonal atmosphere. Owing to the frequent personal contacts and the regular consultation at various levels in the workshop, opinions and observations soon find their way through. In particular, the personnel department is well integrated with the workshop and can in general be relied upon to know what goes on among the staff. (Questionable though such an assumption may usually be in respect of larger establishments, in this special case it is justified.) The consistent impression obtained through the various internal channels of communication and of personal and group consultation is that relations in the workshop are positively good, pleasant, and comradely.

In all the special circumstances, this impression is not surprising; and it is confirmed by the fact that, on the whole, married women can be recruited without difficulty for the Veldhoven workshop. After all, the kind of employment it provides has all the appearance of suiting their particular situation—and seems to do so effectively.

A scientific comparative study, embracing several such workshops and extending to the repercussions on family relationships, would certainly provide interesting further information on the matter.

Conclusion

The Veldhoven experiment may be regarded as conclusive. This is due not least to the fact that it was an experiment in the true sense of the word —a trial of something new.

As shown at the outset, the employment of married women is not yet a general phenomenon in the Netherlands. The characteristics that distinguish married women, sociologically, from other groups of potential workers are the following: they already have a recognized position in society, implying a certain role with its consequential expectations, responsibilities and activities—the role of spouse, housewife, and mother; they have, as a rule, no immediate subjective economic need to be employed outside their homes; and, finally, there is opposition, stemming from traditional standards and opinions, against their employment. In other words: they are already "somebody"; they already have a job; they do not need to seek another away from home; and—in this country—it is not expected, or even considered proper, that they should do so.

Against such a background, what precisely is the social innovation that the Veldhoven experiment has sought to bring about? The answer may be stated thus: by modifying certain components of customary conditions of employment Philips have sought to make employment in this particular workshop better suited to the position and needs of married women (deliberately envisaged as a class of potential workers) so that such women may be more easily motivated to offer themselves as employees. Practically all customary conditions of employment have been modified—the geographical, the contractual, the economic, the organizational, the social, and the physical components. In other words, the novelty is not that Philips should have turned to married women with an offer of employment in a pre-existing setting, but that it should have turned to married women *specifically* with an offer of employment in a *modified* setting.

This approach, which may be called revolutionary in several senses, is indeed new to current patterns of industrial life. It raises various questions, first and foremost what effects the new approach may have on the women concerned, their marriages and families. Only a deliberate investigation can provide an answer to that question; as already pointed out, such an investigation has not been made; so nothing about these particular effects can be stated as certain. However, on the basis of practical experience and theoretical knowledge, conjectures may be put forward on certain important aspects of the matter. The characteristic features of the Veldhoven approach make it reasonably probable that the individual married woman comes to a responsible decision regarding the compatibility of a part-time job with her family obligations; it is also probable that, in the Veldhoven setting, she finds it relatively easy to strike the right balance between her two roles. The proximity of the workshop to her home, the broad freedom to choose her own hours of work (both number and distribution), to determine her own working tempo and to take time off, the personal consultation and the possibility of making appropriate individual arrangements —all this offers scope for combinations to suit each particular case; and from the very beginning the worker receives the full support of the personnel service. Inquiries undertaken elsewhere into the implications of part-time work for married women reveal, in general, significantly more positive than negative experience; positive results may be expected *a fortiori* from a set-up such as that at Veldhoven.

Prospects

More generally speaking, what can be the implications of part-time work for married women, for their marriages and families, and for society?

If a married woman finds a part-time job that she can combine well enough with her family responsibilities, she will at the same time have obtained a second opportunity for contacts and connections and a second activity, which makes a change from her household duties; she will hear new opinions and see new things, get more information, gain experience and with it more ability and recognition. If she adjusts psychologically to having two roles, and also combines them efficiently, she will be integrated into society not only through her husband and family, but also in another and different way; and this will give her a more varied sense of her own personality. It is reasonable to suppose that, for many people, the result may be a greater chance to attain a higher level of general satisfaction. One cannot be sure that such a result will be reached; but several researchers have reported that, where it is reached, great value can accrue, both for the woman herself and for her marriage and family, especially with regard to the children's upbringing.[18] For instance there are indications that part-time employment of the mother has a favorable effect on the position of the elder children in the family—such mothers seem better able to strike a good balance, as educators, between guiding their children and giving them independence in the later stages of their upbringing than mothers who do not work outside the home and see their educational task coming to an end. It is most important that further research be undertaken on the effect of part-time or other work by married women on their marital and family relations.[19]

A second question thrown up by an experiment like that made by Philips at Veldhoven is the important one of the effect on the undertaking itself and on its social policy. One can, of course, hold the view that such a special approach is initially motivated by pure opportunism: when there is a manpower shortage the employer has to adopt a more personal attitude, particularly toward people who, strickly speaking, have no need of him. It is quite true that in an industrial undertaking the temptation to be merely opportunist in social matters is inevitably greater if the objectives seen are almost exclusively economic.[20] If such is the case the market situation and the relative strength of the two parties have only to change to the worker's disadvantage and it is all over with the "personal approach"— which is then seen, retrospectively, to have been just a market tactic: human labor was treated as a mere commodity.

An up-to-date social policy, on the other hand, takes up the challenge of proving that it does not regard men and women as a commodity, as mere manpower, but sees workers as human beings with their own personality, entitled to be respected as such, and fit to bear responsibility toward the undertaking as a whole. That principle has been officially laid down, as far as Philips, Netherlands, are concerned, in a blanket agreement with the trade unions that can always be revised and renewed if necessary. The authors of a modern social policy in industry know that often it is not "what" but "how" which matters. Everyone understands that conditions in modern society are dynamic and that changes constantly occur, some to people's advantage, some to their disadvantage. As undertakings make more effective use of available up-to-date knowledge when determining their social policy, so, when big changes occur, there will be a more

---

18 On this point, see *inter alia*, Jephcott, *op. cit.*, pp. 169 and 179; Zweig, *loc. cit.*; Mary Zeldenrust Noordanus and G. M. van der Kroon, "Arbeid buitenshuis door vrouwen met gezinsverantwoordelijkheid," in *Sociaal Maandblad Arbeid* (Alphen aan den Rijn), 21st Year, No. 1, 1966, p. 53; I. Gadourek, "Tevredenheid in een welvaartsstaat in een tijd van overvloed," in M. Mulder *et al.*, *Mensen, groepen, organisaties* (Assen, 1963), Part 2, pp. 298ff. and 316; F. I. Nye and L. W. Hoffman, *The Employed Mother in America* (Chicago: Rand McNally, 1963); and A. Kornhauser, *Mental Health of the Industrial Worker* (New York: John Wiley & Sons, 1965).

19 See Jephcott, *op. cit.*, pp. 101 and 109; and Zweig, *loc. cit.*

20 See E. Fromm, *Man for Himself* (London, 1950), pp. 67ff.

thorough search for appropriate procedure of consultation and participation in decision making, since it will be understood that such procedures improve the content of the decisions made, modify their unilateral character, and render them more acceptable and effective. Structural changes in the relative strength of the parties will therefore always be a challenge and a test both of the honesty and of the effectiveness of the social policy in any industrial undertaking.

Another aspect of the above-mentioned second question thrown up by an experiment like that of Veldhoven relates to its effect on future management. The following may be said in this regard.

If the situation of abundance in the Western world is consolidated and intensified, probably the structural tendencies indicated in the introduction to the present article will continue and increase in strength. What is now done as, and felt to be, an experiment in an unusual situation for a special class of workers may well turn out also to have had the function of a trial run for a new kind of approach that may soon need to be used on a wider scale for larger classes of workers. Opposing trends—such as shortage of manpower and shorter hours of work on the one hand, capital-intensive automation with an increasing need for continuous operation on the other —are pushing us toward new systems of shift work for all industrial employees. The new shift systems will necessarily comprise four, five, six or even more shifts in each cycle, so that the plant can operate continuously, while each individual has more leisure. Individuals will then be able to combine two jobs more easily, and such combinations are therefore likely to become a widespread phenomenon. Old conceptions of the monolithic undertaking will have to give way all the more rapidly to modern conceptions of the undertaking as a pluralistic whole with complex objectives that can best be served by co-operation between the component parts on the basis of their relative autonomy, these parts being the various functional sectors and interest groups each retaining its own structure and values.[21] Managers of industrial undertakings and other employing units must learn even more thoroughly that social policy in the broadest sense of the term is of no less crucial significance to the success of the unit than its technical and commercial policy.

Consequently, research and a scientific approach will be just as im-

---

[21] See, for example, F. Furstenberg, *Wirtschaftssoziologie* (Berlin, 1961), pp. 52 and 62; J. G. March and H. A. Simon, *Organizations* (New York: John Wiley and Sons, 1958), p. 121; M. Haire, "The Concept of Power and the Concept of Man," in G. B. Strother *et al., Social Science Approaches to Business Behavior* (Homewood, Illinois: Dorsey Press, 1962), p. 163; W. Brown, *Explorations in Management* (London: Heinemann, 1960), pp. 232ff.; R. Dahrendorff, *Gesellschaft und Freiheit* (Munich, 1963), p. 161; W. S. Ross, "Organized Labor and Management," in *Human Relations and Modern Management* (Amsterdam, 1958), p. 101; L. van Outrive, "Deelname aan de macht in de onderneming," in R. F. Beerling *et al., Arbeid, vrije tijd, creativiteit* (The Hague, 1964), p. 64; Likert, *op. cit.;* and F. Voigt and W. Weddigen, *Zur Theorie und Praxis der Mitbestimmung* (Berlin, 1962).

portant in the preparation, testing, correction, and development of a social policy as they already are at the technical and commercial levels.[22] The trade unions movements in the various countries concerned will also have to reorient their policies substantially so as to improve their position vis-à-vis their members and the members and the employers at a time of abundance and individualization.[23] This will become necessary as larger groups of persons are enabled, within their own field, to compose individually appropriate combinations of part-time jobs.

A third question posed by the Veldhoven experiment is none the less intriguing because it is mentioned last. What may be the effect of the experiment for workers in general and for society? To the individual worker such a development brings the opportunity for more intrinsic freedom and independence while doing a given job with a given employer, and also the opportunity to play a more varied role in society and to achieve greater self-expression.[24]

It is not possible, within the limits of the present article, to go into the opportunities and risks of this perspective, which may only be described here as a challenge to the individual citizen to seek with fresh zeal an appropriate development of his personality, his ideals, and his social and political responsibility.

This kind of social reality may already be discerned on the horizon as perhaps the most likely to emerge in the not too distant future.

Discussion Questions

1. How would you evaluate the position of women in the economy of the Soviet Union?
2. Independent of such factors as political freedom, would you regard the American or Soviet woman as having greater options as an economic entity?
3. Discuss the Dutch experiment with part-time female employment.
4. Do you think the Dutch experiment is worth transferring to the United States?

---

22 See, for example, Bennis, *op. cit.,* pp. 179ff.; and Van Zuthem, *op. cit.*

23 See W. Albeda: "Vakbeweging in een veranderende wereld," in *Evangelie en Maatschappij* (Utrecht), September 1960, November 1960, May 1963 and March 1965; P. J. A. Ter Hoeven, *Arbeiderprotest en vakbeweging* (Leiden, 1963); I. P. van Leerdam, J. G. Lulofs, C. Poppe and H. Wallenburg, *Vakbeweging in beweging* (Meppel, 1964); C. Poppe, "De vakbond in het bedrijf," in *N.I.O. Bo-kwartaalbericht* (Breukelen), 8th Year, No. 32, 1966, p. 15; M. van de Vall: *De vakbeweging in de welvaartsstaat* (Meppel, 1963), pp. 102–103; and *Vakbeweging en onderneming* (The Hague: A.N.M.B.-Publikatie, 1965), pp. 18ff.

24 See, for example, R. F. Behrendt, *Dynamische Gesellschaft* (Berne, 1964); Fourastier, *op. cit.;* E. Fromm, *The Sane Society* (New York: Rinehart, 1956); and E. Zahn, *Leven met de welvaart* (Amsterdam, 1962).

Urban Development

America is an urban country. The profound structural change and industrial growth in the United States in the past century has wrought many miracles. The growth of cities around natural areas for commerce, shipping, and finance, has produced not only high levels of affluence, but also meccas of culture: symphonies, museums, and ballets. But growth, as was pointed out earlier, has its costs, and our urban areas speak in perverse eloquence of a distasteful ugliness. Our cities are marked by the "ghettoization" of the black and white poor, areas crowded with people whose sense of desperation and alienation have at times turned the cities into nightmares of rebellion. The streets of many cities, crowded a decade ago with people enjoying the amusements of the night life, have become empty and are viewed as unsafe. City fathers, more concerned with maximizing their tax base than with esthetics, have permitted the rape of their skyline, and the term "Manhattanization" has crept into the vocabulary of city planners who fear that a haphazard construction of downtown buildings will turn their city into an architectural hodgepodge. Driving into downtown New York or Chicago's Loop and home again in the evening demands the patience of Job and is surely an act of courage. The product of industrialization has become a polluted atmosphere and the city sky can be grey even when the sun is out. In short, America's cities have become the least desirable places in this country to live, and the oft-referred to flight to the suburbs is evidence of this repulsion.

It is far easier to criticize what has happened in America's cities than to find solutions; there are no facile answers available. Western Europe has encountered many of the same kinds of problems that our cities have experienced. The two articles in this section demonstrate that America can learn a great deal from the European experience. John Garvey's article provides something of a potpourri of West European attempts to deal with some of these problems. The article by David N. Kinsey describes French efforts to deal with a common U.S. problem, the concentration of economic and related activities in certain major cities.

John Garvey, Jr. is Deputy Executive Director of the National League of Cities and an Associate Editor of Nation's Cities. David N. Kinsey is a *graduate student at the Woodrow Wilson School of Public and International Affairs, Princeton University.*

The French Z.U.P. Technique of Urban Development

DAVID N. KINSEY

An important part of the present French national urbanization policy is the "Z.U.P." (*zone à urbaniser de priorité*) or Priority Urban Development Zone. The new community at Hérouville, outside of Caen, in Normandy, is an example of this innovative French technique for organizing urban development, using a mix of the public and private sectors. Comparison with British and American new town development suggests that it may be possible to transfer some of the Z.U.P.s financial and administrative techniques.

French Urbanization Policy

A basic problem of French urbanization stems from the extraordinarily massive concentration of national activities in Paris and the resulting lack of substantial regional development. This can be attributed to the long tradition of administrative centralization initiated by Louis XIV and Napoleon. Continuing rapid growth in the Paris region has not only drawn down development levels in the rest of France, it has also caused a large shortage of housing and public services in Paris.

Present-day French policy for the Paris region, the 1965 *Schéma Directeur d'Aménagement et d'Urbanisme de la Région de Paris,* or Strategic Plan, was prepared by the Délégation Générale au District de la Région de Paris, a special administrative agency directed by Paul Delouvrier, the Prime Minister's special delegate and first prefect of the Paris Region. Its jurisdiction extends over 5,000 square miles in a 40- to 60-mile radius from Notre Dame. Its primary role is co-ordinating the implementation of its plans for the future of the Paris region. The *Schéma* proposes an axial pattern of growth along a double axis straddling the Seine, from Paris toward Rouen, Le Havre, and Caen. The backbones of the double axis are railway lines and limited-access superhighways. The railway has been electrified to Le Havre and a turbotrain provides swift service to Caen. The superhighways should be completed in the 1970s. The banks of the Seine will be

Reprinted by permission of the *Journal of the American Institute of Planners,* Vol. 35, No. 6. November 1969, pp. 370–375, and by the author. This selection was revised for this volume by Mr. Kinsey.

protected as a giant recreation zone while new communities are created on both the northern and southern plateaux of the river. According to this plan, Paris will provide the same number of jobs, while the new urban centers will offer new jobs as well as residential facilities. The master plan will prohibit further expansion of today's shapeless dormitory-suburbs and will create along the Seine double axis at least eight completely equipped new towns with populations from 35,000 to 300,000. The plan also calls for renovating several existing urban centers, providing an intensive system of regional transportation, restructuring the region's activity, and satisfying recreational and cultural needs for the region's projected 14 million inhabitants. The *Schéma* attempts to relieve much of the congestion of the Paris region. It is a decentralization plan, but it recognizes and capitalizes upon the great attractive power of Paris by diverting new growth into the double axis. Caen and its semi-satellite of Hérouville are at the western terminus of the southern axis designated by the *Schéma*.

The Fifth Plan (1966–1970), approved in 1965, proposed a policy of eight *métropoles d'équilibre,* or regional metropolises, to provide a balance to the attraction of Paris and to stimulate economic development in the provinces. These *métropoles* are loosely-defined urban complexes where renovated central cities, new business and housing centers, and selected national investments in key sectors should promote regional growth around that particular center.

Caen is not an independent *métropole d'équilibre;* it is too closely tied to Paris. However, Caen is most definitely the regional center for the sub-region known as Lower Normandy. The *métropole d'équilibre* policy calls for several of these smaller regional centers to be equipped as relay centers between Paris and the distant provinces. Thus, the growth of Caen and centers such as Rouen, Dijon, Limoges, and Clermont-Ferrand will also be encouraged by national investments.

A third segment of French urbanization policy concerns the large cities —such as Caen, Rouen, Le Mans, Tours, Orléans, Reims, and Amiens— in the Paris Basin, the area within 200 miles of Paris. The Basin includes the Paris Region covered by the 1965 *Schéma* and six other administrative regions: Basse-Normandie, Haute-Normandie, Picardie, Champagne, Bourgogne, and Centre. The past growth of these regions and their principal cities has been thwarted by the attraction of commercial and industrial activity to Paris.

Decentralization policies in the early 1960s stimulated growth in the Basin. As a result, the development of regional centers in the Basin was proposed as an alternative or complementary policy to the *métropole d'équilibre* and *Schéma* plans to check the growth of the Paris region. Such an effort would reduce the net outmigration from the Basin to Paris by attracting people from the rest of France to the Basin itself.

The Sixth Plan (1970–1975) does not make explicit the relative priorities for investments to be made among: (1) new towns for the Paris

Region proposed by the *Schéma*, (2) the eight *métropoles d'léquilibre* and their sub-regional centers, and (3) the cities of the Paris Basin. In any case, the satellite city of Hérouville fulfills the two goals of French urbanization policy, decentralization and the development of regional centers, as it contributes to the three alternate or complementary programs of that policy: (1) it is at the western terminus of the *Schéma's* growth axis, (2) it improves the position of Caen as a sub-regional center for the *métropoles d'équilibre*, and (3) it greatly strengthens Caen's position as a major center in the Paris Basin.

The Z.U.P. Technique

The French government, despite its strongly national form, promotes its urbanization policy by stimulating local authorities, not assuming their roles. The national government provides the financial assistance and increased legal powers necessary for planned urban development. The most important French vehicle for structuring such development is the Z.U.P. technique. A Z.U.P., or *zone à urbaniser de priorité*, is a housing zone whose development is entrusted by a commune (the commune is the basic unit of local administration, similar to a township) to a special development corporation. A Z.U.P. can be thought of as a "semi-satellite," but not a "new town." In January 1967, there were 173 such Z.U.P.s in France, covering 59,000 acres with a capacity for 740,000 dwelling units. The purpose of a Z.U.P. is clearly defined in the Z.U.P. legislation:

A decree of the Minister of Construction can designate a Z.U.P. in those communes and agglomerations where the importance of housing projects will necessitate the creation, strengthening, or extension of public services.

Essential public services are schools, roads, utilities, social, commercial, administrative, and cultural centers. Local and national government authorities recognize that they must furnish most of these services sooner or later during the life of a housing project. A Z.U.P. is delimited so that the arrangement of services and dwellings in a new housing zone will be co-ordinated and organized from the earliest planning stages and the life of its inhabitants will be as normal as possible. This concern for quality and variety of life in a new development, the desire to co-ordinate provision of public services, and the wish to avoid disorderly development are the main purposes of the Z.U.P. technique.

A Z.U.P. may be created by the Minister of Construction, acting at the request of an interested commune, or by a decree of the Council of State. If a Z.U.P. is deemed necessary for the development of a particular region, the prefect of the region, an appointed civil servant-governor, may ask a commune to request a Z.U.P. The request may also be initiated by the commune. A Z.U.P. must lie within one commune's borders, otherwise administrative and legal difficulties arise.

Local authorities are given strong development tools by the Z.U.P. legislation. As soon as the decree delimiting the Z.U.P. is published in the *Journal Officiel,* all new construction—financed by the state—of more than 100 dwelling units in that commune must be built within the delimited zone. A developer of housing outside the Z.U.P. may also be refused a building permit if his intended site is not sufficiently equipped with public services and if an equally suitable site is offered to him within the Z.U.P. The existence of a Z.U.P concentrates housing construction in one sector of a commune so that a comprehensive plan with reasonable costs for necessary public services can be prepared, financed, and implemented.

Local authorities are given the right of pre-emption, or the first option for the purchase of any ground put up for sale in the Z.U.P. within a period of four years—which may be extended for two years—from the date of the decree delimiting the Z.U.P. If the land cannot be purchased by mutual consent, then the purchase price is fixed by regular condemnation procedures. These land acquisition powers limit the land speculation that accompanies any housing project and permit a commune to purchase the land necessary for planned urban development.

Using the Z.U.P. technique to create a viable urban center is an awesome task for many local authorities. Therefore, the definition, development, and management of a Z.U.P. is entrusted to a specialized corporate body that has the necessary administrative and technical services. This body or authority is either a public establishment or a semi-public corporation dedicated to carrying out projects of public interest or operating public services. The latter is known under French law as a *société d'économie-mixte.* At least 50 percent of the capital of a *société d'économie-mixte* must be held by local authorities, such as communes or departments (a large territorial unit of government).

Specialized public financial institutions and private banks provide from 30 percent to 40 percent of the capital, with the rest coming from private and local interests. Activities of these development corporations include: national food distribution markets, superhighways, regional improvement projects, and, of course, urban development.

Financing a Z.U.P.

Z.U.P. status of a development project confers financial advantages on the local government authority. The financial plan for a Z.U.P. must be approved by Committee 2b of the Economic and Social Development Fund (*Fonds de Développement Economique et Social* or FDES) of the Ministry of Finance, before any construction can begin. (See Table 1.)

Financing options available are: (1) loans from the National Land

Table 1. Sources of National Financial Aid for Z.U.P. Construction

Source	Description
FNAFU	Loans to the commune for land acquisition and infrastructure.
Ministries	Capital grants to the commune to subsidize the cost of public facilities and infrastructure.
Caisse des Dépôts et Consignations	(a) Loans to the commune for public facilities and infrastructure.
	(b) Subsidized loans for public housing distributed by the Caisse des Prêts aux Organismes HLM.
Crédit Foncier	Subsidized loans for private and co-operative housing.

Management and Urban Planning Fund, *Fonds National d'Aménagement Foncier et de l'Urbanisme* (FNAFU); (2) capital grant subsidies from national ministries; and (3) loans from the *Caisse des Dépôts et Consignations* and *Crédit Foncier.*

The FNAFU is a special inter-ministry loan-granting fund responsible for land use policy and basic urban infrastructure. It grants loans to local authorities for acquiring land and equipping it with roads and utilities. Loans are made directly to the developing authority, usually a *société d'économie-mixte,* but the commune creating the zone must guarantee the loans. The loans are for two years at 2.5 percent with a possibility of two renewals totaling six years. These loans are repaid by the developing authority as soon as the land of a Z.U.P. has been acquired, equipped, and its lots sold to builders. FNAFU acts as a powerful catalyst for construction of new urban centers by granting loans for land acquistion and most of the infrastructure.

A second source of general construction money is the direct capital construction subsidy of particular facilities by appropriate national ministries. The proportion of these subsidies to the total cost of the particular public facility depends on the facility and the value the national government places on having it included in the Z.U.P. For example, subsidies cover 65 percent of the capital cost of school construction.

A third major source of loan money is the powerful *Caisse des Dépôts et Consignations,* a specialized nationally-owned and managed credit institution which turns short-term savings from savings banks, and pension and insurance funds into long-term credit for government-supported projects such as the development of infrastructure and the construction of public facilities. A commune can borrow from the *Caisse* to finance the local share of capital investments, with loans at 5.25 percent (1962) to 7.25 percent (1971) interest for 15 to 30 years, repaid out of increased local revenues stimulated by population increases from Z.U.P. construction.

Financing land acquisition and infrastructure is necessary so that land can be sold to housing promoters and builders of public facilities. Although most of these costs should be borne by users of the land in order to develop the land to the point where builders will buy lots, someone must pay for the costs of land acquisition and infrastructure. On the average 75 percent of initial costs are borne by land users—25 percent come from public construction corporations and 50 percent come from housing. The remaining 25 percent is evenly divided between direct subsidy from the state and the share assigned to the commune.

French Housing Policy

Because of war damage, age, and increased population, at least 12 million new dwelling units are needed in France in the next 20 years. This is the basic French national housing policy goal. While many of these units are being built in Z.U.P. sectors, there are still three kinds of housing in France: social, private, and co-operative. Social housing, known as 'H.L.M.' or *habitation à loyer modéré* (moderate rental housing), is either publicly or semi-publicly organized and seeks no profits. Private housing, built for profits, may be for rent or for sale as private property, joint property (*la copropriété*), or condominium. Co-operatives, organized to eliminate the profit motive, generally build housing that is superior to most social housing. The national government implements its housing policy by making available several means of financial support(Table 2).

Table 2. Sources of Housing Construction Funds in France

| | Principle Sector Served | | |
Source	Social	Private	Co-operative
Caisse des Prêts aux Organismes HLM	X		
Crédit Foncier		X	X
Employers' 1 percent payroll tax	X	X	X
Private banks	X	X	X

There are four main sources of housing construction funds in France. The first is the *Caisse des Prêts aux Organismes H.L.M.*, a public credit institution owned, funded, and operated by the *Caisses des Dépôts et Consignations*. It grants up to 95 percent of the cost of social housing in 40-year loans at 2.6 percent interest.

The chief source of subsidized loans for private housing is the *Crédit Foncier,* a semi-public bank (a privately-owned joint-stock company with government-appointed directors) which lends funds, in addition to its capital and deposits, raised by issuing debentures. Its loans are made at below market conditions, but they may only cover 30 percent to 50 percent of construction costs. A third source of funds is the *cotisation patronale,* or 1 percent employer's payroll tax, a device requiring all employers of more than 10 employees to invest annually in housing a sum equal to 1 percent of the salaries they have paid during the preceding year. A final major source of construction money is private banks, although they make loans at an expensive interest rate, 10 percent–15 percent, for 12 to 15 years.

Implementation: The Z.U.P. Technique at Hérouville

With a basic understanding of the Z.U.P. technique, we can look at its first major trial at Hérouville. In late 1959, the regional prefect decided to transform a rural village of 1,300 inhabitants in Caen's suburbs into a definitely urban new community for 35,000 residents as part of a regional growth strategy. Caen was 75 percent destroyed in the 1944 invasion of Normandy. The city was largely rebuilt by 1958, but economic development had lagged. The growth strategy called for a limited-access by-pass to connect several housing and industrial zones in Caen's suburbs, and then join the Paris-Normandy superhighway. On March 25, 1960 the Municipal Council of the Hérouville commune accepted the prefect's suggestion to build the largest housing zone in the Caen area. On October 19, 1960 the decree delimiting the Z.U.P. at Hérouville was published. A national competition for the master plan was announced in December 1960, and the winners, the *Union des Architectes-Urbanistes* (UAU) of Paris, were chosen in February 1962. The master plan, as defined by the *Société d'Equipment de la Lasse-Normandie* (SEBN), a *société d'économie-mixte* which is the development corporation for the Hérouville Z.U.P., and as designed by the UAU, calls for the creation of a completely equipped town for 35,000 people in 8,000 dwelling units on 740 acres of former fields. There will be 18 schools for a student population of 11,610 as well as a small commercial center, a local community center, and a youth house in each of the five residential neighborhoods. Churches, dispensary, post office, administrative center, recreation facilities, dormintories for the nearby university, cinema, regional department store, hotel, cafes, banks, and all kinds of shops and offices are planned in addition to dwellings. Construction began in November 1963; one year later the first families moved in. The final financing plan of the Hérouville Z.U.P. was approved by Committee 2b of the FDES in June 1964.

The first school opened in 1965, and by October 1971 the population of the commune had reached 25,000. By January 1972 72 percent of the originally programmed 8,000 dwelling units had been completed. The Master Plan was revised in 1971 after the March 1971 municipal elections and a re-examination of the development corporation's cash-flow problems. Instead of 8,000 dwelling units, 8,600 units are now programmed for the Z.U.P. Housing construction is expected to be finished by 1974, although some public facilities will not be completed before 1976.

Financing the Hérouville Z.U.P.

The total cost of the Hérouville new community was estimated at $184.7 million in 1971. Roughly $98 million, or 53 percent, of the total cost, is contributed by the national government as either a direct capital grant, subsidized loan to the commune of Hérouville, or subsidized housing loan. The major share of land acquisition and infrastructure costs is included in the price of construction lots purchased by public and private builders. However, the state directly contributes 40 percent of the infrastructure cost through loan and grant programs. The estimated $23 million capital cost of publicly financed education, social, administrative, and cultural facilities is met by direct capital grants from national ministries and a local share, which is financed by *Caisse des Dépôts* loans to the commune of Hérouville. On the average, the national ministries provide 65 percent or an estimated $15 million of the capital cost of public facilities. The total cost of the 8,600 dwelling units of housing is estimated at $100 million, resulting in a low unit cost of $11,600. Loans from state-owned banks finance nearly 60 percent of housing construction. There is some state aid for commercial-office and miscellaneous construction, but there is none for the industrial zone. The sources of the $97.8 million state aid include ministerial capital grants and FNAFU, *Caisse des Dépôts,* and *Crédit Foncier* loans. Ministerial capital grants total $20.6 million, only 21.1 percent of total aid, and a mere 10.1 percent of the total cost of construction. The difference between state aid and total construction cost is met with private funds. (See Table 3.)

A Critique of the Z.U.P. Technique

The Z.U.P. technique of urban development has advantages and disadvantages on both national and local levels. Nationally, it permits establishment of priorities for government financing of urban infrastructure and choice of sites for new developments throughout France, in short, a *national industrial development and urbanization plan*. This system of priorities is effective in reducing dispersion of new buildings and high cost of public utilities resulting from such dispersion.

One disadvantage at the national level is the problem of allocation of national investments. A fixed amount of national resources, subsidies, and loans is available for distribution to all urban development projects. Since the strikes in May and June 1968 and the austerity measures after the *franc* crises in November 1968 and August 1969, there are fewer resources available for Z.U.P.s, and progress will be delayed.

The state has three alternative polities it can follow: (1) concentrate its capital investments in a few Z.U.P. developments to equip them quickly and completely; (2) distribute its capital investments widely and sparsely in order to reach a large population; or (3) take a middle-ground stance. Politically this is a moot question, and the obvious, predictable choice is

Table 3. Estimated Construction Cost of the Hérouville Z.U.P. and National Financial Aid

Category	Total capital cost (millions of dollars)	Form of aid	Total aid (millions of dollars)	National aid (percent of total cost)
Land acquisition and planning	3.4	FNAFU advances	1.9	56
Infrastructure	29.3	FNAFU loans Ministerial capital grants Caisse des Dépôts loans for local share	2.8 4.6 4.5	40
Public facilities	23.0	Ministerial capital grants Caisse des Dépôts loans for local share	15.0 8.0	90–10 10–90
Commercial-office space, miscellaneous	14.0	Caisse des Dépôts loans	2.0	14
Industrial zone	15.0	—	—	—
Housing (a) Public	30.0	Caisse des Prêts aux Organismes d'HLM loans to HLM housing promoters	29.0	95
(b) Private	70.0	Crédit Foncier loans, varying from 30–50 percent of construction cost	30.0	43
Totals	$184.7 million		$97.8 million	53

the second alternative. However, in a centralized national administration somewhat removed from provincial pressures, economic planners may prevail over politicians. Such was the case at Hérouville. The Z.U.P. at Hérouville was the first major one in France and the first to benefit from a national competition for its master plan. Normandy has the highest emigration in France and greatly needed the economic boost of a well-equipped Z.U.P. A *mystique* about Hérouville developed in Paris in the early 1960s, and promises of large capital grants and loans were made by the ministries. However, not all the promises were kept. Theoretically, by promoting the Z.U.P. technique the state commits itself to financing much new urban development and thus strains its resources.

Another disadvantage at the national level is an expected lack of strict inter-ministry co-operation and commitment on subsidies. Although Committee 2b of the FDES must approve the financing plan, individual ministries may renege on their agreements to subsidize projects. At Hérouville subsidies were actually granted an average of eighteen months later than they had been promised; on some projects the amount of the subsidy was reduced. The development corporation, the SEBN, could do nothing about these delays or changes except wait and hope for the best. As a result, the social centers, youth centers, some schools, and the Z.U.P. center were not ready for the first residents.

There are many advantages for local authorities in the Z.U.P. technique. Land acquisition is merely an administrative process. The development corporation is given sufficient powers and access to funds to do its work efficiently. The financial plan is coherently organized, and the master plan receives the aesthetic consideration of the *Conseil Supérieur d'Urbanisme et d'Architecture.* Every effort is made to create an environment where the inhabitants will be adequately housed and serviced and happy.

There are, however, disadvantages at the local level. A small commune with a Z.U.P. is dependent on the state. Its debt is monumental due to its extensive contribution to infrastructure and public facility costs. In the future it can expect increased operating costs—balanced, however, by increased tax receipts. It has no real flexibility and cannot break away from national control because of financial limitations. In order to receive a national subsidy to cover municipal budget deficits, the commune must make economies in its local operations, according to dictates of the state.

By 1969 the growth rate of the Hérouville Z.U.P. began to decrease. New housing starts dropped, in part due to the poor economic health of the Caen area. Also, new housing was not concentrated in the Hérouville 'Priority' zone; instead it sprawled and dispersed itself in all directions around Caen. The strong governmental backing that was responsible for initiating the Z.U.P. dissipated. Changes in political winds affected the operation's progress. By 1971 both the development corporation and the commune faced difficult cash-flow problems. FNAFU and *Caisse des Dépôts* loan payments were overdue. The Z.U.P.s financial planning experienced a major revision in 1971–1972.

Yet, in spite of these difficulties and the disadvantages of the Z.U.P. technique, the system has worked in Hérouville. There are thousands of families who are better housed than they were before living in Hérouville. They have a better than average level of services and amenities. Life in Hérouville could be better, but it certainly is not bad.

In short, a Z.U.P. is a strange combination of: (1) public initiative that creates the zone; (2) public capital that finances infrastructure, public facilities, and housing loans; (3) private capital that seeks profits; and (4) various organizations that construct the new urban center. Unquestionably it is an example of a modern mixed economy.

Comparison with American Experience

American planners are sufficiently aware of Swedish and British development techniques, but French methods are less known. A comparison of French Z.U.P. technique with American experience at Columbia, Maryland, may reveal Z.U.P.s utility as a means of structuring urban development. In the Columbia case, one finds that: (1) there was no applicable national urbanization policy; (2) land acquisition without expropriation powers was expensive and had to be very secretive; (3) the Rouse organization was effective as a developing authority but had no help from the national government; (4) relations with local authorities of Howard County were good because of the skill of the Rouse organization; (5) Columbia was adequately financed, again with no credit due the national government; and (6) the human environment was well-planned and is succeeding. However, Columbia is the exception rather than the rule in the U.S.A.

The Hackensack Meadowlands Development Commission, created in January 1969 by the state of New Jersey, is another American approach to the challenge of urban development. Nearly 18,000 acres of vacant meadows lie in the heart of the New York metropolitan area, north of Newark, New Jersey. Problems of low elevation, tidal flooding, conflicting ownership claims, political fragmentation, pollution, and garbage have impeded development for many years. The Hackensack Meadowlands Development Commission has the strong planning, title-settling, tax-sharing and financial powers necessary to solve these problems and coherently develop the valuable Meadowlands. This commission's development technique is much like the Z.U.P. methods. It, too, is a combination of public initiative, public capital and bonds, and private capital. However, this commission is a unique approach to a unique problem. It is too early to see how well it will work. Nevertheless, its general principles: (1) tax-sharing and regional planning to supersede political fragmentation; (2) independent financial capability; and (3) strong land-use and development controls, are applicable in other situations as the Z.U.P. technique is applicable throughout France.

An encouraging note on the part of the federal government is Title IV,

"Land Development and New Communities," of the Demonstration Cities and Metropolitan Development Act of 1966 and the New Community Development Act of 1970. Title IV expanded the Federal Housing Administration (FHA) mortgage insurance program for privately financed land development by (1) authorizing the Secretary of the Department of Housing and Urban Development (HUD) to insure mortgages to finance "new communities," and (2) increasing the maximum amount of mortages permitted.

Under the 1970 Act the following new communities have federally-guaranteed financing: Jonathan, Minnesota ($21 million), Maumelle, Arkansas ($7.5 million), St. Charles Communities, Maryland ($24 million), Park Forest South, Illinois ($30 million), Flower Mart, Texas ($18 million), and Cedar Riverside, Minnesota ($24 million). There is a ceiling of $50 million on any single guarantee per new community. Total guarantees may not exceed $250 million each year. The Z.U.P. technique is superior to the American efforts to encourage new community development, since the French policy includes much more than loan guarantees.

Given the differences between U.S. and French economic and social settings, is the Z.U.P. technique a feasible prototype for structuring urban development in America? The French setting is a modern welfare economy with strong capitalistic and socialistic tendencies. The American setting has produced limited socially oriented legislation in spite of the residual belief in the conventional wisdom of American laissez-faire capitalism. We do have considerable experience with a mixed economy. Yet the Z.U.P. technique, depending as it does on extensive national financial commitments through direct subsidies for public services and massive loans from national credit institutions, is *not* directly applicable in the American setting until several changes are made. Since 1937, it has been generally conceded that the federal government is primarily responsible for promoting the general welfare. If the federal government finally takes vigorous action meeting that responsibility, by providing direct subsidies for educational, social, community, administrative, cultural, health, youth, and recreational facilities and by a strong financial commitment to a national housing policy, then American success with the Z.U.P. technique is possible. The Z.U.P. technique could be best used for concentrating development in new urban centers such as Columbia, Maryland, as opposed to allowing unguided growth to occur around metropolitan areas. For example, a modification of the Z.U.P. technique could be used to implement construction of the 100 new communities proposed in 1969 for the United States by the year 2000 by the National Committee on Urban Growth Policy or the Growth Units proposed in 1972 by the American Institute of Architects' National Policy Task Force.

In short, the Z.U.P. technique is a well-organized administrative and financial formula for structuring urban development. National priorities and urban investments are organized; land acquisition is facilitated; strong development corporations are created; and complete financing is arranged on generous terms at the national level. Unless political, economic, and administrative factors stall the progress of a Z.U.P., development can proceed guaranteeing that new housing projects will be served by the public facilities necessary to permit growth of a complete city.

Postscript: From Z.U.P to Z.A.C.

The Z.U.P. technique fell under criticism in 1968. A survey of Z.U.P.s throughout France showed that the cost to promoters of improved land in a Z.U.P. was much higher than improved land elsewhere, due to the high standards of Z.U.P. infrastructure development. As a consequence, the Z.U.P.s "filled up" slowly, causing cash-flow problems and modifying their social composition. The proportion of public HLM housing, which was to be limited to an average of 40 percent of a Z.U.P.s dwelling units, often reached 60 percent–70 percent since private promoters preferred to build elsewhere—and governmental authorities acquiesced. Thus the financial planning statements for all existing Z.U.P.s were to be revised in 1968, and future Z.U.P.s were to meet market demand, location, and profitability criteria.

The Z.A.C. (*zone d'aménagement concerté*)—Concerted Development Zone—technique then modified and has now replaced the Z.U.P. technique. The Z.A.C. technique incorporates changes in the ground rules governing French urban development. Theoretically, administrative red tape is reduced as the locus of decision making is decentralized from Paris to the prefects for all Z.A.C.s of under 10,000 dwelling units. Secondly, the definition of appropriate developers has been broadened to include private, profit-oriented individuals and corporations, as well as the traditional commune and development corporation of the Z.U.P. technique.

Unlike the Z.U.P., the iniative for creating a Z.A.C. may come from the national as well as the local government. In fact, for exceptional circumstances the national government may create, finance, and build a Z.A.C. over local opposition.

The decree creating a Z.A.C. defines its perimeter, and names the type of developer chosen. A Z.A.C. may be developed by either a commune itself, a development corporation with a concession from a commune, or a private, profit-oriented developer.

The developer must present three documents for approval by the authority that legally created the Z.A.C., usually a prefect, before the concession contract is issued: (1) a plan for the provision, financing, and staging of public facilities, specifying the developer's share of the capital investment, (2) an estimated financial plan, including cash-flow analysis, and (3) a land-use plan (P.A.Z.—*plan d'aménagement de la zone*). The land-use plan must include existing land-use restrictions (right-of-ways) and American-style zoning regulations (land-use, densities, building heights, site occupation coefficients). The Z.U.P. technique required a specific master physical plan for the zone; the Z.A.C. requires only a general, looser zoning regulation. The estimated financial plan is similar to the Z.U.P. financial plan presented to the FDES, which also examined the public facility program for a Z.U.P. However, FDES approval is only necessary for large Z.A.C.s of greater than 10,000 dwelling units.

Land acquisition for a Z.A.C. proceeds in the same manner as for a Z.U.P., except that there is no right of pre-emption in a Z.A.C. However, a private developer with a Z.A.C. concession cannot directly condemn land that he cannot acquire on the open market. But a commune or development corporation may condemn the needed land and transfer title to the private developer as long as the transfer price is at least equal to the condemnation cost plus expenses. This major change in the ground rules gives private developers access to condemnation power when it is needed to assemble large sites.

Front-money to finance land acquisition and early development expenses is available to public Z.A.C. developers, just as in the Z.U.P. technique. The *Caisse des Dépôts* now offers six-year loans at 6 percent with a 3-year deferred repayment. The national government guarantees most of these loans, so that developers pay only 3 percent interest. The loan-granting procedure for *Caisse des Dépôts* loans is decentralized to the regional prefects who thus have the power to create a Z.A.C. and distribute *Caisse des Dépôts* loans to acquire and improve the land. Private Z.A.C. developers do not benefit from the low-interest *Caisse* loans; the Z.A.C. technique presumes the existence of a large private investment capital market. Private Z.A.C. developers do not have access to the $34 million annual short-term *Caisse des Dépôts* credit used by development corporations which are subsidiaries of the *Société Centrale pour l'Equipement du Territoire* (SCET—a subsidiary of the *Caisse des Dépôts*). This short-term credit keeps the cash-flow moving.

The financing of public capital investments in Z.A.C. infrastructure depends upon the nature and location of the investment, as in a Z.U.P. Prefects decide upon the distribution of most capital grants from national ministries for infrastructure construction. However, difficult decisions on major Z.A.C.s are made in Paris. As in a Z.U.P., the capital financing of public community facilities is shared by national ministries and communes. However, certain ministries program their capital grants in a deconcentrated manner—prefects are alloted annual lump sums from which they then program the distribution in their region. The local share of infrastructure and public facilities construction costs is financed, as in the Z.U.P., by long-term *Caisse des Dépôts* loans.

Finally, two contracts govern the realization of a Z.A.C. The concession contract between the commune and the public or private developer defines the local share, developer's share, and expected national capital grant arrangements in the financial planning. Secondly, a contract between the commune and the national government, represented by the prefect, provides a guaranteed schedule for funding the agreed upon capital grants.

By January 1971 there were 217 Z.A.C.s in France, including 53 in the Paris region. There were major policy changes from Z.U.P. to Z.A.C. The private sector is more explicitly included in public-purpose urban development. The national government is making a greater effort to decentralize decision making and co-ordinate public capital investments, so that France can better control her urban development.

———

For complete notes, see the original version of this article in the *Journal of the American Institute of Planners, XXXV*, No. 6, November 1969, p. 375.

What Can Europe Teach Us About Urban Growth?

JOHN GARVEY, JR.

A wealth of urban knowledge in Western Europe is waiting to be shared.

Urban techniques from abroad can be translated, imported, and adapted right here by any American whose mind is not self-confidently closed in the mistaken belief that our country knows all there is to know about urban policy setting and problem solving.

There's a tendency by some to discount European urban experience because of a belief that the problems of the American city have no equal. Discrimination, affluence, race, status, poverty, the impact of the private car, leisure time, urban decay, regionalization, congestion—these are not confined to our country.

There are lessons to be learned in Europe. There's fresh thinking there, too, on urban problems, such as: cities as regional relay centers; abandonment of the sales tax in favor of the value added tax; the determined rebuilding of dying cities; a central city builds a new town, a non-contiguous portion of itself within its own suburban area; a country links redevelopment to expansion; supra-municipalities; a municipal home advisory located in shopping centers; the reconciliation of the cost of public facilities to build-up areas; building "suburbs" within city limits; the concept of the dominant and the subservient community; experiments with old-fashioned, mixed land uses in newly built areas; an area-wide medical data system; the separation of administrative boundaries from political boundaries; the concept of declared growth patterns; a downtown masters the automobile by narrowing, not widening its streets; administrative concepts keyed to the scale and pace of urbanization; and the community trust.

Relationships not yet recognizable in this country—such as the importance of urban efficiency to the national product—are met with effective measures abroad. Other new techniques can be found in such fields as: the role of industry in reaching the goals of a quality environment; the extended city-region single system concept; fringe plans for peripheral growth; the search for a new urban form; relationships of transit to predetermined density; and justifying urban growth investments by a relationship and a co-ordination rationale.

These are all examples of the ways by which the countries of Western Europe are shaking themselves loose from their twentieth century traditionalism. Their sights are now set on their population demands for the year 2000.

Reprinted from *Nation's Cities,* April 1969, pp. 13–18, 31, by permission of the publisher.

The following attempt at a summarization of new ideas and concepts does not do justice to the urban dynamics involved, to the hope and enthusiasm, to the priority importance of urbanization one finds in talking to European officials. Such a summarization reflects, but does not do justice to the most important ingredient of all: the thinking processes and the pioneering spirit of stimulated European officials.

Regional Policies

In Western Europe, an American visitor cannot help but be impressed with a series of determined breakthroughs in developing new regional policies.

Holland is developing its eastern regions to minimize the flow of population into its present great cities and their environs. The less developed eastern regions are being promoted by accelerated public resource development and subsidies to industries.

France is redressing the imbalance created by the high concentration of the Paris metropolitan area by stimulating the growth of eight large provincial urban complexes by 1985. The concept of counter-magnets is being applied to these centers, each free from dependency upon Paris. Priorities will be given to equip each with "high level" facilities for culture, research, higher education, medical care, government, and communications. For each regional metropolis to be effective, it must have relay centers equipped to transmit their influence and that are connected to them by rapid means of communication.

England is pursuing the development of a regional plan for the entire southeast, involving major new cities, expansions of cities, and an enlargement of greenbelts. The concept is to prevent private capital from spreading endlessly to the countryside.

The Netherlands is considering another form of administration, the supra-municipal organization, for the city-region. Under this concept, policy for the city-region can be laid down while maintaining the essential function of the municipal councils. The municipal councils do not lack the strength to fulfill their individual tasks. The missing ingredient, co-ordinated action, would be supplied by the supra-municipal body.

Greater stress is placed upon the importance of a co-ordinated regional attack on the patterns and problems of urbanization by Western European countries than by the United States.

France has a National Commission for Integrated Develpoment, a recognition that the national economy does not expand at the same rate everywhere. It is felt that planning for France must be highly inter-regional. Great stress is placed upon prospective environmental planning and the control of urbanization. Metropolitan areas are viewed twofold: in their urban renewal and their balanced sense.

Sweden is empowered to take the initiative in the formation of regional planning federations. It seeks to achieve desirable economic balance by regions, not by towns within a region. It has formulated the concept of the dominating and the subservient communities, between whom any perfect competition is out of the question.

The Copenhagen regional area is using as the basis of its development a private initiative "finger plan" prepared in 1947. Transit, housing, and other developments are allowed along the fingers with green space preserved between the fingers, permitting open country to push in toward the center of Copenhagen.

In France, consultative bodies advise regional prefects as to economic development and expansion plans.

New Towns

Our conception of new towns may be the types of fringe developments we have seen spring up in our suburbs, particularly since the end of World War II. These one-class neighborhoods with a thin layer of economic variation and no subsidized, low-cost housing are not new towns. New towns are communities of residence and employment, of culture and of recreation, in convenient relation to each other and to existing cities, and usually built with certain environmental objectives in mind.

England has been the pioneer country (since 1946) in new and expanding towns development. Some have the mistaken belief that much of the growth of British urban areas has been resolved by the building of new towns. This is far from a correct impression. Perhaps 5 percent of the growth of population has gone into new and expanding towns so far.

Great Britain's new town program (24 designated since 1946) has been designed mainly to encourage the gradual dispersal of industry and population from congested cities. France's new towns program (eight urban complexes to be equipped as regional metropolises by 1985) was designed mainly to counterbalance the growth of the capital city.

Stockholm's most successful efforts have been in the development of five "sub-communities," or district centers, four within Stockholm's city limits. Dubbed locally as "sleeping towns," these independent suburbs, as they are also called, are light on industry. Each features major shopping facilities, all connected by rapid transit. The fifth sub-community, Järva, is located in portions of five municipalities, one of which is Stockholm. A five-city co-ordinating committee has been founded for acquisition and planning. Järva may eventually become a town of its own.

In the Uusimaa Province of Finland, six national private organizations formed a Housing Foundation which has since assembled three new town sites (Tapiola, Espoo Bay, and Porkkala). Tapiola is now completed and winning international attention for its principles and achievements. The Foundation then proceeded to prepare a comprehensive developmental plan for the entire province to the year 2010, a private initiative plan. In addition to the three new towns, the plan envisions the expansion of four others.

Denmark's concept of new towns is "city sections" with decentralization as the principle objective. These sections are to be linked up with the existing metropolitan area in such a way that the region functions as an integrated whole, permitting easy access to the city center. This "city sections" plan is not similar to the satellite town principle for it is based upon a concept of a great traffic axis, along which are placed large centers with employment and supporting populations.

"Sub-centres" in Amsterdam are reserved for displacement of homes and industries, in keeping with a 15-year decentralization plan (in lobe form) to accommodate overflow. The "city fringe plan," a master plan of future growth, is the basis of city extensions and sub-center developments.

Redirection of Urbanization

Urban sprawl can be controlled, reshaped, thinned out, and redirected. Needless urban spread is being resisted and its trends outwitted in Western European countries. The recipe is not an easy one, for solutions involve greater use of ingredients we are not used to using: preservation of nature by permanent public green space, public ownership of land, greater involvement of the national government in planning and in development decisions.

In the various Western European countries, the national concepts of urban development are largely based upon the same fundamental principles (avoiding excessively high concentrations; developing regional centers, new towns, etc.). The differences are in the methods of implementation. The central problem appears to be a search by each country for ways to control urbanization in an acceptable form.

France uses "priority urbanization zones," which can apply to sections or entire towns to guide the direction of development projects, a method of providing for the financing of public facilities and amenities for the inhabitants. Sweden does not give its landowners an unconditional right to open their properties to dense development. Such requests for development must be found to be in the public interest.

Amsterdam gives recognition to the larger scale on which administrative authorities must think and decide. This has consequences for the administrative organization.

The concept of urban hubs in France is established as a settlement principle in underdeveloped or renovated areas. These hubs, which are to serve populations of 300,000 to 1,000,000 each with a complete range of urban components, are to be located on two major growth axes.

Copenhagen's city center is hoping to retain its existing compact and close-knit character by the carefully planned placement of "city-sections" in the outer reaches of its regional finger plan. The functions and enterprises for which central location is not absolutely essential will be removed.

The design of Stockholm's "sub-communities" has followed traditional concentration of special functions, such as residential areas, industrial areas, commercial, etc. Many people are protesting vigorously, believing such layouts to be dull and unimaginative—even if parks and footpaths connect various sections. They want to go back to the densely built-up, old-fashioned type of town with streets surrounded by shops, entertainment, small industries, etc. Such mixed uses seem more lively and have more diversity, they say.

Amsterdam's regional problem is the need to guide and control the use of space. Without this, there will be a vast area of continuous urban development in which the balance between built-up and unbuilt-up areas will be destroyed.

Denmark's regulation of built-up areas establishes three zones (inner, intermediate, and outer). Lands in the latter can be held a number of years in agricultural use. This zone has also been called a waiting zone. In Denmark, the Ministry of Culture is responsible for the preservation of nature.

Reforming Local Government

Amsterdam is building its own new town (Bijlmermeer), a non-contiguous section to the south of the city's limits, added to Amsterdam by Parliament for the 12-year period of development.

It was felt that the metropolitan area of Helsinki, Finland, should be viewed as a uniform area within which administration should be organized so that activities of a lower character are managed by the communities in the area. The central administration should be responsible for comprehensive duties affecting the area as a whole.

France viewed its traditional, local administrative institutions as a bottleneck to effective regional economic planning and action, and, in 1960 grouped these into 21 districts. In 1961, Sweden outlined a central government proposal whereby 900 local governments would come together in large enough clusters to sustain a diversified economy. The units have been reformed into 282 voluntary linkages and Sweden is now considering setting a target date for compulsory merger of the 282 units.

The Royal Commission on Local Government in England is expected to make its recommendations on the structure of local government this year. The Association of Municipal Corporations, in an effort to break with the traditions of the past, has proposed to the commission that local authorities be empowered to form "community trusts," a flexible, non-structured mechanism, both advisory or policy setting, for local area opinion gathering and decision making, and serving as a focus for local needs and customs.

Revitalization of Dying Municipalities

France attempts to encourage industrial locations near medium-sized towns to maintain a certain degree of job stability in the region.

In Amsterdam, areas suffering from loss of industry, serious unemployment, etc., are rebuilt and expanded.

France is studying ways by which industrial dispersion, together with rural planning, can help small towns and rural centers.

Public Facilities and Services

In Stockholm, five new sub-community developments followed rapid transit lines, rather than the reverse. The object was to first create the density that can support rapid transit, and then string the communities on a radial plan along the transit line.

Stockholm locates branches of its home advisory service program in major shopping centers.

Increasing provision for malls has been made in Swedish cities. A growing consensus shares the view the automobile does not fit into the innermost portions of the city. Measures have been taken to narrow some streets and convert them to malls.

Urban Renewal

France permits "Deferred Planning Zones" to facilitate the implementation of urban renewal projects. A community can take 12-year options on the land it needs for its development projects. In Sweden, such long-range acquisitions may also be designated. Cities can acquire these gradually and may even fix them up for interim occupancy.

Sweden is determined to preserve her urban cores as regional centers, realizing the need for drastic surgery if these cores are to continue to function is administrative, commercial, and cultural centers.

Though urban renewal in Amsterdam costs roughly 10 times as much as urban expansion, the city is determined to give a great deal of attention to the renewal of those quarters which are out of date. Amsterdam draws a close relationship to its renewal and its expansion programs.

Industrial Dispersal

The role of industry, in most Western European countries, is viewed as a helpful instrument in reaching the basic goals of the environment. Special concessions are made, encouraging industrial locations that aid inadequately developed regions.

Housing

We have not yet established the kinds of housing institutions found in Western Europe which are able to plan long-range programs or assume responsibility for continuing development. The many small builders in the U.S. are in no position to conduct meaningful research which only contributes to rising housing costs and shortages of low-income housing. We must revolutionize our housing production.

The Scandinavian countries have outdone us, particularly in advances in the housing industry. In Sweden, two large public co-ops build 25 percent of the housing volume. There, construction workers can count on sustained employment and the trade union itself encourages mechanization.

Municipal Land Policy

Urban land is an extremely valuable resource which we are too careless with. Our philosophies favor a system whereby ownership can be short-lived and speculative and with it, the best interests of the community and the best economic social values. The concept of optimum development of land is in widespread use in Western Europe where land is regulated like a public utility.

In Sweden, Stockholm has been purchasing land for over 60 years and now owns one-third of the original, central city and 85 percent of all the rest as well as much land outside. Because of this ownership, Stockholm has been able to lead building development along rational lines. When municipal properties are developed by private enterprise, the land is leased and not sold.

Municipalities are the largest owners of land in the Netherlands for housing and related purposes, and they buy land long before they develop it. If the acquisition is in accordance with the extension plan, compensation is based on over-all value after development. This has kept the price of land for city extensions low.

Land ownership in Denmark is primarily private though a few municipalities are considerable land owners. An annual land increment tax is levied on the increase of land values. This has not reduced the selling price of land. Since conditions of a seller's market exist, purchasers pay both the full price of land plus the land increment tax. This tax is now being reconsidered since it has been severely criticized.

In France, much of the land is privately owned though in urban areas, the proportion in public ownership is tending to increase. Sweden taxes the profits from property resold within 10 years of its purchase. This tax does not appear to result in a reduction of land prices.

Some local authorities in Great Britain own considerable acres of urban land. A characteristic of land tenure is the use of the leasehold system whereby the free holder grants a substantial interest in land to a leaseholder. This technique is particularly good in redevelopment since local authorities can combine the powers of landlord with those of a planning authority, enabling them to share in financial success, while at the same time attracting private investment.

Fiscal Policies

Indirect taxation on the value-added principle has been gaining ground in recent years. In January, Sweden adopted the value-added tax to replace the sales tax. Practically all Swedish consumption of goods and services will be taxed under the new system, compared to two-thirds of consumption under the sales tax. Principally designed to aid Swedish exports, the tax applies to the value added at each phase of production and distribution (the sales tax was levied only at the sale to the final consumer). This value-added tax, also under consideration in Britain and Norway, has been in effect in Denmark.

In the face of ever increasing land prices, Great Britain created a Land Commission to buy and sell land for development to local authorities and other public developers as well as private developers. In addition, the commission was given the responsibility to collect a betterment levy, amounting to 40 percent of the development value, as imposed on the seller of land. The concept behind the levy is that when the value of, or interest in, a piece of land increases as a result of decisions made by the community (such as the installation of essential services, the granting of planning permissions, etc.), the community is entitled to take at least a share of that development when realized.

To a greater extent than in our country, the local governments of Western Europe depend upon shared revenues from their central governments. This is an increasingly important potential for our state governments for it removes from local governments an over-dependence upon inadequate taxing sources. For example, Amsterdam's tax base is not affected should one of its major industries move outside of its limits. Jobs are not a part of the tax base. This minimizes tendencies of local governments at fiscal zoning and permits locations of industries, jobs, and people based upon economic and social considerations and not fiscal considerations.

What are the major options in public policy available in the coming 20 to 30 years? What do we want to achieve? Where are we headed? Can we control the major trends that shape our future? The countries of Western Europe are giving these questions about their future deep thought. By remaining flexible, they are keeping their options open. They are trying to stay on top of the pace and scale of urbanization.

Ever hear of an organization known as "Group 85"? It's not a choral group, but a high level advisory body in France which has selected 1985 as the significant year in that country's urban, industrial, and agriculture future. The French Man of Tomorrow—his individual, group, and consumption needs—is being calculated closely. The findings are largely dictating guidelines for environmental planning.

How does a country make the best use of its affluence? Sweden is taking a comprehensive look at this question and the effect of its standard of living on its environment. Its visionary officials are also considering the three-dimensional city, attempting to capture the potential of the state of building technology.

In Great Britain, local authorities are required to prepare 20-year development plans, to be reviewed at least once every five years. Local communes prepare five-year flexible plans in Sweden. As far back as 1935, Amsterdam took a comprehensive look at future policies on the use of land, with population and other projections to 2000. Called the General Extension Plan, its projections have since been revised.

The planning policy of the Netherlands "is in keeping with the position the year 2000 already occupies in the minds of people in different walks of life." Though it is difficult to form a reliable picture of the changes about to occur in the present system of values and standards, such uncertainties do not relieve a person of the duty to look ahead, according to Netherlands policy.

Paris maps out guidelines to 2000 within which it sets specific goals to be reached in 10-year increments. It is accompanied by an investment plan under which work is started on infrastructure—highways, parking, rail, water, colleges—in order to lay the groundwork for guiding urban development toward the longer-term targets.

Denmark has 36 town development boards, each made up of a number of municipalities. Each must prepare a general pattern of development for 15 years. Such planning permits growth by stages, reconciling costs of needed public facilities.

Conclusion

The observations in this article are taken from a 17-day travel and study visit last fall to six Western European countries: Denmark, Finland, France, Great Britain, The Netherlands, and Sweden. The visit, under the auspices of the Commission on Urban Growth, concentrated on new town inspections. This summarization is based on those observations plus information obtained from as many meetings on the side as the travel schedule would permit with national municipal association representatives, municipal and national officials, professional local government and new town corporation officers, labor, business and academic officials, etc.

At best, this summary reflects the benefits of a windshield survey. But, more importantly, what it represents is the wealth of urban experience lying near the surface, easily explorable, time permitting. Officials in every country visited were most friendly, co-operative, and eager to engage in honest give-and-take discussions on the philosophy and the practice of urbanization—mistakes as well as successes. Any discerning American urban generalist could mine the applicable gems of this vast body of urban knowledge in Western Europe.

All that need to be given is a willingness to do the same and to share our experiences.

Discussion Questions

1. Discuss the French Z.U.P. technique, its goals, and its advantages and disadvantages.
2. In what ways have the West Europeans approached the problems associated with rapid urban growth?
3. What lessons do the two articles suggest for America's urban problems?

Poverty and Welfare

One out of every five Americans is poor. In addition, there are a substantial number of families in this country who are one step from poverty if a sickness or a layoff should occur. Until the early 1960s poverty was one of those unfortunate conditions of life to which we gave very little thought. Then, having discovered the other America in the early 1960s, we began to fight a war against poverty. Unfortunately, we also began to fight a war in Asia and it received a higher claim on national resources. The poor's need for these resources is no less justified today than it was yesterday. The President's Family Assistance Plan, designed to put a floor on income, is an attempt to ultimately turn the lie to the comfortable belief that the poor will always be with us. But the $1,600 guaranteed annual income not only fails to meet the government's own standards of a minimum standard of living, it also fails to meet the standard necessary to provide a level of income which would eliminate the crisis of fear which accompanies poverty.

It is arguable that the American philosophical outlook of individualism has colored our view of what should be done to solve the poverty problem. It is clear that other nations have approached the problem quite differently from the United States. The article by John Chandler offers some comparative measures of poverty and then describes some of the various approaches to the poverty problem abroad. The second article compares social-security programs in several countries and deals with the philosophical differences among those countries which have designated social security as a way of providing economic security.

John H. Chandler is Chief of the Division of Foreign Labor Statistics, Office of Foreign Labor and Trade, Bureau of Labor Statistics, U.S. Department of Labor. Gaston V. Rimlinger is Professor of Economics at Rice University.

Perspectives on Poverty: An International Comparison

JOHN H. CHANDLER

Where does the United States stand, and where do Europeans stand, with regard to poverty?

In making such a comparison, two opposing attitudes or myths can affect our objectivity. One is the myth of European infallibility. Loosely, it may be claimed that Europe has coped with poverty much longer than we have, and the Europeans have more experience with the problems of living together in a compact industrial society.

The opposite myth is that of American superiority. This begins with the fact that we have greater abundance and economic power, and moves to the conclusion that, if we still have social and economic problems, those problems must be much worse in other countries.

The following sections examine a few facts about economic and social conditions on both sides of the Atlantic—conditions that relate in some way to the concept "poverty." Because of measurement differences that exist from country to country, many of the comparisons must be regarded as indicative rather than precise findings.

Income

The most elementary measure is to compare per capita income. In 1965, U.S. per capita income was $2,893. (See Table 1.) In Sweden, Switzerland, and Canada, income averaged between $1,800 and $2,000, or about the same as the average for nonwhites in the United States. In the major European countries, France, Germany, and the United Kingdom, the average was about $1,450, in Italy $900, and in Japan $700.

Such comparisons do not tell very much, however. First, in another country the purchasing power of a given income may be much higher than in the United States, and indeed this is the case as shown by several studies. Real per capita consumption in Japan is about twice as high as the estimate based on official exchange rates, according to a study by the Organization for Economic Cooperation and Development. Similarly, real consumption in Europe is 15 to 40 percent higher than indicated by currency conversions at the official exchange rates.

Then there are the numerous differentials that can be found within countries. Data from a purchasing power map issued by the Chase Manhattan Bank illustrates differences in purchasing power among European provinces and departments:

Reprinted from the *Monthly Labor Review*, February 1969, pp. 55–62.

	Per capita income	
	High province	Low province
Belgium	$1,231	$801
Denmark	1,481	972
France	2,019	532
Germany	1,550	606
Italy	944	272
Netherlands	1,143	731
Sweden	1,848	987
United Kingdom	1,887	539
United States family income, 1959:		
Tunica County, Miss.	——	1,260
Owsley County, Ky.	——	1,324
Montgomery County, Md.	9,317	——

Similar results can be shown by industry or occupation. Generally, the differentials are narrower in Europe than in the United States, except perhaps for the earnings differential by sex.

Poverty is a relative matter, and the most significant income measure, perhaps, is the dispersion of net income among families, by decile or quintile group. A few years ago we made an attempt to analyze income dispersion and concluded tentatively that the dispersion is greater in the United States than in Germany, Sweden, or the United Kingdom. In the United States, net annual income in 1960–61 was $2,575 for those households at the top of the lowest income quintile, and $8,596 for those at the bottom of the highest income quintile. The low income figure was 30 percent of the high income figure—lower than in Germany (where the low income figure was 35 percent of the high income), Sweden (57 percent), or the United Kingdom (48 percent). The lowest-income fifth in the United States received a 5.0-percent share of total household income after taxes, compared with 6.4 percent in Germany, and 8.3 percent in the United Kingdom. Thus in terms of either comparative dispersion or aggregate income, there was apparently a greater inequality in income distribution in the United States than in the other countries.

Several others have attempted to analyze income dispersion, also with inconclusive results. Irving Kravis found that in the early 1950s Denmark, the Netherlands, and Israel had less income inequality than the United States. Great Britain, Canada, and Japan had about the same degree of inequality, and Italy had greater inequality.

There is also disagreement about the redistribution effects of government programs. On the one hand, it can be demonstrated that the combination of a progressive tax system and a regressive benefit system results in greater equality of net income. On the other, if we examine all types of

Table 1. Per Capita National Income in Selected Countries, 1965 (in U.S. dollars)

Country	Per capita national income
United States	$2,893
Argentina	740
Australia	1,620
Brazil	217
Canada	1,825
Chile	515
France	1,436
West Germany	1,447
Israel	1,067
Italy	883
Japan	696
Korea	88
Mexico	412
Netherlands	1,265
Nigeria	63
South Africa	509
Switzerland	1,928
United Kingdom	1,451
Venezuela	745
Viet Nam	113

SOURCE: United Nations Monthly Bulletin of Statistics, October 1967, pp. xx–xxii.

subsidies provided by government, not just the social programs, the results can turn out differently. The question of income distribution and redistribution obviously needs more study. This has been acknowledged by the United Nations as well as by U.S. statisticians.

Another approach is to measure the percent of GNP spent on social programs in different countries. An International Labor Organization study in 1960 showed that the United States spent 6.3 percent of GNP on social security, while leading European countries spent from 11 to 16 percent.

Consumer Expenditures

One may recall Engel's Law to the effect that, as income increases, the proportion of income spent on necessities diminishes. Engel's coefficients can be worked out for food alone, or for other groupings of basic expenditures such as food, shelter, and clothing. Our consumer expenditure survey shows that, on the average, American households spent 53 percent of income in 1960–61 on the three basics, slightly less than the percentages reported for other countries. (See Table 2.)

Table 1. Family Consumer Expenditures for the United States and Eight Other Industrial Countries *

Country and date	Survey coverage	Percent distribution of expenditures					
		Total	Basic expenditures				All other
			Total	Food	Shelter	Clothing	
United States: 1960–61							
White	All households.	100	52	24	18	10	48
Negro		100	57	25	19	13	43
Household income under $3,000:							
White	Urban households.	100	63	29	27	7	37
Negro		100	64	29	25	10	36
Household income, $3,000–$7,499:							
White	do	100	54	25	19	10	46
Negro		100	57	25	19	13	43
Household income, $7,500 and over:							
White	do	100	50	23	16	11	50
Negro		100	53	21	16	16	47
Canada 1964	do	100	56	25	20	11	44
Japan 1965	do	100	57	38	8	11	43
France 1963–64	Worker households.	100	61	39	12	10	39
West Germany 1963–64	do	100	62	37	14	11	38
Italy 1963–64	do	100	68	43	15	10	32
Netherlands 1963–64	do	100	61	34	13	14	39
Sweden 1958	All households.	100	58	33	14	11	42
United Kingdom 1964	do	100	54	29	16	9	46

* It has not been possible to adjust for differences in definitions and coverage, which may be substantial in some cases.
SOURCE: European Economic Community Statistical Office, various national publications, and U.S. Department of Labor, Bureau of Labor Statistics.

The U.S. superiority according to Engel's coefficient is, although perceptible, very small. When we examine the three basics separately, we find that U.S. and Canadian consumers spend much less of their income on food and more on shelter than do consumers in Europe.

Low Income Households

In analyzing the lowest income quintiles of four Western European countries compared with the United States, it is found that in 1960–61, the lowest income groups in the United States spent an average of 53 percent of after-tax income on food and shelter alone, compared with an average for all United States households of 45 percent. As expected under Engel's Law, the poorest households in all these countries spent a larger proportion of total income on these two "basic necessities" than the average household. However, the proportion spent was smaller among poor households in the United States than in any of the other countries, with Sweden a close second. (See Figure 1.) The significance of these relationships is that, as a rough generalization under Engel's Law, the lower the proportion of income spent for food and housing, the less "poor" are the families concerned. From this standpoint, therefore, the poorest group in the United States was not as poor as the comparable group in France, Germany, or the United Kingdom.

Expenditures on shelter, as a proportion of all expenditures, were generally higher at each income level in the United States than in the four European countries, where housing programs for the poor are more extensive. Food expenditures, on the other hand, took up a smaller part of household income in the United States than in Europe.

A few additional facts about household expenditures emerge from the expenditure data in money terms shown in Table 3. First, it is not surprising that total cash expenditures, as well as cash expenditures in each consumption category, rise according to income level. The amount spent on food and shelter rises more gradually, however, than the amount spent on discretionary items. It is also found that those in the lowest quintile appear to spend more than their incomes, whereas those in the upper quintiles show considerable savings. In addition, the inequalities in family expenditures between quintile groups seems to be greater among urban than rural households.

Many questions arise in appraising the expenditure data described above, some dealing with technical aspects of the surveys and others calling for more facts such as sources of income, services rendered free, household composition, and the quantity and quality of goods actually received by the households. Most of these cannot be answered without more intensive study. Additional facts are available from the surveys, however, which may shed light on conditions in each country.

The average size of household in each income quintile is particularly

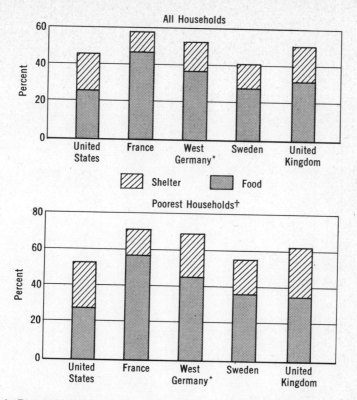

Figure 1. Expenditures for Food and Shelter as a Percent of Total Expenditures in the United States and Other Countries.

* West German data for "All households" applies to middle-income households; for "Poorest households," to low-income households.
† Lowest income quintile.

significant because it makes possible an estimate of average expenditures per capita as well as per family.

The proportion of expenditures on prime necessities may be influenced strongly by differences in the average size of households among the five countries, as well as by subsidies or other national programs that do not show up as household income or expenditure. By way of illustration, the average size of household in the United States was larger than in Sweden or the United Kingdom and smaller than in France. Therefore, the household demands for food and shelter would be greater in France and the United States than in Sweden and the United Kingdom.

Another consideration is that the characteristics of households were quite different from one income quintile to another. The lowest income quintile in each country had the lowest average number of household members (2.14 persons in the United States, 2.40 in France, 1.71 in Sweden,

Table 3. Average Annual Household Income and Expenditures by Income Quintile, United States and Four European Countries

Country and year	Average, all quintiles	Quintile				
		Lowest	Second	Third	Fourth	Highest
All Households						
United States, 1960–61:						
Average income (in dollars)	$6,246	$1,693	$3,658	$5,485	$7,547	$12,852
Total expenditures	5,053	1,959	3,527	4,802	6,144	8,832
Percent spent:						
Food*	24	29	26	25	24	22
Shelter†	18	24	20	18	18	16
France, 1956–57:						
Average income (in new francs)						
Total expenditures	Fr 7,830	Fr 2,906	Fr 5,302	Fr 7,312	Fr 9,492	Fr 14,138
Percent spent:						
Food	46	57	54	50	47	38
Shelter	11	14	12	11	11	12
West Germany, 1961: ‡						
Average income (in Deutschmarks)	—	—	DM 295	DM 818	—	—
Total expenditures	—	—	279	671	—	—
Percent spent:						
Food	—	—	46	37	—	—
Shelter	—	—	23	15	—	—
Sweden, 1958:						
Average income (in kroner)						
Total expenditures	SKr 13,989	SKr 5,978	SKr 9,344	SKr 13,437	SKr 15,450	SKr 25,732
Percent spent:						
Food	25	37	32	28	26	19
Shelter	12	18	13	12	12	10

Country and year	all quintiles	Lowest	Second	Third	Fourth	Highest
United Kingdom, 1962: **						
Average income (in shillings)	413s.	128s.	267s.	359s.	483s.	827s.
Total expenditures	352	151	261	327	417	603
Percent spent:						
Food	31	35	34	34	31	27
Shelter	16	27	19	17	15	13
Rural Households						
United States, 1961 (rural farm):						
Average income (in dollars)	$4,732	$937	$2,381	$3,917	$5,780	$10,644
Total expenditures	3,595	1,977	2,436	3,433	4,326	5,803
Percent spent:						
Food	24	27	27	24	24	22
Shelter	15	17	15	15	15	15
France, 1956–57:						
Average income (in new francs)						
Total expenditures	Fr 7,707	Fr 3,890	Fr 5,485	Fr 7,118	Fr 8,794	Fr 13,249
Percent spent:						
Food	54	62	62	59	54	47
Shelter	10	9	8	9	10	12

* Food includes cost of food prepared at home, food away from home, meals or food received as payment in kind, and imputed value at retail prices of home-prepared food. Excludes alcoholic beverages and tobacco products.

† Shelter includes cost of rent, repairs on rented dwellings, interest on mortgages for owned dwellings, taxes, insurance, and repairs on owned dwellings, operating and maintenance costs for vacation homes and cabins, cost of fuel, light, and water, and other operating and maintenance costs.

‡ West Germany: information available for "low" and "middle" income households. From 1961 Federal income tax records, estimated that low income households fall in second quintile. Middle income have been placed in third quintile. Average monthly.

** Average weekly.

Note: Dashes indicate data not available. Because of rounding, sums of individual items may not equal totals. No adjustments have been made for differences in definitions and coverage.

SOURCE: United States—Consumer Expenditures and Income Surveys: Urban United States, 1960–61 (U.S. Department of Labor, Bureau of Labor Statistics, 1964). BLS Report 237–38 and Supplement 3, Part A to BLS Report 237–38, and unpublished data of the U.S. Department of Agriculture; France —Compendium of Social Statistics, 1963 (United Nations, 1963), pp. 582–583; West Germany—Statistisches Jahrbuch, 1963 or [Statistical Yearbook, 1963] (Statistisches Bundesamt [Federal Statistical Office], 1963), p. 517; Sweden—Hushallens Konsumtion ar 1958 [The Consumption of Households in 1958] (Kungl. Socialslyrelsen [Sweden Social Welfare Board], 1961), pp. 138–147; United Kingdom—Family Expenditure Survey, Report for 1962 (Ministry of Labor, 1963).

and 1.64 in the United Kingdom). For three countries with income data by composition of household, the lowest income quintile shows a surprisingly low average number of children. In the United States, the average was 0.58 children under 18 per household, in Sweden 0.36 children, and in the United Kingdom 0.22 children.

On the other hand, the number of aged persons in the lowest quintile was disproportionately high. The number of aged persons, 65 or over, exceeded the number of children in low-income households in at least two of the countries. In the United States the number of aged persons was 0.61 per household and in the United Kingdom 0.88 per household, for the lowest income quintiles. The preponderance of elderly people in low-income households is particularly significant in view of budget studies that show lower levels of need for the elderly.

Other Measures

The question might be asked, what level of satisfaction is gained by consumers in different countries, regardless of what they may spend on particular necessities? Despite its importance, income is not the only measure of poverty, and maybe not the best measure. There are several measures of physical and social well-being that serve as indicators of poverty conditions, for example, mortality rates. We find that mortality is lower in many European countries than in the United States, especially for males. Life expectancy at birth is about 69 years for American men, 71 for Dutch men, and 72 for Swedish men. For women, it is 74 years in the United States, 76 for the Dutch, and 76 for the Swedes.

Infant mortality, another measure of poverty, is higher in the United States than in 16 countries. (See Table 4.) Here is a matter where the United States is clearly in need of improvement. The belief that our poor performance is due solely to higher infant mortality in our nonwhite population is not supported by the facts. Nine of the 16 countries show a lower infant mortality rate than the rate for the U.S. white population.

In the field of nutrition, minimum standards have been suggested by the United Nations Food and Agriculture Organization (FAO), but not yet fully accepted. The FAO standard for daily calories per person is 2,600, a level that is amply exceeded by the average consumption in the United States and Western Europe. The American diet is generally higher in animal proteins and sugar than the European diet, and lower in grains, fish, cheese, and butter. The American consumes about the same amount of fresh fruits and vegetables as the European. On balance, it is virtually impossible to judge which country has the superior diet, since the amount and variety of food consumption seems ample in both areas. A more pertinent question is whether a significant number of people in either area are missing out on the adequate diet enjoyed by the great majority. This question cannot be answered because of data limitations, but we know from recent reports that

Table 4. Infant Mortality Rates,* Selected Countries, 1965

Country	Rate	Country	Rate
United States	24.7	Israel	27.4
White	21.5	Italy	35.6
Nonwhite	40.3	Japan	18.5
Argentina	60.7	Jordan	42.0
Australia	18.5	Mexico	60.7
Belgium	24.1	Netherlands	14.4
Bulgaria	30.8	New Zealand	19.5
Canada	23.6	Panama	44.7
Chile	107.1	Peru	90.7
China (Taiwan)	22.2	Philippines	72.9
Cuba	37.7	Poland	41.8
Czechoslovakia	25.3	Romania	44.1
Denmark	18.7	Spain	37.3
Finland	17.6	Sweden	13.8
France	22.0	Switzerland	17.8
East Germany	24.5	USSR	27
West Germany	23.8	United Kingdom (England	
Guatemala	94.6	and Wales)	19.6
Hong Kong	23.7	Venezuela	47.7
Hungary	38.8	Yugoslavia	71.5

* Number of deaths of infants under 1 year of age per 1,000 live births.
SOURCE: Demographic Yearbook, 1966 (New York, United Nations, 1967).

segments of the U.S. population are seriously malnourished or underfed.

The quality and quantity of housing, as measured by such standards as presence of piped water, electricity, and indoor plumbing, and the extent of overcrowding, may also be considered as measures of well-being. With respect to inside piped water, this convenience is found in 93 percent of occupied U.S. dwellings (99 percent of urban dwellings and 79 percent of rural dwellings). This rate is surpassed in Germany, Switzerland, and the United Kingdom. The rate in Sweden is slightly lower and in France considerably lower than the U.S. rate. Electricity is present in over 99 percent of U.S. dwellings, as well as in several European countries. Ninety percent of all occupied dwellings and 98 percent of urban dwellings in the United States have flush toilets. Only the United Kingdom has a higher percentage of dwellings containing this essential plumbing feature. Over 88 percent of U.S. dwellings have baths, a rate that is surpassed only in Australia.

Thus the United States ranks high among nations in its housing conditions, but may be surpassed in some respects by the leading European countries.

Education level is not a direct measure of well-being, but it correlates quite closely with income level. Illiteracy rates are 2 percent or less in the United States and several European countries. At successive levels of edu-

cation, the precentage of enrollment in the United States is significanuy
higher than in most other countries. This is particularly true at the college
level, where the U.S. enrollment rate is more than double the rate in most
other countries. It is in education that the United States most clearly excels
in relation to the rest of the world.

The U.S. unemployment rate is still somewhat higher than the rates in
Europe, although the contrast is not as great as it was in the early 1960s.
(See Table 5.)

Table 5. Unemployment Rates * in Eight Industrial Countries,
Adjusted to U.S. Concepts

Country	1959	1963	1967
United States	5.5	5.7	3.8
White	4.8	5.0	3.4
Nonwhite	10.7	10.8	7.4
Canada	6.0	5.5	4.1
France	2.8	†2.4	†3.3
West Germany	1.6	.4	†.9
Great Britain	3.1	3.4	†3.1
Italy	5.7	2.7	3.8
Japan	1.9	1.1	†1.1
Sweden	‡	1.7	†2.2

* Percent unemployed.
† Preliminary estimates based on incomplete data.
‡ Not available.

Note: With the exception of Great Britain, all of the adjusted rates are based primarily on
data derived from labor force surveys similar to the U.S. monthly labor force survey. The
adjusted rates for Great Britain, which has not conducted a labor force survey, are based
on a comprehensive 1962 comparative study of British and U.S. unemployment rates.
Although the data are adjusted for all known major definitional differences, it should be
recognized that it has been possible to achieve only approximate comparability among
countries. Nevertheless, the adjusted figures provide a better basis for international comparisons than the usually published figures, which are based on labor force and unemployment definitions that differ from country to country and dissimilar methods of computing
unemployment rates.

In summary, U.S. economic averages and education level are generally
favorable compared with Europe. Average income is higher, measures of
abundance (autos, TV sets, refrigerators, housing) are higher. However,
events have shown that U.S. abundance is not reaching all social levels.
Social and demographic averages do not show a superiority in the United
States. The U.S. performance respecting longevity, infant mortality, literacy,
nutrition, illegitimacy, and unemployment is less favorable than performance in some other countries. The distribution of benefits, both social and
economic, may be more uniform in Europe, although the evidence is not
conclusive.

Policies and Programs

No European country has a multidimensional program like our "War on Poverty." Yet the Northern European countries probably have a greater variety of programs to assist the economically weak than we have in the United States.

The primary means for overcoming poverty in Europe are the numerous programs for maintaining general economic health. These programs range from flexible fiscal policy through area development, including counter-cyclical spending, investment incentives, economic planning, incomes policies, price restraining measures, and regional co-operation through such bodies as the European Economic Community and the European Free Trade Association. The active efforts to maintain general prosperity and growth are a powerful weapon against poverty and deprivation. During general prosperity the task of providing assistance to those in need becomes more manageable.

The trend in assistance is upward in Europe as well as in the United States. Assistance programs tend to be liberalized over time rather than made more restrictive.

The Europeans seem to emphasize programs to prevent or forestall hardship. Manpower policies are designed to avoid unemployment, maintain income stability, create jobs, and facilitate access to jobs. Programs include work projects (public works), standby works plans, public purchasing during slack periods, contraseasonal employment incentives, investment reserve funds, encouragements to labor mobility, investment incentives, development of depressed areas, export stimulation, placement service, and career guidance and counseling. To deal with the traditional immobility of European labor, incentives are given to employers (tax exemption, training allowances, loans, wage subsidies) for locating in labor surplus areas. To encourage employee mobility, incentives such as relocation allowances, housing, transfer allowances, and differential wage payments (for coal miners) are offered.

European countries realize the need for broadening educational opportunities. One step has been to raise the minimum working age in several countries, although it is still quite low in most countries. Financial aid to students is being extended and allowances are furnished to parents in some cases. Vocational education and retraining is nurtured with allowances, and often at no loss of unemployment benefits so that income is maintained. In many countries, vocational training and apprenticeship are considered an extension of general education. Contrary to the American practice favoring increased general education and free vocational choice at maturity, the entry age into apprenticeship, commonly 14 or 15, is much lower than in the United States. An apprentice in Europe may start at a wage as low as 10 percent of the journeyman rate; in the United States he earns from 50 to 90 percent of the journeyman rate. Customarily, a large proportion of school leavers in Europe obtain public vocational guidance and accept apprenticeships.

Other European programs are aimed at promoting independence and self-sufficiency among workers. For example, low-cost loans have been provided for purchase of homes, and savings plans provide bonuses if withdrawals are not made for specified periods.

Then there are social insurance measures to alleviate or forestall the effects of poverty on individuals. These measures are numerous, as they are in the United States. Unemployment benefits are provided and, in recession periods, have been extended beyond usual time limits. Emphasis is placed on value-creating assistance, such as public works, training, furnishing of tools, and rehabilitation. Each European country has pension plans for the elderly, for widows, the handicapped, and disabled veterans. Most also have statutory family or children's allowances, which may add one-third to the average earnings of households.

The Europeans have gone far in relaxing the links between contributions and benefits. Many benefits, such as children's allowances and medical care, are provided from general tax revenues. In the United Kingdom, the "cradle to grave" security provided under the Beveridge Plan does not include any means test for benefits. Similar schemes operate in Denmark, Sweden, Finland, and Iceland.

Finally, for cases not reached by social insurance, there are public assistance programs, as in the United States. In several countries, municipalities are required to organize assistance programs. Special attention is given to children and to rehabilitation. The individual causes of poverty are so varied that social diagnosis can play a major role in providing the right kind of help. Cited causes include old age, sickness, physical handicap, mental retardation, maladjustment, inadequate training or education, irrational consumption habits, wastefulness, divorce, broken homes, alcoholism, drug addiction, and others. Often the causes are multiple. The social worker has been used extensively in Europe to identify such problems and to aid in their solution. The aim is to restore the individual or family to constructive life wherever possible.

Possible Lessons

The economic and social programs described here illustrate the diversity of activities undertaken in Europe to avoid or mitigate poverty. No single country undertakes every such program, nor are many of the programs universal. Also, many of the programs have their counterparts in the United States. Possibly some lessons can be gained from the Europeans, nevertheless, since many of the countries do not show the symptoms of poverty to any great degree although their economic resources are more limited than ours.

The European countries show a willingness to experiment, to try out novel programs. Some may fail, of course, or may not be applicable to U.S. conditions. Others may provide the type of pilot experience worth studying further.

European programs for youth are conspicuously different and, in some ways, apparently more successful than U.S. programs. The child in Europe receives a measure of protection through the children's allowance that is not available here. Although in most European countries his opportunities for higher education and his chance of upward social and economic mobility are very limited, his chances of leaving school with a skill or vocation are much better. As a youth he is encouraged at an early age to obtain occupational training that will fit him for an adult job. As a result, the transition from school to work occurs much earlier—for better or for worse—and is much smoother than in the United States, judging from comparative unemployment levels.

The role of the employment service is more dominant in Europe. In addition to placement activities, the service may engage in counseling, training, nation-wide referral, relocation, initiation of public works, and participation in national economic policy decisions.

Several European schemes are aimed to maintain income when the breadwinner is unable to provide. While income is maintained, major efforts are made to rehabilitate the breadwinner, restore him to productive life, or enable other family members to find work. The principles of prevention and self-help are given top attention in fighting poverty, which is consistent with the historic European attitudes that the community shall accept responsibility for the poor, but that able-bodied persons shall be responsible for themselves.

Social Security and Society: An East–West Comparison

GASTON V. RIMLINGER

Social security is shaped by an interplay of forces which vary over time and between countries. Recent studies have analyzed the role of some of these factors in the development of social security systems. This paper takes a broad comparative view of the interplay of forces, with the hope of identifying the patterns that have emerged in different environments.

Reprinted from *Social Science Quarterly,* Vol. *50,* December 1969, pp. 494–506, by permission of the publisher and author.

Economic Protection as a Social Right

It might be appropriate to begin with a look at alternative economic guarantees a society may offer. These include the right to earn an income, the right to income maintenance, the right to opportunity, and the right to defend one's economic interest. The right to earn an income may be in the form of the right to work or the right to own land and capital. Socialist countries tend to guarantee the right to work but severely restrict the right to own income-producing property. The right to opportunity is a more general way to look upon the right to earn an income. Today, the right to opportunity includes certainly the right to education, training, health care, rehabilitation, counseling, placement, and so forth. The right of individuals to defend their economic interests, especially through group action, has been seen as an alternative to protection provided by society. Before Bismarck turned to social insurance, he promoted the workers' right to organize in the hope that this might provide some protection against the bourgeoisie. Until the 1930s, American trade unions were opposed to social insurance on the grounds that it was their function, not the state's, to protect the American worker.

A few words may be added regarding the right to work. One of the knottiest problems in the development of income maintenance programs has always been the handling of the able-bodied worker. Historically, his right to relief has been tied to his duty to work, insofar as work was usually made a condition of relief. Relief for the able-bodied worker therefore implied recognition of his right to work. This conception of the right to work, in the sense of *droit au travail,* was strongly supported by the left wing during the French revolutions of 1789 and 1848. It has also figured prominently in socialist ideology since then and has become enshrined in the Soviet Constitution as one of the basic rights of Soviet citizens. Not by accident does the same Constitution proclaim the duty to work, in terms of the biblical principle: "He who does not work, neither shall he eat." Another conception of the right to work, the *droit de travailler,* in effect access to work, is part of the liberal heritage of the eighteenth century. Its main support at that time was again in France, where it served as a weapon against restrictive guilds and the absolutism of the Crown. Today, this same conception of the right to work is contained in the famous Section 14(b) of the Taft-Hartley Act, where it is intended to limit trade-union restrictions on the free labor market.

These two conceptions of the right to work—that of the Soviet Union and that of the United States—illustrate one of the fundamental differences in the provision of social rights in a free-enterprise market economy and a socialist planned economy. In the market economy, the emphasis is on freedom of contract. Ideally, the freely competitive market distributes income in a manner that is consistent with the most efficient allocation of resources, which tends to maximize aggregate income. Unfortunately, the market mechanism does not provide for nonparticipants in the productive process. It is necessary therefore to supplement the primary income distribution of the market with a secondary system of redistribution and transfers. This raises the possibility of a conflict of distributive principles. Market distribution is based on contract, but contract-based distribution has only limited applicability to those who are not actively in the labor market. It applies only to the extent that secondary distribution consists of transfers derived from previous contractual relationships or of advances based on future contractual commitments. Within these limits, it is usually impossible to provide the full array of social rights a modern state deems desirable. It becomes a question therefore of how far a society is willing to deviate from the contractual rights and distribute income on the basis of rights associated with status.

Since the eighteenth century, the Anglo-American-French tradition has emphasized individualistic contractual rights, consistent with the political philosophy of the "Social Contract." The German tradition of paternalistic government, on the other hand, was more congenial to the development of income distribution based on social status. This tradition, which emphasizes the collective over the individual interest, is also dominant in the socialist state. In theory, a centrally planned command economy can concentrate on collective goals and achieve the most efficient allocation of resources quite independently of the returns to the owners of productive factors. It could therefore allocate income as it pleases to meet whatever social objectives it chooses. In practice, of course, the ultimate communist distribution principle "to each according to his needs" cannot be met so long as people are more responsive to material incentives than to ideological exhortation. While this limits the authorities' freedom of income distribution in the Soviet Union, they are at least not hampered by individualistic traditions. The absence of any contractual ties, in fact, gives the Soviet planners great leeway to adjust the distribution of social income to meet the needs of the state, the party, or the economy, as they see them.

Poor Laws

It was in response to the social and economic changes engendered by industrialization that one country after another found it necessary to shift from the old systems of poor relief to modern programs of social insurance and public assistance. With advancing industrialism and the democratization of political power, the old poor laws had become inappropriate. It has to be understood that even in countries like England, where there was a recognized "right to relief" under the Poor Laws, this meant only that the national state had imposed upon the local community a duty to provide relief. The emphasis of the Poor Laws was not on the rights of the individual but on the welfare of the community; poor relief was a sanitation measure. The strong deterrents attached to the receipt of relief made the

Poor Laws an instrument which the ruling groups used to inculcate habits of work and industry among the needy.

The poor law in the West (and for that matter, in Russia, too) was an attempt to reform if not the character at least the behavior of those in need. It looked upon poverty, especially in the case of able-bodied individuals, as evidence of some personal shortcomings which needed to be corrected. The ruling group's perception of these shortcomings and of the anticipated consequences of relief changed over time, but there was always an argument as to why it was harmful for society to make the poor comfortable. The arguments have not died. Perhaps there is some truth in them. But they have lost their conviction in today's industrial society. The poor laws, after all, where expected to apply only to a small minority living at the margin of society. They were ill-suited to deal with the problems of economic insecurity of large groups of normally self-supporting individuals who may be temporarily disabled or unemployed, or have become too old to compete in the labor market. When social investigations showed that age, illness, and involuntary unemployment were the greatest causes of poverty among a wage-working population, social means of protection that were free from the punitive stigma of the poor law became inevitable.

Germany: The Paternalistic Heritage

Germany was the first country to introduce large-scale social insurance programs. Bismarck's dominant concerns were to woo the workers away from socialism and to preserve the country's authoritarian monarchy. The creation of social security rights was a response to pressure from below; but the rights were justified and shaped from above. Bismarck had a genuine paternalistic interest in the welfare of the workers. His emphasis, however, was on the duty of those who rule to protect the ruled, rather than on the rights of the ruled. Bismarck and the feudalized upper bourgeoisie who supported his welfare program thought of the workers' rights to protection mainly as a counterpart of the laborers' duty of obedience and deference. It is somewhat ironic that the initiators of modern social rights were looking backward to the duties of the loyal subject rather than to the privileges of modern citizenship. Social rights were introduced partly as a compensation for the weakness of political rights.

This frame of reference naturally had an impact on the nature of the rights that were granted. The thrust of the program was to protect the "economically weak" who were also politically dangerous. It was a program primarily for the industrial workingman. Initially, it had little or nothing to offer the salaried employee, the artisan, the agricultural laborer, and the peasant. Some of them were in great need of protection, but they were neither organized nor dangerous. The level of protection aimed at in the early German system was barely sufficient to alleviate hardship. It was not intended to maintain a customary standard of living or a designated national minimum. This aim was consistent with Bismarck's political objectives. With regard to financing and administration, Bismarck argued strongly for state financing and for administrative control in the hands of a centralized state bureaucracy. He feared that if the workers had to pay, the desired impact on them would be lost. On both the financing and the administrative issues Bismarck had to accept compromises as his bills went through the Reichstag. The state, the employers, and the workers shared in the cost and the administration of the health and old-age programs. With the exception of the Social Democrats and the feudalized big industrialists, there was a general feeling that workers ought to share in the cost of social insurance. The Social Democrats, who had mixed feelings about the attempt to bribe the working class, demanded benefits equal to full wages, to be paid for completely by the employers but administered by the workers. In reality, they did not expect these demands to be met, nor did they think genuine economic security would be provided for the workers until socialism replaced the existing order.

In subsequent years the character of the original programs changed considerably. Already, before World War I, the system had lost its strict industrial working class orientation. Coverage was extended to include salaried employees, and benefits were improved. But it remained a system of social rights which had its limits set by an authoritarian regime. The passing of the old order and the upsurge of popular political forces after World War I led to reform demands. During the mid-1920s the whole system of social rights was the subject of lively debate, with reform proposals ranging from complete and universal protection to complete abolition of social protection. As a result, social rights were expanded, especially through protection of the unemployed, but the burden of social income redistribution now became a politically divisive issue. It is significant that it was the financing of unemployment insurance that broke the back of the right-left political coalition in 1930—a break which opened the road to the Nazi regime. Hitler used social insurance to support his political objectives, but the major reforms that were planned were never introduced.

After World War II a complete reformulation of social rights had become inevitable. East Germany followed the Soviet path. West Germany put its economic faith in the Social Market Economy, a system which tries to blend the stimuli of the market with the social concerns of the state. The new West German social security system reflects these tendencies, as well as a new concern with equality. It is a cradle-to-grave system for everybody, but it has shed the old paternalism. It emphasizes the individualistic insurance principle of relating benefit levels to contributions. The ideological emphasis is no longer on the state's but on the individual's contribution. The stress is not on redistribution from rich to poor, but on transfer from productive to nonproductive citizens according to previous performance. Benefit levels are geared not to mere alleviation of hardships, or attainment of a minimum standard, but to the maintenance of whatever standard an individual may have achieved through his own work. Solidarity between generations is a keynote. It is highlighted through systematic pension adjustments to the growth in national income. The system tries to solidify not to alter the stratification derived from the division of labor.

Britain: The Egalitarian Tradition

Differentiated benefits and contributions have always characterized German social security. In this respect it presents a sharp contrast to the British system, which has a tradition of flat benefits and flat contributions. This latter tradition, which emphasizes equal social rights regardless of individual economic merit, goes back to the beginnings of the modern British welfare state. The movement which led to the 1908 Old-Age Pension Act had its roots in the late nineteenth century struggle for greater social equality. In 1885 the extension of the franchise further democratized political power, there was a new militancy of the less skilled elements of the working class, a new social consciousness became evident among elements of the upper and middle classes; as a consequence, reform of the poor law had become irresistible. Yet, the mood of reform was hardly revolutionary; its main insistence was on the "national minimum," the right to a minimum standard of existence. This social egalitarian orientation, as well as the precedents of the poor law and private charitable organizations, established the pattern of flat minimum benefits. Another factor which helped to promote the idea of a national minimum was the mounting concern in the early twentieth century with national efficiency. The maintenance of a national minimum of health and vigor was believed to be essential to the preservation of the country's economic and political position.

On the matter of financing there was considerable division of opinion. The Socialists demanded that all programs be made universal and noncontributory, but there was resistance from those who feared encroachment of the state upon individual freedom and from those who were concerned with protecting the Exchequer against seemingly boundless fiscal responsibilities. There has always been a widespread feeling in Britain, and for that matter in Germany, that the individual ought to contribute at least part of the cost in order to preserve a sense of social responsibility. Nevertheless, the 1908 Pension Act was made noncontributory, partly because its purpose was to rescue the aged poor from the curse of the poor law, and partly to placate the friendly societies which feared state competition for the workers' meager savings. On the other hand, the health and unemployment insurance programs of the 1911 National Insurance Act were made contributory. The Liberal leaders, David Lloyd-George and Winston Churchill, who pushed these reforms were more concerned with national efficiency than with philanthropy or social reform.

The egalitarian and national minimum concepts established by these early programs received their fullest formulation in the famous Beveridge Report of 1942. This was a comprehensive statement of the citizen's social right to freedom from want and of the means to implement it. Its central idea was the national minimum: "Social insurance should aim at guaranteeing the minimum income needed for subsistence," Beveridge declared. He strongly advocated egalitarian social insurance, regardless of earnings. "All insured persons, rich or poor, will pay the same contributions for the same security; those with larger means will pay more to the National Exchequer and so to the state share of the Social Insurance Fund." This approach, he argued, "has been found to accord best with the sentiments of British people." He added that there was growing support for the principle that "in compulsory insurance all men should stand together on equal terms, that no individual should be allowed to claim better terms because he is healthier or in more regular employment." Along with this Dunkirk-inspired posture and an emphasis on society's responsibility for the welfare of the individual, Beveridge expressed the traditional British concern for individual freedom and responsibility. This concern was behind his insistence on providing only minimum benefits and keeping the system contributory. "Management of one's income," he observed, "is an essential element of a citizen's freedom." He believed that guaranteeing the minimum would give the citizen both the freedom and the incentive to provide more for himself and his family. With regard to worker contributions, he noted that "insured persons should not feel that income for idleness, however caused, can come from a bottomless purse."

The fundamental features of the Beveridge proposals were enacted into law between 1945 and 1948. At that time these laws gave Britain one of the most comprehensive health and social security systems in the world. Since then one of its fundamental features, the egalitarian benefit, has been discarded. With growing affluence during the postwar years, there arose increasing dissatisfaction with a system that almost necessarily tied benefits to a level somewhat below the lowest common wages. In 1959 Britain introduced a second layer of wage-related pensions to supplement the national minimum. It may be worth noting that during the same year Sweden also altered her traditional, egalitarian system in favor of a wage-related pension and cash sickness benefits.

The United States: The Individualistic Tradition

In Europe we have seen a varying balance between individual and social interests. In the United States the balance has been heavily weighted in favor of individual interest. The traditional emphasis on self-help and individual achievement, the identification of state intervention with loss of freedom and destruction of economic vitality, the lack of class solidarity, the hostility of organized labor to governmental competition, and an optimistic faith in boundless opportunities—all of these factors created an environment in which advocating compulsory social protection of the individual was more likely to invite political retribution than reward.

It is significant that until the 1930s the only kind of nondeterrent social protection that had gained general acceptance was compensation for industrial injuries. Workmen's compensation was supported by all the major parties in the 1912 campaign, and was even before then officially endorsed by the National Association of Manufacturers and many trade and employer associations. The reason for this exception is rather simple. Workmen's compensation, even though compulsory, could easily be treated as a police and profits problem, rather than a social welfare problem. It could be divorced from social rights and duties and presented as a matter of industrial efficiency. The accident-prevention programs which were induced by workmen's compensation appealed to employer self-interest. John R. Commons, one of the guiding lights of the early compensation movement, explained that the "appeal was made to a new kind of 'efficiency,' efficiency in preventing accidents, by which the cost of production could be reduced, with the result that prices need not be increased." The success of the workmen's compensation campaign in the second decade of the century gave false hope to the social insurance advocates, mainly social workers and intellectuals, that the efficiency then could serve as a vehicle for introducing other forms of social insurance, especially health insurance. Economists and statisticians, like Irving Fisher and I. M. Rubinow, calculated the return in productivity that improved health care through health insurance would provide. This was an appeal for social protection not for the sake of social rights but for the sake of productivity. Unfortunately, the economic gains from better general health are primarily social rather than private. In this sense, the effects of health insurance are unlike those of workmen's compensation. In the individualistic American environment the absence of demonstrable private gains made compulsory action difficult.

During the 1920s the efficiency theme was applied to old-age pensions and unemployment insurance. The emphasis now was on the private gains, through improved efficiency made possible by timely retirements and through regularization of employment. To the extent that the arguments had validity, they could justify voluntary private measures but not compulsory governmental action. Quite a few private schemes were introduced with the enthusiastic support of the American Management Association. Their significance lies not in what they achieved, but in the models they provided when social action on a large scale became unavoidable in the 1930s.

The main programs of the Social Security Act of 1935, pensions and unemployment benefits, were patterned after plans that had been tested in a private interest setting. The underlying idea was to violate in the least possible way the market principle of an exchange of benefits for contributions.

The system had to be as consistent as possible with the principle of efficiency maximization through profits. In the case of unemployment insurance this led to the adoption of the Wisconsin plan (similar to the "American Plan" supported by the American Association for Labor Legislation), which put the entire cost on the employer and made his tax a function of the amount of unemployment he caused. This was exactly parallel to workmen's compensation, and a similar result was expected in the form of a reduction of unemployment. The unemployment tax was expected to induce improved management. Moreover, in this manner it was argued, each employer would pay for his unemployment, not for that of other employers. Benefits were based on wages and the length of previous employment. The economic merits of the scheme were and still are controversial, but its advocates had no doubt that it was highly suitable for America. Commons, whose life-long goal was to build institutions that would utilize the profit motive in the social interest, declared: "It is extraordinarily an individualistic and capitalistic scheme." Another member of the Wisconsin school described the plan as "enlighted individualism," which involved "the least change in private business consistent with the government's vital interest in steadier employment and income. . . ."

The individualistic element was even more pronounced in the structure of the old-age pension program. The crucial concept here was the *contributory-contractual principle*. Even in the depth of the depression, the spokesmen for the program found it necessary to emphasize again and again that protection for the aged was not to be a matter of governmental benevolence but a matter of individual, contractual rights. Such rights protect freedom, they felt, while governmental benevolence threatens it. The emphasis, therefore, had to be on contractual equity rather than social justice, which meant that benefits had to be geared as closely as possible to contributions by and for the worker, with a minimum of redistribution. In testimony on behalf of the social security bill, J. Douglas Brown, then a member of the technical staff, explained that "a contributory-contractual plan uses the method of thrift to protect workers" and that "by contributing the individual worker establishes an earned contractual right." As should be clear, this idea of an *earned contractual right* as a rationale for a contributory system is quite different from Beveridge's concern with the maintenance of a sense of individual responsibility. In spite of Franklin D. Roosevelt's oratory about freedom from want, the idea of social rights was still suspect in America. One way out was to make social security appear as a kind of self-help scheme, which would threaten neither individual initiative nor individual freedom. In Brown's words, "We wanted our government to provide a mechanism whereby the individual could prevent dependency through his own efforts." The government was to provide merely the mechanism for self-help, not a new conception of the citizen's social rights.

It was not possible, of course, to adhere completely to the logic of the contributory-contractual principle and to the precedents of private welfare plans. Some redistribution in favor of low income receivers and people near retirement was unavoidable. But in America (unlike Europe), the government did not make any contribution from general revenue toward the cost of social insurance. Since contributions were from the beginning levied only on the lowest part of earnings, there has always been a regressive element in the American system. When benefits were liberalized in 1939, by adding survivorship and dependents' benefits, the tendency toward regressiveness was increased. The recent substantial raises of the tax base have reduced, but by no means eliminated, all of the regressive features of the system. So long as there is no contribution from progressive taxes, we will have a system in which the poor and the rich bear the same financial burden for the protection of the poor. Its great "virtue" is that it forces the poor to protect themselves and thereby protects the more affluent members of our society.

USSR: The Collective Approach

The contrast between East and West has been most emphasized by Soviet writers. One of them notes the following differences: in the USSR, social security "is a factor in the improvement of life and of the material and cultural position of the working class; it is one of the levers for the uplifting of all those who work." In the West, on the other hand: "Its substance lies in the use of pacifiers . . . to protect capitalist property against encroachment from the poor." And he goes on: "What underlies social security in Capitalist countries is not the needs of man, nor the right to secure old age, but the interest in profits, the interest in strengthening the capitalist mode of production by way of partial concessions to the worker." Wrong-headed as this interpretation may be, it is nevertheless partially correct. In the West we have found varying degrees of individual and social responsibility for protection from want; in the USSR the emphasis is exclusively on social responsibility. Reliance on the state rather than self-help is the keynote of Soviet welfare.

The difference is closely associated with the differing explanations of poverty in the Western tradition and in Marxist thought. The former concentrated on the shortcomings of the individual while the latter focused exclusively on the failures of the economic system. Before coming to power, the Bolsheviks, like other Socialists, insisted on the principle that it was the Capitalist system that was the cause of insecurity; therefore, it was up to the ruling class to provide and pay for the workers' protection. Their right to comprehensive, free protection derived from the fact that they were being exploited by the Capitalists. The kind of social security system that this implied was spelled out by Lenin at the 1912 Prague Conference of the Russian Social Democratic Workers' Party. He cited the following principles: (1) state social security had to protect against all risks of income loss, (2) it had to cover all workers and their families, (3) it had to pay full compensation of lost earnings, (4) all costs had to be borne by employers and the state, and (5) there had to be a unified system of administration (as opposed to separate programs for separate risks) under the complete control of the insured workers. These principles have remained the touchstone of Soviet social insurance. They were embodied in a bill prepared by the Bolsheviks in 1914 and in the social security proclamation issued by the Bolshevik leaders only five days after the seizure of power. In 1936, the right to comprehensive social protection for all Soviet citizens was incorporated into the Constitution.

In the development of Soviet social security these principles have been adapted to the economic and political needs of the hour. While Soviet writers charge that under capitalism social security serves mainly the purposes of the ruling class, there is no country in which welfare programs have been so closely tailored to the needs of those in power as they have in the Soviet Union. The promise of November 1917 to establish without delay a comprehensive program of social insurance for all workers and for all urban and rural poor was soon pushed into the background under the impact of civil strife. Soviet social insurance began, effectively, in 1921 on a less than comprehensive scale. It applied only to wage and salary earners. The self-employed were excluded. It was not until 1964 that the mass of agricultural workers, the *kolkhoz* members, were included in the state pension and temporary disability programs.

While it is not possible to review here the details of the Soviet social security system, some of its outstanding characteristics should be noted. One aspect which Soviet spokesmen often point to with naive pride is the absence of contributions by the workers. The official ideology stresses the fact that benefits are a gift from the state, an expression of its deep concern for the average citizen. Soviet legal experts note that there is no contractual relationship in their social insurance; only the state has an obligation, not the worker. A worker is entitled to social insurance because of his status as a worker, not because he or his employer paid contributions. Initially, there was not even a test of an individual's attachment to the work force. The idea of a service requirement was gradually introduced during the 1920s—at first, mainly to determine the eligible status group. With the beginning of the five-year plan era, the service requirement became a determining factor in the granting of benefits.

In 1929, the social insurance agencies were ordered to reorganize their work in order "to achieve every possible support for the growth of labor productivity and every encouragement for shock work and socialist competition, to heighten the struggle against absenteeism and labor turnover, and to aid in the formation of cadres and the strengthening of labor discipline." In 1930, unemployment benefits were summarily abolished, and the unemployed sent to any available jobs. In the following years the service requirements were considerably tightened, with particular emphasis being placed on the length of unbroken service in the same establishment.

Workers who moved from job to job were penalized with lower benefits and denied benefits altogether during the first six months of a job. Workers in important industries and shock workers were given preferential treatment. In 1933, the trade unions were given the dominant role in the day-to-day administration of social insurance for active members of the force. While most workers belong to a trade union, those who do not are entitled to temporary disability at a rate of 50 percent of what is paid to union members. The unions were ordered to use social insurance in a manner which would strengthen labor discipline, reward the zealous, and punish the loafers. This certainly was an ironic development for workers in a country which had accepted the principle of management by the insured.

The disciplinary character which Soviet social insurance acquired during the Stalin five-year plans was relaxed after his demise, although its productivity objectives were retained. The vast improvement of pensions in 1956 gives the country a system with a better balance between productivity and welfare objectives. Until then the maximum pension for the vast majority of pensioners was below a minimum subsistence level, which forced most of them to continue to work. Today the Soviet pension scale provides benefits which are a higher percentage of wages for most workers than in the United States. Like almost all Soviet benefits, pensions are still highly differentiated and incentive oriented; they offer special bonuses for long and steady work and higher rates and lower retirement ages for dangerous or difficult work. Workers in the Far East and Far North are singled out for privileged treatment. Since 1930, the Soviet authorities have emphasized, and sometimes pushed to extremes, the differentiation of benefits. Only since 1956 are pensions weighted in favor of low income receivers. In their rejection of egalitarian rewards, the Russians are like the Americans, and very much unlike the British and the Swedes.

Today Soviet citizens enjoy a comprehensive and unified system of health care and social security rights. According to studies by the International Labor Office, the Soviet Union in 1963 spent 10.2 percent of its Gross National Product on social security, which is substantially more (relative to GNP) than the 6.2 percent spent by the United States. On the other hand, the USSR rates behind countries like West Germany (15.3 percent), France (14.6 percent), Sweden (13.5 percent), and the United Kingdom (11.2 percent).

Concluding Comments

In comparative analysis there are two opposite dangers: one is to overstress differences in order to bring out contrasts; the other is to exaggerate similarities in order to highlight unity. Keeping these pitfalls in mind, we must take note of a remarkable convergence. In spite of vastly different starting points in terms of ideologies, social, economic, and political conditions, the countries surveyed have ended up with remarkably similar systems of income protection. The American, German, or Soviet pensioners waiting for the postman to bring their monthly social security benefit certainly have something important in common. But as we look beyond the technical similarities of the programs, as we examine their social and economic context, we find that significant differences remain. These are embedded in the degree of protection, the conditions under which rights are awarded, and the meaning attached to them.

One decisive factor in the historical process by which social rights are granted is the emphasis society places on individual versus collective interests. Whether a government is more or less representative does not necessarily affect the extent of social rights granted but has a great deal to do with the structure of these rights. The less representative a government, the more it is inclined to manipulate the rights to suit the objectives of the ruling group. Social rights have inherent limitations; they extend certain dimensions of freedom but necessarily curtail others; they may increase social equality, but beyond a point only at the cost of economic incentive. These are the considerations which account for both differences and similarities in the patterns of East and West.

Discussion Questions

1. How would you compare the countries of the U.S., Great Britain, West Germany, and the Soviet Union in their perceptions of social security?
2. What programs have the Europeans used to fight poverty?
3. How would you evaluate the success of America's anti-poverty measures in comparison with foreign programs?